International Adventures

Film Europa: German Cinema in an International Context
Series Editors: **Hans-Michael Bock** (CineGraph Hamburg);
Tim Bergfelder (University of Southampton); **Sabine Hake**
(University of Texas, Austin)

German cinema is normally seen as a distinct form, but this new series emphasizes connections, influences, and exchanges of German cinema across national borders, as well as its links with other media and art forms. Individual titles present traditional historical research (archival work, industry studies) as well as new critical approaches in film and media studies (theories of the transnational), with a special emphasis on the continuities associated with popular traditions and local perspectives.

The Concise Cinegraph: An Encyclopedia of German Cinema
General Editor: Hans-Michael Bock
Associate Editor: Tim Bergfelder

International Adventures: German Popular Cinema and European Co-Productions in the 1960s
Tim Bergfelder

INTERNATIONAL ADVENTURES

German Popular Cinema and
European Co-Productions in the 1960s

Tim Bergfelder

Berghahn Books
New York • Oxford

First published in 2005 by

Berghahn Books

www.berghahnbooks.com

© 2005 Tim Bergfelder

Library of Congress Cataloging-in-Publication Data

Bergfelder, Tim.
    International adventures: German popular cinema and European co-productions in the
1960s / Tim Bergfelder.
        p. cm.
    Includes biographical references.
    ISBN 1-57181-538-4 (alk. paper)
        1. Motion picture industry--Germany (West)--History. 2. Motion pictures--Germany
(West)--History. 3. Coproduction (Motion pictures, television, etc.) I. Title.

PN1993.5.G3B37 2004
384'.8'0943--dc22

2004052961

British Library Cataloguing in Publication Data

A catalogue record for this book is available from
the British Library.

Printed in the United States on acid-free paper

ISBN 1-57181-538-4 hardback

CONTENTS

List of Illustrations   vii

Acknowledgements   ix

1 Introduction   1

Part I: Historical and Cultural Contexts

2 From Rubble to Prosperity: Reconstruction of a National
   Film Industry   19
3 From National to European Cinema   53
4 The Distribution Sector   71
5 Film, Television, and Internationalisation   88

Part II: Case-Studies

6 Artur Brauner's CCC: Remigration, Popular Genres,
   and International Aspirations   103
7 Imagining England: the West German Edgar Wallace Series   138
8 From Soho to Silverlake: the Karl May Westerns   172
9 Beyond Respectability: B-Film Production in the 1960s   207

10 Conclusion: the End of an Era?   237

Appendix: Filmography of 1960s Genre Cycles   251

Bibliography   263

Index   271

LIST OF ILLUSTRATIONS

2.1. Habsburg Romance and the Heimatfilm: Romy
Schneider and Karlheinz Böhm in *Sissi* (1955).   41

2.2. Teen stars Peter Kraus and Conny Froboess in the
Schlagerfilm *Wenn die Conny mit dem Peter* (1958,
When Conny Met Peter).   45

3.1. Romy Schneider in the Franco-German co-production
Ein Engel auf Erden/Madame Ange (1959).   62

3.2. Imitation James Bond: Tony Kendall (real name
Luciano Stella) as 'Kommissar X'.   68

4.1. Ilse Kubaschewski, West Germany's female film tycoon.   77

4.2. Michèle Mercier in *Angélique* (1964), co-financed by
Kubaschewski's Gloria.   80

4.3. Constantin and the sex film boom: still from
Schulmädchenreport (1968, Schoolgirls Report).   86

6.1. Remaking Weimar Cinema: Ruth Leuwerik as Renate
Müller in *Liebling der Götter* (1960, Darling of the Gods).   113

6.2. Artur Brauner (right) in 1958 with Fritz Lang and
actress Debra Paget.   120

7.1. Producer Horst Wendlandt (left); director Alfred Vohrer
is second from the right.   150

7.2. Klaus Kinski in *Die toten Augen von London* (1962,
The Dead Eyes of London).   154

7.3. Eddi Arent in a publicity still for *Der Hexer* (1965, The Ringer). 155

8.1. West German cinema's 'dream couple' Pierre Brice (left)
and Lex Barker (right) in a publicity still from *Der Schatz
im Silbersee* (1962, The Treasure of Silver Lake).   182

9.1. The West German Jayne Mansfield: Barbara Valentin
in the early 1960s.   210

9.2. A well-behaved James Bond? George Nader as Jerry Cotton
in *Schüsse aus dem Geigenkasten* (1965, *Tread Softly*).   216

9.3. Tsai Chin and Christopher Lee in the Spanish-West
German-British-Italian co-production *The Castle of
Fu Manchu* (1968).   221

9.4. Ruth Gassmann as *Helga* (1967).   223

ACKNOWLEDGEMENTS

This book began as a research project at the University of East Anglia in the early 1990s. I would like to thank Charles Barr for his support, inspiration, and advice in helping me to bring the initial project to completion. Andrew Higson and Erica Carter provided insightful and constructive criticism, important suggestions for redirection, and encouragement, which significantly helped to transform the original thesis into this book. Hans-Michael Bock, Sabine Hake, and the editorial team at Berghahn proved invaluable in giving the manuscript its final shape, and they added detailed information and corrected a number of factual inaccuracies. My special thanks to Eric Rentschler and Anton Kaes and all the participants of the 2002 German Film Institute at Dartmouth College, the experience of which gave my manuscript a number of new dimensions in the final stages of writing. Many other colleagues and friends have contributed to this book through suggestions, helpful advice, and comments at conferences, in research seminars, and in private discussions. Particular thanks are due to Deniz Göktürk, Joseph Garncarz, and Peter Krämer; to colleagues and friends at Southampton; and to Bill Marshall, Robynn Stilwell, Mette Hjort, Maggie McCarthy, and Randall Halle, who have commented on earlier versions of material appearing in this volume. I am grateful to the School of Modern Languages at the University of Southampton for granting me a semester's study leave for completing the book.

A number of archives and institutions were crucial in tracing primary and secondary sources. I am grateful to the staff at the British Film Institute, the library staff at the University of East Anglia and the University of Southampton; Evelyn Hampicke from the Bundesarchiv/Filmarchiv in Berlin (now Potsdam); everyone at CineGraph (Hamburg); and Rüdiger Koschnitzki and Claudia Dillmann at the Deutsches Institut für Filmkunde (now Deutsches Filminstitut) in Frankfurt-on-Main. The DIF was also invaluable in tracking down and supplying the illustrations in this book. I have been unable to trace or contact the copyright holders of these images. If notified the publisher will be pleased to rectify any errors or omissions at the earliest opportunity. I fondly recall my meeting with the late Horst Wendlandt, who granted me a lengthy interview in 1993 and who supplied me with promotional material about his company Rialto.

My greatest personal debt is to my mother and my brother – this book is dedicated to them.

All translations from German in this book are, unless otherwise indicated, my own. Italicised film titles indicate original release titles. Film titles that are not italicised indicate a literal translation (by myself) of the original title in those cases where no English release title exists, or alternatively where no English release title could be traced.

Shorter, or alternative, versions of parts of this book have previously appeared in the following publications: *Cinegraph. Lexikon zum deutschsprachigen Film. Lieferung 29*, ed. Hans-Michael Bock (Munich 1997); *Musicals – Hollywood and Beyond*, eds. Bill Marshall and Robynn Stilwell (Bristol 2000); *Cinema and Nation*, eds. Mette Hjort and Scott McKenzie (London and New York 2000); *The German Cinema Book*, eds. Tim Bergfelder, Erica Carter, and Deniz Göktürk (London 2002); *Light Motives. Popular German Cinema*, eds. Maggie McCarthy and Randall Halle (Detroit 2003).

Chapter 1

INTRODUCTION

A cinema full of people implies base instincts (Vlado Kristl).[1]

When I began, over a decade ago, to embark on a study of the West German film industry in the 1950s and 1960s, its popular genres and its international dimensions, my research was motivated by what I perceived to be significant gaps and critical misconceptions in histories of German cinema. Much of postwar West German film, from the end of the 'Third Reich' to the consolidation of the New German Cinema in the early 1970s, was, at least in terms of academic analysis and especially in the anglophone context, an almost complete *terra incognita*, reduced to a few dismissive comments in standard textbooks and histories. Timothy Corrigan's summary of the first two postwar decades of West German film production as a domestically moribund and internationally irrelevant 'Bavarian cottage industry' was perhaps the most quoted of these generalisations.[2] The fact that a particular historical period has not been analysed in any depth is of course not enough reason on its own to claim its importance. However, the long-standing neglect of postwar West German cinema between 1945 and the late 1960s is harder to understand when one discovers that the cinema before Oberhausen was far from being the fatally ailing industry usually portrayed in historical accounts. During the 1950s, for example, national cinema attendance figures for domestic productions experienced an all-time peak, while the decade also witnessed an upsurge in productivity. These facts on their own do not give any indication about the quality of the films of the period in question, of course, but at least they suggest the significance of this medium for its target audiences at the time, and as such should merit the attention of anyone interested in the way films function in their immediate social and historical context. A closer look at the 1960s, meanwhile, reveals that, despite the legendary declaration of the Oberhausen Manifesto in 1962 of the death of 'Daddy's cinema', for most of the decade it was the commercial cinema of popular indigenous and European genre cycles that dominated West German screens and audience preferences, until it was eventually sidelined in the early 1970s, not by the internationally acclaimed films of the New German Cinema, but by Hollywood. This, though, is hardly the impression that one gains from reading a survey of West German cinema in the 1960s, published in the early 1990s, which spends roughly five pages out of thirty-seven on the 90 per cent of the decade's releases (the period's popular genres), and the remaining thirty-two pages on the handful of début films of the emerging *auteurs* of the New German Cinema.[3] While the author cannot completely ignore the popular films' domestic dominance in the 1960s, he summarily dismisses them with the somewhat illogical argument that 'the financial success of these series concealed how bad cinema's situation actually was in Germany'.[4]

In part, the deliberate neglect in critical writings on New German Cinema of the preceding era of film-making can be explained by a partisanship of those critics for the *auteurs* of the 1970s, who never tired of articulating their antagonism towards the West German films and filmmakers of the 1950s and 1960s. The New German Cinema's rejection of the old guard of German film producers was theoretically informed by the cultural pessimism of the Frankfurt School, and consequently the indigenous commercial cinema became either the ghostly projector of a haunted national psyche that Siegfried Kracauer had evoked in *From Caligari to Hitler* or the embodiment of Adorno's and Horkheimer's reviled and tainted culture industry.[5] Moreover, the rhetoric of the New German Cinema was often instinctually informed by an élitist disdain for lowbrow forms of mass entertainment *per se*, a disdain that originated in the cultural hierarchies of the German *Bildungsbürgertum* (educated bourgeoisie), the social class the majority of New German Cinema's *auteurs* and critics emerged out of, and which, despite many New German film-makers' ostensible anti-bourgeois politics, significantly shaped their aesthetic values. Symptomatic in this respect are the tone and wording of the previously mentioned survey of the 1960s, which denounces the popular films of the period as *naiver Rummel* (naïve fairground attraction), *greller Klimbim* (garish junk), and *Kinderkram* (child's stuff).[6]

To a certain extent, the New German Cinema's antipathy towards 'Daddy's cinema' centred primarily on the fact that it was 'Daddy's', and only secondarily on its merits or otherwise as 'cinema'. In other words, this was a symbolic act of rejection of a politically compromised parental generation, projected wholesale, and without taking hostages, on to the films, film-makers, and not least (as avant-garde director Vlado Kristl's comment above amply documents) the audiences of an indigenous popular cinema.[7] What was originally meant as a polemical intervention, carefully orchestrated for dramatic effect in the context of the cultural politics in the 1960s and 1970s, became subsequently transcribed, including exaggerations, half-truths, and outright inventions, as 'objective', and endlessly reproduced, history. As a result, German cinema's history was condensed, and appeared to be reducible, to three emblematic moments – 'the innovative use of the camera in expressionist films of the early twenties; the unprecedented politicization of the entire cinema apparatus during the Third Reich; and the emergence of a "new wave" cinema in the seventies that combined innovative aesthetics with socially conscious narratives'.[8]

Left out of this ideal trajectory was not just postwar West German cinema before Oberhausen. The cinema of the German Democratic Republic (GDR) from the late 1940s to the end of the 1980s, too, was for a long time a barely known entity, often relegated to the status of a strange and eccentric sideline, out of which very occasionally an *auteur* of stature (e.g. Konrad Wolf) emerged. Only after the end of DEFA as a viable film company and the end of the GDR as a separate German state has the history of East German cinema come out of the shadows, and over the last decade, it has become one of the most prolific areas of research in German film studies.[9] The cinema of the Federal Republic in the 1950s and 1960s, in contrast, characterised by hierarchies of popular genres and stars and reliant on a strategy of formulaic repetition rather than aesthetic or narrational experimentation, could hardly, even with the best intentions, be reclaimed as innovative. The period appeared to lack *auteurs*, or better it lacked *Autoren* in the German sense of the word as arbiters of high culture and art cinema, since the more flexible criteria of either the French or American *auteur* theories might well have been utilised to rehabilitate the careers and *oeuvres* of such industry stalwarts as Hans Deppe, Harald Reinl, Jürgen Roland, or Alfred Vohrer, to name but a few possible candidates. Indeed, the only West German directors active and reasonably prolific in the commercial industry in the 1950s and 1960s who have, until recently, been critically analysed at any length are Helmut Käutner and Wolfgang Staudte.[10] Significantly these are two film-makers whose most important work is commonly perceived to predate the 1950s and 1960s, who were not tied to particular popular genres, and who frequently produced what could be termed 'prestige' pictures. It is worth remembering that most studies of German cinema until relatively recently were primarily text, or *Autoren*, based, with few analyses of film economics, studios, producers, or popular genres. The preference of exclusively text-based modes of critical analysis, however, has proved to be a particular stumbling-block for the evaluation of the 1950s and 1960s, where individual texts and directors mean ultimately less than, or at least are impossible to comprehend without a knowledge of, the generic and industrial regimes, let alone the wider cultural and social contexts, these texts and film-makers were part of.

This leads me to the third reason why the films of the 1950s and 1960s have been perceived as lacking in substance and worth, namely their alleged absence of political commitment, and their diffuse relation to issues of national representation. It is indeed undeniable that most popular West German genres of the 1950s and 1960s, from the *Heimatfilm* with its seemingly intact rural communities and scenic landscapes, to the

Gothic thrillers, exotic adventure films, and westerns of the 1960s, are escapist in their ideological function for contemporary audiences and resolutely non-realist in their mode of representation. As such, these genres do not lend themselves easily to the kind of critical approach that perceives films as a direct and mimetic reflection of specific national developments, and which only values those films that didactically engage in a critical, or 'progressive', political discourse *vis-à-vis* the social and political realities of the time.[11] With some notable exceptions, the 'real' postwar West Germany, its economic, industrial and social reconstruction, its positioning in the politics of the Cold War, and its gradual processing of the Nazi trauma and concomitant guilt, is conspicuously absent in the popular genres of the period, and can, at best, be read only obliquely in the period's films' narratives and visual representations.[12] Moreover, while the films of the 1950s, in particular the *Heimatfilme*, may still conform to conventional notions of national cinema in their overall indigenous mode of production and in their (however inauthentic and clichéd) references to indigenous cultural traditions and iconographies, the films of the 1960s, frequently realised as multinational co-productions and set in an imaginary American Wild West, or in an equally constructed Gothic Britain, Asia or Africa, challenge the very validity of national cinema as a means of classification.

What all of this suggests is that the study of the popular cinema of the 1950s and 1960s requires different critical parameters from the ones that have been traditionally employed. Although German film criticism has generally been slow in reacting to international trends in film theory and history, there is now a growing body of work, which has moved on from an exclusively *auteur*-based analysis of selected, aesthetically as well as politically worthy, masterpieces towards the study of genres, stars, studios, producers, audiences, and cultural contexts, or in other words has moved from a traditional film aesthetics towards a sociology of cinema. Meanwhile, a number of publications initiated by conferences organised by the Hamburg-based research centre CineGraph in the early to mid-1990s has opened the debates of German national cinema up to a wider international academic community and focused its research on the interrelations between German and various other European film industries.[13] In this, CineGraph's efforts have been mirrored by the (so far four) conferences on popular European cinema at the University of Warwick, in Punkaharju (Finland), and in Stockholm; and the publications that have resulted from these, which have significantly shifted the debate on transnational collaboration, at least in the European academic context.[14] In terms of interpreting these phenomena, critical paradigms have developed from an indebtedness to the Frankfurt School's cultural pessimism towards greater nuances with regard to the potentially progressive and liberating functions of popular culture, which has often been facilitated by the engagement with anglophone academic traditions such as cultural and film studies, but also by a revisionist reinterpretation of Weimar film theory.[15]

Among these new interventions, a number of important revisionist studies on the West German cinema of the 1950s and 1960s have been published since the 1990s. In Germany, of particular significance were two volumes on German postwar cinema published in 1989 and 1991 by the Deutsches Filmmuseum in Frankfurt.[16] The two volumes deal respectively with the period 1946 to 1962 and 1962 through to the 1970s. While one may want to question this chronological break (it seems to have been dictated solely by the caesura of the Oberhausen Manifesto, which, at least in its immediate influence on production and reception patterns, was in retrospect more a symbolic than a real turning-point), the books' selection of essays on genres, stars, and film economics have been hugely influential in engendering a re-evaluation of the period. Equally important was the publication of Claudia Dillmann's study on Artur Brauner and his Central Cinema Company (CCC), a groundbreaking investigation into one of postwar cinema's most resilient producers, but even more importantly the beginning of a long-term project of archiving Brauner's extensive business correspondence, which has become a unique and invaluable resource for anyone studying the commercial industry of the 1950s and 1960s.[17]

However, perhaps the most crucial intervention on the cinema of the postwar period, and the most wide-ranging in its implications, has been, at least in the German academic context, Joseph Garncarz's *Populäres Kino in Deutschland. Internationalisierung einer Filmkultur, 1925–1990*.[18] In this impressive and exhaustive *Habilitationsschrift*, Garncarz takes issue with one of the most persistent myths of German cinema, namely, that following the Second World War, or earlier, the indigenous film infrastructure was taken over by Hollywood distribution companies and that audience preferences immediately followed suit. The notion of an encroaching colonisation and Americanisation and the concomitant irrelevance and impotence of the indigenous film industry had first been argued by Thomas Guback and Kristin Thompson, and was later supported by Thomas Elsaesser, surveying the prehistory and industrial preconditions of the New German Cinema.[19] Although articles prior to Garncarz's thesis had already doubted the received wisdom of this scenario,[20] it was down to Garncarz to systematically prove, by drawing on contemporary sources, such as data from exhibitors and box-office success rankings, that German audiences on the whole resisted American domination until the early 1970s, and up to this point preferred either indigenous productions and stars (until the late 1950s) or a mix of German and European films (throughout the 1960s). Garncarz not only fundamentally revised the perception of the postwar West German industry from being the butt of condescending jokes to being a serious subject of study, but also questioned the all-too-familiar scenario of Hollywood's unbroken cinematic hegemony in Europe, with fundamental consequences for the study of European cinema and its relationship to the American film industry in a wider sense.

In the anglophone context, too, some influential new research on post-war German cinema has been undertaken over the past decade. Heide Fehrenbach and Robert Shandley, for example, have shed new light on the early postwar years.[21] Fehrenbach's book provides a largely institutional history, documenting the way in which the American military authorities during the occupation and, later on, pressure groups such as Germany's two churches exerted their influence on the selection, distribution, and exhibition of films in the late 1940s and 1950s. Fehrenbach's account provides invaluable and fascinating new insights into the legal and ideological wranglings between the various groups involved in assuming control over the West German media after the war. Fehrenbach positions their strategies, values, and, not least, objections within the context of the Cold War on the one side and the reconstitution of national German identity on the other. As an institutional history, Fehrenbach's book tends to adopt a slightly top-down approach, in which the intentions and aims of the American military, the churches, the imperatives of the Cold War, and the agenda of the West German Federal government are mapped perhaps too neatly on to the supposed reception by German cinema audiences (I shall expand on this point in the second chapter of this book). None the less, Fehrenbach's solid historical research has contributed more to an understanding of the postwar period than many exclusively text-based studies that have preceded her work.

Robert Shandley, in contrast, adopts almost the opposite approach to that of Fehrenbach. Concentrating exclusively on the cycle of *Trümmerfilme* (rubble films) made between 1946 and 1949, his book is inevitably more based on textual and generic analysis than Fehrenbach's. Shandley's main argument, too, is to revise earlier conceptions of the postwar years, in particular the role the rubble films played in Germany's coming to terms with the Nazi past. Shandley rejects the suggestion, frequently made during the 1970s and 1980s, that it is only with the advent of the New German Cinema that issues of the Nazi past were articulated in German films. Shandley does indeed make a strong case, even though not all of his close textual readings are uncontentious, such as his analogy of postwar films with the generic mode of the western.[22]

One of the possible reasons why the *Trümmerfilm* and the years from 1945 to 1950 more generally, have proved attractive to scholars, and why this era has been at the forefront of a wider historical revisionism of the postwar period is that these are subjects that can be reconciled with familiar research topics in German Studies – the Nazi past and its legacy, a cultural mode of intense soul-searching, national identity, and the threat (or liberation) of Americanisation. The 1950s and 1960s, in comparison, are still relatively under-researched, perhaps precisely because they do not conform in the same way to traditional research agendas in German studies. In many aspects the blatant and often shrill consumerism of the period does not match any of the above issues at all and may therefore require different critical emphases and frameworks. Erica Carter has suggested one such avenue with her study on the (re)construction of gender positions in the 1950s in a variety of media, from magazines and fashion to films, thus placing her filmic examples within a wider, intertextual, force field of consumer choices and behaviour.[23] Johannes von Moltke's ongoing research of the *Heimatfilm*, meanwhile, has extended the parameters of his subject by stressing the continuities of the genre across different periods, and in this follows more recent insights in German film history that the trajectory of the indigenous cinema is marked far more than has previously been assumed by continuities than by ruptures.[24]

Interventions such as the ones mentioned above still remain fairly isolated and do not necessarily indicate that there has been a radical paradigm shift in preferences, priorities, or conceptualisations of German cinema in general. A case in point is the anthology *Perspectives on German Cinema*, comprising a selection of essays primarily compiled from the journal *New German Critique*.[25] Contributions on popular cinema, even for the ever-popular Weimar period, are scarce in what is after all a fairly extensive tome. The only article dealing with West German cinema of the 1950s (or, indeed, the whole period between 1945 and the Oberhausen Manifesto) is also the only one that attempts a radical review of precisely the kind of German film historiography that is likely to have informed the editors' choices for this anthology.[26] Significantly, Tassilo Schneider's 'Reading Against the Grain: German Cinema and Film Historiography' comes with a number of intellectual 'health warnings'. The anthology's editors preface Schneider's essay with a number of questions, including the following: 'How does Schneider's call for greater scholarly focus on Nazi and post-Nazi German cinemas, which he designates the products of an extreme ontological lapse, ultimately reinscribe the opposite notion, "low culture", toward a likewise problematic aestheticising of World War II and the Holocaust?'[27] Leaving aside for a moment Schneider's own position, this quote is revealing. Apart from the highly dubious implication that a 'scholarly focus on Nazi cinema' automatically equals an 'aestheticising of World War II and the Holocaust', what is perpetuated here is a rather questionable, if familiar, symmetry between 'low culture' and Nazism and an equally problematic conflation of Nazi cinema with what is tellingly reduced to as 'post-Nazi' cinema, as if German history and cinema after 1945 possessed no identity (or indeed identities) beyond the legacy of the 'Third Reich'.

Schneider's argument, expressed in a number of articles in the early to mid-1990s and expanded in his as yet unpublished Ph.D. thesis, deserves further, and detailed, attention here.[28] This is not only because of its highly polemical, and remarkably accurate, diagnosis of the state of German film historiography and because it provides one of the most insightful, intelligent, and passionate accounts of the 1950s and 1960s and its popular genres in English so far, but also because Schneider's argument is ultimately trapped in the same paradigms it seeks to overcome. Schneider argues that German cinema, similarly to other European national cinemas, has been almost exclusively equated in critical discourse with 'art' cinema and *auteurs*, whereas American cinema is synonymous with popular cinema and genres. Thus, whereas the study of Hollywood has increasingly privileged cinema's social, historical, and industrial determinants and its international reach (and the textual polysemy of its films), national film cultures in Europe have been discussed according to paradigms of culturally discrete artistic movements, determined textual or formal meanings, and individual creativity. According to Schneider, however, the analysis of German cinema differs from the treatment of other national film industries, in that aesthetic criteria have been conflated with notions of national identity. Schneider notes that:

> discussion of German cinema has always suffered from a rarely acknowledged inherent contradiction: the presupposition that they are dealing with a cinema of singular artistic 'masterpieces' (which have been chosen by the critic on the basis of their aesthetic relevance, in fact their very singularity, or uniqueness) has never prevented writers from using the very same texts as a basis from which to embark on rather ambitious attempts to assess Germany's cultural history, to construct an image of its national identity and self-understanding, and to diagnose the social and psychological condition of its movie-going inhabitants.[29]

For Schneider, the obvious culprit and reference point for this kind of approach is, not surprisingly, Kracauer and the Frankfurt School, against whose verdicts German 'cultural criticism has been held hostage'.[30] Yet Schneider reserves his strongest criticism for a largely Anglo-American historiographical tradition associated with, and supportive of, the New German Cinema, which, according to Schneider, has helped to muddy and falsify German film history.

Drawing on debates from Anglo-American genre criticism, Schneider suggests that 'methodological strategies developed in the study of popular American cinema ... provide us with a more comprehensive understanding of these texts and their relationship to social, cultural, and ideological contexts'.[31] According to Schneider, critical practice needs to focus on textual (and wider generic) features and to extrapolate from these not only a relationship to a defined social and historical context, but also the expression or manifestation of particular 'ideological conflicts'. Schneider is careful not to suggest that interactions between texts and ideology are easy or unambiguous to determine, yet he queries reception studies or audience research as a methodological framework:

> In order to account for a particular audience's response to a specific body of films at a particular time and place, it might be necessary to address not only the particular generic texts in question, but also their context, specifi-

cally their interrelationship with (and their audience's consumption of) other cultural products or signifying practices. Such an endeavour, however, is bound to fall victim to all the theoretical problems that any attempt to reconstruct historical audiences and their reading practices is subject to. In order to avoid these problems, I suggest a different route of analysis, one which conceives of popular postwar German cinema as a function of specific generic determinants which, in turn, emerged in response to specific ideological pressures.[32]

During the 1990s, the advantages and limitations of textual versus contextual analysis as a tool of film criticism were widely debated in Anglo-American film academia, without much resolution, and creating two distinctive camps in the process. Certainly, reception-based approaches have initiated a significant reorientation in the academic writing on American cinema history[33] and have been commonly applied to the study of television. For the critical evaluation of European, and particularly German, cinema, however, textual-based models have remained far more common.[34] While I agree with Schneider that reception-based models do pose methodological problems, the same (if not more so) applies to the potential arbitrariness and ahistoricity of textual readings. Thus, while Schneider may be right about the 'theoretical problems' of reconstructing historical audiences, there are, arguably, equally problems with his own suggestion that films 'respond' to 'ideological pressures'. For example, in Schneider's account, the 1950s represent a period in which a patriarchal social order 'had' to be reestablished and relegitimated in West German society. To this context, genres such as the *Heimatfilm* responded by presenting patriarchal authority figures and, more generally, by a 'thematic preoccupation with familial struggle, problems of parental authority/legitimacy, and generational conflict'.[35] Schneider's only evidence for his assumptions over societal conflicts, however, is deduced from the films' narrative constructions.

In a similar vein Schneider sees the 1960s as a period in which West Germany's 'economic miracle' of the previous decade begins to show signs of social divisions. Therefore, for Schneider, 'what distinguishes the films of the 1960s from those of the previous decade is a significant realignment of narrative positions and functions along gender and class lines'.[36] The fact that many of the popular genres in postwar West German cinema frequently neither are set in nor explicitly refer to contemporary West German society, is for Schneider a 'function of an ideological effect worked out in generic terms: far from simply evading or suppressing German social reality, the genres that dominated German theaters in the 1960s worked, on the contrary, to open up narrative spaces within which the contradictions of that reality could be articulated and negotiated'.[37]

This correlation of shifting generic and narrative features with wider shifts and trends in postwar West German society is both suggestive and productive. One may question, though, the way in which the ideological pressures of the two decades can be so succinctly compressed into a narrative of 'patriarchal relegitimation' (which, in principle and methodology, does not differ that much from the historical narratives of earlier accounts). Secondly, although Schneider sees contemporary social and political agendas as being coded within and mediated by specific generic conventions, he shares the assumption with his predecessors that an explicitly 'national' meaning (however hidden or camouflaged) can be extrapolated from popular films by way of textual analysis without much recourse to the social conditions and contexts in which these texts were produced and consumed (not to mention the subsidiary texts of marketing and promotion and the intertextual references that accompanied them).

In this book, my argument is meant to contribute to a hopefully ongoing exploration of the 1950s and 1960s, not to provide a definitive account of the period. While it is necessary to study the development of the West German industry from 1945 into the 1950s in order to understand the emergence of industrial and generic patterns in West German film culture after the Second World War, the main emphasis of the text and its core case-studies, centres on the 1960s. This is partly to 'liberate' the popular cinema of the decade from the critical limbo in which it has been placed owing to the previously mentioned traditional chronology, which sees the period simply as the dawn of the New German Cinema. The 1960s, however, also hold another attraction in that their products may be used to question the critical tenets of national cinema. Thus, rather than seeing the developments of the West German film industry in the postwar era as an exclusively national concern, my book attempts to place this history within the wider parameters of European film history. The 1960s provide an interesting case study in this respect, because it is a period of intense cultural hybridisation and internationalisation in European cinema at large, in terms both of production practices and industrial contexts, and of audience preferences. It is in these aspects that the national film history I am describing hopefully expands into a transnational one, or at least intersects with the histories of other national cinemas such as those of France, Great Britain, or the former Yugoslavia. Overall, my book sets out to identify transnational processes and practices at both an international and a localised level. While there are admittedly a number of different contexts through which this interaction between the international and the local might have been studied, I have chosen in this book to focus specifically on and to write a history of the hitherto under-researched areas of production practices and distribution patterns and particular areas of contemporary reception. I am well aware that, even in dealing only with these issues, I am covering the proverbial tip of the iceberg.[38]

My approach has been particularly influenced by the work of scholars in reception studies and new American film history.[39]Analyses based on studies of reception and research into audience preferences and negotiations may help to retain and sometimes even reinforce a sense of cultural specificity, and yet they undermine the notion of an essentially and a priori knowable audience, 'national' or otherwise. However, given the complexity of theoretical, methodological, and logistical issues, one of the central aims of my book is to suggest not a single critical methodology (and thus becoming entangled into the textual/contextual controversy I outlined above), but to propose a number of frameworks according to which both national specificities and transnational interactions during the 1960s may be revisited. The study of popular genres requires attentiveness both to the material contexts of production, distribution, and exhibition and to the textual operations of the films themselves. The issue of co-productions demands the acknowledgement that economic considerations interact with specifically national developments, but that they are equally informed by the dynamics of an international media market. The context of diasporic communities, meanwhile, which I discuss in chapter 8 in relation to the producer Artur Brauner and his work with remigrant directors, needs to account for the various political, personal-biographical, and economic determinants of such experiences, and there is a need to find a critical mode that is able to convey these trajectories.

This book does not propose any overriding and generalising claims for the period under discussion that could be summarised into a snappy conclusion. There are, however, a number of concerns that run through the various parts of this book. The first is the realisation how impossible it is to compartmentalise the history of German cinema into decades, since every genre, every production company, and every cultural source extends, from the vantage point of the historical period in question, into the future as well as into the past. The extraordinary longevity not only of specific genres, but also of endlessly recycled stories, over decades, in some cases approaching a century, emerges as one of the enduring patterns in German popular culture, which, despite frequent claims to the contrary, has remained remarkably independent, despite the powerful influences of Americanisation and globalisation. Independence, though, should not be mistaken for national parochialism, and does not preclude international cross-fertilisation. The second theme that runs through the book has to do with the textuality of these generic formats. What unites such seemingly disparate genres as the *Heimatfilm* of the 1950s, the Gothic Horror of the Edgar Wallace series, the Karl May western, and the exotic adventure films and spy thrillers is their creation of an escapist utopia that deliberately does away with national constraints. Notable, too, is their particular approach in both narration and *mise en scène* to space and time. In these stylistic and narrational characteristics, the genres again point backward to the cinema of attractions of the silent period, and they point forward to what we now define as post-modern devices.

In terms of overall structure, this book divides into two major sections. Part One (Industrial and Cultural Contexts) aims to provide a materialist history of West German postwar cinema from 1945 to the 1960s. Chapter 2 outlines the macroeconomic situation of both the West German and the international film industry that facilitated and encouraged national producers and distributors to embrace 'internationalist' practices. I look at the way in which the West German film industry not only consolidated itself internally after the Second World War and responded to its decentralisation enforced by the Allied powers, but also at the way in which the West German film industry corresponded to wider developments in the relationship between European cinema and Hollywood. Drawing on contemporary surveys and comments as well as recent academic studies of the immediate postwar period, I also consider the reception of indigenous and foreign films by West German audiences. Critical evaluations of the immediate postwar reconstruction of German cinema have frequently emphasised the 'renationalising' aspects of this process. What interests me, however, is how, already in the first postwar years, ideological and political concerns about a 'national film culture' competed with public and industrial demands for internationalisation.

In chapter 3 I document how West German film policy in the 1950s was balanced between the political agenda of the West German government to reinstate a national film industry and the increasingly international composition of the West German film market. I discuss the influence that closer European integration, and particularly the aftermath of the Treaty of Rome, had on financing, subsidies, and production strategies of the West German film industry. This chapter also covers prevalent perceptions and discourses in different national film industries about the cultural as well as economic potential and merit of an international mode of production. Drawing on contemporary debates in West German and British trade papers, I suggest that marked differences existed in different industrial contexts regarding the practices of co-productions and the transnational transfer of labour.

Chapter 4 introduces the West German distribution sector and charts the developments and changing strategies of the two most significant distribution companies, Gloria and Constantin, while chapter 5 discusses the relationship between the film industry and the emergent mass medium of television. The 1950s and 1960s witnessed gradually changing media preferences from cinema to television. Consequently, an understanding of the development of the film industry in this period is incomplete without an understanding of how these two media interacted. I argue that, in its generic priorities and in its marketing, the West German transnational cinema of the 1950s and 1960s was in a constant dialogue with television, and vice versa. Like the film industry, television pursued a strategy of internationalisation, by promoting Hollywood films within a framework of cultural education, by creating a demand for American TV formats, and by promoting an idea of Europe through trans-European co-production strategies.

Whereas Part I is concerned with macroeconomic factors, Part II looks at specific genres and production companies in greater detail. The producer Artur Brauner, whom I discuss in chapter 6 is one of the pioneers of international collaboration among West German producers of the postwar period. The trajectory of his short-lived British subsidiary, CCC-London, illustrates the risks of adapting to different production practices and of second-guessing explicitly national, rather than international, audience preferences or market demands. Brauner quickly abandoned his British subsidiary and refocused his activities on co-productions in a continental European framework. The case of Brauner, an exiled Polish Jew with a number of international contacts based on similar experiences, also illustrates how the practice of inter-European cooperation interlinked with a dispersed and diasporic Eastern European film community and with the legacy of the political upheavals of the Second World War. I look at the trajectories of a number of former exiles, predominantly directors (Gottfried Reinhardt, Ernst Neubach, Fritz Lang), who worked for Brauner during this period. My argument is that these patterns of remigration were largely motivated by an attempt to internationalise film production and to revive the generic strategies of the Weimar period.

Chapters 7 and 8 are concerned with production company Rialto's Karl May and Edgar Wallace adaptations, the two longest and most successful generic cycles of the West German film industry in the 1960s. In these two chapters I focus on the close relationship between popular literary fiction and popular cinematic genres during this period, as well as going back to the origins of this relationship. I am particularly interested in how this relationship was exploited in terms of promotional strategies. The two genres, moreover, also interlinked with other developments in consumer culture. As in other national contexts, West Germany of the 1960s experienced the contradictory influences of a proliferating youth culture (often informed by American role models) and, on a more general level, shifting leisure habits, which included greater mobility and increased spare time. These general shifts in social behaviour significantly informed the stylistic and promotional patterns and the reception of popular film genres. My discussion of the Karl May and Edgar Wallace series emphasises their interaction with areas such as tourism and youth culture.

The Karl May and Edgar Wallace series furthermore illustrate in interesting ways how specifically national cultural expectations and a more transnational imagination could interact and how such 'international' narrative formulae were received in different markets. The Karl May films adapted the novels of a German author of the late nineteenth century and represented, for its German audiences, a specifically indigenous imagination of the American Wild West. In Britain and America, however, the Karl May series was received according to the parameters of the Hollywood western. The Edgar Wallace series adapted the work of an early twentieth century British crime novelist and reformulated it according to current German perceptions of Britain. In their historical, geographical, and cultural setting, the Karl May and Edgar Wallace series distanced themselves from the social and political context of postwar West Germany. In this respect, these popular genres can be seen as escapist and as articulating a more general evasion of Germany's contemporary situation and recent past. At the same time, it was precisely the series' strategy of blurring cultural distinctions and historical specificities that made these cultural forms internationally viable.

Chapter 9 looks at other industrial variants informing transnational activities. Whereas Rialto and Artur Brauner's CCC represented established and financially relatively stable outlets, there were a large number of smaller-scale (or B-film) producers who also participated in transnational ventures. I introduce a number of selected case-studies (among them Wolf C. Hartwig's company Rapid and the Anglo-West German connections of the British producer Harry Alan Towers). I look at the various generic formulae these producers pursued over the 1960s (from exotic adventure films and spy thrillers to soft porn), and how these generic formulae fitted international modes of financing and production. Chapter 10, finally, provides both a conclusion and an outlook on what subsequently to the 1960s became of the generic formats and protagonists of the preceding chapters.

Notes

1. Quoted in Joe Hembus, *Der deutsche Film kann gar nicht besser sein. Ein Pamphlet von gestern. Eine Abrechnung von heute*, Munich 1981, p. 264.
2. Timothy Corrigan, *New German Cinema. The Displaced Image*, Austin 1983, p. 2.
3. Norbert Grob, 'Film der sechziger Jahre. Abschied von den Eltern', in *Geschichte des deutschen Films*, ed. Wolfgang Jacobsen, Anton Kaes, and Hans-Helmut Prinzler, Stuttgart andWeimar 1993, pp. 211–248.
4. Ibid., p. 214.
5. On the influence of Kracauer, Adorno, and Horkheimer on the historiography of German cinema, see Tim Bergfelder and Erica Carter, 'Introduction', in *The German Cinema Book*, ed. Tim Bergfelder, Erica Carter, and Deniz Göktürk, London 2002, pp. 1–12.
6. Grob, in Jacobsen et al., *Geschichte des deutschen Films*, pp. 214 and 218.
7. Kristl's contempt for mass audiences has remained consistent over the years. The title of one of his films in the 1980s was *Tod dem Zuschauer* (Death to the Spectator, 1983).
8. Marc Silberman, *German Cinema. Texts in Context*, Detroit 1995, p. ix.
9. See, e.g., *'Sie sehen selbst, sie hören selbst': Die DEFA von ihren Anfängen bis 1949*, ed. Christiane Mückenberger, and Günter Jordan, Marburg 1994; *Das zweite Leben der Filmstadt Babelsberg, DEFA 1946–1992*, ed. Rolf Schenk, Berlin 1994; *DEFA: East German Cinema, 1946–1992*, ed. Seán Allan and John Sandford, New York and Oxford 1999; *Moving Images of East Germany*, ed. Barton Byg and Betheny Moore, Washington 2002.
10. See *Käutner*, ed. Wolfgang Jacobsen, Hans-Helmut Prinzler, Berlin 1992; and *Staudte*, ed. Eva Orbanz, Hans-Helmut Prinzler, Berlin 1991.
11. Exemplary for this kind of approach are, e.g., Barbara Bongartz, *Von Caligari zu Hitler – von Hitler zu Dr. Mabuse? Eine 'psychologische' Geschichte des deutschen Films von 1946 bis1960*, Münster 1992, and Kirsten Burghardt, 'Moralische Wiederaufrüstung im frühen deutschen Nachkriegsfilm', in *Positionen deutscher Filmgeschichte*, ed. Michael Schaudig, Munich 1996, pp. 241–276.

12. See, e.g., Fritz Göttler, 'Westdeutscher Nachkriegsfilm. Land der Väter', in Jacobsen et al, *Geschichte des deutschen Films*, pp. 171–210.
13. See, e.g., *London Calling. Deutsche im britischen Film der dreissiger Jahre*, ed. Jörg Schöning, Munich 1993; *Schwarzer Traum und weiße Sklavin: Deutsch-dänische Filmbeziehungen 1910–1930*, ed. Manfred Behn, Munich 1994; *Fantaisies russes: Russische Filmemacher in Berlin und Paris 1920–1930*, ed. Jörg Schöning, Munich 1995; *Hallo? Berlin? Ici Paris! Deutsche-französische Filmbeziehungen 1918–1939*, ed. Sibylle Sturm and Arthur Wohlgemuth, Munich 1996.
14. See, e.g., *Popular European Cinema*, ed. Richard Dyer and Ginette Vincendeau, London 1992; *Encyclopedia of European Cinema*, ed. Ginette Vincendeau, London 1995; see also Tim Bergfelder, 'Reframing European Cinema. Concepts and Agendas for the Historiography of European Film', *Lähikuva*, no. 4 (Popular European Cinema Issue), Winter 1998, pp. 5–18.
15. Bergfelder and Carter, in Bergfelder et al, *The German Cinema Book*, pp. 7–8.
16. *Zwischen Gestern und Morgen. Westdeutscher Nachkriegsfilm 1946–1962*, ed. Jürgen Berger, Hans-Peter Reichmann, and Rudolf Worschech, Frankfurt am Main 1989; *Abschied von Gestern. Bundesdeutscher Film der sechziger und siebziger Jahre*, ed. Hans-Peter Reichmann and Rudolf Worschech, Frankfurt-on-Main 1991.
17. Claudia Dillmann-Kühn, *Artur Brauner und die CCC. Filmgeschäft, Produktionsalltag, Studiogeschichte 1946–1990*, Frankfurt-on-Main 1990. Apart from Dillmann-Kühn's book, there are very few studies of individual postwar film producers. Another exception is *Luggi Waldleitner. Fast ein Leben für den Film*, ed. Carola Hembus, and Monika Nüchtern, Munich 1983.
18. Joseph Garncarz, 'Populäres Kino in Deutschland. Internationalisierung einer Filmkultur, 1925–1990' (Habilitationsschrift, University of Cologne 1996). See also his 'Hollywood in Germany: The Role of American Films in Germany' in *Hollywood in Europe. Experiences of a Cultural Hegemony*, ed. David W. Ellwood and Rob Kroes, Amsterdam 1994, pp. 94–135.
19. Thomas Guback, *The International Film Industry*, Bloomington 1969; Kristin Thompson, *Exporting Entertainment. America in the World Film Market 1907–1934*, London 1986; Thomas Elsaesser, *New German Cinema*, London and Basingstoke 1989.
20. See, e.g., Martin Loiperdinger, 'Amerikanisierung im Kino? Hollywood und das westdeutsche Publikum der fünfziger Jahre', in *Theaterzeitschrift*, no. 28, Summer 1989, pp. 50–60.
21. Heide Fehrenbach, *Cinema in Democratizing Germany. Reconstructing National Identity after Hitler*, Chapel Hill 1995; Robert R. Shandley, *Rubble Films. German Cinema in the Shadow of the Third Reich*, Philadelphia 2001. For yet another perspective on the same period, see Ursula Hardt, *From Caligari to California. Eric Pommer's Life in the International Film Wars*, Providence and Oxford, 1996.
22. Shandley, *Rubble Films*, pp. 31–46.
23. Erica Carter, *How German is She? Postwar West German Reconstruction and the Consuming Woman*, Ann Arbor 1997.
24. Johannes von Moltke, 'Evergreens. The *Heimat* Genre', in Bergfelder et al., *The German Cinema Book*, , pp. 18–28.
25. *Perspectives on German Cinema*, ed. Terri Ginsberg and Kirsten Moana Thompson, New York 1996.
26. Tassilo Schneider, 'Reading Against the Grain. German Cinema and Film Historiography', in Ginsberg and Thompson, *Perspectives*, pp. 29–48.
27. Ibid., p. 27.
28. Tassilo Max Schneider, 'Genre and Ideology in the Popular German Cinema 1950–1972', (PhD diss., University of Southern California 1994).
29. Schneider, in Ginsberg and Thompson, *Perspectives*, pp. 30–31.
30. Ibid., p. 37.

31. Tassilo Schneider, 'Somewhere Else. The Popular German Cinema of the 1960s', *Yearbook of Comparative and General Literature*, no. 40, Bloomington 1992, p. 76.

32. Ibid., p. 79.

33. See e.g., Miriam Hansen, *Babel and Babylon: Spectatorship in American Silent Film*, Cambridge 1991; Janet Staiger, *Interpreting Films. Studies in the Historical Reception of American Cinema*, Princeton 1992; Barbara Klinger, *Melodrama and Meaning. History, Culture, and the Films of Douglas Sirk*, Bloomington 1994; Thomas Austin, *Hollywood, Hype and Audiences. Selling and Watching Popular Film in the 1990s*, Manchester 2002.

34. Exceptions include Jackie Stacey, *Star Gazing. Hollywood Cinema and Female Spectatorship*, London 1994; Annette Kuhn, *Cinema, Censorship and Sexuality*, London 1988; Sue Harper, *Picturing The Past. The Rise and Fall of the British Costume Film*, London 1994. In German film criticism, see, e.g., Helmut Korte, *Der Spielfilm und das Ende der Weimarer Republik: Ein rezeptionshistorischer Versuch*, Göttingen 1998.

35. Schneider, 'Somewhere Else', pp. 80–81.

36. Ibid., p. 81.

37. Ibid., p. 80.

38. For example, I could have dealt with a number of other protagonists who were equally (perhaps in certain aspects even more) important to the ones I have chosen to cover, including producers such as Luggi Waldleitner, Franz Seitz, or Kurt Ulrich.

39. Staiger, *Interpreting Films*.

PART I

Historical and Cultural Contexts

Chapter 2

FROM RUBBLE TO PROSPERITY: RECONSTRUCTION OF A NATIONAL FILM INDUSTRY

1945–1949: Continuities and New Beginnings

In histories of German cinema the years between 1945 and 1962 have frequently figured as a period of missed opportunities and meek and unsuccessful attempts to break with the past, as a period of American political colonialism and cultural colonisation, and as the beginning of a 'crisis' in the West German film industry which to some extent is seen to have persisted to the present day.[1] Judging by the basic economic indicators, and particularly considering the extent of devastation within the German film industry in 1945, the recovery of the German film sector after the war was in fact remarkable. While the resumption of German film production was initially rather slow, by 1954 West Germany had become the world's fifth-largest producer. Distribution companies and exhibition outlets doubled in number within less than two years after the end of the war. Audience figures rose from 150 million in 1945 to 474 million in 1950, and these trends were sustained well into the 1950s (audience figures reached their peak in 1956 with 817 million). In 1960 cinema admissions in Germany were still the second highest in Europe (Italy being in first place, the U.K. in third place, followed by Spain and France).[2] The development of the German film market in the first ten postwar years thus differed significantly from economic patterns in other countries.

In the United States and Britain, the film industries emerged from the war in a financially prosperous position. In both countries, box-office earnings reached an all-time peak in 1946. Yet both Hollywood and the British film industry experienced an almost immediate and sharp decline thereafter. Hollywood was faced with the economic pressures of decartelisation (the Paramount decree in 1948), political problems (the ramifications of the House Un-American Committee, or HUAC, hearings), and rapidly changing habits of leisure and consumption (including the steady rise of television). Between 1946 and 1956, American box-office revenues dropped by 23 per cent, and the gross revenues of the major companies fell by 26 per cent. Unemployment in Hollywood was high throughout the 1950s.[3] In postwar Britain, on the other hand, government-imposed austerity measures and Britain's dependence on an ailing American industry severely damaged the indigenous film sector, leading, in 1949, to the worst crisis in British film production since 1936 and to the closure of a number of studios.[4]

In postwar West Germany, in contrast, the international financial aid pumped into its economy, the political motivations behind occupation policies (namely, the necessity of a strong and stable Western ally on the Cold War border), and finally a number of state-sponsored support schemes and subsidies in the early to mid-1950s, helped to cushion the reconstruction of the West German film market and delayed the effects of the crisis in the global film economy until the late 1950s.

During the Nazi period, the German film industry had increasingly been transformed into a monolithic and monopolistic state enterprise, known from 1941 under the acronym UFI, or Ufa Film GmbH.[5] When the Allies took over the administration of Germany in May 1945, the first priority – at least of the Western Allies – was to initiate a process of democratisation and denazification. All communication media, such as the press, radio, and film, came under Allied control, and were to be used in an extensive national re-education programme, before they were returned to a vetted and private German ownership. The entirety of UFI's management structure and all employees were made redundant. The restructuring process was coordinated by the American Information Control Division (ICD), a branch of the Office of the U.S. Military Government for Germany (OMGUS).

By Allied decree, all remaining cinemas were closed in the first two months after the end of the war, but were allowed to reopen thereafter. However, owing to the Nazi policy of expropriating real estate and property from German Jews and other nationals, claims to ownership of cinemas and companies had to be re-evaluated or reversed. In the meantime, the Allied authorities retained ownership. Similarly, German production personnel and management had to undergo an ideological vetting process before they were allowed to resume their activities. Given the almost complete control the Nazis had had over the German film industry, there were few professionals left (except returning exiles) who were not compromised by having worked for UFI.

While the German film industry was thus temporarily halted, American and British distributors were able to enter the vacuum created in the German film market. Of all the films screened in Germany between 1946 and 1948, 26 were new German productions, 84 were re-releases from the UFI back catalogue, and 312 were films from other countries, the majority from Britain and France. J. Arthur Rank established a German base between 1945 and 1948 with Eagle-Lion and Rank Distribution in British-controlled

Hamburg, while the interests of the major Hollywood studios were coordinated by the Motion Picture Export Association (MPEA, a branch of the Motion Picture Association of America, MPAA) from offices in Munich and Frankfurt.[6]

The military authorities and the commercial distributors had clearly divergent agendas. For the ICD, film was primarily an educational tool, and it favoured the production and distribution of documentaries and newsreels intended to confront the German public with its past and to trigger an admission of responsibility. In the first postwar years, the ICD regularly coordinated public screenings of documentaries presenting concentration-camp footage, forcefully encouraging the German audiences to engage with this material. This encouragement could on occasion take the form of coercion, but was mostly achieved by a 'stick-and-carrot' principle, in that educational documentaries were shown in tandem with more entertaining features. In some areas attendance was rewarded by increased food rations. High-profile names from the film industries of all the Western Allies were employed to supervise or in other capacities contribute to these documentaries, including figures such as Paul Rotha, Jacques Prévert, Billy Wilder, Alfred Hitchcock, and Josef von Sternberg.[7]

In many historical accounts of the postwar reconstruction of Germany, the enforced screenings of 'atrocity' documentaries feature as highly emblematic events. Many fictional films too, from Basil Dearden's British film *Frieda* (1948), via Samuel Fuller's Hollywood B film classic *Verboten!* (1958) to Margarethe von Trotta's *Die bleierne Zeit* (1981), have depicted the screenings of documentaries such as *Die Todesmühlen* (1945) as both cathartic experiences and a significant stage in the Germans' re-education and 'retraining' for democracy. In reality, however, such mandatory screenings proved not very effective, if not counter-productive, to their intentions. As Heide Fehrenbach has noted, 'most Germans were unprepared to undertake a thorough soul-searching at the command of an alien victor; and many were so consumed by their own (admittedly substantial) physical needs that they preferred to consider themselves the true victims of war'.[8]

The feature films supplied by the commercial distributors were of a different order altogether. Whereas the documentaries were seen to have both a punitive and an educational function, feature films were meant as enticing advertisements for the merits and rewards of democracy (or, in the case of the Soviet zone, communism). The military authorities reserved the right to veto the distribution of individual films according to their suitability, blocking films that were deemed to hold the potential of provoking unrest or which portrayed Allied countries in a less than positive light. According to Heide Fehrenbach, Hollywood classics such as *The Grapes of Wrath* (1940) and *Gone With the Wind* (1939) 'were rejected out of hand by the ICD and the Office of War Information (OWI) due to their subject matter, and in the case of the latter, the portrayal of "objectionable...Negro incidents"'.[9] In the British sector too, a number of films were withheld by the distributors on request from the military authorities, ranging from

David Lean's Dickens adaptation *Oliver Twist* (1948) due to its potential of being read as anti-Semitic, to films depicting Britain's criminal underworld, such as *Brighton Rock* (1948).[10]

Apart from these restrictions, the decision over the selection of films distributed in the Western zones rested with the distributors, whereas in the Soviet zone the state-regulated Sovexport company closely co-ordinated the distribution of Soviet war and propaganda films with the military authorities. In the British zone, Rank relied on films that had been recent box-office successes at home, particularly Gainsborough's costume melodramas. Between 1946 and 1948 Rank distributed *Madonna of the Seven Moons* (1944, German release title: *Madonna der sieben Monde*), *The Magic Bow* (1946, *Paganini*), *Caravan* (1946, *Gefährliche Reise*), *The Wicked Lady* (1945, *Frau ohne Herz*), and *Love Story* (1944, *Cornwall Rhapsodie*), but also David Lean's production *Great Expectations* (*Große Erwartungen*, 1946).[11] Many of these films proved to be extraordinarily successful with postwar German audiences. There are a number of explanations for this success: most of the films were set in a past safely distant from the recent war, and often in attractively colourful and exotic, but primarily European, locations such as Italy (*Madonna of the Seven Moons, The Magic Bow*) and Spain (*Caravan*). Some of the films (e.g., the Dickens adaptation *Great Expectations*) were based on familiar classics of European literature and culture, while the Gainsborough films were mostly adapted from florid romantic novels, a literary genre which had a direct counterpart in German popular culture, especially in the work of the eminently prolific Hedwig Courths-Mahler (1867–1950). Moreover, it has often been noted that the visual style of the Gainsborough films, their *mise en scène* and cinematography, borrowed significantly from the Ufa aesthetics of the 1920s (indeed, a number of German émigrés were among the films' technical crews).[12] In this respect, it is possible to suggest that both the look and the content of the British imported films conformed to aesthetic expectations, and followed familiar conventions, for German audiences.

Pam Cook, Sue Harper, and other feminist historians of British cinema have argued that the Gainsborough melodramas targeted a female audience with their narratives of transgressive female sexuality, fetishised masculinity on display, and visual excess at a time of austerity, and that these films performed an important emancipatory function for British women during the war.[13] It is easy to see how the Gainsborough films could have appealed in similar ways to German women after the war, who, after all, represented a substantial proportion of the cinema-going public at the time. German women, too, had been empowered, albeit forcedly, in the aftermath of the war, and now formed the bedrock of the physical as well as psychological reconstruction of Germany out of the urban ruins. Coming in the wake of a political regime that had specifically repressed female self-determination and self-expression, the Gainsborough films, in contrast, created and celebrated a 'world in which the expression of psychological and emotional states is dominant – indeed a world in which expressivity itself is paramount'.[14] Pam Cook has particularly emphasised the films' investment in 'fantasies of loss of identity',[15] which expressed an underlying 'unease with fixed boundaries of national identity, a desire to be someone else and elsewhere'.[16] In the grim reality of post-1945 Germany, such desires and expressions of unease must obviously have struck a chord with many Germans. Indeed, when German film production recovered, the most popular genres for the next twenty years were frequently those that, like the Gainsborough melodramas, articulated a potential of escaping the constrictions of national identity.

While the Rank Organisation had thus found, whether by accident or by design, a winning formula, American distributors followed a different strategy. Owing to the fact that since 1941 no American films (nor, for that matter, any films from other Allied countries) had been publicly shown in Germany, the postwar German film market provided a highly profitable opportunity to reuse older material, mostly from the early 1940s, which had come to the end of its commercial life in the home market. As Ursula Hardt has stated, 'the Americans were in no hurry to undermine their market potential and were holding back more contemporary quality films for economically more opportune times in Germany'.[17] Among the first American films shown to postwar German audiences the majority consisted of war films celebrating American heroism (*The Navy Comes Through*, 1942; *Action in the North Atlantic*, 1943; *Air Force*, 1943, *The Sullivans*, 1944) and sentimental pieces of Americana (*Abe Lincoln in Illinois*, 1940; *Young Tom Edison*, 1940; *The Human Comedy*, 1943; *Going My Way*, 1944), the rest being a fairly haphazard mix of musicals, comedies, biographical dramas, and thrillers, such as *The Maltese Falcon* (1941) and Alfred Hitchcock's *Shadow of a Doubt* (1943).[18]

It is clearly unlikely that so shortly after their defeat many Germans would have warmed much to narratives depicting triumphant American war heroes. Heide Fehrenbach has noted that a number of Hollywood war films were withdrawn from circulation after hostile audience reactions had been reported to the military authorities.[19] Moreover, resentment towards American culture, which had been fostered throughout the Nazi period, was still widespread (particularly among the older generation), and was to some extent exacerbated by the humiliating experience of occupation. Finally, the American distributors apparently took no account of gender-specific generic preferences among German audiences. Thus, it is perhaps not surprising that the most successful Hollywood films in postwar Germany came to be, more by default than by design, those which focused on either historically removed or universal human-interest stories, such as the biopic *Madame Curie* (1943) or the religious epic *The Song of Bernadette* (1943, based on a novel by émigré novelist Franz Werfel). Significantly, like the British imports, the settings and main protagonists of both films were European, rather than American, and they centred on female protagonists.

While American and British distributors began to establish themselves in the German market, the military authorities were still uncertain of how to reorganise the indigenous industry. The German film industry was among the obvious targets for the wider political objective of a decartelisation of the German economy. At least on paper, the UFI assets had the potential of comprising a vast media empire. The memory of UFI's part in the Nazi war of propaganda was vivid in the minds of military officials, while the precedent of Ufa's challenge to Hollywood's hegemony in the 1920s, and of the ban on the import of American films after the outbreak of war troubled the American film industry.

Practically, however, the UFI assets were almost impossible to reunify. A large part of the German film industry's studios, such as the Ufa complex of Babelsberg near Potsdam and the Tobis studio in Johannisthal in the south-east of Berlin, were in the Soviet-occupied zone. Prior to the end of the war, in April 1945, the Soviets had appropriated these facilities, which had been damaged in Allied bomb raids, and allegedly looted their remaining technical equipment and film stock. The studio at Johannisthal was used for the dubbing of Russian films, distributed by the Soviet company Sojusintorgkino. After the Allied victory and after Cold War divisions became more pronounced (and with them the prospect of a more permanently divided Germany), the facilities in the East were used to create DEFA in May 1946, a separate East German film monopoly with its centre at Babelsberg.[20]

This left the smaller and more dispersed facilities in the Western, and mainly American zones, such as the Tempelhof studios in central Berlin, and the Bavaria studios in Geiselgasteig near Munich, which in the immediate postwar period were used to store U.S. Army trucks and to house misplaced persons. As with the studio facilities, the exhibition sector was divided between East and West. Only half of the cinemas in existence in the Western territories in 1944 were still functional in 1945, many of them in rural areas that had escaped excessive bombing raids.

Production was delayed not only by the priority given to the denazification process and the effective work ban for most indigenous film personnel, but also by a shortage of film stock and by defunct technical equipment. Factories supplying raw film stock had either been destroyed during the war or were out of reach in the Soviet zone (such as the Agfa factory in Wolfen near Bitterfeld). UFI's large back catalogue (comprising the output of Ufa, Terra, Bavaria, and Tobis, and dating back to the 1920s) was, where films had not been destroyed, lost, or looted, in the process of being checked for its political suitability. Among the first films to be re-released were Ufa musicals and comedies.

The disentangling and reorganisation of the German film industry thus posed a number of problems for the Allied administration. It became trapped between the conflicting objectives of German politicians and filmmakers who were eager to resume an autonomous and strong national film industry, and of Hollywood's major studios intent on keeping competition neutralised. The decartelisation of the UFI assets within the framework of building a competitive, free-market film economy (which, of course, gave a significant advantage to established American companies over German competitors, who had to start from scratch) was actively pursued by the Allied authorities. A group of German trustees was appointed to manage the assets and maintain their value. Ironically, as Klaus Kreimeier has pointed out, the trustees managed the UFI legacy so well that its value increased.[21] Thus, while the Americans worked for a sell-off in parts, the German hope ultimately rested on a resumption of a centralised and vertically integrated film industry. Vertical integration, however, was precisely what the American authorities wanted to avoid.

After several years of uncertainty, the American and British military government finally ratified in September 1949 a law for the future of the UFI assets. 'Lex UFI' stipulated that the assets were to be liquidated by the trustees within eighteen months and sold to the highest bidder. Conditions for the sale included that no single prospective buyer was allowed more than one studio or three cinemas, that former managers or executive-board members of UFI-related companies were barred from bidding, and that the commercial use of the acronyms Ufa or UFI were banned. While there was no prospective buyer to be found under these conditions, the UFI trustees worked to increase the assets' value by renting out studio facilities, acquiring further exhibition outlets, and selling films from the UFI back catalogue to distributors. The re-release of old Ufa, Tobis, and Terra classics proved to be a profitable business; in 1949 125 films from the back catalogue were distributed, a third of that season's total number of films on offer in Germany. By 1951 the number had risen to 174.[22]

The strange saga of UFI's apparently ongoing dismantling, coupled with its simultaneous expansion and steady increase in value, was to continue for the next decade. Most of the Allied conditions regarding decartelisation declared in the 'Lex UFI' were ignored or reversed in subsequent legislation by the West German federal government. Despite several attempts of interest groups from within the film industry to acquire at least parts of the UFI assets, the West German government sanctioned in 1956 the sale of the whole package to a consortium of banks for a price that was between an estimated 30 and 45 million DM below the assets' actual value. Klaus Kreimeier has suggested that the motivation for this transaction was purely political, in that the West German government wanted to re-establish a representative centralised national film industry, and the return of the Ufa diamond as a symbol of a proudly national film culture.[23] A year before the UFI transaction, West Germany had re-established a national army, equally projecting a regained national self-confidence on the world stage. As it turned out, the UFI sale came at the worst possible moment. Between 1956 and 1959 audience figures in West Germany went down from 817 million to 671 million, rapidly decreasing in the following years. The revived Ufa only just about survived into the 1960s, before it was sold off once again in 1964 to the Bertelsmann corporation, which was more interested in Ufa's back catalogue of music than in producing films. UFI's back catalogue of feature films and documentaries was sold in1966 to the government-backed Friedrich-Wilhelm-Murnau-Stiftung.[24]

While the legacy of the German film industry was being administered and shifted around rather than put to productive use, the Allied postwar administration's second task was to rebuild a new industrial base for future German film production. Allied law stipulated that all branches of film business had to be licensed by the military authorities following a process of ideological vetting. The U.S. Military Government Film Control Officer in charge of this licensing procedure in the American zone was no stranger to the German film industry. Erich Pommer had been one of the most important producers of the Weimar period, and he had overseen the making of such classics as *The Cabinet of Dr Caligari* (1919), *Metropolis* (1927), *The Last Laugh* (1925), and *The Blue Angel* (1930), before emigrating to Hollywood via Paris and London.

Pommer seemed an ideal choice to deal with the specific problems facing the German film industry after the war.[25] Already in the aftermath of the First World War he had been influential in restructuring German film production and reviving its international reputation following national defeat. During the 1920s and early 1930s he had been able to negotiate and balance national interests, American inroads in the German market, and the transnational endeavours of the Film Europe initiative.[26] The experience of exile had not dampened Pommer's best intentions for the redevelopment of the film industry in his country of origin, but it had created an equally loyal commitment to American political objectives for postwar Germany. This balanced perspective made Pommer ultimately susceptible to suspicions and accusations from both sides.

Among the four Allies, the Americans entered the process of licensing new companies rather reluctantly, and only after the Soviets, British, and French had taken the first initiative. Prior to Pommer's appointment, the Soviets had established DEFA as a licensed company in the East where production resumed very quickly, resulting in the first postwar German feature film *Die Mörder sind unter uns* (The Murderers Are Among Us) in 1946. British authorities had granted licences to Camera Film GmbH, an enterprise of the director Helmut Käutner (who had kept a low profile during the Nazi years with a number of apolitical melodramas and comedies), and Studio 45, both Hamburg-based production companies. The French authorities in their administrative section of Berlin issued a licence to Artur Brauner's company CCC.

In the case of the companies approved of by Pommer in the American sector, nearly all of the newly licensed film-makers and producers had previously worked in the German film industry and were well known to Pommer, but there were significant biographical differences. Günther

Stapenhorst, a former Ufa manager, had returned from exile to found Carlton Film in Geiselgasteig. Josef von Baky (Objectiv Film), on the other hand, had been a highly prominent director of entertainment films during the Nazi period, and he had been in charge of Ufa's 25th anniversary blockbuster *Münchhausen* in 1942. Fritz Thiery, who was appointed trustee of the UFI asset Bavaria and founded Helios Film, and the director Harald Braun (Neue Deutsche Film GmbH) equally had previous Ufa connections.

Pommer was pragmatic enough to realise that, for any indigenous activity to resume, distinctions had to be made between committed Nazis and opportunist fellow-travellers. Furthermore, the spectre of an emerging East German film industry, capable of producing communist propaganda, gave further incentive to abandon too draconian vetting decisions and to speed up the reconstruction process in the West. Between 1945 and 1948, the period in which the licensing requirements operated, the number of new companies in the Western zones grew steadily to fifteen production companies and over forty distributors. In the same period, the number of cinemas in the Western zones grew from 1,150 in 1945 to nearly 3,000 by 1948.[27]

Pommer's responsibilities did not end with licensing procedures, but also included the restructuring of production facilities and the control over new film scripts and proposals in terms of their content, the ultimate aim being the foundation of a self-regulatory code of practice for German film production (an issue to which I shall return in the next section). Given the damaged state of studios such as Tempelhof, their lack of equipment, and the precarious and uncertain political status of Berlin, Pommer concentrated his efforts in rebuilding facilities in the Bavaria studios in Geiselgasteig, with most of Pommer's licensees being based in or near Munich. Under Pommer's supervision, the former dominance of Berlin as the capital of German film production thus gradually shifted to Munich. Although Berlin later became a significant production base again, the dispersal of the German film industry among separate locations persisted for decades, where Berlin provided mainly production initiatives and companies, but where the capital investment in distribution and studio facilities was concentrated in Munich and Frankfurt.

The films produced in the Allied zones between 1946 and 1948 under licence agreements all show signs of the difficult production conditions under which they were made. Quality of sound and film stock was very often poor. While films made in the newly refurbished Geiselgasteig studios and Neubabelsberg could at least provide some kind of production values, films shot in the Western sector of Berlin and in Hamburg frequently had to rely on location shooting alone. The constant backdrop of ruined cities, the films' melancholy mood, and the focus on issues of postwar reconstruction and the Nazi past quickly earned these productions the label *Trümmerfilme* (rubble films). Pommer believed that the films' shortcomings in production values could be an advantage: 'Germany is poor. It's the great chance for the reputable German film. We must want the essential.

All pomp and spectacular wizardry has to disappear. Mass movies? No. Stars? Not really necessary. The decisive factor is the script. The idea. The development of the idea. Poverty can have a productive effect'.[28]

Pommer's vision for the 'reputable German film' may have lacked specific aesthetic or political ideas, but in principle and in its aims this concept of film production was not too dissimilar from the objectives of the contemporary neo-realist movement in Italy. Like the German rubble films, but with a much clearer aesthetic and political agenda, neo-realism propagated a cinema of scarcity and a purist focus on the 'essential'. Following the American release of Roberto Rossellini's *Roma, Citta Aperta* (1945), Italian neo-realism came to epitomise in America, but also in other European countries, a significant departure in film style and production and the emergence of what would come to be labelled 'European Art Cinema', with its distinctive exhibition context, the art-house circuit.[29] Pommer's production strategy of the rubble film was thus not only aimed at supplying the indigenous market, but at raising the reputation of the German film internationally through culturally prestigious and stylistically 'modern' and 'realistic' films. This could then have the effect of opening up foreign markets more generally for German productions. A similar strategy of countering international hostility towards Germany through the concept of an alternative 'art cinema' had motivated Pommer's production of *The Cabinet of Dr Caligari* in the aftermath of the First World War. Pommer's strategy initially proved right, as the rubble films were overall critically well received abroad (particularly in Scandinavian countries – less so, however, in the United States) and frequently compared with their more famous Italian counterparts.[30]

Among the German public, however, the rubble films faced disappointed and even hostile reactions. For the intellectual élite, the rubble films of the postwar period only superficially, if at all, resembled Italian neo-realism. Instead they saw in these films a continuation of an old Ufa style and aesthetics, manifesting itself in overblown visual symbolism and stilted, theatrical acting styles. The fact that the same directors and actors who had been responsible for the glitz and glamour of Nazi cinema now specialised in rags and rubble was noted with some irritation. In a contemporary review of *Und über uns der Himmel* (1947, And the Heavens Above Us), a drama of returning war veterans with a catchy title song, starring one of Ufa's biggest stars, Hans Albers, and directed by Josef von Baky of *Münchhausen* fame, the influential critic Friedrich Luft noted dryly: 'The cinephiles in the audience would have wished not for routine, but for something new, and revolutionary. Instead we get Hans Albers, for a change, among ruins'.[31] The rubble films' political content was not seen as sufficient to address the moral problems and dilemmas of the postwar period, and their filmic style was seen as inappropriate. Commenting on the first, Soviet-commissioned, rubble film, *Die Mörder sind unter uns* (1946), Luft complained that 'the film is mostly tortuous. Behind every shot rises the wagging finger of a forced symbolism, and a wider picture is buried under a myriad of isolated symbols. Especially since this is the first attempt to deal with the present, clarity and an uncompromising argument would have been appropriate'.[32]

While for German critics the rubble films did too little in addressing the postwar social and ideological context, contemporary mass audiences had precisely the opposite complaint. The majority of Germans were confronted with ruins and destruction on a daily basis, and they were confronted with their moral guilt in the ongoing Allied re-education programmes. In this context, the rubble films with their settings and high moral tone were likely to be met with a certain fatigue, if not outright rejection. An article in the newly launched German weekly magazine *Der Spiegel* commented on an audience discussion following the première of the rubble film *Irgendwo in Berlin* (1946, Somewhere in Berlin), stating that

> What emerged was that a large part of the 'normal' cinema audience rejects the topical content, the 'true-to-life' quality of the new film. And that in spite of the respect they have for it otherwise. Real life, it was said, and notably by women, too, was sad enough today. In the cinema, people would like to relax, to 'forget', and not to be reminded of everyday misery. People no longer wanted to see ruins and homecoming prisoners of war in rags … They wanted more cheerful images.[33]

Pommer had speculated on the rubble films' export potential, but he ignored or misinterpreted the conflicting demands of German audiences. In any case, the term 'rubble film', which turned from being a useful label for marketing German films internationally to being, domestically at least, a summation of what audiences did not want to see, was always something of a misnomer. In fact, very much like Pommer's earlier marketing concept, 'Expressionist cinema', the generic unity of the rubble film begins to dissipate on closer inspection. Few of the films conventionally listed as belonging to the cycle had much to do with the problems of postwar urban destruction at all, while a number were in fact dealing with the immediate Nazi past. More pointedly, despite their often contemporary settings, hardly any of the films are 'about' the present in the way most of Italian neo-realist films were, but are more concerned in bridging a compromised past with the promise of a bright future through the process of redemption. Stylistically there is very little consistency across individual films and film-makers. The cycle ranges from portentously symbolic films such as *Die Mörder sind unter uns*, to self-reflexive and whimsical films about the vocation of film-making after the war (*Film ohne Titel*, 1947, Film without a Title), and comic and satirical oddities, such as *Berliner Ballade* (1948), and Helmut Käutner's surreal *Der Apfel ist ab!* (1948, The Apple has Fallen Down).[34] Already in 1947, Käutner, one of the most established directors associated with the rubble film, had declared that German audiences had no interest in a significantly new departure or in a rigidly defined aesthetic dogma for German cinema.[35] For the remainder of his long and successful career, Käutner would be mostly content in being a prolific, but resolutely mainstream and non-political, film-maker. The German intellectual élites, meanwhile, turned their backs on German cinema for most of the next twenty years, barely acknowledging that it even existed.

Pommer's ideas for a nationally defined art cinema, in terms both of a coherent industrial strategy and of a clearly delineated narrative content, were met with fierce opposition from the American industry. It was in the MPEA's interests to slow down the reconstruction of the German film industry in order to achieve its main aim, namely the monopoly of American distributors in the German market. Ursula Hardt has outlined in detail the various manoeuvres by which the MPEA attempted to discredit and replace Pommer and the campaigns directed against him in the American trade press.[36] Despite these interventions, Pommer retained the confidence of the military authorities, and he was able to persist with his plans until he finally relinquished his duties in May 1949. The military authorities in Germany had the unenviable mission of stabilising an independent German economy (including the film sector) while being politically pressured at the same time to support American economic interests.

The MPEA was founded as an export cartel in 1945, with the explicit aim of gaining a stronghold in overseas, and particularly European, distribution.[37] As the domestic troubles of the American film industry grew, the organisation's global ambitions became increasingly significant. With the support of successive American governments, the MPEA was able to exploit the absence of import restrictions in defeated countries such as Germany and Italy and to ensure that restrictions would not be adopted again. In Allied countries financially dependent on American investment, such as Britain and France, the MPEA was in a position to dictate the terms by which quota regulations operated, exemplified by the Anglo-American and Franco-American film agreements, both signed in 1948.

The substantial control the American film industry gained in the postwar years over European markets can hardly be disputed. What is much more open to revision is how German audiences responded to American products. Heide Fehrenbach has argued that 'the interwar fascination with American culture faded once it became associated with the unilateral policies of military occupation. Harkening back to their pre-war habits, Germans in the U.S. zone demanded freedom in the form of consumer choice and scorned the exclusive presence of Hollywood films in their theaters'.[38] An interesting insight into German audience preferences and consumer choice of the immediate postwar period is provided by a 1949 survey conducted by the market research institute Emnid (founded in 1945, the institute's acronym stands for Erforschung der öffentlichen Meinung; Marktforschung; Nachrichten; Informationen; and Dienstleistungen). The survey supports, but also modifies, Fehrenbach's conclusion according to demographic distinctions.[39]

Given the under-representation of adult men owing to war imprison-ment, injury, or death, women and adolescents comprised the majority of cinema-goers during the postwar years. Among different social groups, the most avid film-goers were blue- and white-collar workers, followed, by some margin and in ranking order, by the self-employed, freelance pro-fessionals, civil servants, pensioners, farmers, and farm labourers. In terms of generic preferences, blue-collar workers listed adventure stories, social drama, and crime films among their priorities. White-collar workers pre-ferred social drama, 'erotic' films (frequently a synonym for French and British productions), and historical narratives. The other groups repeated the same generic categories in a different order, although some also men-tioned film operettas, a staple genre of both the late Weimar and the Nazi periods.

Asked about the 'best contemporary German film', 67 per cent of all respondents were unable to provide an answer, while 72 per cent could name their favourite foreign film. When asked, however, about the best film seen all year, 33 per cent came up with a German title, while only 28 per cent decided on a foreign product. What this indicates, then, is that the respondents of at least this particular survey preferred foreign films to the rubble films characterising contemporary German film production, and yet that older German films in circulation were preferred over imports. Preference for German over foreign films was also more strongly articulated among the lower classes, such as blue-collar workers and farm labourers.

If one cautiously accepts the findings of this survey as reasonably rep-resentative (and studies of later periods – for example, those undertaken by Garncarz – do suggest continuities), one could argue that German audi-ences clearly supported the change in German film production towards popular genres that was under way by 1949. Among the contemporary German films mentioned positively, the most popular were two produc-tions that pointed towards a development beyond rubble narratives: *Fre-gola* (1948), a film combining elements of the musical and crime film genres, and starring the former Ufa star Marika Rökk, and *Tromba* (1949), a circus melodrama.

As can be expected, gender differences seem to have played a signifi-cant part in generic preferences. Among contemporary, and post-rubble, German films, the women in the survey tended more towards sentimental and melodramatic productions that had a main female protagonist, such as the previously mentioned *Fregola*, *Hofrat Geiger* (1948), where a young woman is reunited with her long-lost father, and *Das verlorene Gesicht* (1948, The Lost Face) which, in its subject matter of trauma-induced schiz-ophrenia, appears to have been modelled on the plot of the recently released British hit *Madonna of the Seven Moons* (1944). Men, on the other hand, tended more towards male-centred narratives, such as *Tromba*. In the groups of white-collar workers and the self-employed, male correspondents were also more open to 'topical' and 'culturally prestigious' films with a contemporary subject, such as *Liebe 47* (1949, Love '47), a drama about the homecoming of a war veteran, and *Ehe im Schatten* (1947, Marriage in the Shadows), a tragic tale of a Jewish–Non-Jewish marriage between two actors during the Nazi period.

Similar preferences are evident in the differing reception of foreign films. In this category women listed as their favourites the previously mentioned *The Song of Bernadette* (1943), starring Jennifer Jones as the saint from Lourdes; the French Biblical epic *Fabiola* (1948), set in Roman times and starring Michèle Morgan; and *Madonna of the Seven Moons* (1944). Among male correspondents, films featured were William Wyler's *The Best Years of Our Lives* (1946) and the Laurence Olivier production of *Hamlet* (1948). Again these examples indicate that male viewers showed a greater interest in a 'realistic' representation of contemporary social issues (as opposed to the more 'escapist' preferences confessed to by the female respondents). Men also preferred films that centred on male protagonists with whom they could identify. Although *The Best Years of Our Lives* had an American setting, the depicted dilemmas facing home-coming soldiers were in many respects comparable to the German situation, while the film's representation of nurturing women and physically and psychologically scarred men was remarkably similar to the rubble film's gender politics. The mention of a film such as *Hamlet*, on the other hand, indicates how much notions of cultural respectability and prestige appear to have influenced cinema-going preferences among men.

The picture that emerges from the survey regarding the popularity of indigenous and international stars is quite complex. All of the top German stars in the survey were favourites from the Ufa period, the most popular male actors being Willy Birgel, Hans Albers and Theo Lingen, while the best-loved female stars listed were Marika Rökk, Kristina Söderbaum, and Hilde Krahl. Taken together as a group, these six actors represented a wide range of the normative masculinities and femininities that had been offered by Ufa during the Nazi period. When asked about the best 'international' stars and given the choice to include German names as well, the respondents showed little confidence in the international box-office pulling power of their indigenous talent. Only the Swedish-born Ufa star Zarah Leander (who had not appeared in any film since 1943) and Hildegard Knef (one of the few genuinely 'new' German stars) were seen to have any 'potential'.

The list of 'best international stars' provides a curious mix of new and older favourites. Among male stars, Gainsborough's Stewart Granger (*Madonna of the Seven Moons*) led by a wide margin, followed in ranking order by Clark Gable, James Mason, Bing Crosby, Charles Boyer, Jean Marais, and Douglas Fairbanks Sr (a silent film star who had died ten years earlier!). Topping the list of female stars were Hollywood's Greta Garbo (inactive since 1942), Ingrid Bergman, and Marlene Dietrich, followed by British Margaret Lockwood. Further down the list were Leander and Knef, Rita Hayworth and the French actress Danielle Darrieux. This rather odd compilation of names may suggest a number of things. First, the popularity of American stars was often not based on contemporary film-going experience, but dated back to an earlier period of engagement with Hollywood cinema, namely, the 1920s and 1930s. Apart from Crosby, Bergman, and Hayworth (who does not feature very prominently anyway), none of the other American names listed were essentially stars of 1940s Hollywood and few of their older films were distributed in postwar Germany. Thus, while Garbo may have been placed as the top foreign female star, only two of her films were actually in circulation during the occupation period (*Ninotchka*, 1939, and *Two-Faced Woman*, 1941), both of them trailing behind Ufa re-releases and other foreign films in terms of popularity. Secondly, German audiences overall seemed to prefer Hollywood stars with a distinctly European appeal, as is indicated by the ranking of Garbo, Bergman, Dietrich, and Boyer. Thirdly, among foreign stars, popularity seems to have been fairly evenly distributed between American, French, and British actors. In fact, at least at the time of the survey, the British were particularly strongly represented (Granger, Mason, Lockwood), and this popularity persisted well into the next decade. Stewart Granger especially was placed among the top ten of popular male stars from the late 1940s until 1954.[40] Female British stars, such as Margaret Lockwood, Phyllis Calvert, and Jean Simmons, also frequently outclassed Hollywood competition well into the 1950s.[41]

The popularity of British films with postwar German audiences is further borne out by the rather curious result of the survey's enquiry about the best film director. Forty-seven per cent of all responses named J. Arthur Rank (listed simply as Arthur Rank) in this category. In second place was the notorious Nazi propagandist Veit Harlan. Helmut Käutner, among the culturally more ambitious directors of indigenous postwar films, came near the bottom of the list.

The results of the Emnid survey help to revise and challenge a number of established assumptions about postwar German cinema, its audiences, and the films in circulation. With regard to Hollywood films in the postwar German market, Klaus Kreimeier, subscribing to a view of a gradual American colonisation of the German psyche, has suggested that 'if only for their quantity, they satisfied the entertainment needs of the defeated and impoverished Germans, and influenced their view of the world and their desires. With the American imports, the American way of life crept into the daydreams of the masses and indoctrinated them with a message of an omnipotent economy, and of the virtues of ruthless individualism'.[42] Heide Fehrenbach (at least in her assessment of the immediate postwar occupation period) arrives at exactly the opposite conclusion. Charting the development of the German film industry from the late 1940s into the 1950s towards popular entertainment and indigenous genres such as the

Heimatfilm, she perceives instead an instinctive resistance of German audiences in the postwar years to Hollywood and the American way of life, a resistance that only begins to erode in the mid-1950s. Drawing on different data, Joseph Garncarz comes to a very similar conclusion, although he dates the erosion of a preference for national products slightly later.[43] For Fehrenbach, 'Hollywood never addressed German audiences as Germans, with reference to their national past, present, or future', resulting in a nearly complete rejection of American films and a preference for indigenous products, both past and present.[44]

Despite their differences, both Kreimeier's and Fehrenbach's accounts provide a fairly homogenised view of 'the German audience' in the immediate postwar period. For Kreimeier, the German public is a passive entity without a clear identity, helplessly subjected to outside political and economic imperialism and susceptible to cultural and ideological indoctrination. Fehrenbach's concept of the postwar audience, on the other hand, invokes the idea of a shaken, but otherwise relatively stable, national community, asserting its rights to an indigenous culture and national identity through consumption preferences.

The Emnid survey from 1949 suggests a more complex picture of German audiences during this period. It certainly indicates that postwar German cinema-goers were not immediately bowled over by Hollywood's economic might, genres, stars, and production values. German audiences were highly discriminating in deciding which American genres and films they liked. Furthermore, these preferences did not necessarily correspond to current American product differentiations or specific generic trends. As the categories mentioned in the Emnid survey indicate (social drama, adventure, erotic films), German perceptions seem to have been rather fluid with regard to generic distinctions. This would make it difficult for Hollywood companies in the German market for years to come to assume the same production, distribution, and marketing patterns as in the American home market.

Certain Hollywood genres, particularly the American musical, met with an almost complete lack of interest at the German box office, a trend that persisted throughout the 1950s and 1960s. The western was almost exclusively confined to children's matinees (a fact that in itself raised concern among German educationalists, who worried about the genre's brutalising effects on children), making only the most simplistic formats, such as B-film serials, financially viable. Hollywood's 'quality' or 'adult' postwar westerns, on the other hand, were largely ignored. For the Emnid correspondents in 1949, it was rather atypical studio productions, such as *The Song of Bernadette* (1943), and older, sometimes no longer active, stars, such as Fairbanks and Garbo, that were appreciated over more standard Hollywood genres or more contemporary stars.

The Emnid survey, however, also illustrates that German audience preferences, far from comprising a cohesive national taste, were subject to substantial differences along gender, class, and generational lines. These differences are not only important in assessing the reception of foreign (and not just Hollywood) films, but also significant in view of changing indigenous production strategies. Given the particular consumer strength of female audiences, their preference for genres such as melodrama to some extent dictated the development of certain generic patterns throughout the next decade. It is therefore suggestive to read the critical decline of the German cinema from the late 1940s onwards in connection with its perceived 'feminisation'.

Fehrenbach rightly points out that 'national cinematic culture was understood to be suffering from the effects of the shoddy taste of a consumer group that was not sufficiently cultured – not sufficiently masculine, that is – in its critical faculties'.[45] On the other hand, the Emnid survey reveals a very broad and eclectic range of tastes and preferences, encompassing both indigenous and foreign films. This eclecticism, however, suggests that, far from having been stubbornly 'resistant' to outside influence, German audiences were, within certain parameters, willing to expand their cultural horizons or competence. The male and female correspondents of the survey were evidently capable of negotiating their preferences for older and recent German films with the different appeal of American, British, and French productions, and of contextualising these different priorities within the framework of a film culture that was clearly understood as being international. In other words, while popular indigenous films may have been 'dominantly' preferred, it does not follow that German audiences were ignorant of or necessarily hostile to other cultural conventions. As the success of the Gainsborough melodramas with German audiences indicates, however, there are certain patterns that can be perceived with regard to generic and thematic preferences, at least as far as popular cinema is concerned. What worked with postwar German audiences were films that were recognisably 'European' in their use of locations and narratives, but which simultaneously detached these locations and themes from any 'realism' through elements of historical distance, romantic fantasy, and stylistic exaggeration.

Studies of how specific audiences engage with indigenous and foreign films frequently rely on hegemonic categories of either a 'dominated' or a 'nationally resistant' audience. What is denied in both cases are the influences of diversity, personal agency and, perhaps most importantly, the possibility that audiences may have different registers for understanding, comparing, and appreciating different cultural conventions at a given time. While many studies of postwar German cinema have frequently pointed to its parochial nature and to the allegedly nationalist undercurrents of indigenous production, I would suggest instead that already in the first postwar years under occupation rule the notion of rebuilding national film production was balanced by an increasingly internationally minded audience, a fact that was acknowledged by producers and distributors alike.

National Intervention in the 1950s

Following the foundation of the Federal Republic in 1949, the Allied control over the German film market gave way to a free-market economy. The West German film industry responded favourably to the changed situation; between 1946 and 1948 forty films had been made, while in 1949 alone the number went up to sixty-two.[46] The number of production companies and distributors, no longer subject to vetting procedures, also rose rapidly after 1949. Far from being free of restrictions, however, the West German film industry faced a new set of interventions into its affairs, this time from the federal government and political lobbying groups and taking the form of censorship and film subsidies.

Ideas for a national institution to regulate film content had first been aired by Erich Pommer during his time as American film control officer between 1946 and 1949. Given the way in which the German film industry had been used for propaganda purposes during the war, Pommer envisaged a politically neutral, democratically balanced, and centralised body, based on the self-regulatory model of the American Production Code and its executive body, the Production Code Administration. Among the Allied powers, objections to a centralised German film-control institution were initially raised by the French, who preferred the idea of regionally based control committees, composed of members from certain interest groups, such as education authorities, the churches, cultural organisations, and trade unions, with only a minority representation of the film industry itself. The notion of regionality corresponded to the political reconstruction of Germany, with its emphasis on regional autonomy within a federal framework. However, what ultimately motivated French resistance was 'that French officials feared industry self-censorship would result in hostility to the French product (since imported films would also be subject to review by the censorship board) and that the historical competition between the two countries would be carried over to the sphere of economics and culture in a way that would disadvantage French interests'.[47]

While French objections were soon overcome owing to French economic dependence on America, Pommer's plans met with equal resistance from the emerging West German political and cultural establishment. West German politicians also proposed a greater influence of local authorities and the two main churches on film control (particularly with regard to youth protection and the preservation of moral values). Pre-empting a final decision on the exact nature of a national censorship board, both the West German film industry and public interest groups coordinated their ambitions in forming strategic alliances and associations. It is during this period that self-appointed moral guardians, such as the Aktion Saubere Leinwand (Action for a Clean Screen) were founded, as well as Catholic and Protestant film publications and clubs.

After several attempts at reaching a compromise between the divergent interests had failed, a final agreement was reached in 1949 with the establishment of the Freiwillige Selbstkontrolle (Voluntary Self-Control), or FSK, based in Wiesbaden. Until the 1970s, no indigenous or foreign film could be released in West Germany without the FSK's approval. The FSK was not only responsible for issuing age certificates, but could also demand cuts or prohibit films in their entirety, and it advised producers on how to avoid contentious matters such as sexual explicitness or political suitability. To some extent, the FSK complied with American principles, as Fehrenbach has noted: 'Industry representatives occupied four out of six seats on the Working Committee, which would review all films before their release in Germany, and eight out of fifteen seats on the Main Committee, which was responsible for settling contested decisions'.[48] The remaining non-industry representatives were recruited from the state ministries of culture, the churches, and federal youth-protection agencies. Significantly, the specific motivations behind FSK decisions were to be exempted from public scrutiny, which since the FSK's inception has continued to raise questions and public debate about the institution's accountability and hidden agenda.[49]

The FSK settlement of 1949 was only grudgingly accepted by West German politicians and church leaders, as they reserved the right to review film-control mechanisms if they fell short of the functions they envisaged. Once in place, however, the FSK was unlikely to be replaced or significantly changed. In years to come, religious or right wing lobbying groups would concentrate instead on eroding the commission's authority by rallying dissent and organising public protest actions against individual FSK decisions. Heide Fehrenbach has detailed such strategies in the national 'scandal' caused by the release of the melodrama *Die Sünderin* (1950, The Sinner). In its subject-matter of prostitution and suicide, and in its (albeit barely perceptible) representation of female nudity, the film was singled out for its 'corrupting influence', and its release was accompanied by widespread public protests and riots, and the resignation of the two church representatives within the FSK.[50]

In 1949 the Catholic publication *Filmdienst*, which reviewed all current films in circulation, established its own system of evaluation, advising its readers on whether films were worthy or unworthy, which frequently depended on whether films complied with church dogma. The case of the British film *Black Narcissus* (1947), centring on a group of Catholic nuns based in a remote Himalayan mountain mission who become adversely affected by their surroundings, is instructive in indicating the publication's priorities. In recent years the film has been recognised as a visually and narratively sophisticated melodrama, as well as a showcase for the craftsmanship and auteurist vision of its creators, Michael Powell and Emeric Pressburger. At the time of its West German release, however, the *Filmdienst* review condemned the film for its supposed defamation of nuns' lives. Even a subsequently revised review, still in print today, opines that the film is 'dubious because it uses religious life simply as a colourful backdrop'.[51]

State interference manifested itself not only through federal involvement in censorship, but also through state subsidies for film production. The currency reform of 1948 had diminished the financial protection provided by the occupation economy and left the mostly small to medium-sized indigenous film companies short of funds. Support from Konrad Adenauer's new conservative government for the indigenous film market was rather ambivalent. On the one hand, a newly imposed entertainment tax stunted growth in the exhibition sector. On the other hand, the state provided tax relief for 'culturally prestigious' films.

In 1951 the Filmbewertungsstelle der Länder (Film Evaluation Board) or FBW was founded, which was designed to award aesthetically or thematically 'outstanding' films with the distinction of being 'valuable' or 'very valuable'.[52] Both indigenous and foreign films were eligible for these awards, which essentially were latter-day versions of the Nazis' system of Predicates, and for subsequent tax relief. However, as with the decisions of the FSK, the criteria of what constituted value were not outlined in public and seemed not always to be clear or consistent. One study claims that throughout the 1950s the FBW, in line with Cold War politics, preferably rewarded films that had a militarist or anti-Communist agenda, or which were at least politically innocuous.[53]

Apart from such post facto control, however, the state also intervened more directly in film production. Already in 1949 individual federal states provided financial aid for film production on differing conditions. In Bavaria, the regional government covered distributors' losses on individual films through underwriting guarantees. In Berlin, on the other hand, film-makers received fully repayable loans at a favourable rate of interest.[54] In 1950, the federal government intervened with its own financial aid package for the indigenous industry. A lump sum of 20 million DM was made available, to be distributed by a government commission with representatives from the Ministries of Finance, Economy, and the Interior. An advisory council of five members (three politicians from both houses of parliament, one film industry representative, and one journalist) was to negotiate with ministry officials on the economic viability of individual proposals.

It quickly became apparent, however, that projects were judged not only according to their financial potential. As Jürgen Berger has noted, screenplays were sent back for 'improvements' on moral or political grounds and casting choices were overruled in cases where individuals were seen as politically inopportune (for example, where actors or directors had worked on East German productions).[55] A blanket ban affected all East German imports up till 1954, after which an extensive ideological vetting process was put into place.[56] This underhand blacklisting reflected in particular the agenda of the Ministry of the Interior, which was at the fore-front of Cold War politics during this period.

The federal guarantee scheme in operation between 1950 and 1953 was directed at producers, who had to undergo a laboriously bureaucratic process of approval that included both a lengthy application procedure and continual supervision during production. Producers had to submit a final script, cast and crew lists, a shooting schedule, a distribution contract, the evidence of bank loans, and the assurance that they could cover 20 per cent of the production costs out of their own funds. Subtracting the 20 per cent as the producer's personal risk, the guarantee scheme covered 35 per cent of the initial budget in the event of box-office losses. In return, producers had to concede the rights of ownership and future use to a government-appointed trusteeship. Furthermore, producers were obliged to use studio facilities that were already in existence in 1950, which more or less exclusively covered the UFI assets, and which indicates that the long-term aim of this measure was to revive Ufa as a national industry monopoly. Between 1950 and 1953 the federal government provided guarantees for eighty-two productions, rejected forty-four proposals, and lost approximately 9 million DM from the initial 20 million in the process.

In 1953 the federal government approved a second guarantee scheme, this time with a lump sum of 50 million DM. The practice of vetting scripts on political as well as economic grounds continued. The significant difference from the earlier scheme was that guarantees were only granted to proposals that included eight or more films, a condition that favoured distributors and forced producers into an increasing dependence on them. As a result, independent production outlets began to shrink by the mid-1950s. Furthermore, the new guarantee scheme stipulated that distributors could retain fixed percentages of the production costs as their own profit. These two aspects effectively meant that distributors applying for federal guarantees were encouraged not only to increase the number of films on offer, but also to raise production costs.

In 1954 the annual number of indigenous productions had risen to 142. However, the new guarantee scheme also meant that distributors had to rely on ever more substantial backing through bank loans, and the increased risk factors led to a succession of bankruptcies in the indigenous distribution sector, which would become a defining feature of the West German film industry well into the 1970s. By 1955 the guarantee scheme was phased out, having lost the government an estimated 30 million DM.

Popular Genres and Cinema in the 1950s

As the previous section has made explicit, the combined pressures of political and religious interests and the film industry's economic dependency in the early to mid-1950s determined a mode of production that favoured consensual entertainment over politically or socially controversial material. Moreover, this corresponded, as the 1949 Emnid survey had already suggested, to dominant audience preferences at the time. By the early 1950s, the majority of indigenous films were the so-called *Heimatfilme* (25 per cent of all the films made), followed by melodramas (frequently featuring saintly doctors), operettas, and comedies.

The West German *Heimat* (or homeland) film of the 1950s is arguably one of the most quintessentially German genres, since its very name attests to its rootedness in indigenous locations and cultural traditions. It is, as Johannes von Moltke has argued, an explicitly 'spatial' genre, connected to a particular construction of space, which connects it with spatial genres from other cultural contexts, such as the American Western, *film noir*, or the British 'heritage' film.[57] More accurately described as a generic hybrid, the *Heimatfilm*, at least in its most prominent manifestation during the 1950s, combines romantic and/or family melodrama (the films' plots often focused on generational conflict), intermittent comedy, and music (often, but not exclusively, of the folk variety) against the backdrop of an idyllic countryside. Nearly all of the *Heimatfilme* of the period display a marked priority of 'scenery' and location in relation to narrative progression, a priority that manifests itself in an obsessive use of panoramic long takes and digressive shots of animals and mountain vistas which occasionally blur the distinction between fiction film, nature documentary, and holiday home movie. Principal locations of the genre are the Bavarian Alps, the Black Forest, Lake Constance, or the Lüneburg Heath. Austrian landscapes provided the scenic backdrop for a whole subgenre of the nineteenth century Habsburg costume romance, epitomised by the hugely successful *Sissi* film trilogy, starring Romy Schneider as the empress and former Bavarian princess Elizabeth of Austria. Meanwhile, former territories in the East (e.g., Pommerania, Silesia, Eastern Prussia), celebrated by the Nazis as the pivotal German frontier of blood and soil and territorial expansion, are conspicuously absent from the films of the postwar period, even though refugees from these areas feature, sometimes prominently, in the films' narratives.

In critical histories of postwar German film, the *Heimatfilm* has been the linchpin for the perceived provincialism and parochialism of German commercial cinema, and there is no single genre on which as much condescension has been heaped, often without any significant recourse to a detailed study of the genre or individual films in question. The *Heimatfilm* has been until very recently, as von Moltke correctly identifies, the quintessential 'bad object' of German film historiography.[58] Apart from persistent derision of the genre's perceived aesthetic shortcomings, there are a number of interlocking ideological objections that have been raised against the *Heimatfilm*. First, the genre's insistence on the concept of *Heimat* so soon after the compromised use of the term under the Nazis allegedly attests to the genre's (and by implication its audience's) inherently nationalist sentiment. In this respect, the *Heimatfilm* has been perceived as nothing more than a simple continuation of the 'blood-and-soil' cinema of the Nazi years, which itself is preceded by the 1920s and early 1930s *Bergfilm* or mountain film (this continuity in ideological content can further be 'proven' by a continuity in the film-making personnel associated with the genre, many of whom span the mountain films, the Nazi years, and the 1950s). Indeed, as von Moltke has amply documented, the genre's iconography and principal narrative convention, can be traced even further back to the Wilhelmine era.[59] The *Heimatfilm* has, moreover, been criticised for avoiding critical engagement with the recent national past, and for realigning the restoration of postwar national identity with traditional models of gender hierarchies and moral norms, which, according to the genre, are best represented by a rural lifestyle, governed by ancient traditions, and religious and seasonal duties and requirements.

While it would be pointless to construct a revisionist view of the *Heimatfilm* as inherently politically progressive or subversive, the above critique of the genre seems similarly misdirected. First, the return to the notion of *Heimat* in 1950s cinema is hardly comparable with the determined nationalism of the Nazi years (and of the 'blood-and soil' cinema that is often seen as a direct precursor to the *Heimatfilm*). In fact, it is precisely its non-

Figure 2.1. Habsburg Romance and the Heimatfilm: Romy Schneider and Karlheinz Böhm in *Sissi* (1955). Deutsches Filminstitut (DIF), Frankfurt-on-Main.

political and escapist possibilities that made *Heimat* such an appealing concept for film-makers and audiences alike. Georg Seesslen has noted that the *Heimatfilm* demarcated a geo-psychological movement 'from the East associated with defeat and guilt to the South associated with love and redemption',[60] in other words, the genre allowed its audiences to escape the consequences of both the Nazi era and the postwar division of Germany into two states. The genre's emphasis away from life-or-death allegiances to the concept of national identity towards individualistic self-determination is clearly perceptible in the films' tone and mood, which are rational and secular where the mountain films of the 1920s and 1930s were often laden with mysticism and fatalistic endurance. Compare also the archetypally brooding heroes of the 1920s and 1930s (e.g. Gustav Diessl) with the resolutely 'normal' protagonists of the 1950s, embodied, for example, in the rather unheroic star personae of Rudolf Prack or Claus Holm.

Seesslen's argument above indicates that it would be wrong to deduce from the word Heimat an emphasis on stasis in the films in question; on the contrary, the genre is about mobility to such an extent that already by the mid-1950s it overlaps with and sometimes is indistinguishable from its twin genre, the *Ferienfilm* (holiday film). Years before the West German travel boom commenced, the *Heimatfilm* transported its audiences away from the drabness of West German physical and political reconstruction into a cheerful outdoor utopia that had its indoor equivalent in the dream kitchens and living-rooms of mail-order catalogues. The *Heimatfilme* were primarily targeted at and appealed to urban and predominantly female audiences (and, without doubt, the fact that the *Heimatfilm* was perceived as a 'female' genre has played a significant part in the way the genre has been critically pigeon-holed and reviled over the years). Meanwhile, public reactions to *Schwarzwaldmädel* (1950, Black Forest Girl) in the Black Forest suggested that audiences in rural areas resented their portrayal on screen as backward and whimsical provincials.[61] The *Heimatfilm* constructed and celebrated a world in which the technological and social progress of modernity could without major problems be negotiated and harmonised with a rural and pre-industrial Arcadia. The magical link in creating this utopia and thus fundamentally transforming, in effect eliminating, the separation of urban and rural spheres was the growing service industry of tourism. While in its narratives the *Heimatfilm* often centred on the dichotomies between a 'healthy' countryside and the corrupting influences of urban life, the genre simultaneously marked out its locations for tourist development and addressed its audience as potential holiday-makers and as consumers within an emerging leisure society. The *Heimatfilm* did not propose, as has often been claimed, a regressive and reactionary movement towards a pre-modern way of life. On the contrary, as both Seesslen and von Moltke have previously argued, the genre explicitly endeavoured to reconcile modernity and rural idyll in a utopian theme park based on the principles of entertainment and distraction.

The postwar *Heimatfilm* both responded to and accelerated the development of mass tourism, in similar ways in which, as Nancy Nenno has argued, the mountain film of the 1920s and 1930s had helped to promote alpine sports tourism.[62] Postwar poverty and reconstruction priorities had delayed the re-emergence of travel and tourism until the early 1950s. In 1954, 85 per cent of all holiday journeys undertaken by West Germans were to domestic destinations, a pattern that would, at first gradually and then dramatically, reverse in the 1960s and 1970s.[63] Promotional discourses surrounding the *Heimatfilme* often encouraged audiences to visit the locations depicted in the films. Conversely it is known of at least one famous example, *Der Förster vom Silberwald* (1954), that it was financially supported by the Austrian tourist authorities with the explicit agenda to advertise Austrian holiday resorts.[64] In this respect, the rural Arcadia the *Heimatfilm* portrayed was both incentive and eventual reward for its (mainly urban) audience's individual efforts in West Germany's economic and social reconstruction, rather than simply a representation of an idealised national culture. Indeed, soon after regained affluence made it possible, a vast number of West Germans flocked to national and later international tourist resorts to find physical and spiritual regeneration. Particularly from the mid-1950s onwards, the promotion of films according to the appeal of specific locations (whether at home or abroad) became increasingly linked to the development of tourism. In other words, the film industry's imaginary 'elsewhere' and the tourist industry's actual travel provisions fed on and could refer to each other in terms of tie-ins, promotions, and consumption patterns.

In its explicit alignment with a tourist discourse, the *Heimatfilm* thus suggested a pleasurable escape from the constraints of both the present, and of history more generally. At the same time, as we have seen, the genre was hardly the unreconstructed paean to traditional rural living and patriarchal primacy it is often made out to be. While essentially committed to eventually consensual and conservative resolutions (between the generations, between the city and the countryside, between the sexes), the narratives of the *Heimatfilm* are littered with dysfunctional families, all marked by deep-seated conflicts and problems, which are remarkably similar to the dilemmas facing the protagonists of Hollywood's family melodramas during the same period.[65] The 'idyll' of the 1950s *Heimatfilm*'s principal locations is nearly always deconstructed through human intervention in the course of the films' plots, only to be reconstituted in the end, not in its pure and untouched form but as another compromise construction. The *Heimatfilm* is thus a genre where one can find the validation of patriarchy alongside the celebration of female emancipation, pleas for the conservation of traditional living next to the promotion of rampant consumerism, and torrid family relations against the scenic backdrop of a tourist idyll. It is precisely this persistent drive towards ideological compromise, reconciling what are in reality irreconcilable differences, which in turn has confounded many ideological readings of the genre.

While the *Heimatfilm* of the 1950s borrowed narrative tropes and visual elements of previous cinematic genres as well as literary predecessors, other popular genres of the period drew their main inspiration and motivation from other media, particularly from the music industry and the new medium of television. Out of this new context of intertextuality emerged the other quintessential 1950s indigenous genre, the *Schlager* (or 'chart hit') film.[66] Television and radio, rather than cinema or stage, became the predominant media for musical revues, which, alongside the new formats of hit parades and chart shows, quickly established a new generation of younger performers and artists, as well as a rapidly developing market for recordings, jukeboxes, and fan magazines (for example, the teen publication *Bravo*). In the second half of the decade, televised international events such as the San Remo Festival and the Eurovision Song Contest (first staged in 1956) helped to create both a taste and a market for an increasingly cosmopolitan popular music scene.

Apart from the essential requirements of light-hearted or sentimental lyrics and a catchy tune, the *Schlager* was actually a widely inclusive category for various musical and performance styles and influences. Among the best-loved of the vast number of *Schlager* stars of the 1950s and 1960s was rugged Freddy Quinn, an Austrian who reinvented himself in the image of a stereotypical Hamburg sailor, singing shanties, Country-and-Western songs, and other sentimental ballads, usually about the contradictory desires of wishing to be elsewhere and of returning home from long seafaring journeys. Equally popular was Peter Alexander, a slick Austrian crooner with a repertoire ranging from operetta to swing and folk song. Finally there was the energetic Italian Caterina Valente, who apart from all of the above could also sing Italian ballads and imitate Ella Fitzgerald's 'scatting' vocals and, if required, could tap-dance, waltz, or boogie-woogie. It was musical performers such as these who became West German cinema's most bankable stars in the second half of the 1950s and who accelerated the industry's propensity and audience demand, for internationalism.

The *Schlagerfilm* was less a self-contained genre in its own right than an extension of and advertisement for the leisure industries and entertainment media from which it emerged. Indeed, the star vehicles for Quinn, Alexander, and Valente more or less constituted subgenres in their own right, and were less concerned with generic consistency and more with giving their stars ample opportunities to display their various talents. The films were frequently set against the backdrop of scenic foreign locations, such as the Adriatic Coast, the French Riviera, or the island of Capri, thus further continuing the East-South movement initiated by the *Heimatfilm*. By the end of the 1950s, *Schlagerfilme* made up a quarter of all West German productions, amalgamating not only diverse musical styles but also different cinematic genres: 'Like a chameleon, the *Schlagerfilm* adapted itself to all new trends and U-turns of a hysterical consumer market, venturing out of its original context of the revue genre, and entering into wild combinations with the *Heimatfilm*, the "beach holiday" film, the thriller, the Western, and later soft porn'.[67]

This generic and musical adaptability also enabled the *Schlagerfilm* to bridge an emerging generational and gender gap among cinema audiences. By the mid-1950s urban youth had begun to embrace American popular culture, epitomised by rock 'n' roll, fashion items (such as leather jackets, jeans, and petticoats), motor bikes and rebel icons such as Elvis Presley, James Dean, and Marlon Brando. Fehrenbach argues that 'American-style consumption became the weapon of choice in the postwar generation's protest against parental prescriptions for proper socialisation', seeking 'a transformation of identity through a transformation of the body'.[68] Teenage street gangs (the so-called *Halbstarken*) were indeed seen by the cultural and political establishment as a serious social problem, especially after youth riots erupted in a number of cities in 1956.[69] Although couched in relatively conformist moral conventions and narrative resolutions, Hollywood films such as *The Wild One* (1954), *Rebel Without a Cause* (1955), *Blackboard Jungle* (1955), and *Rock Around the Clock* (1956) functioned as subversive texts for young film-goers (of course, not just in West Germany), partly due to the charisma of their stars (Brando, Dean, Sidney Poitier), and partly owing to their reference to and use of the iconography, fashions, and music of the emerging subculture of rock 'n' roll.

Figure 2.2. Teen stars Peter Kraus and Conny Froboess in the Schlagerfilm *Wenn die Conny mit dem Peter* (1958, When Conny Met Peter). Deutsches Filminstitut (DIF), Frankfurt-on-Main.

In West Germany the release of these four Hollywood imports was surrounded by public debate and press hype, which added to their box-office success and convinced the indigenous film industry that youth audiences were a new and distinctive consumer group to be reckoned with. After the social drama *Die Halbstarken* (1956) had introduced brooding youth rebels to West German cinema in the form of Horst Buchholz and Karin Baal, the *Schlagerfilm* responded by introducing the much tamer teen stars Peter Kraus and Cornelia ('Conny') Froboess. Their films, such as *Wenn die Conny mit dem Peter* (1958, When Conny Met Peter) and *Conny und Peter machen Musik* (1960, Conny and Peter Make Music), were standard teen comedies, which featured petticoated girls and boys with greased back hair, whose main pastime is making 'hot music' in Daddy's garage, playing the guitar, swivelling hips, and singing toned down U.S. rock 'n' roll hits (often referred to as 'jazz') with German lyrics. The promotional slogan for *Wenn die Conny mit dem Peter* set the agenda: 'Be young and stay young with plenty of music'. Permanently upbeat, and overall clean and safe, Conny and Peter were popular with young and older audiences alike, subtly introducing American musical styles and youth fashions into the *Schlagerfilm* repertoire, while at the same time defusing generational tensions and differences.

The mid-decade success of the four previously cited teenager-oriented American films and of U.S. stars such as James Dean and Marlon Brando indicates early signs of a significant change in audience preferences in West Germany. In the early postwar years, as I have outlined previously, Hollywood films initially had little impact in terms of box-office results. However, following the foundation of the Federal Republic, the influx of foreign and particularly American films had increased dramatically. Attempts to introduce quota regulations in the first years of the republic had failed, largely as a result of West Germany's political and economic dependence on the United States. A proposal by the West German government in 1950 to restrict American imports to 100 films per year was rejected by the Allied High Commission. The MPEA and the West German film industry subsequently agreed on 200 films per year, but only a couple of years later the number had risen to 250.[70]

The best performance of a foreign film in the early 1950s was achieved by the Anglo-American production *The Third Man* (1949), its success with domestic audiences certainly in part due to its Viennese setting, and to the participation of German-speaking actors such Paul Hörbiger, Ernst Deutsch, Erich Ponto, and Siegfried Breuer.[71] Between 1950 and 1953 only four purely Hollywood films reached the annual top ten, the Esther Williams musical *Bathing Beauty* (made in 1944), *Conquest* (made in 1938), a Greta Garbo vehicle set during the Napoleonic wars and featuring French actor Charles Boyer as Bonaparte, Hitchcock's Gothic thriller *Rebecca* (1940), and the Cecil B. De Mille circus spectacle *The Greatest Show on Earth* (1952).[72] Considering the findings of the Emnid survey in 1949 that female audiences constituted the majority of cinema-goers, and that overall they preferred 'soft' genres such as melodrama, the box-office success in the early 1950s of indigenous melodramas and the *Heimatfilm* and also of foreign variants of these, indicates that women continued to be the dominant cinema going force.

Erica Carter has suggested that, for women during this period, cinema represented a 'part of everyday experience' whereas, for men, it was perceived as a specialist interest or hobby.[73] Noting women audiences' interest in commercials and advertisements accompanying main features, Carter points to its significance:

> in the context of a film culture that in general emphasized the links between film, female consumption, and the commodity form. Women film stars were used regularly in advertising and fashion photography to promote fashion and beauty products as specifically feminine consumer cultural forms. The postwar cinema, in other words ...acted as a symbolic vehicle for new models of consuming femininity.[74]

By 1953, a noticeable demographic shift among audiences occurred. The number of male cinema-goers, and particularly those from white-collar professions and with an educated background, increased. According to Fehrenbach, they:

> constituted a large proportion of the audience for quality American films. They should not be classified too readily as willing subjects for cultural Americanization, however, for although they were avid consumers of quality films, they exhibited no firm preference for any particular national product. After Hitler, cinematic cosmopolitanism became the mark of an enlightened German who was seeking to shed the chauvinism of a shameful past.[75]

However, generic preferences shifted not only towards 'quality' films, but more generally towards male-oriented genres, both indigenous and foreign. While the *Heimatfilm* continued to feature among the best-performing films, it became increasingly accompanied by genres such as war and adventure films. In the season 1954/55 an indigenous war film (*08/15*) for the first time outperformed the most popular *Heimatfilm* of the year (*Der Förster vom Silberwald*, The Forest Ranger from the Silver Forest). In 1957/8 it was another (foreign) war film that for the first time in the postwar period superseded indigenous competition, the Anglo-American *The Bridge on the River Kwai*. In the same year, two other British war films had a strong impact on the West German box office, significantly both featuring 'positive' and heroic German protagonists, *The One That Got Away* (starring Hardy Krüger as a German soldier intent on escaping a British prisoner-of-war camp during the Second World War) and *The Battle of the*

River Plate (a film about the sinking of the 'Graf Spee', and featuring a dignified Peter Finch as a German captain).[76]

Since the early 1950s, American and British distributors had learned from the experience of the immediate postwar era that West German audiences resented the representation of 'ugly' Germans in foreign imports. Joseph Garncarz has documented how several Hollywood films were re-edited and redubbed for their West German release.[77] In the dubbed version of Alfred Hitchcock's *Notorious* (1946), a group of Nazi spies trying to get access to uranium were remodelled into communist conspirators meddling in drugs. In the case of *Casablanca* (1942, released in West Germany in 1952) any reference to Nazis was excised (and with it the part of Conrad Veidt's Nazi commander), turning the film into the story of a fugitive scientist who is sought because he destroyed his own invention, a weapon of mass destruction. Where negative characters were identified originally as German, such identifications were cut, as in the case of *I Confess* (1952), *The African Queen* (1951), and *Arsenic and Old Lace* (1944). Significantly, as Joseph Garncarz has documented, the majority of such variations were initiated by the American distributors themselves. Only in a minority of cases had the FSK demanded changes or the West German dubbing studios acted without authorisation.

Such novel strategies and incursions notwithstanding, until the late 1950s indigenous productions consistently outperformed foreign competition at the box office. However, the success of genres such as the *Heimatfilm* and *Schlagerfilm* does not necessarily prove that 1950s audiences had a particularly strong proclivity towards films expressing national sentiment. If anything, the *Heimatfilm* evaded issues of national identity by dispersing it into regional specificities and by transforming indigenous traditions and communities into sites of leisure and consumption. The *Schlagerfilm*, on the other hand, thrived on cosmopolitanism, or at least on the promise of it. Referring to the socio-political climate of 1950s West Germany, Georg Seesslen has argued: 'The 1950s could have chosen to be either "new" or "old", instead the decade settled for something which was neither new (the utopia of a genuinely democratic fresh start) nor old (a seamless continuity from the Nazi period, only without the symbols and the power potential), but rather a third way in between'.[78]

Genres in 1950s West German cinema bear out this argument. Alternately provincial and eagerly cosmopolitan, they can be seen as the cultural products of a society unsure about its identity, negotiating a legacy of national guilt, self-pity and defeat with renewed confidence, mobility, and affluence. Popular cinema positioned itself *vis-à-vis* this context by creating a particular, nationally specific, form of escapism that not only evaded the Nazi past and the problems of the present, but established a specific temporality in between. Common to many West German films of the 1950s and the 1960s are thus narratives that leave at least modern audiences wondering not only where but also when they are supposedly set; narratives that rely on, but get irrevocably lost in, nostalgic, but often disorientating, and even jarring flashbacks; and narratives that are suspended between the wish to move forward and the temptation to linger on spectacle and reverie.

Audience preferences of indigenous and foreign films in 1950s West Germany, though divergent according to gender, generational, and educational difference, all seem to be based on a rejection of traditional concepts of 'German identity'. The political and cultural agenda of the 1950s was to establish a new social consensus precisely not, as has often be argued, through a restoration of national identity, but by embracing global consumerism. This agenda went alongside the promotion of a collective amnesia about the immediate past. The popular film genres of the 1950s and 1960s actively contributed to this discourse, and supplied its narratives and images. American distributors too colluded with this objective, removing from their products any negative portrayals of Germans. In the early 1950s the project of consumerism was to some extent still regulated by a rationalised economy and linked to consensual norms and traditional values such as domesticity. However, as soon as the propagated ideal of consumerism became congruent with real spending power by the mid-1950s, a multitude of separate consumer groupings and different, self-assertive consumer choices emerges. Internationalisation, both with regard to cultural production and in terms of audience taste, became a crucial aspect of this proliferation process.

Notes

1. Examples for this historical evaluation can be found in Michael Dost, Florian Hopf, and Alexander Kluge, *Filmwirtschaft in der BRD und Europa. Götterdämmerung in Raten*, Munich 1973; Timothy Corrigan, *New German Cinema. The Displaced Image*, Austin 1983; Thomas Elsaesser, *New German Cinema. A History*, London and Basingstoke 1989.
2. All figures taken from Hans Günther Pflaum and Hans Helmut Prinzler, *Cinema in the Federal Republic of Germany*, Munich and Vienna 1983; and the annual yearbooks *Filmstatistisches Jahrbuch*, published by the Spitzenorganisation der deutschen Filmwirtschaft (SPIO).
3. Tino Balio, 'Retrenchment, Reappraisal, and Reorganisation', in *The American Film Industry*, ed. Tino Balio, Madison 1985, pp. 401–412.
4. Robert Murphy, 'Rank's Attempt on the American Market, 1944–9', in *British Cinema History*, eds. James Curran and Vincent Porter, London 1983, p. 176.
5. Still one of the most comprehensive studies of Nazi film economics and propaganda is Julian Petley, *Capital and Culture. German Cinema 1933–1945*, London 1979.
6. Peter Pleyer, *Deutscher Nachkriegsfilm, 1946–1948*, Münster 1965, p. 35.
7. For a textual analysis of some of these films, see Marie-Hélène Gutberlet and Holger Ziegler, 'Re-educate Germany by Film', in *Frauen und Film*, no. 61, 2000, pp. 197–226.
8. Heide Fehrenbach, *Cinema in Democratizing Germany. Reconstructing National Identity after Hitler*, Chapel Hill and London, 1995, p. 57.
9. Ibid, p. 55.
10. Robert Peck, 'The Banning of *Titanic*: A Study of British Postwar Film Censorship in Germany', *Historical Journal of Film, Radio, and Television*, vol. 20. no. 3, 2000, p. 428.
11. Dost et al, *Filmwirtschaft in der BRD und Europa*, p. 149. See also Joseph Garncarz, ' Abbildung 8: Erfolgsfilme des Jahres 1948', in 'Populäres Kino in Deutschland.

Internationalisierung einer Filmkultur, 1925–1990' (Habilitationsschrift, University of Cologne, 1996), p. 126.

12. Cf. Tim Bergfelder, 'The Production Designer and the *Gesamtkunstwerk*', in *Dissolving Views. Key Writings on British Cinema*, ed. Andrew Higson, London 1996, pp. 20–38.

13. Cf. Sue Harper, *Picturing the Past. The Rise and Fall of the British Costume Film*, London 1994; and Pam Cook, *Fashioning the Nation. Costume and Identity in British Cinema*, London 1996.

14. Pam Cook, 'Neither Here Nor There. National Identity in Gainsborough Costume Drama', in Higson, *Dissolving Views*, p. 60.

15. Ibid., p. 62.

16. Ibid., p. 61.

17. Ursula Hardt, *From Caligari to California. Eric Pommer's Life in the International Film Wars*, Providence and Oxford, 1996, p. 166.

18. Fehrenbach, *Cinema in Democratizing Germany*, pp. 261–264.

19. Ibid, p. 54.

20. My chapter concentrates predominantly on the developments in the Western zones. For further details on the situation in the East, see, e.g., Dieter Wolf, 'Gesellschaft mit beschränkter Haftung', in *Babelsberg. Ein Filmstudio, 1912–1992*, ed. Wolfgang Jacobsen, Berlin 1992, pp. 247–271, and *'Sie sehen selbst, sie hören selbst': Die DEFA von ihren Anfängen bis 1949*, ed. Christiane Mückenberger and Günter Jordan, Marburg 1994.

21. Klaus Kreimeier, *Die Ufa Story*, Munich 1992, pp. 434–438.

22. Dost et al, *Filmwirtschaft in der BRD und Europa*, pp. 101–103.

23. Kreimeier, *Die Ufa Story*, pp. 444–452.

24. Hans-Michael Bock and Michael Töteberg, 'A History of Ufa', in *The German Cinema Book*, ed. Tim Bergfelder, Erica Carter, and Deniz Göktürk, London 2002, pp. 137–138.

25. The position of Film Control Officer had been initially offered to another Hollywood émigré, Billy Wilder, who resigned and suggested Pommer as his successor, see Hardt, *From Caligari to California*, p. 172.

26. Wolfgang Jacobsen, *Erich Pommer. Ein Produzent macht Filmgeschichte*, Berlin 1989, pp. 39–45.

27. *Filmstatistisches Jahrbuch 1954–55*, ed. Goetz von Pestalozza, Wiesbaden 1954, pp. 89–91.

28. Quoted in Hardt, *From Caligari to California*, p. 180.

29. Cf. Janet Staiger, 'With the Compliments of the Auteur. Art Cinema and the Complexities of Its Reading Strategies', in *Interpreting Films. Studies in the Historical Reception of American Cinema*, Princeton 1992, pp. 178–196.

30. Critical responses to rubble films in Copenhagen and by the American press, quoted in *Trümmer und Träume. Nachkriegszeit und fünfziger Jahre auf Zelluloid*, ed. Ursula Bessen, Bochum 1989, pp. 126–127.

31. Friedrich Luft, review of *Und über uns der Himmel*, in *Die Neue Zeitung*, 1947, reprinted in *Zwischen Gestern und Morgen. Westdeutscher Nachkriegsfilm, 1946–1962*, ed. Jürgen Berger, Hans-Peter Reichmann, and Rudolf Worschech, Frankfurt 1989, p. 342.

32. Ibid.

33. Anon., 'Stimmen aus Parkett und Rang: Man mag keine Ruinen', *Der Spiegel*, 6 January 1946.

34. For a much closer textual analysis of these and other films in the cycle, see Robert Shandley, *Rubble Films. German Cinema in the Shadow of the Third Reich*, Philadelphia 2001.

35. Helmut Käutner, 'Demontage der Traumfabrik', *Film-Echo*, no. 5, June 1947.

36. Hardt, *From Caligari to California*, pp. 182–190.

37. Thomas Guback, 'Hollywood's International Market', in Balio, *The American Film Industry*, pp. 463–487. See also Thomas Guback *The International Film Industry*, Bloomington 1969.

38. Fehrenbach, *Cinema in Democratizing Germany*, pp. 61–62.

39. Anon., 'Männer für Sentiment – Frauen für Sensationen', *WAZ*, 16 December1949.

40. Cf. Garncarz, 'Starerfolgsranglisten', in 'Populäres Kino in Deutschland', pp. 396–412. Interestingly, Granger's German popularity declines exponentially as his career shifts from British to Hollywood productions. Nevertheless, Granger's remarkably consistent

appeal during these early years may well explain why West German producers were so
eager to cast him in European co-productions in the 1960s.

41. Ibid.
42. Klaus Kreimeier, 'Die Ökonomie der Gefühle. Aspekte des deutschen Nachkriegsfilms',
in Berger et al, *Zwischen Gestern und Morgen*, p. 12.
43. Garncarz, 'Populäres Kino in Deutschland'.
44. Fehrenbach, *Cinema in Democratizing Germany*, p. 163.
45. Ibid., p. 149.
46. Dost et al, *Filmwirtschaft in der BRD und Europa*, p. 103.
47. Fehrenbach, *Cinema in Democratizing Germany*, p. 71.
48. Ibid., p. 89.
49. Martin Loiperdinger, 'Filmzensur und Selbstkontrolle', in *Geschichte des deutschen Films*,
ed. Wolfgang Jacobsen, Anton Kaes, Hans-Helmut Prinzler, Stuttgart and Weimar 1993,
pp. 479–499. See also Martin Loiperdinger, 'State Legislation, Censorship, and Funding',
in Bergfelder et al, *The German Cinema Book*, pp. 148–157.
50. Fehrenbach, *Cinema in Democratizing Germany*, pp. 92–118.
51. *Lexikon des internationalen Films*, ed. Klaus Brüne, Reinbek 1991, p. 3346.
52. Loiperdinger, in Jacobsen et al, *Geschichte des deutschen Films*, pp. 496–497.
53. *Der deutsche Heimatfilm*, ed. Wolfgang Kaschuba, Tübingen 1989, p. 78.
54. Dost et al, *Filmwirtschaft in der BRD und Europa*, p. 104.
55. Jürgen Berger, 'Bürgen heisst zahlen – und manchmal auch zensieren', in Berger et al,
Zwischen Gestern und Morgen, pp. 80–91.
56. Klaus Kreimeier, *Kino und Filmindustrie in der BRD. Ideologieproduktion und Klassenwirk-lichkeit*, Kronberg 1973, p. 194.
57. Johannes von Moltke, 'Evergreens. The Heimat Genre', in Bergfelder et al, *The German Cinema Book*, pp. 18–28.
58. Ibid., p. 18.
59. Ibid., p. 20.
60. Georg Seesslen, 'Durch die Heimat und so weiter. Heimatfilme, Schlagerfilme und
Ferienfilme der fünfziger Jahre', in Berger et al, *Zwischen Gestern und Morgen*, p. 155.
61. Kaschuba, *Der deutsche Heimatfilm*, pp. 87–88.
62. Cf. Nancy P. Nenno, '"Postcards from the Edge": Education to Tourism in the German
Mountain Film', in *Light Motives. German Popular Film in Perspective*, ed. Randall Halle
and Margaret McCarthy, Detroit 2003, pp. 61–84.
63. Peter Schnell, 'The Federal Republic of Germany: A Growing International Deficit?', in
Tourism and Economic Development. Western European Experiences, ed. Allan Williams and
Gareth Shaw, London and New York 1988, p. 197.
64. Gertrud Steiner, *Die Heimatmacher: Kino in Österreich 1946–1966*, Vienna 1987, p. 162.
65. Interestingly, Douglas Sirk, the acknowledged master of 1950s Hollywood melodrama,
had directed in the 1930s in Germany a proto-*Heimatfilm*, *Das Mädchen vom Moorhof* (The
Girl from the Marsh Croft, 1935), which was remade in 1958.
66. Cf. Manfred Hobsch, *Liebe, Tanz, und 1000 Schlagerfilme*, Berlin 1998.
67. Robert Fischer and Joe Hembus, *Der neue deutsche Film 1960–1980*, Munich 1981, p. 190.
68. Fehrenbach, *Cinema in Democratizing Germany*, p. 168.
69. Uta G. Poiger, 'Rebels with a cause? American popular culture, the 1956 youth riots, and
the new conception of masculinity in East and West Germany', in *The American Impact on
Postwar Germany*, ed. Reiner Pommerin, Providence and Oxford 1995, pp. 93–125.
70. Martin Loiperdinger, 'Amerikanisierung im Kino? Hollywood und das westdeutsche
Publikum der fünfziger Jahre', *Theaterzeitschrift*, no. 28, Summer 1989, p. 52.
71. Ibid., p. 57.
72. Joseph Garncarz, 'Hollywood in Germany: The Role of American Films in Germany', in
Hollywood in Europe. Experiences of a Cultural Hegemony, ed. David W. Ellwood and Rob
Kroes, Amsterdam 1994, pp. 124–125.

73. Erica Carter, *How German is She? Postwar West German Reconstruction and the Consuming Woman*, Ann Arbor 1997, p. 175.
74. Ibid.
75. Fehrenbach, *Cinema in Democratizing Germany*, p. 165.
76. Garncarz, in Ellwood and Kroes, *Hollywood in Europe*, pp. 125–126.
77. Joseph Garncarz, *Filmfassungen. Eine Theorie signifikanter Filmvariation*, Frankfurt and New York 1992, pp. 94–123.
78. Seesslen, in Berger et al, *Zwischen Gestern und Morgen*, p. 140.

Chapter 3

FROM NATIONAL TO EUROPEAN CINEMA

From the mid-1950s to the late 1960s, most European film industries witnessed a decline in purely national productions and a rise in bilateral, or multinational co-productions. In 1953, of the 104 films produced by West German companies, only fifteen had foreign involvement. These figures would fluctuate throughout the decade but went dramatically up in the early 1960s. Between 1963 and 1964 alone the number of co-productions more than doubled, and for the rest of the decade they consistently outnumbered purely indigenous films.[1] Similar developments occurred in Italy and France.

In the face of declining audience figures and American distribution dominance, co-production strategies provided, at least in theory, an opportunity to boost productivity, to share production costs, and to increase the number of cinema-goers. It would be mistaken, however, to assume a coherent or consistent 'European' defence strategy against Hollywood behind this mode of production, at least as far as the film industries were concerned. In fact, many European producers of the 1960s preferred American cooperation over inter-European agreements, where such cooperation was available. Thus, the Italian producer Carlo Ponti argued:

> The American film industry produces less films and needs more than ever before the cooperation of internationally minded producers, in order to fill the gaps in their home and international markets. We in Italy can no longer produce films for the Italian markets. The costs are too high, and we can't get our money back at the Italian box-office alone. We need American capital, we need the American market, and we need American companies to distribute our films globally.[2]

Throughout the 1960s, European co-production ventures were made alongside Hollywood's so-called runaway productions, films that were shot on cheaper European locations with cheaper technical crews and studio facilities (Samuel Bronston's epics such as *King of Kings*, 1961, *El Cid*, 1961, and *The Fall of the Roman Empire*, 1964, are prominent examples). Countries such as Italy and Spain in particular benefited from such productions as their studios worked to full capacity (rented out to American and European companies), which in turn aided a boom in indigenous productivity and employment. In West Germany and France, on the other hand, Hollywood expansion was mainly focused on the distribution sector, which hardly benefited the indigenous industry. Thus, divergent economic interests between different European industries with regard to Hollywood intervention significantly determined attitudes towards European cooperation, and these interests weighed strongly against national and European cultural policies.

Whither Europe?

Throughout the 1950s and 1960s, the issue of European cooperation was widely and heatedly discussed in the West German trade press. The idea of transnational cooperation between European film industries was of course far from new – in fact, much of film production, from before the First World War through the 1920s and early 1930s and even to some extent continuing into the Second World War, had been explicitly international. The strategy of bilateral or joint production initiatives between European film industries resumed shortly after the war against the background of European integration policies and American competition. By 1949 the Western European Union (WEU) had established a Non-commercial Cinema Subcommittee with the brief to 'promote the exchange of documentary film, service film networks, sponsor central film libraries' acquisition of scientific and educational films, and the possibilities for joint European productions'.[3] The European institutions' attitude towards commercial film production was rather ambivalently positioned between the drive towards economic liberalism and free trade and, on the other hand, the promotion and protection of national specificities.

A document of the Organisation for European Economic Cooperation (OEEC) stated in 1960 that it was 'necessary to preserve national film production as a significant expression of national cultures',[4] while a European Council directive in 1961 demanded the abolition of all quota regulations in member states of the European Economic Community (EEC), thereby effectively undermining the intentions of the OEEC.[5] While the newly formed pan-European institutions pursued both long-term cultural and economic goals, European film industries were more interested in concrete and immediate economic benefits. Regular discussions between the European industry (through its representative body the Committee of European Film Industries, or CICE) and European political institutions took place throughout the 1950s and 1960s with the recurrent theme of defining the 'national film' against the economic necessity of international cooperation, and in some cases, the quite overt agenda of establishing a trans- or even supranational European cinema. During the same period,

European co-productions were also regularly on the agenda at the meetings of the Fédération internationale des associations des producteurs de films (FIAPF), the international association of film producers, of which the Motion Picture Association of America (MPAA) was the most powerful member. Understandably, the question of co-productions in this context concentrated particularly on the pursuit of American co-productions with Europe. Significantly, despite all these discussions and a number of individual agreements between EEC (and later European Union) member states, a pan-European law for co-productions was never agreed upon.

In 1949 France and Italy had been the first European countries to sign a co-production agreement, in order to boost production and to balance the quantity and steady influx of American imports. Between 1949 and 1964 alone, 711 films were produced under the French/Italian agreement, a number that since then has risen to 1,500 today. As Anne Jäckel has argued, 'the system worked well because co-producers came from countries with cultural affinities, a similar industrial and institutional framework, comparable schemes of incentives and markets which could claim, until the 1980s, a more or less equal potential. Such fruitful cooperation not only led the two countries to sign agreements with other partners, but encouraged other countries to follow their example'.[6]

Except for France and Italy, co-production agreements between other countries initially developed rather slowly and on a cautious and experimental basis during the early 1950s. By the end of the decade, however, and particularly following the foundation of the EEC in 1957 with its directive of abandoning trade barriers between member states, most European film industries had established co-production agreements with each other. Furthermore, from 1957 onwards, the practice of relatively unregulated bilateral cooperation became increasingly replaced by bureaucratically minute joint arrangements between governments, setting out detailed contingency plans and guidelines for co-production. After the ratification of the Treaty of Rome, the nature of these arrangements depended to a great extent on EEC membership; for example the West German/Spanish co-production agreement in 1960 was still coupled with strict and mutually protective contingency regulations, whereas the relationship between the West German, French, and Italian industries was much more flexible with regard to such restrictions.[7]

Co-productions were potentially lucrative, but they also involved laborious bureaucratic procedures for producers.[8] First, they required an initial proposal (idea, script, stars) that had to appeal equally in two or more European countries, and they needed mutual agreement between two or more European producers. These proposals had then to be approved in each contributing country as a 'national' production, in order to benefit from potential state support funds. The higher levels of state support in countries such as France, Italy, and Spain, usually advantaged production partners from these countries over those from West Germany. Although all of the co-production agreements were based on the assumption of equally shared investment, in practice the relation was more uneven and frequently balanced at a 70/30 per cent share.

The responsibility for co-ordinating and supervising a co-production contract was held by the Export-Union in West Germany and by the industry umbrella organisations Unifrance and Unitalia in France and Italy. Co-production contracts aimed at parity between contributing countries and stipulated their involvement in exact detail. Prospective markets for distribution were divided into 'language territories'. In the case of France, this included former and present colonies and francophone countries in Europe and elsewhere. Italy included Malta and former Italian colonies in Africa. Switzerland, owing to its multilingual status, was subdivided as a market between West Germany, France, and Italy. Co-production contracts also outlined the exact number of national personnel (both cast and crew) involved and the cost, length, and extent of their involvement. It is often with these details where national disagreements would occur.

Once the details had been agreed upon by the co-production partners, the contract (if it involved West German interests) had to be supported by the Export-Union and then passed on to a special branch of the Federal Ministry of Trade, based in Frankfurt, for final approval. In order to get this approval, producers had to submit a detailed budget, a definitive cast and crew list, a shooting schedule (including specification of location or studio work), proof of the acquisition of copyrights, and a final script. Once the film had been completed, the final cut was checked again against the approved proposal and, where the film had deviated from it, the Ministry of Trade could (and did) demand either cuts or reshoots. It is clear from these stipulations that they left producers with very little room to improvise or to react to unforeseen circumstances during the production process. West German producers and their co-production partners frequently complained about this form of state intervention and about a level of bureaucracy that was perceived to be higher and more inflexible than in other European countries. The fact that co-productions were approved by an industry-external and explicitly political body was not unique to West Germany. In France the approval came from the Centre National de la Cinématographie (CNC), while in Italy the ultimate decision also rested with the government in the form of the Ministerio del turismo e dello spettacolo. What complicated the West German situation was, as Martin Loiperdinger has suggested, that the final authority was often divided between the Ministry of the Interior, the decisions of which, particularly during the height of the Cold War, were frequently coloured by ideological considerations, and the Ministry of Trade, which had more straightforwardly economic motivations.[9]

Between 1949 and 1964, the total number of European co-productions (including bilateral, joint and tripartite productions) came to 1,091. The majority of these films were popular genre products, but it is worth reiterating again that the frameworks of co-production also aided the art-cinema sector from the 1950s onwards and benefited directors as diverse as Orson Welles, Federico Fellini, Pier Paolo Pasolini, and Luchino Visconti. This does not necessarily mean that all industry sectors equally supported this development. Even in the case of the most successful and amicable bilateral partnership, between France and Italy, there were frequent instances of disagreement, and the most vociferous criticism in many cases originated with the trade unions.[10] Henri Back, secretary of the French Cinema Technicians Union, argued that:

> the producers are trying to form a European cinema. Their plan is the auto-financing of films at European level. This, if it goes through, will enable them to film in any member country. Since conditions in both Italy and Germany are at a lower level than those obtaining in France, our studios will get the thick end of the stick.[11]

Similar sentiments prevented the British film industry from entering into co-production agreements. While British distributors were largely in favour of developing stronger European ties and lobbied successive governments to that effect, the political establishment and film unions proved far more resistant, which reflected the British Left's more general rejection of European integration during this period. In a particularly hostile article for the journal *Film and Television Technician*, affiliated with the Association of Cinema and Television Technicians (ACTT), the Labour MP Hugh Jenkins (and former assistant general secretary of the British actors' trade union Equity) condemned the 'incestuous Common Market' as 'Western European chauvinism' and 'continentalism', setting the tone for most debates on European co-production.[12]

In the same journal, editor and producer Sidney Cole, one of the founding members of ACTT, had earlier expressed his concerns about the free mobility of labour, and increased American dominance, which he perceived would follow the integration of European film industries. Cole summed up the by now familiar reservations about the international film:

> the kind of cosmopolitan film which has been made in great numbers in Europe in the last few years, highbudgeted spectaculars with international casts, many of which might have been made on the moon for all the relation they bear to any recognisable specific European culture and tradition ... the deathly elimination of the best kind of native film, that springs from the roots of a country and expresses something of the living reality of its people.[13]

Compared with the large number of Anglo-American productions in the 1960s (some of which included participation from continental European producers), exclusive co-production ventures between British and other European companies without American input remained rare and limited in scope and, because of a lack of official agreements, institutional support and guidelines, commercially risky. A co-production agreement between Britain and West Germany was only signed in the early 1970s after Britain had joined the EEC. The Anglo-French agreement signed in 1965 has resulted, as Anne Jäckel has calculated, in on average one film per year since its inception.[14] Anglo-Italian arrangements were slightly more common in the 1960s, and, since both markets were strongly dominated by U.S. interests, were often coupled with American investment, as for example in the case of Michelangelo Antonioni's *Blow-Up* (1966). There are, however, a large number of 1960s British films whose national origins and business interests (including the crucial area of distribution) are far less easy to disentangle, and where a national label can only be applied haphazardly.

West German Co-Productions: Moving Towards Internationalisation

In West Germany, it became increasingly apparent by the late 1950s that the ambitious government plans to re-establish an autonomous and centralised national film industry had failed. State interventions, such as the disastrous handling of the UFI assets and the costly and paralysingly bureaucratic state subsidy schemes, had proven counter-productive. After the guarantee schemes had been phased out by the mid-1950s, there were few institutional support mechanisms left for West German film producers at home. These included the previously discussed tax relief for films awarded by the Filmbewertungsstelle der Länder (FBW); the *Deutsche Filmpreis* (Federal Film Prize) annually awarded by the Ministry of the Interior; and the *Drehbuchprämie* (Script Reward), a 200,000 DM reward for outstanding or promising scripts, judged by a government commission. Rewards such as these gave incentives to and prioritised productions that were seen to boost cultural and national prestige.

However, at least up to the mid-1960s, this did not mean that the government encouraged an aesthetically innovative form of home-grown cinema. Judging by the films rewarded throughout the 1950s and early 1960s, government officials envisaged the ideal film primarily as being politically consensual, aesthetically conventional, and rooted in high cultural traditions. Middlebrow adaptations of literary classics (e.g., *Buddenbrooks*, 1959, based on Thomas Mann's novel) and biopics of historical figures (e.g., *Stresemann*, 1956) dominated the list of rewarded films. In an interview published in the trade paper *Film-Echo*, a representative from the Ministry of Trade outlined the crucial function of a nationally defined industry:

> It is the task of the German government to perceive film as a significant element of German cultural politics, and to support the German film and the German film industry. We have to realise that the German film as a cultural artefact and as a mediator of thoughts and ideas is predestined to represent German thinking and our way of life, both at home and abroad.[15]

Industry representatives predictably responded with impatience and frustration to such sentiments. The producer Alexander Grüter argued: 'Cinema is still regarded by our government as a somewhat indecent institution. They have forgotten that film is a tough business and has nothing to do with sentimentality. There is far too much talk about culture'.[16]

As a reaction against what they perceived as élitism and interference, the Spitzenorganisation der deutschen Filmwirtschaft (Central Association of German Cinemas, or SPIO) and the trade paper *Film-Echo/Filmwoche* set up in 1964 the *Goldene Leinwand* (Golden Screen) award to acknowledge the economic success of any indigenous or foreign film that attracted 3 million cinema-goers within eighteen months. It is notable that few *Goldene Leinwand* recipients were simultaneously rewarded with government prizes, indicative of a division in German film culture between commercial interests on one side and cultural aspirations and political considerations on the other that was to last for decades. Given the disdain of the authorities for mass culture and the generally low level of state support, however, nationally independent film production ceased to be a viable economic strategy for commercial producers.

West German distributors, on the other hand, were faced with a film market that had become increasingly saturated with foreign investment and products (owing to the government's failure to establish quota regulations) and with a national audience that, from the early 1960s onwards, increasingly demanded a greater variety of both indigenous and international films. The acceptance, popularity and box-office success of foreign films increased significantly during the 1960s, and the dominant position of indigenous products began to wane. However, changed audience preferences did not necessarily advantage Hollywood products.[17]

In 1960, only one American film (*Ben Hur*, 1959) made it into the top ten, which was otherwise dominated by indigenous productions. In the following year, the only reasonably successful American films, the Doris Day vehicle *Lover Come Back* (1961) and the Walt Disney production *The Absent-Minded Professor* (1961), were not only outperformed by West German films – the most popular film of the season was a Swedish comedy, *Änglar, finns dom?* (1960, Do Angels Exist?). Sweden again cornered top position in 1964 with Ingmar Bergman's *Tystnaden* (1963, The Silence), a success built on notoriety, as the film faced boycotts from the Catholic Church and elicited widespread debate and public riots. British (or at least Anglo-American) films also did well at the West German box office throughout the 1960s and frequently outperformed the competition of solely American-produced films. All of the James Bond films were top box-office hits in West Germany, as were Ken Annakin's *Those Magnificent Men in their Flying Machines* (1965), Richard Lester's Beatles vehicle *Help!* (1965), and Antonioni's art-house hit *Blow-Up* (1966). If one considers David Lean's *Doctor Zhivago* (1965), which reached top position in 1966, as an Anglo-American co-production, then the first all-American production to outperform all other competition in postwar West Germany was, as late as 1969, *The Love Bug* (1969), featuring a humanised Volkswagen beetle. Overall, the picture of the West German film market in the 1960s remained evenly balanced between West German, co-produced, and foreign films.

In contrast, the performance of West German films in other countries was relatively limited, and the only substantial export markets were German-speaking countries, such as Austria and Switzerland. In order to coordinate and improve foreign distribution and sales, the main industry bodies, the Verband deutscher Filmproduzenten (Association of German Film Producers), the Verband deutscher Filmverleiher (Association of German Film Distributors), and the Interessengemeinschaft deutscher Filmexporteure (Interest Group of German Film Exporters), had in 1954 created the umbrella organisation Export-Union, which also advised producers on co-production ventures.[18] The head of the Export-Union in the 1960s was the Romanian-born producer Carol Hellmann, a veteran of the 'Film Europe' initiatives in the late 1920s and 1930s with established international contacts, particularly in Italy, France, and Britain (where his brother Marcel had been working as a producer since the 1930s).

State support for film exports was erratic and half-hearted at best, and from its inception the Export-Union lacked the clout of similar institutions in France and Italy.[19] In the early 1960s, the Ministry of the Interior provided a one-off lump sum to support the dubbing of indigenous productions for export purposes (the so-called *Synchron-Million* or dubbing million). However, unlike the dubbing facilities that translated foreign films into German, the quality of the dubbing of German films into other languages was often poor. Moreover, without continual support, the Export-Union was soon again left with few funds to promote German films abroad. Throughout the 1950s the export earnings of German productions rose slowly but steadily, from 7.6 million DM in 1953 to 27 million in 1960. After a temporary fall in 1961 and 1962, export revenues reached their peak in 1964 with 31 million DM.[20]

West German producers thus faced considerable obstacles in entering into co-production agreements. West Germany did not have the same 'cultural affinities' that existed between Italy and France, its industrial infrastructure was far more fragmented than in neighbouring countries, it lacked the financial incentives and state support schemes France and Italy could rely on, and it was hampered by federal bureaucracy and cultural élitism. During the boom period of European co-productions in the late 1950s and 1960s West Germany contributed in terms of overall investment less than either Italy or France (though more than Spain).[21]

In the majority of cases films were not shot in West German studios but in the country of one of the co-production partners. Hollywood's 'runaway productions' of the 1960s largely bypassed West Germany as a potential production base as well. One notable exception was Stanley Kubrick's First World War drama *Paths of Glory* (1957), produced by Kirk

Douglas' company Bryna for United Artists, which was shot partly on German location, with a largely German technical crew as well as German supporting actors. A rather low-key attempt by Warner Bros. in the mid-1960s to establish a West German production subsidiary was the company Rhein-Main-Film, in all likelihood not much more than a cover for tax manoeuvres or an attempt to strengthen Warner Bros.' distribution interests. In any case, the company did not witness much activity, apart from its financial contribution to the spaghetti western, *Il Bastardo* (1968), which was largely an Italian production, and the Cold War spy thriller *The Defector* (1966), which at least was shot on location in Germany, but which had practically no impact at either the West German or any other box office, and whose only marginal point of interest today is that it includes Hollywood star Montgomery Clift's last film role.[22] There were other West German – American co-productions during the 1960s, but they remained a rarity, much to the chagrin of West German producers and of studios eager to rent out their facilities to Hollywood companies.

What West Germany could of course provide from an outside perspective, at least up to the early to mid-1960s, was a sufficiently lucrative exhibition sector with still relatively sizeable audiences (despite the dramatic decline in precisely this sector over the previous years). A widespread strategy of West German companies partaking in co-production was therefore the practice of *Schreibtischproduktion* (desk production) where actual West German involvement was minimal and difficult to trace and largely limited to the negotiation of distribution rights. The practice of minority involvement, constituting a practically fictitious form of co-production, was frequently criticised in the West German trade press. A leading article in *Film-Echo* in July 1960, entitled 'What does European film mean?' argued: 'Does a film with minority German involvement become a European film? No. It remains a foreign production. We think that we ought to take more care of the German film'.[23]

Representatives from the production sector, however, were less interested in the unconditional protection of the national film, nor were their motivations necessarily linked to idealistic concepts of European integration or 'cultural affinities':

> In the age of political integration, co-productions are inevitable and necessary. Indeed, they provide the only strategy to boost the cinema economically, and to secure a film's success at the box office. Worries that the artistic input might suffer in purely economic considerations might be justified. But much more important is to find the foundations for workable joint productions with any country in the world which is willing to cooperate and where co- or tripartite productions promise to be financially viable.[24]

West Germany had established contacts with other European film industries since the early 1950s. Its main partners were France and Italy, followed by Austria, Spain, and Yugoslavia. One of the earliest co-productions West

Germany entered into was the West German-Belgian bilateral production *Le Banquet des fraudeurs/Bankett der Schmuggler* (1951, The Smugglers' Banquet), a light-hearted satire on European trade barriers, written by Charles Spaak, brother of the then president of the European Council, and starring the eminent Belgian and German actresses Françoise Rosay and Käthe Haack. The film was partly financed through European funds, and underwritten by the West German government guarantee scheme.[25]

Franco-West German co-productions were also initiated at the beginning of the 1950s, following the signing of a bilateral agreement in 1951. A co-production agreement between West Germany and Italy soon followed in 1953. Early examples for Franco-German cooperation included Julien Duvivier's *Marianne de ma jeunesse/Marianne* (1954) and *Escale à Orly/Zwis-*

Figure 3.1. Romy Schneider in the Franco-German co-production *Ein Engel auf Erden/Madame Ange* (1959). Deutsches Filminstitut (DIF), Frankfurt-on-Main.

chenlandung in Paris (1955, Stopover in Orly). Both films were also under-written by the German federal government's guarantee scheme.[26] The majority of Franco-West German co-productions until the late 1950s con-sisted of romantic comedies, but there were also a number of more ambi-tious (though not necessarily more successful) projects aimed at fostering Franco-German reconciliation, such as Helmut Käutner's military satire *Die Gans von Sedan/Sans tambour ni trompète* (1959, The Goose of Sedan), starring Hardy Krüger and Jean Richard.

One problem with many of these co-productions was that, while a num-ber of French stars were popular with audiences in West and often also East Germany (for example, Jean Marais, Gérard Philippe, Brigitte Bardot, and comedians such as Louis de Funès and Fernandel), the reverse was seldom the case. Among the few German stars to become popular with French audiences was the Austrian-born Romy Schneider. The *Sissi* trilogy between 1956 and 1958 had made Schneider a top star in German-speak-ing markets, and the films also sold very well in other European countries, including France. Schneider relocated to France in 1958, and appeared in Franco-West German co-productions such as *Ein Engel auf Erden/Madame Ange* (1959), *Christine* (1959), and *Katia* (1960). These films drew on Schnei-der's 'sweet girl' persona, established through her West German and Aus-trian productions, but adapted it to a distinctly French context. Significantly, the West German box-office revenues of these films were considerably below Schneider's previous productions, and her subsequent transformation into an international character actress with a far more mature and ambivalent image in art films by Luchino Visconti (*Bocaccio 70*, 1962) and Orson Welles (*The Trial/Le Procès/Der Prozess*, 1962, a Franco/West German/Italian co-production based on Franz Kafka's novel) met with almost complete rejection by West German audiences.[27] Other top stars with an established star image, such as Maria Schell (who by the late 1950s also appeared in French and Hollywood productions), Curd Jürgens, or O.W. Fischer, experienced a similar indifference at the West German box office, where their foreign or co-produced films did not conform to indigenous conventions or audience expectations. A good example is the adaptation of the Vicki Baum best seller (and remake of the Hollywood film *Grand Hotel*, 1932), *Menschen im Hotel/Grand Hôtel* (1958), a Franco-West German star vehicle for O.W. Fischer and Michèle Morgan, which flopped in both countries.

As these examples indicate, co-productions could not rely exclusively on the transnational attraction of already established national stars. Fur-thermore, the concept of a purely indigenous star system, particularly in West Germany, became increasingly eroded in the late 1950s and early 1960s by foreign actors appearing not only in co-productions but also in 'purely' West German films. Industry representatives perceived as central the issue of how far West German audiences could be persuaded or better, deceived into accepting foreign stars or co-produced films as 'German':

> We know that the majority of audiences are not interested in the names of directors, or in production categories, but respond exclusively to narratives and actors. Everyone is surprised to find out that several of 'our' stars actually can't speak any German, but that they have to be dubbed. Therefore the key issue has to be dubbing. A professionally dubbed foreign film may possibly appear more German than a German co-production where less care has been put into the translation.[28]

Apart from the issue of foreign, linguistically restricted actors, the other central question addressed in the above statement is what kind of film (in terms of genre or narratives) a commercially successful co-production should be. The trade paper *Film-Echo* argued that 'the only type of film that has any box-office potential internationally is the spectacular film with attractive production values and a big budget. The majority of our usual "small fry" is on the other hand practically unsaleable.'[29] Given the financial constraints of European producers by the late 1950s, what was needed for the coming decade was a predictable mode of production, built on easily reproducible or repeatable generic formulae that could appeal to a large number of European audiences, and which might even be exported outside Europe. One generic model that fitted this strategy was the peplum film which the Italian film industry had been producing (often jointly with France, but also, occasionally, with American investment) since the mid-1950s, made relatively cheaply and quickly through an assembly-line mode of production.

The Genre Factory: Popular European Cinema in the 1960s

Popular European genre films of the 1960s present a number of methodological problems in categorising them into a coherent whole. First, as I have argued earlier, despite the fact that co-production agreements frequently gave the impression of fairly evenly distributed involvement, the reality was that in most cases one country would assume a dominant role in initiating and producing a given project. West Germany's main co-production partners during the 1960s were (in descending order) Italy, France, and Austria. The latter was the most established and traditional ally for West German producers. Germany and Austria had traditionally strong cultural affinities, and the Austrian film industry had always been almost symbiotically linked to its bigger neighbour and dependent on German distribution.

For most of the postwar period, Austria and West Germany functioned as a combined, more or less integrated market for German-language productions. Many of the most popular 'German' *Heimatfilme* of the 1950s had in fact been produced in Austria and, conversely, West German productions (alongside Hollywood films) dominated Austrian screens. The Viennese operetta had been one of the consistently popular musical genres of

German-language cinema since the early sound period. Furthermore, German directors and stars frequently worked on Austrian films, and vice versa, and some of the most popular 'indigenous' stars of German cinema during the 1950s, such as O.W. Fischer, Romy Schneider, and Peter Alexander, were in fact Austrian.

The potentially lucrative West German market particularly motivated smaller European countries, with a limited indigenous industry and market, to enter into co-productions with Germany. This applies, for example, to sporadic co-productions with Belgium, the Netherlands, Denmark, Switzerland, and Romania. Co-productions with Spain and Yugoslavia, on the other hand, were largely motivated by these countries' provision of cheap production facilities and services, which made them attractive to a number of European (and Hollywood) producers. In addition, Spain had a sizeable exhibition sector, while Yugoslavia opened up wider markets and distribution opportunities in the Eastern bloc. In the case of co-productions with France and Italy, countries with a healthier industrial infrastructure, Germany frequently featured as a junior partner (increasingly so as the decade progressed), often within a tripartite arrangement.

The issue of national origins frequently depends on the genre in question. Thus, while a large number of 'spaghetti westerns' were co-financed by West German and French companies and may also have included cast and crew members from these countries (the actor Klaus Kinski, in particular, owed his extremely prolific international career during the 1960s to these productions), the overall creative input remained with Italian directors, technical personnel, and producers. The same applies to a number of West German/Swedish co-productions in the late 1960s. The German publishing success of the 'Pippi Longstockings' children's novels by Swedish author Astrid Lindgren motivated West German producers to invest in a film series, shot in Sweden with a largely Swedish cast and crew. However, apart from financial aid and the casting of a number of German actors (most notably Margot Trooger as the child heroine's main adversary, the spinster Fröken Prysselius), the main artistic and creative input was provided by Swedish personnel.

Other genre cycles (such as the Karl May westerns and Edgar Wallace adaptations) were initiated by West German producers and filmed by predominantly German crews. In some cases, co-productions may have also been motivated by more idiosyncratic or personal reasons, as in the case of Artur Brauner's co-productions with Britain and Israel. One genre, however, where a dominant national involvement is almost impossible to determine, is the mid-1960s secret agent/spy thriller in the James Bond mould, where investment, cast and crew involvement, and production locations were evenly spread between France, West Germany, Italy, and Spain (often also including other production partners from Asia or the Middle East).

A second problem in discussing popular generic patterns among European co-productions in the 1960s is that, unlike 'classic' Hollywood genres,

European popular films of this period are much more difficult to contain within stable generic categories. 'Adventure films', for example, a term commonly used by West German producers, distributors, and exhibitors during the 1960s, are a rather fluid category, and referred in turn to historical 'swashbuckler' movies, Italian-style peplum films, and biblical epics, and exotic adventure films in a contemporary setting. With regard to the latter variant, the 'adventure' film would frequently overlap with spy thrillers, equally set in exotic locations. Given their rather vague iconography, 1960s adventure films occasionally included the most incongruous hybrids, for example *Samson und der Schatz der Inkas* (1964, Samson and the Inca Treasure) where the muscleman from the ancient world finds himself in South America searching for an Inca treasure. To complete the incongruity, the cast also includes Austrian ski champion Toni Sailer.

Crime, horror, costume melodrama, and the sex film also rarely defined 'pure' genres and were more often used as narrational components in hybrid combinations (one particularly productive exponent of the sex/horror film was the Spanish director Jesus Franco). Next to such 'straight' hybrids were innumerable genre parodies, drawing on the conventions of all the other major genres in circulation. More generally, European popular genres of the 1960s were frequently characterised by narrative overkill, pastiche, and repetition, which makes them easy to ridicule in retrospect and accounts for the critical disdain in which they are commonly held. One reason for the generic excesses of European co-productions of the 1960s has been identified by Christopher Frayling as a 'certain competitiveness between rival production companies working within a given genre, which in turn sometimes led to a type of internal pressure towards bizarre experimentation'.[30] Kim Newman has argued that 'the pattern of Italian commercial cinema reveals an overlapping succession of generic cycles ... During the short life span of any individual cycle, an often incredible number of similar films are rushed through production and into distribution before the format wears thin and its popularity fades. The period of overlap between cycles often accounts for intriguing hybrids'.[31]

Similar patterns can be observed in the West German co-productions of the 1960s, perhaps not surprisingly, given West German producers' close interaction with Italian partners. In order to determine generic patterns during the 1960s and the dominance of certain genres over others, one has to take into account both overall consistency and quantity and temporary boom periods. What is clearly apparent is that the dominant genres of 1950s West German cinema (in particular the *Heimatfilm*) were virtually abandoned in the co-productions of the 1960s. A notable exception is West German co-production with Austria, which by and large stuck to established genre formulae, such as comedies, musicals, and even occasionally the *Heimatfilm*. Overall, however, the predominant genres of the 1950s became replaced by genres that were at best insignificant in the previous decade among home-grown products.

The most dominant genre among West German co-productions of the 1960s became the crime film, particularly in its Gothic/Victorian variant, exemplified by the Edgar Wallace adaptations. Significantly this type of crime film was a genre where German production involvement was strong and where films were frequently shot in local studios by German crews, at least up to the mid-1960s. By the late 1960s, the dominant location for co-produced crime films shifted to Italy and Spain. Between 1959 and 1972, more than a hundred releases in total can be grouped into this category and the average number of crime films remained fairly consistent throughout the decade. This corresponds to an equally consistent number of crime films among purely indigenous productions during this period.

Following the crime film in terms of overall quantity, the two other dominant genres among West German co-productions in the 1960s are the western and the adventure film. While German westerns had been made during the silent and pre-war period,[32] the first postwar venture of German producers into this genre was in 1962 with the Karl May adaptation *Der Schatz im Silbersee* (The Treasure of Silver Lake), a co-production with France and Yugoslavia, the latter providing the locations. With the Karl May films developing into a series and spawning numerous imitations, the number of German-initiated westerns rose rapidly within the next two years, reaching its peak in 1965 with thirteen films, nearly a quarter of all the co-productions of that year. Following the discontinuation of the Karl May series in 1966, however, the subsequent decline in German-initiated westerns was as rapid as their rise and, for the rest of the decade, co-produced westerns were almost exclusively Italian 'spaghetti westerns'. Adventure films, evenly balanced between German and foreign-initiated variants, provided a stable and consistent percentage among co-productions in the early to mid-1960s, experiencing a boom period between 1964 and 1966, before disappearing almost completely after 1968.

Other popular genres follow similar patterns of temporary boom periods and rapid demise. The spy thriller, alongside its generic cousin the adventure film and the equally male-oriented western, dominated co-productions between 1965 and 1967, while being more or less insignificant both at the beginning and at the end of the decade. The spy thrillers only took off after the Europe-wide box-office success of the James Bond series. In West Germany, the Bond series was so successful that its distributor United Artists re-released older entries in tandem with the latest production.[33] European producers desperately tried to emulate the Bond formula. As Kim Newman has rightly pointed out:

> although to many, the James Bond films represent the epitome of Anglo-American movie-making, they were expressly aimed at a multi-national audience from very early on. The casting of guest stars from the German (Gert Fröbe, Lotte Lenya), French (Claudine Auger) and Italian (Ursula Andress, Daniela Bianchi, Adolfo Celi, Luciana Paluzzi) popular cinema did much to give the series an international feel. If the European spy thrillers

ever managed to struggle out of the shadow of Bond, it had more to do with moments of sex and sadism permissible in Europe than with expanse of budget or imagination.[34]

Horror and sex films became more prominent in the late 1960s among West German co-productions, the former mainly through Italian-initiated productions (Italy had established its own brand of horror film since the late 1950s), while the latter was represented mostly by West German-initiated projects. Comedies provide an interesting variation to these patterns.

Figure 3.2. Imitation James Bond: Tony Kendall (real name Luciano Stella) as 'Kommissar X'. Deutsches Filminstitut (DIF), Frankfurt-on-Main.

Overall, they were not strongly represented among co-productions in terms of quantity and in terms of average numbers per year, and yet they do add up in terms of consistency. As with crime films, comedies continued to provide a significant percentage of indigenous productions during this period, and they were in the majority among Austrian-West German co-productions.

A number of conclusions can be drawn from these patterns. In the early 1960s, the production of different genres among co-productions was fairly evenly balanced, with no particular genre being dominant overall. This situation changed between 1964 and 1966, when adventure films, spy thrillers, and westerns made up more than half of all the co-productions during this period. In 1969, in contrast, nearly a third of all co-productions were sex films. The West German contribution (in terms of creative input, investment, and production facilities) was more pronounced in the early 1960s, became overtaken by Italian, Spanish, and French involvement between 1965 and 1967, and was again temporarily more pronounced during the sex-film boom of the late 1960s. However, by this time, the overall number of co-productions had gone down. From 1959 to 1966 the number of West German co-productions had risen steadily, reaching its peak in 1966 with fifty-five films. By the end of the 1960s, however, the annual number of co-productions levelled at below thirty. Although co-productions remained an important industrial strategy for many European companies, the 1970s would be primarily characterised by an increasing chasm between state-funded, nationally conceptualised, art cinema and the renewed onslaught by Hollywood major studios in European markets.

Notes

1. Anon., 'Die Exportsituation des deutschen Films', *Film-Echo/Filmwoche*, 25 June 1966, p. 26.
2. Quoted in Michael Dost, Florian Hopf, and Alexander Kluge, *Filmwirtschaft in der BRD und Europa. Götterdämmerung in Raten*, Munich 1973, p. 22.
3. Paul Hainsworth, 'Politics, Culture and Cinema in the New Europe', in *Border Crossing. Film in Ireland, Britain and Europe*, ed. John Hill, Martin McLoone, and Paul Hainsworth, London and Dublin 1994, p. 13.
4. Anon., 'Beispiel kulturwirtschaftlicher Förderung',*Film-Echo*, 3 December 1960.
5. Dost et al., *Filmwirtschaft in der BRD und Europa*, p. 13.
6. Anne Jäckel, 'European Co-Production Strategies. The Case of France and Britain', in *Film Policy. International, National and Regional Perspectives*, ed. Albert Moran, London and New York 1996, p. 87.
7. Reg.-Dir. Dr. Leitner, 'Das deutsch-spanische Filmabkommen', *Film-Echo*, 3 December 1960.
8. Anon., 'Wie entsteht eine Coproduktion?', *Film-Echo/Filmwoche*, 13 March 1963, continued on 3 April 1963.
9. Martin Loiperdinger, 'State Legislation, Censorship, and Funding', in *The German Cinema Book*, ed. Tim Bergfelder, Erica Carter, and Deniz Göktürk, London 2002, pp. 154–155.
10. Anne Jäckel, 'Dual Nationality Film Productions in Europe after 1945', *Historical Journal of Film, Radio and Television*, vol. 23, no. 3, 2003, p. 233.

11. Anon., 'French Union Secretary's Warning on Common Market', *Film and Television Technician*, December 1962, p. 215.
12. Hugh Jenkins, 'The First Fifty Days of Labour Rule', *Film and Television Technician*, January 1965, pp. 4–5.
13. Sidney Cole, 'Danger Ahead', *Film and Television Technician*, January 1962, p. 4.
14. Jäckel, in Moran, *Film Policy*, p. 87.
15. Anon.,'Beispiel kulturwirtschaftlicher Förderung'.
16. Jutta W. Thomasius, 'Produzent sagt der Nachtausgabe: Höchste Zeit für Film-EWG', *Frankfurter Nachtausgabe*, 24 April 1963.
17. Joseph Garncarz, 'Hollywood in Germany: The Role of American Films in Germany', in *Hollywood in Europe. Experiences of a Cultural Hegemony*, ed. David W. Ellwood, and Rob Kroes, Amsterdam 1994, pp. 126–128.
18. Hans-Günther Pflaum and Hans Helmut Prinzler, *Cinema in the Federal Republic of Germany*, Munich and Vienna 1983, p. 81.
19. Cf. Joachim Lembach, *The Standing of the German Cinema in Great Britain after 1945*, Lampeter 2003, pp.131–139.
20. Anon., 'Die Exportsituation des deutschen Films', *Film-Echo/Filmwoche*, 25 June 1966.
21. C.C. Schulte, 'Coproduktionen sichern Europas Film', *Film-Echo/Filmwoche*, 22 January 1965.
22. Dost et al., *Filmwirtschaft in der BRD und Europa*, p.21.
23. F.E., 'Was heisst Europäischer Film?', *Film-Echo*, 6 July 1960.
24. Horst Axtmann, 'Internationale Zusammenarbeit als zwingendes Gebot', *Film-Echo/Filmwoche*, 23 June1967.
25. Jürgen Berger, 'Bürgen heisst zahlen – und manchmal auch zensieren', in *Zwischen Gestern und Morgen. Westdeutscher Nachkriegsfilm 1946–1962*, ed. Jürgen Berger, Hans-Peter Reichmann, and Rudolf Worschech, Frankfurt 1989, p. 92.
26. Ibid., p. 94.
27. Sabine Gottgetreu, Andrea Lang, and Ginette Vincendeau, 'Romy Schneider', in *Encyclopedia of European Cinema*, ed. Ginette Vincendeau, London 1995, p. 378.
28. Axtmann, 'Internationale Zusammenarbeit', *Film-Echo/Filmwoche*.
29. Anon., 'Kleine Fische sind unverkäuflich', *Film-Echo*, 25 February 1960.
30. Christopher Frayling, *Spaghetti Westerns*, London 1981, p. 73.
31. Kim Newman, 'Thirty Years in Another Town: The History of Italian Exploitation', *Monthly Film Bulletin*, vol. 53, no. 624, January 1986, p. 20.
32. On silent German Westerns, see Deniz Göktürk, *Künstler, Cowboys, Ingenieure. Kultur- und mediengeschichtliche Studien zu deutschen Amerikatexten 1912–1920*, Munich 1998. For a study of the 1930s German western *Der Kaiser von Kalifornien* (1936, The Emperor of California), see Frayling, *Spaghetti Westerns*, pp.19–27; and Lutz Koepnick, 'Siegfried Rides Again. Nazi Westerns and Modernity', in *The Dark Mirror. German Cinema between Hitler and Hollywood*, Berkeley 2002, pp. 99–134.
33. N.W., 'James Bond – Das Phänomen', *Film-Echo/Filmwoche*, 7 April 1965, p. 6.
34. Kim Newman, 'Thirty Years in Another Town: The History of Italian Exploitation, Part II', *Monthly Film Bulletin*, vol. 53, no. 625, February 1986, p. 51.

Chapter 4

THE DISTRIBUTION SECTOR

Given the overall fragmented industrial infrastructure of the European film industries after 1945, it is perhaps inevitable that in most countries a hierarchical system evolved in which the distribution sector led the industry. Owing to favourable conditions and preferential treatment during the Allied occupation following the end of the Second World War, American and British companies had managed to establish important positions in the West German distribution sector. The most significant British company was Rank, which performed extremely well against American competition. Following its initial successes in the postwar years with Gainsborough melodramas, Rank continued to be a major distributor in West Germany throughout the 1950s and 1960s. In the 1967/8 season its programme, comprising thirty films, outperformed any single U.S. distributor.[1] Major Hollywood distribution subsidiaries in West Germany during this period included Warner Bros., Centfox (20th Century Fox), M-G-M (Metro-Goldwyn-Mayer), United Artists, Paramount, Universal, and Walt Disney. In 1963, German company Bavaria became a subsidiary of the Hollywood studio Columbia, with its own distribution arm, Columbia-Bavaria. Columbia-Bavaria differed from other U.S. distribution subsidiaries in that it offered not only Hollywood films but also West German features and European co-productions. Among the films distributed (and co-produced) by Columbia-Bavaria was, for example, Helmut Käutner's *Lausbubengeschichten* (1964, Little Rascals' Tales) a nostalgic and whimsical portrait of everyday life in nineteenth century Bavaria, based on the childhood memories of popular Bavarian author, playwright, and humorist Ludwig Thoma (1867–1921). The film was immensely successful, and spawned a series of similarly themed films that lasted into the 1970s. Bavaria's other major asset was its studio facilities in Geiselgasteig near Munich. This studio complex, the biggest and best equipped in West Germany at the time outside Berlin, was predominantly used from the late 1950s for television productions, but also occasionally for domestic and international films. An example for the latter is the M-G-M/King Brothers production *Captain Sindbad* (1963), a children's adventure film starring

West German teen star Heidi Brühl alongside an international cast, and made with a predominantly West German technical crew. The casting of Hollywood actor Guy Williams in the male lead may have taken domestic audience preferences into account, as he had been a resounding success in the 1957–1959 TV series "Zorro", which was theatrically released in West German cinemas by the German distribution company Gloria.

While the presence of American companies cannot be disputed and it is also clear that their solid financial background and the lack of quota regulations in West Germany allowed them to operate fairly securely and to provide a consistent supply, their overall influence on the West German market during the 1950s and 1960s needs to be put into perspective. The American companies' aim to dominate the West German market through quantity (oversupply) and quality (production values) met, as previously outlined, a far more selective response from West German exhibitors and audiences than is normally acknowledged. Throughout the 1960s, no single American company managed to gain overall dominance in the West German distribution sector.

Among American companies, M-G-M supplied up to the mid-1960s the largest annual quantity of films in the West German market, peaking in 1963/4 with thirty-seven releases. The box-office performance of M-G-M's almost exclusively American products, however, was varied and frequently fell below exhibitors' expectations. By the 1967/8 season, M-G-M had been overtaken in its annual programme not only by American competitors Centfox (the West German representative of 20th Century Fox), and Paramount, and by the British Rank Organisation, but more significantly by the West German company Constantin, which distributed sixty-two feature films as against M-G-M's seventeen.

In the domain of the big-budget Hollywood blockbuster (particularly biblical or other historical epics, which had represented one Hollywood genre that had proved consistently popular with European audiences since the silent film era), the American companies had a distinct advantage, owing to more calculable risk, over their European competitors. As far as small and medium-budget features were concerned, however, West German and other European distributors very much held their own and often outperformed their U.S. rivals. In order to do so, West German distributors had to invest in production to be able to offer attractive film packages. Standard practice for deals between distributors and exhibitors was the 'block-booking' system, whereby cinema-owners agreed to take a specified amount of films from a distributor without knowing in detail what these packages entailed (in part because the films had not yet been made). Exhibitors could reasonably expect that the packages would include a number of high profile productions, but also lesser films, often comprising what in the Hollywood system are called B-films. The practice of 'blind' block-bookings, negotiated prior to production and clearly dependent not only on a given distributor's reputation but also on a substantial amount of trust on the side of the exhibitor, gave distributors the financial guarantees necessary for bank loans and production advances from investors. Judging by West German cinema-owners' comments in the trade press and their ranking of individual distributors, it is clear that throughout the 1960s they overall preferred the range of films offered in the programmes of domestic distributors (which included the bulk of indigenous and European productions) over American ones, and that they also preferred to negotiate with West German distribution partners. Significantly, the only American subsidiary that did consistently well in exhibitors' polls was Columbia-Bavaria, with its more internationally oriented programme, and its – at least in part – German pedigree.

Distribution remained a potentially profitable but also volatile and highly risky business throughout the 1960s. Of the main West German companies operating in this period, few survived into the 1970s and many of them had already ceased to exist by the mid-1960s.[2] A first significant wave of company closures occurred in 1961/2 with the bankruptcy or liquidation of Union, Atlantik, Neuer Filmverleih, Stella, Loewen, Europa, and Prisma. Schorcht, which had distributed some of the 1950s greatest box-office hits, lost its direction after the death of its founder Kurt Schorcht in the late 1950s and went out of business in 1965. Significantly, all of these distributors had previously been involved in the 1950s government guarantee schemes.

The year 1965 also saw the demise of Piran, which was briefly and unsuccessfully relaunched as Lord. Inter, on the verge of collapse since the early 1960s, made a brief recovery during the sex-film boom of the late 1960s, before disappearing a couple of years later. Another significant casualty of the mid-1960s was Hanns Eckelkamp's Atlas, which had specialised in the distribution of European art cinema (Ingmar Bergman, the French *nouvelle vague*) and 'quality' American films and had been one of the few supporters of and investors in the emerging directors of the New German Cinema. Atlas collapsed in 1967 and was subsequently reduced to a more modest outlet with an educational brief, supplying 16mm copies of international film 'classics' to private film clubs and schools.

To some extent, this reduction of companies and the subsequent oligopoly of only a handful of distributors were an inevitable and possibly even necessary consequence of a market that had been unnaturally oversaturated for several years. By the mid-1960s, the Bertelsmann Publishing Group became a significant shareholder in several West German distribution outlets, following its acquisition of a large part of the UFI assets in 1964. What could have turned out to be a desirable reorientation towards industry concentration and consolidation, however, became a frantic process of company acquisitions and sales. Bertelsmann's strategy was geared towards short-term profit rather than production investment that could have turned its affiliated companies into financially viable and competitive outlets. Bertelsmann's long-term aim was to consolidate its publishing base, while branching out into multimedia interests, which included television and record companies. Film production and distribution, on the other hand, were of far lesser importance to the Gütersloh-based corporation. Bertelsmann became less the saviour than the receiver and undertaker of the West German distribution sector, and this accelerated a renewed American attack on the West German market. When Nora, a dominant distributor during the 1950s, failed to make a successful transition into the 1960s, Bertelsmann acquired majority shares in the ailing company, but sold them in 1968 to Commonwealth United, an American media group. Nora declared bankruptcy a year later. Bertelsmann also took over Pallas (quickly ceasing business thereafter) and became, from 1965 onwards, the majority shareholder of Constantin.

A result of American oversupply and German distributors' response to this was an oversaturation of a market that at the same time saw a drastic decline in cinema-goers. The federal government's *Filmförderungsgesetz* (Film Subsidy Bill) of 1967, passed against opposition from directors of the New German Cinema and from West German exhibitors, overheated this situation even further. The government acknowledged that the main authority within the West German film sector rested with the distributors, and the *Filmförderungsgesetz* reflected this balance of power. Thus, the bill imposed an additional tax burden on the already moribund exhibition sector and reallocated these tax revenues to subsidise film distribution.[3] What enraged the main protagonists of the New German Cinema movement was that the bill included, as a prerequisite for financial support, a so-called *Referenzfilm* (reference film) that had proved to be a financial success at the box office. This crucial proviso of the subsidy bill effectively barred newcomers from receiving financial assistance, while it encouraged established distributors to expand their programmes (increasingly comprised of co-produced or totally foreign films) for no other reason than to secure financial advances for subsequent projects. These short-term strategies began increasingly to threaten the survival of the distributors' traditional allies, the exhibitors, and the advantages of the subsidy bill for distributors were short-lived. The changing fortunes and strategies of survival of the West German distribution sector can best be illustrated by a closer look at the two most successful companies in the 1960s, Ilse Kubaschewski's Gloria, and Constantin.

The Case of Gloria

Among West German film distributors in the 1950s and 1960s, Ilse Kubaschewski, with the outward appearance of an ordinary postwar German housewife, must rank as one of the most unlikely of film tycoons. Yet 'Kuba', as she was both affectionately and respectfully referred to in the film industry, was a figure of formidable influence and power. Moreover, she most typically exemplified the social mobility and the *Zeitgeist* of the West German 'economic miracle', a spirit of dogged determination and resentfulness of change, which Rainer Werner Fassbinder decades later portrayed so perceptively in *Die Ehe der Maria Braun* (1978, The Marriage of Maria Braun).

Kubaschewski was a woman with defiantly conservative and lowbrow tastes, a broad Berlin accent, and a shrewd understanding of finance. Born in 1907 as Ilse Kramp, a postman's daughter, in a working-class district of Berlin, she began her career working as a typist for Paul Czinner's production company and later for the modestly successful distributor Siegel-Monopol Verleih.[4] In the 1930s and early 1940s this outlet had carved out a small niche market left by the oligopoly of the increasingly state-dependent major companies Ufa, Tobis, Terra, and Bavaria, by specialising in low-budget, folkloristic fare aimed at provincial audiences. After the creation of the state monopoly UFI, the company was shut down in 1942, and Kubaschewski acquired a small suburban cinema, which she ran with the help of her extended family. Shortly before the Russian attack on Berlin in 1945, she moved to Bavaria. After the war had ended, Kubaschewski quickly resumed her activities in southern Germany, aided by a number of circumstantial advantages. Given her hitherto low-profile career, her political record was relatively untainted, and yet her professional expertise was undisputed. Moreover, her husband since 1938, Hans Kubaschewski, a former Ufa branch manager, was conveniently working for the American military authorities, advising them on the issuing of licences to politically opportune producers, exhibitors, and other film personnel.

Together with Luggi Waldleitner (who would also become a significant player in the postwar West German film industry), Kubaschewski took over a provincial cinema in Oberstdorf, Bavaria, for the next four years, during which time she recognised that Ufa rereleases fared better at the box office than the newly imported American and French products. With a bank loan of 30,000 DM, Kubaschewski founded her distribution company Gloria in 1949, specialising at first in the acquisition of old German box-office hits before venturing into contracts with production companies. In 1953 she founded her own production outlet, Divina, and two years later her empire also included a number of prestigious first-run cinemas.

Gloria's corporate strategy in the 1950s and 1960s was to a large extent based on Kubaschewski's prior professional background in mainly provincial or suburban exhibition and distribution and on her personal taste in films, which she perceived as being representative of the average German cinema-goer at large (a perception that, at least during the 1950s, proved remarkably accurate). Gloria's target audience was assumed to be primarily female, and the distributor tried to reach this clientele with florid and sentimental advertising campaigns that blurred the distinction between film promotion and romantic fiction. Kubaschewski's trust in and reliance on her female constituency also explains why Gloria only reluctantly moved into producing more 'male' genres. Eventually the company did, and 'Kuba' had one of her greatest distribution successes with the *08/15* cycle, a series of films centred on the battle experiences of ordinary German soldiers during the Second World War.

The genres Gloria most strongly supported and specialised in during the 1950s, were *Heimatfilme* and female-centred melodramas. Producers (which included Artur Brauner's CCC, Luggi Waldleitner's Roxy, and Kurt Ulrich's Berolina) were instructed to make films that featured musical numbers, comic elements, romance, happy endings, and plentiful images of an idyllic countryside. In terms of production personnel, Gloria epitomised the ethos of Adenauer's 'no experiments' era: it distinctly preferred established Ufa directors over younger talent, and its contracted stars tended to be those who had been tried and tested during the Nazi era. This latter priority did not always pay off, as is evident, for example, in Gloria's failed attempts to revive the flagging careers of ageing Ufa favourites such as Zarah Leander, Marika Rökk, and Kristina Söderbaum. On the whole, however, Kubaschewski's business instinct proved right, as *Heimatfilme* such as *Grün ist die Heide* (1951, Green is the Heath), and film operettas, such as *Kaiserwalzer* (1953, Emperor Waltz), resulted in unprecedented box-office profits. By the mid-1950s West German cinema had once again established a roster of home-grown and indigenously popular stars, such as Ruth Leuwerik, Maria Schell, Sonja Ziemann, Lilli Palmer, and Curd Jürgens, that Gloria could draw on. By the late 1950s, Gloria's initial starting capital of 30,000 DM had grown into a fortune of 25 million DM, largely invested in real estate, and the company had an annual turnover of 30 million DM.[5]

To a large extent, this success was, of course, due not only to Kubaschewski's populist tastes, but also to her extremely tight calculations and tough negotiations with producers and production personnel, leaving them with only the smallest of profit margins. Unlike most of her competitors, Kubaschewski refrained from entering into the government guarantee schemes discussed in the previous chapter and thus retained her independence both from state intervention and from high-interest-rate bank loans.

Gloria's image as the quintessential distributor of *Heimatfilme* and other domestic fare during the 1950s, seems to suggest precisely the parochial "Bavarian cottage industry', which has become the stereotypical impression of postwar West German film companies as a whole. However, this image is only partially true, and obscures the fact that the company responded very early to the increasingly international dimension of the West German film market. Following his work for the U.S. military authorities, by the late 1940s Kubaschewski's husband had become the manager of Warner Bros.' West German distribution subsidiary. From 1959 until his death in 1961, Hans Kubaschewski was the trustee of the former UFI asset Bavaria, laying the groundwork for closer cooperation with major Hollywood studios, which would eventually lead to the merger of Columbia and Bavaria in 1963. The Kubaschewskis strongly supported each other's business interests. Hans Kubschewski's international connections and advice served to complement his wife's more parochial outlook and helped to diversify Gloria's profile.

Figure 4.1. Ilse Kubaschewski, West Germany's female film tycoon. Deutsches Filminstitut (DIF), Frankfurt-on-Main.

Since most of the major American companies had already established their own distribution subsidiaries in Germany, Gloria, through Hans Kubaschewski's mediation, established business contacts with the American B-film studio Republic in 1950 and eventually became its West German distributor until Republic's demise in 1958. The American studio sold its output in large packages, which consisted of both current productions and Republic's back catalogue, previously unseen in Germany. More profitable for Gloria than the predominant westerns in these packages, however, was Republic's TV series "The Adventures of Fu Manchu" (1956), with individual episodes edited from their original one-hour format into dubbed, feature-length films, and released theatrically in West Germany. A flexible repayment agreement with Republic and the guaranteed profit from the relatively cheaply acquired American films ensured that Gloria gained continual financial solvency from this deal. Gloria employed a similar strategy when it managed the West German distribution of the previously mentioned Walt Disney TV series "Zorro" (1957–1959). Apart from managing American products, Gloria also showed a good instinct in acquiring the West German distribution rights for other foreign films, the biggest success being Fellini's *La Dolce Vita* in 1959. Such imports should, of course, not be mistaken as evidence for Gloria's reverence for esteemed European art-house *auteurs*. Gloria's promotion campaigns in such instances would be more than likely to highlight the films' erotic attractions rather than their artistic qualities, and Gloria showed no scruples either in arbitrarily cutting or renaming foreign films or in changing their narrative emphasis through 'creative' dubbing. Only rarely did Gloria encounter much opposition for such practices, but the company did face a court injunction in 1972 brought by Italian director Luchino Visconti, who vetoed planned cuts of his film *Ludwig* (1972), a production that Gloria had co-financed, presumably on the mistaken assumption that the film would cater to the nostalgia industry surrounding the mad Bavarian king of the nineteenth century, and that it would repeat the box-office success of a previous West German production on the same subject in 1955.[6] Unlike the earlier film, *Ludwig II* (which had principally been a star vehicle for O.W. Fischer), Visconti's *Ludwig* explicitly referred to its main protagonist's homosexuality, which was hardly in line with Gloria's morally conservative image. The film's over-length and stately pace, moreover, made it an economically dubious proposition for distributor and exhibitors alike.

Co-productions featured in Gloria's programme from the late 1950s, even though Kubaschewski's first experiences had not been too encouraging. Wolfgang Staudte's *Die Dreigroschenoper* (1962, The Threepenny Opera), for example, adapted from Bertolt Brecht's play, co-produced with France and shot in three language versions, was an unmitigated financial as well as critical disaster, despite, or perhaps because, of a bizarre cast that included Curd Jürgens, Sammy Davis Jr., and Lino Ventura. Compared with other major distributors of the 1960s, Gloria subsequently followed generic trends and fashions in European co-productions (such as the western, crime thrillers, and horror, spy, and soft-porn films) much more erratically and half-heartedly. While acknowledging the popularity of these genres and trying to cater for new adolescent and male cinema-goers, Kubaschewski's own priority remained, at least during the first half of the decade, with her core target audience of, by now, middle-aged housewives. The major domestic releases distributed by Gloria in the early 1960s continued to be *Heimatfilme*, musicals, women's melodramas, and comedies, the latter three genres very often set against the scenic backdrops of Mediterranean seaside resorts.

Co-productions sponsored and distributed by Gloria during this period followed a similar pattern and were largely high-class melodramas aimed at a domestic female audience. Advertised by Gloria as its 'most promising' feature for the 1964/5 season, for example, was the Italian portemanteau film *I tre volti* (1964, The Three Faces), co-financed by Gloria primarily because one of the film's three segments starred the Shah of Iran's ex-wife, Soraya, whose fortunes and tribulations had become a permanent feature in West Germany's tabloid and illustrated press.[7] Despite such advance publicity, however, the film was a box-office flop, and is today remembered only because Michelangelo Antonioni directed one of the film's other segments. Other Gloria co-productions included the CCC film *Axel Munthe, der Arzt von San Michele* (1962, Axel Munthe, the Doctor of San Michele), based on the autobiography by a Swedish physician and globetrotter that had been a best seller since its publication in 1929. The novel had achieved its cult following primarily owing to its religious symbolism and quasi-mystical message. The film, on the other hand, emphasised more pictorial qualities, focusing on upper-class expatriate residents on the island of Capri, and starring 1950s idol O.W. Fischer opposite Italian film stars Rossana Schiaffino and Valentina Cortese.

Gloria's most profitable venture into co-productions, however, was the historical costume cycle *Angélique*, a series of five Franco-West German-Italian co-productions between 1964 and 1967 (a sixth film, announced in 1968 by Divina as *Angélique, die Rebellin*, was abandoned prior to production). The films were based on the bestselling novels by French author Anne Golon and starred Michèle Mercier as the resourceful eponymous heroine embroiled in romantic intrigues during the reign of Louis XIV. Although principally speaking a French enterprise (in the sense of having primarily French casts and technical personnel), the *Angélique* series became a crossover success for Gloria in West Germany and helped to balance a number of misguided acquisitions. The films' indebtedness to female-centred romantic fiction and their casting of German stars (such as 1950s screen idol Dieter Borsche) in supporting roles managed to attract Kubaschewski's traditional constituency, while their risqué erotic content and episodes of swashbuckling adventure were designed to appeal to younger and male audiences. The first three *Angélique* films were awarded the *Goldene Leinwand* (Golden Screen) for audience figures of over 3 million cinema-goers, though overall the cycle fell below the popularity levels of other series, such as the Edgar Wallace crime thrillers and Karl May westerns.

Gloria hoped that the *Angélique* series would, eventually, spawn a new generic and box-office trend of slightly bawdy costume romances. To this end, the company invested in the American/West German *Fanny Hill* (1965, based on John Cleland's long-censored erotic classic), and in the Franco-West German/Italian *Cathérine – Il suffit d'un amour/ Cathérine – Ein Leben für die Liebe* (1968), made by *Angélique* director Bernard de Borderie and, like *Angélique*, based on a bestselling historical romance novel (in this case, by Juliette Benzoni). Neither of these films, however, managed to repeat the phenomenon of the earlier cycle, even though Gloria's evaluation of the genre's box-office potential proved accurate, as the costume drama was transformed into a significant subgenre of the sex-film boom (more on this in chapter 9).

Following the decline of the *Heimatfilm* in the 1960s, and despite Kubaschewski's pragmatic but not overly enthusiastic attitude towards new generic trends, Gloria nevertheless remained one of the most important West German distributors during the decade, albeit with a less clearly defined company profile than in the 1950s. Unlike its main rival Constantin, Gloria failed to maintain a distinctive programme strategy through exclusive contracts with producers and through successful series formulae

Figure 4.2. Michèle Mercier in *Angélique* (1964), co-financed by Kubaschewski's Gloria. Deutsches Filminstitut (DIF), Frankfurt-on-Main.

(with the exception of *Angélique*), and its marketing was uninspired and anachronistic. According to Manfred Barthel, another mistaken strategy was to rely too heavily on the attraction of established stars, while simultaneously saving on other production costs. Well into the 1960s, the majority of Gloria releases were shot in black and white, which did not help to lure audiences away from the equally black and white but increasingly dominant medium of television.[8] Gloria's main rival, Constantin, on the other hand, quite specifically capitalised on and publicised the use of attractions such as colour and wide-screen formats.

Gloria's success since the 1950s had always depended on its exhibition networks and its established contacts with cinema-owners, a relationship that was given a much higher priority than stable contracts with producers. In the latter half of the decade, however, the company, with a steadily decreasing annual programme and dwindling revenues from shrinking exhibition outlets, was more or less desperate for any film to distribute. By the end of the decade, the Gloria programme included material Kubaschewski would in all likelihood have indignantly rejected ten years earlier, such as the Anglo-West German feature *Burn, Witch, Burn* (1970, *Hexen bis aufs Blut gequält*, also known internationally as *Mark of the Devil*), a sadistic sexploitation horror film starring Udo Kier and Herbert Lom, and co-directed by former 1950s *Heimatfilm* heartthrob Adrian Hoven.

By this time, Gloria was one of the few remaining West German distributors that had originated in the immediate postwar period. Kubaschewski was one of the few founding figures of the postwar German film industry who had managed to remain independent and to retain overall power and a stable team within her company, unlike many of her competitors, who had experienced a much quicker turnover of staff, company profile, and managerial control. This stability, however, exemplifying the spirit of the 1950s, which emphasised individual enterprise tempered by risk avoidance, may well have contributed to Gloria's increasing stagnation and decline by the late 1960s, exacerbated by Kubaschewski's personal inability to change with the times and to pursue new audience constituencies more aggressively. In a report on Gloria's activities, the trade paper *Film-Echo/Filmwoche* noted pointedly in 1966: 'One gets the impression that nothing has changed in this company, but that people work here persistently and undeterred, not simply to survive or to stay in the game, but to be at the top. The work is done quietly and thoroughly, but maybe a bit too quietly'.[9] Gloria just about managed to survive into the 1970s, before Kubaschewski sold the company in 1973 to an American TV outlet, Project Seven Inc., and she subsequently disappeared from the film scene altogether, except for the occasional guest appearance at premières and social events. Kubaschewski lived to witness, from the vantage point of a financially very secure retirement, several further U-turns of the commercial film sector before her death in 2001.

The Case of Constantin

Compared with Gloria, which represented continuity from the 1950s to the 1960s and cautious, reluctant change, Constantin was the West German distributor that most quintessentially represented the changed film culture and social climate of the 1960s. Whereas other distributors decreased the number of films on offer, the quantity of Constantin films grew steadily throughout the decade. Whereas Gloria mainly pursued the traditional audience constituency of the 1950s, Constantin deliberately targeted a younger market with new genres, a decidedly cosmopolitan approach towards production, and aggressive marketing and brash advertising campaigns. In the early 1950s, the company had been a modestly successful distributor among many. Like Gloria, Constantin had in the 1950s avoided being drawn into the government guarantee schemes and entered the 1960s without substantial debts. By the late 1960s, Constantin dominated West German distribution, with only Gloria as a serious domestic competitor. For the New German Cinema, Constantin and its distribution policies represented everything that was wrong with the traditional film industry. As late as 1975, when Constantin was virtually defunct and the New German Cinema at its height, Wim Wenders' *Kings of the Road* included the following line of dialogue, quoted by Christopher Frayling in his book on spaghetti westerns: 'Nearly all the films we see are made by Constantin and the big American studios. Better no cinema at all than that.'[10]

Constantin was founded in 1949 by Waldfried Barthel and Preben Phillipsen, initially as a distribution outlet for Hollywood products by United Artists and Columbia. Phillipsen had an interesting background in both the German and the Danish film industry. His father, Constantin Phillipsen, had been a pioneer in Danish film exhibition. After an apprenticeship in the late 1920s at Ufa and the Pathé studios in Paris, Phillipsen junior founded the distribution company Constantin in Copenhagen in 1933. After the war he became one of the founders of the West German distributor Constantin and also operated a production outlet, Rialto, in Denmark. While Rialto's early films were made for the Danish market, by mid-decade the emphasis shifted towards a strategy to produce films mainly for the West German market and more specifically for the West German Constantin. During the 1960s, Rialto became associated with postwar Germany's most successful genre formulas, the Edgar Wallace films and, later, the Karl May series. Phillipsen's international contacts proved invaluable for Constantin's European expansion in the 1950s and by the end of the decade the company had branches in Rome, Warsaw, and Paris. Meanwhile, Phillipsen's business partner Waldfried Barthel, known as 'der Konsul' in the industry, was responsible for the company's production profile and public image.

During the 1950s Constantin distributed small to medium-sized domestic genre productions, lacking the production values and star names companies such as Gloria could offer. It also balanced its programme fairly evenly between indigenous and imported films.[11] These included both the bread-and-butter fare of Italian peplum features or the 'Lemmy Caution' action-film series from France, starring Eddie Constantine, and art features, such as Fellini's *La Strada* (1954). British critic Robin Bean attested to Constantin's commitment to its art-film range by noting that 'Constantin, which distributes many westerns, sponsored a Czech film week in Munich … very much to its credit, with a lavish brochure on the programmes and biographies of the directors, which is more than British distributors do for their art'.[12] During the 1960s Constantin continued its dual strategy – next to experimental films, such as Luis Buñuel's *Viridiana* (1961), Roman Polanski's *Knife in the Water* (1962), and Alain Resnais' *Last Year At Marienbad* (1962), it also distributed in West Germany the French comedies starring Louis de Funès, who would maintain his popularity with German audiences for the next two decades.[13]

Constantin's meteoric rise in the late 1950s and its consistent dominance in the 1960s have been explained by its former head of publicity, Manfred Barthel, as being based on a number of corporate strategies.[14] Unlike its competitors, for its domestic range Constantin commissioned as a rule not established production companies and personnel, but younger (albeit resolutely commercial) talent and emerging production outlets. Rather than spending money on stars of previous decades, it built up its own stable of new stars, very often recruited from television. Thus it was Constantin that created and promoted the careers of directors such as Jürgen Roland, producers such as Horst Wendlandt and Wolf C. Hartwig, or actors such as Joachim Fuchsberger, Heinz Drache, and Hansjörg Felmy. In return, they were frequently bound to Constantin in exclusive contracts. In some cases it is difficult to determine whether the invention or agency for a particular project or for a whole product line (such as series and sequels) originated with the notional production company or with Constantin. In many cases it is very likely that it may have been the latter. Rather than investing in production values, such as mass scenes, expensive sets, or costumes, Constantin focused instead on novel technology and marketing. Its products were almost exclusively in colour and frequently released in wide-screen formats. During the sex-film boom of the late 1960s, it even experimented briefly with stereoscopic, or three-dimensional, cinema (known popularly as 3-D). In contrast to the more modest and restrained lobby-card advertising of other companies, Constantin introduced glossy and garishly colourful posters and press books with lurid headlines, titillating illustrations, and hyperbolic slogans. Compared with Gloria's conservative approach to marketing, emphasising middle-class respectability and wholesome family values, Constantin's marketing thrived on sensationalism and on its promise of action-packed entertainment, notoriety, and scandal.

This form of marketing was directly linked to Constantin's generic profile. Although the company was actually very diverse in the kinds of films it offered (as proved by its art-film range), in the 1960s Constantin became most closely associated by the public with a specific cluster of popular genres and production companies. At the outset of the decade, Constantin still included established domestic genres such as the *Heimatfilm* in its programme, but overall it prioritised new generic trends, such as crime, horror, westerns, and sex films, and emphasised their appeal through increased marketing efforts. Among the popular film cycles initiated or adopted by Constantin in the 1960s, three cross-generic trends can be identified. The first is the pattern of adapting popular literary fiction (often, but not exclusively, of the pulp or *Groschenheft* variety) to the screen and marketing these films with specific reference to the audience's familiarity and appreciation of these sources. This applies to Rialto's Edgar Wallace and Karl May cycles and to Harry Alan Towers' Fu Manchu films, based on 'classic' popular novels originating in the first half of the century, but which had been successfully recycled by West German paperback publishers prior to the films. While Constantin's marketing stressed the modernity and youthfulness of these genres, one major characteristic of popular German films during the 1960s was their recycling of older traditions of mass culture, and particularly those from the 1910s and 1920s. Other incentives for popular genres came from indigenous pulp novels, as in the case of the Rolf Torring, Kommissar X, and Jerry Cotton films.[15]

The second trend was to incorporate sexual titillation and to market relatively explicit erotic content across the company's generic spectrum; as Joseph Garncarz and Thomas Elsaesser note, Constantin 'took the sex film out of the porn shops, making them respectable to adult movie audiences'.[16] The way for this trend had been paved in the late 1950s with the productions of Wolf Hartwig's Munich-based company Rapid, which in the early 1960s became one of Constantin's most prolific and profitable production outfits. A sexually more explicit, and arguably more exploitative, combination of alleged sex education and comedy would characterise most of the late-1960s sex boom, from which Constantin also made a significant profit. Again, as with the literary adaptations, Constantin frequently took its cue from and exploited references to other media, such as social surveys (as in the Schoolgirls Reports) and tabloid stories. I shall analyse Hartwig's mode of productions, and especially the Schoolgirls Reports, in greater detail in chapter 9.

The third trend at Constantin was towards an increasingly European rather than purely German profile in programming. Already in the 1950s the company's output had evenly balanced domestic and foreign productions. From the 1960s onwards, these two categories became more and more blurred, with an increase in co-productions. In 1960, Constantin had advertised in its annual programme twelve West German and ten foreign films. For the season 1962/63, it distributed only seven purely foreign productions, but its slightly misleadingly labelled 'German-language' programme of twenty-four films consisted predominantly of dubbed co-productions, mainly made in France, Italy, and Spain, but with varying degrees of West German investment or artistic contribution. This pattern would remain for the rest of the decade, with a steady increase in co-productions and foreign acquisitions and a simultaneous decrease in exclusively West German productions. This trend was only reversed at the very end of the decade, largely owing to the mushrooming of – mostly home-grown – sex film series.

Constantin's corporate strategy towards product differentiation was to assign nominally independent producers the status of what in the American studio system one would have called a 'production unit'. Although Constantin did have its own production subsidiary, Terra (not to be confused with the Nazi film company of the same name that operated in the 1930s and 1940s), this outlet never became an actual or semi-independent producer (as, for example, in the case of Gloria's offshoot Divina), but provided more of an umbrella organisation for Constantin's affiliated producers both at home and across Europe. The basic function of this mode of production was effectively to exploit the specific production expertise in various popular generic formulae to their full potential. Sequelisation of one-off box-office hits and the creation of generic cycles, which characterises not just West German film production during the 1960s but European cinema more generally, were consequently more rigidly adhered to at Constantin than by any other German distributor.

Nearly all of the successful genre series in the West German market of the 1960s were distributed and co-financed by Constantin. Through its exclusive contract with Preben Phillipsen and Horst Wendlandt's Rialto, and Heinz Willeg's Allianz, it had a monopoly on the Edgar Wallace, Karl May, and Jerry Cotton cycles. The films of Hartwig's Rapid and Harry Alan Towers were also mostly distributed by Constantin. Following the box-office success of the Karl May westerns, Constantin invested in and supported the Italian 'spaghetti western', beginning with Sergio Leone's 'Dollar' films. Constantin offered financial support and guaranteed West German distribution and marketing in return for the inclusion of German actors (e.g., Marianne Koch, Klaus Kinski, and Sieghart Rupp in Leone's productions). Where successful genre formulae had been established by other distributors, Constantin either bought up the rights for sequels or the respective production units. After Gloria had distributed the first *Kommissar X* films, Constantin took over the franchise and commissioned five more sequels. Two sequels of the phenomenally successful semi-documentary sex education film *Helga* (1967) were also distributed by Constantin.

In terms of management and overall control, Constantin was far less centralised and stable than its main competitor Gloria. Of the company's two founding figures, Preben Phillipsen had resigned from his management post in 1955, though he remained affiliated to Constantin through his Danish–West German production company Rialto, which would in the

1960s become Constantin's most significant supplier under Horst Wendlandt's management. In 1965 the Bertelsmann Publishing Group became the majority shareholder of Constantin. Barthel remained nominally in charge, but the official management role went to Herbert Schmidt, who had been chief accountant at Bertelsmann headquarters in Gütersloh for several years, and who had also been briefly appointed as manager of one of Ufa's remaining assets, Universum Film AG, another Bertelsmann acquisition.

Bertelsmann's strategy at Constantin was to further increase the company's annual output, but without increasing production investment. This spreading of finance meant an overall cut-back on production costs, and subsequently the abandonment of certain genre formulae that no longer proved cost-effective (the Karl May series was the first and most prominent casualty, subsequently followed by the Edgar Wallace and Jerry Cotton cycles). Instead the home-grown sex-film boom provided a temporary solution by supplying a large number of quickly and cheaply made films. Bertelsmann's priority of quantity over quality made Constantin's programme look on the surface fairly healthy in the late 1960s, but the large number of releases simply no longer corresponded to decreasing exhibition outlets and dwindling audience figures. Exhibitors began to resent the oversupply of films that were almost impossible to distinguish from each other, particularly in the case of spy thrillers and sex films.[17]

Figure 4.3. Constantin and the sex film boom: still from *Schulmädchenreport* (1968, Schoolgirls Report). Deutsches Filminstitut (DIF), Frankfurt-on-Main.

When Bertelsmann realised that its strategy did not pay off, it decided to sell its shares in 1969. Negotiations with Commonwealth United and, later, Cinerama, both American media groups, fell through. When Waldfried Barthel eventually bought back the 60 per cent share majority from Bertelsmann in 1971, Constantin was moribund, just about kept alive by its sex-film profits. In 1976 the company was taken over by the Gierse Group, but was declared bankrupt a year later. The liqueur manufacturer Eckes bought the remaining assets and relaunched a Neue Constantin in 1977. Two years later, in 1979, Barthel died: his and Philippsen's company, however, or rather the brand name Constantin, would witness a phoenix-like reappearance over the next two decades under the guidance of producer-manager Bernd Eichinger, as I will outline in chapter 10.

Notes

1. All figures compiled from annual lists in the trade paper *Film-Echo/Filmwoche*.
2. On distribution companies' trajectories in the 1960s, see Joe Hembus and Robert Fischer, 'Chronik 1960-1980', in *Der neue deutsche Film 1960–1980*, Munich 1981, pp. 268–278.
3. On the 1967 bill, see Alexander Kluge, 'Das Filmförderungsgesetz vom 1.Dezember 1967 und seine Folgen', in *Filmwirtschaft in der BRD und in Europa. Götterdämmerung in Raten*, ed. Michael Dost, Florian Hopf, and Alexander Kluge, Munich 1973, pp. 121–123.
4. Anon., 'Ilse Kubaschewski. Det greift ans Herz', *Der Spiegel*, 23 January 1957.
5. Manfred Barthel, 'Die Kinokönigin und ihr Gloria-Verleih: Ilse Kubaschewski', in *So war es wirklich. Der deutsche Nachkriegsfilm*, Berlin 1986, p. 63.
6. Michael Töteberg, 'Gloria, die Schnulzenkönigin', in *Der rote Korsar. Traumwelt Kino der fünfziger und sechziger Jahre*, ed. Thomas Bertram, Essen 1998, p. 153.
7. hjw, 'Gloria: 64/65 aufwendiger denn je', *Film-Echo/Filmwoche*, 16 May 1964, p. 5.
8. Barthel, *So war es wirklich*, p. 71.
9. Horst Axtmann, 'Informativer Besuch in Verleihhäusern', *Film-Echo/Filmwoche*, 17 December 1966, p. 7.
10. Christopher Frayling, *Spaghetti Westerns*, London 1981, p. 115.
11. Anon,, 'Constantin: 12 deutsche und 10 ausländische Filme', *Film-Echo*, 13 August 1960, p.1070.
12. Robin Bean, 'Sex, Guns, and May', *Films and Filming*, vol. 11, part 6, 1965, p. 55.
13. Anon., 'Constantins 3,5 Millionen-Programm', *Film-Echo/Filmwoche*, 8 April 1964, p.5.
14. Barthel, *So war es wirklich*, pp. 74–76.
15. Anon., 'Unverwüstlich: James Bond-Edgar Wallace-Jerry Cotton', *Film-Echo/Filmwoche*, 22 December 1967, p.11.
16. Joseph Garncarz and Thomas Elsaesser: 'Constantin', in *Encylopedia of European Cinema*, ed. Ginette Vincendeau, London 1995, p. 93.
17. nn, 'Kommissar X soll Jerry Cotton nicht ins Gehege kommen. Die Angebote der Verleiher müssten unterschiedlicher sein', *Film-Echo/Filmwoche*, 2 March 1966, p. 4.

Chapter 5

FILM, TELEVISION, AND
INTERNATIONALISATION

Although distribution companies played a significant role in changing West German audience preferences towards international films in the 1960s, television played an even greater part in the gradual acculturation of the German public with respect of American (and more generally 'foreign') narrative models and generic conventions. This acculturation of course eventually determined the preferences for foreign (and particularly American) films not just on the small screen, but also in the cinema. In negotiating different cultural conventions and different media, German audiences, and in particular the younger generation, became increasingly media-literate in distinguishing cultural differences, and they used them for specific purposes. In other words, the transnational film culture in both West German cinema and television of the 1960s responded to and facilitated an increased cultural and media competence in its audiences.

As in other countries, the development of television and the changing relationship between film and television in Germany were determined by economic imperatives and technological change. In aesthetic and technological terms, the histories of cinema and television have frequently been seen as distinct from each other, coinciding only in so far as the rise of one mass medium paralleled the decline of the other. Charles Barr, on the other hand, writing on the history of British television drama, has pointed to the convergence of the two media in terms 'not only of institutional framework, economics of consumption ... but of "language" and aesthetics'.[1] For Barr, this convergence was motivated primarily by technological change, in particular by the introduction of the 'Ampex' videotape recording system in 1958, which increasingly made television's early live dramas obsolete.

As in Britain, the shift from the 'immediacy' and 'naturalism' of live transmission to the adoption of 'cinematic principles and qualities' was a contested one among practitioners and theoreticians of television in both East and West Germany. These debates and technological changes affected not only the development of dramatic formats on television, but also the narrational, promotional, and production strategies of the film industry in the 1960s. I shall concentrate here mainly on three major issues: the technical and personal cooperation between television and film producers, the similarities and convergences between televisual and cinematic genres, and the internationalisation of television programming and its relationship to the internationalisation of the film industry.

Television had been established in Germany since the mid-1930s. The Nazis had widely publicised the first regular television programme worldwide in 1935 (with a fairly limited reach, concentrated mostly in Berlin). Television had also been used for live transmissions during the 1936 Olympic Games in Berlin.[2] For the early German television pioneers, the main characteristic of the new medium was 'the live production, the principle of simultaneous production, transmission, and reception',[3] though in future years the medium was more often used for less expensive canned compilations of Ufa films, which functioned as early versions of advertising trailers.[4] On the whole, however, the technologies of television and film during this period were still distinct, as no means of recording electronic images had yet been developed. As a more reliable and consistent tool for state propaganda, the Nazis' preferred mass medium was radio and by the beginning of the war developments in television transmission had more or less come to a halt. Unsurprisingly, though, the postwar development of German television followed on from its early experiments, and many of the pioneers of West German television were veterans of 1930s broadcasting.[5]

Like the German film industry, the broadcasting sector had, for the first postwar years, been under the control of the Allies and had been subject to similar vetting procedures. In the British-occupied zone, the North-West German Broadcasting Station (NWDR), modelled by its first director Hugh Charleton Greene on the ethos and principles of the Reithian BBC, was one of the first German stations to resume (initially only radio) transmission, soon to be followed by other smaller regional services. After the Allies had relinquished control in 1948, these stations joined forces in 1950 to form the Arbeitsgemeinschaft der öffentlich-rechtlichen Rundfunkanstalten in der Bundesrepublik Deutschland (ARD), or Association of Public Service Broadcasters in West-Germany, combining the regional broadcasters' independence with nationally centralised coordination.[6]

Postwar transmissions (initially on an experimental basis) had begun in 1950. On Christmas Day 1952, the NWDR started regular, daily transmissions with a programme lasting initially for about two hours each evening, and consisting of news bulletins, TV dramas, and quiz shows. The first national transmission by the ARD went on air in November 1954. These early formats were supported by state subsidies and revenues from viewers' broadcasting licences. From 1956 onwards, commercial advertising became another important form of revenue, in temporally designated and separately scheduled advertisement 'blocks'.

The film industry's policies towards television initially (at least until the mid-1950s) displayed a feeling of superiority towards what was seen as a short-lived and imperfect technological gadget. Indeed, during the early years the quality of televised images was poor and transmissions frequently broke down. On the other hand, the industry's umbrella organisation SPIO had already in 1952 founded a committee to coordinate talks with television executives, and to study the new medium's performance. As the importance of television grew throughout the 1950s, however, divergent interests emerged among the different branches of the German film industry.

The most vociferous opposition to television came, predictably, from the exhibition sector, where audience figures dwindled by the end of the decade, seen by cinema-owners as a direct result of the competition by the new medium. Already in the late 1940s, the trade paper *Film-Echo*, aimed at exhibitors, had reported on the rise of television in the United States and had issued warnings of similar developments in Germany. During the mid- to late 1950s, a number of more entrepreneurial exhibitors attempted to capitalise on television's novelty value by offering large-screen projections of televised events. This practice could work at a time when television ownership was still fairly limited; yet at the same time it accelerated the demand for privately owned sets even further. The so-called *Aktualitäten-Kinos* (actuality cinemas) were banned by a court order in 1959.[7]

For film production companies, and especially for those that owned studio facilities, on the other hand, television was perceived as a lifeline in the face of the decline in indigenous film production in the late 1950s and early 1960s. Film producer Artur Brauner founded in 1959 a company subsidiary whose explicit aim was to negotiate rentals of his Spandau studio and to produce programmes (TV dramas, folklore comedies, and quiz shows) for broadcasting corporations. In the early 1960s, Brauner's CCC-Television supplied German TV companies, mainly the recently established Zweites Deutsches Fernsehen (ZDF), with approximately thirty productions each year. In this period, CCC's profits from its television activities made up between one-third and half of the studio's income.[8]

By mid-decade, television still needed supplies by external companies in order to fill production gaps, but TV stations were no longer willing to rely on independent, but not fully television-compatible, studios. Instead they invested in the acquisition of their own facilities. CCC's Spandau-based complex was among the last of the independent German studios not to be controlled either by television or by multinational media conglomerates, such as Bertelsmann, or by American companies. From the late 1950s, the Bavaria studios in Geiselgasteig were used by the regional broadcasters Süddeutscher Rundfunk (SDR), and Westdeutscher Rundfunk (WDR), while the former Ufa studios in Berlin-Tempelhof were leased out to ZDF.[9] CCC's Spandau studios thus faced competition not only from older facilities transformed into television production outlets, but also from the creation of new studios, specifically tailored to television's needs. In 1966, the centrally located studio of the Berlin broadcasting service Sender Freies Berlin (SFB) had opened, making Brauner's suburban and comparatively outdated facilities increasingly obsolete for television companies. With the number of cinema films shot at Spandau also declining (the majority of CCC's productions of the mid- to late 1960s were made in Italian or Spanish studios), Brauner reduced the staff and facilities at Spandau to a bare minimum in 1970.[10]

By the mid-1960s, television's absorption of most of the film industry's production facilities was more or less complete, making the relationship between televisual and filmic narratives even more ambivalent and contentious. In the early years of television, television's function was perceived to lie primarily in providing live transmissions of public events, information, and non-narrative formats, such as game shows, and news bulletins. One of the specifically televisual narrative formats was the *Fernsehspiel* (TV drama), usually based on classic stage dramas or adaptations of well-known novels, which were transmitted live either from a studio or from a theatre performance. Karl Prümm has characterised the cultural ambitions of the TV drama as 'a negation of the medium film, from which television distanced itself in order to culturally legitimate itself. The primary models of the TV drama were the stage and the radio play …What was denied was the character of television as a mass medium, through a rhetoric that emphasised "privacy", "proximity" and "intimacy"'.[11] The majority of the literary sources adapted, however, were not German, but predominantly American, French, and British. As Siegfried Zielinski has argued, this preference needs to be understood within the context of a 'strategy of cultural policy which was closely linked to the political endeavour of integrating the Federal Republic into the Western system'.[12]

By the mid-1950s, television executives, producers, and directors increasingly perceived TV drama as a stylistically and technologically restrictive format. Until 1958, the two major modes of production had been live transmission, an ephemeral practice without archiving properties, and the use of film recording, the major disadvantages of which were that it was expensive, and that it could not be used for simultaneous transmission.[13] The introduction of the Ampex videorecording system, first tested in Germany in 1958 and from 1959 regularly used for news programmes, affected the attitude of television producers towards the use of live transmissions for dramatic formats. Hans Gottschalk, a programme editor for the SDR, argued that 'the essence of television is, as it is in the cinema, the succession of images, their movement. Therefore, the basic principles of an "art of television" cannot be different from the art of film'.[14]

By the end of the 1950s, TV drama became gradually superseded by the *Fernsehfilm* (TV film), indicating a shift towards emulating cinematic storytelling principles. Like TV drama, the TV film was still embedded in the context of high cultural aspirations and while its style became more cine-matic, it still largely drew on 'prestigious' sources, such as stage plays and novels. *Fernsehspiel* and *Fernsehfilm* apart, however, German television also ventured into more populist formats. Following the first family soap opera ('Die Schölermanns'), launched in 1955,[15] the crime series 'Stahlnetz' (Steel Net) began transmission in 1957 with semi-documentary stories about the West German police. The series was undoubtedly inspired by the similarly constructed and titled U.S. series 'Dragnet', which was first transmitted on radio in 1949, and ran on American television from 1951 to 1959.

The 1959 production 'Soweit die Füsse tragen' (As Far As Feet Carry), advertised as a *Fernsehroman* (TV novel) exemplified how far television had moved away from the stage-bound early TV drama and its aesthetic ambi-tions. The epic, six-part, serial told the story of a German prisoner of war who escapes through the snow storms of Siberia, with sinister Soviet sol-diers in pursuit, before he finally returns to his home in Bavaria. Shot on film partly on location in Lapland and Switzerland, and partly at Geisel-gasteig's Bavaria studios, the serial was based on the best-selling memoirs of a real-life escapee and drew on the style and narratives of contemporary war films in German cinema, such as *08/15* (1954) or *Hunde, wollt ihr ewig leben?* (1958, Dogs, Do You Want To Live Forever?). One contemporary critic argued, 'television is capable of retelling novels in more detail and more faithfully than the film industry. It can take its time: one year in planning, and ten weeks of transmission (with two-week gaps in between). Above all, a television production is cheaper than a commercial film produced for the cinema'.[16] With today scarcely fathomable audience figures of 90 per cent of all registered television viewers, 'Soweit die Füsse tragen' became one of the first of the so-called *Strassenfeger*, implying that such television events liter-ally emptied the streets in the evenings. The serial was overwhelmingly mauled by the critics, though not so much for its hard-line anti-communism nor for its politically equally dubious rehabilitation of the 'ordinary' Ger-man soldier, as for its aesthetic populism. What is interesting about the con-temporary critical reception of the serial is the kind of cultural tradition in which it was placed, being labelled a 'Siberian Karl May story' and seen as following 'the serial fashion of the silent film era'.[17]

Such comments indicate that television anticipated the predominant production strategies of German film production in the 1960s, or, perhaps more accurately, that German cinema began to conform to the formats and conventions of its major competitor. Television became a source from which the film industry borrowed not only genre formats but also pro-duction personnel. Fritz Umgelter, the director of 'Soweit die Füsse tra-gen', would in the 1960s direct several of Constantin's Jerry Cotton films, an attempt by the film industry to produce a German, cinematic equiva-lent to American TV crime series such as 'The Untouchables'. The influ-ences between television and film, however, were decidedly reciprocal. Rialto's Edgar Wallace series was at least in part an attempt to emulate the

success of previous German TV crime series, such as 'Stahlnetz'. Rialto
employed actors who came directly from television and were certainly
cheaper than established film stars. It is very likely that the Wallace films
also speculated on their recognition value from formats such as
'Stahlnetz'. A number of early Wallace entries were directed by Jürgen
Roland, a former crime reporter who had been a driving artistic force
behind 'Stahlnetz'. Whereas 'Stahlnetz', however, had focused on straightforward domestic police work, the Wallace films added an 'exotic' English
dimension, and melodramatic plots. In turn, television responded in the
early 1960s with its adaptations of a number of novels by another British
crime author, Francis Durbridge. Durbridge can be regarded as one of the
first postwar European crime novelists whose popularity and book sales
were significantly enhanced by television versions of his work. In Britain,
several of Durbridge's novels were adapted for television in the 1950s and
1960s. In the first West German Durbridge thriller, the serial 'Das Halstuch' (1962, The Scarf), a whodunit set among British high society, the
television audience was invited to participate, over several instalments, in
guessing the murderer. The serial became a phenomenal success.[18] The
surprise casting in 'Das Halstuch' of Dieter Borsche, a saintly screen icon
of 1950s cinema, as a killer had a drastic impact on the actor's subsequent
screen career, as the Wallace series employed him from then onwards as a
deranged villain.

West German cinema's emphasis in the 1960s on wide-screen technology, colour, and spectacular outdoor and foreign locations has to be seen
as an attempt to differentiate itself from the relatively studio-bound and
black and white images of television. Up to the late 1960s, West German
television could not compete with the production values and locations of,
for example, the Karl May westerns. It was also too strongly regulated by
a family-based moral consensus to follow the film industry into the
domain of the sex film. Instead, television ventured into popular genres
that the West German film industry largely ignored during the 1960s and
which fitted more closely into its studio-based mode of production.
Among the most successful of these ventures was the science-fiction series
'Raumpatrouille' (1966, Space Patrol), featuring the futuristic adventures
of the spaceship 'Orion', whose multinational crew somehow resembled
the similarly diverse cast of the contemporary U.S. series 'Star Trek'.

As far as the transmission of feature films previously released in the
cinema is concerned, West German television's strategy was initially fairly
erratic. In the early 1950s, cinema films featured only marginally in programme schedules, and largely functioned as fill-ins. In fact, few of these
films were explicitly promoted as attractions, and they were often not even
advertised under their title but under the general category of 'main feature'. In the majority, these feature films were either older German productions, or foreign films, such as Robert Flaherty's *Nanook of the North*
(1922), which was introduced as a *Kulturfilm* (cultural film), terminology

that recalls Ufa's educational documentaries. This uneven output was due not only to early broadcasting's emphasis on live formats, but also to the fact that broadcasters had a limited choice of films at their disposal.

Owing to the complex financing system of the West German film industry in the 1950s, which I outlined earlier, the revenues of distributors were directly linked to cinema audience figures. Because of this, distributors were not only reluctant to supply TV stations, but they effectively enforced a television embargo for current or recent West German films which could still be re-released in the cinema. It was, above all, film distributors and exhibitors who throughout the 1950s and 1960s polemicised against what was dismissed as a *Pantoffelkino* ('slippers cinema'). Only in 1965, at a time when the balance of power had already irreversibly shifted towards television, did the film industry finally negotiate with ARD and ZDF a *Grundsatzvertrag* ('Declaration of Principle') that gave TV stations access to more recent West German productions.[19] This package consisted of popular productions from 1960 to 1964, but excluded, for example, the Karl May and Edgar Wallace films which were still being shown in cinemas.

The isolation of West German television from feature-film supplies had been gradually eroded since the mid-1950s. UFI's back catalogue of pre-1945 productions, which had already been given a new, and successful, theatrical lease of life in cinemas in the postwar years, were transmitted by the ARD from 1954 onwards, capitalising on the continuing popularity of stars such as Hans Albers, Hans Moser, Heinz Rühmann, and Willi Forst. Towards the end of the 1950s, the feature film became a significant element of programming and was moved to prominent positions in the weekend schedules. Given the lack of supply of more contemporary indigenous productions, however, individual stations increasingly began to rely on foreign imports.

Television executives could not necessarily expect a widespread or immediate audience acceptance of foreign films. As argued previously, indigenous productions certainly dominated film exhibition throughout the 1950s. Television's strategy was therefore to create a demand for foreign films and to educate and train its audience in 'learning' and accepting their conventions. Television programmers pursued a dual strategy in promoting non-German films. On the one hand, foreign art films – for example Fellini's *Le notte di Cabiria* (1957, transmitted in a dubbed version in West Germany in 1961) – were aimed at an already established culturally educated audience of cinephiles. Throughout the 1960s, when West German exhibitors focused primarily on popular genres, the majority of European art films, including East European ones, had their première on television. Klaus Brüne, who was in charge of the ZDF's feature-film programme in the 1960s, argued that 'Karl May and James Bond belong to the cinema audience. For a broadcasting station, it is the experimental film that is successful'.[20]

While the notion of the 'experimental film' encompassed mainly European art cinema, West German television also promoted Hollywood films. From 1960 on, television stations had managed to circumvent the indigenous distribution channels and bought feature films directly from foreign suppliers or secured long-running licences, thus allowing for repeat transmissions. Even in the case of Hollywood films, stations nevertheless presented their foreign imports in a framework of cultural education. Through genre-specific, theme-oriented, or director-focused retrospectives, it instructed its viewers in film history and repositioned the perception of Hollywood in general and previously ignored figures such as John Ford or Howard Hawks in particular. Thus, the German television première in 1968 of Howard Hawks' *Red River* (1948) was accompanied by the following, slightly paternalistic, introduction:

> The idea is to confront an audience that normally would not switch on their set to watch a western on a Saturday night, with an exceptional example of this art form and to awaken an interest in this genre. Western and gangster films are not a necessary evil of programming but an integral element of our overall remit which is exercised with careful selection and appropriate placement.[21]

Television's initially enforced reliance on foreign feature films eventually became a consistent strategy. Thus, television assumed the role of both a repertory and an art cinema, and as an educational outlet disseminating film-historical knowledge.[22] This strategy was part of the increasing internationalisation that characterised TV stations' approach towards other programme formats. Eager to shed its image of a provincial, second-class medium, German television emphasised its international standing both through imports and through giving its shows and variety programmes a 'cosmopolitan' air. This new 'cosmopolitanism' manifested itself in an increasing number of non-German show hosts and in trans-European co-productions, such as sports events, the Eurovision Song Contest, and pan-European game shows such as 'Jeux Sans Frontières' (German title: 'Spiel ohne Grenzen').[23] The first collaboration between European television networks had been a BBC transmission from Calais in 1950. Following the 1953 British coronation, which was simultaneously transmitted in Britain, France, Germany, and the Netherlands, European co-productions became more frequent, and led to the rather loose 'Eurovision' grouping of national networks in 1954. As Siegfried Zielinski has noted, 'the majority of these programmes consisted of sports events. Anything more adventurous would have shattered the political-ideological consensus of the different European competitors'.[24]

One of the first successful American TV-series imports on German television had been 'The Adventures of Rin Tin Tin' in 1956, scheduled in the afternoon and clearly directed at a children's audience. Later imports such as 'Circus Boy' ('Corky und der Zirkus'), 'Fury', 'My Three Sons' ('Vater unser bestes Stück'), 'Flipper', and 'Lassie', fulfilled similar programming functions. By the early 1960s, the American imports seemed to 'grow up' with their original audience, and were moved to more prominent transmission slots in the late afternoon and evening. Thus, German television began to import American crime series, such as '77 Sunset Strip', 'The Untouchables', and 'Sea Hunt', and western series, such as 'Laramie', 'High Chaparral', and 'Bonanza', whose main audience constituency was teenagers. This generational trajectory continues throughout the rest of the decade with either American or British series, such as 'The Saint', 'The Avengers', and 'The Persuaders', the latter a far greater success in continental Europe, including West Germany, than in Britain and the United States. By this time, foreign TV series had moved to the most attractive time-slots on West German television.

While in terms of film stars, teenagers oriented themselves throughout most of the 1960s towards indigenous models, a very different picture emerges of teenagers' preferences with regard to television, evident in the way the teen publication *Bravo* featured television stars. Very early on in the 1960s, German television performers, such as the comedian Willy Millowitsch and the quiz-show host Hans-Joachim Kulenkampff, were being replaced in terms of popularity by foreign stars. Among these were Edd Byrnes ('77 Sunset Strip'), Roger Moore ('The Saint'), Patrick Macnee and Diana Rigg ('The Avengers'), Mike Landon ('Bonanza'), and David McCallum ('The Man from U.N.C.L.E.'). The most popular star was Robert Fuller of the western show 'Laramie', which was transmitted in Germany from 1959 to 1965 (and then in repeats until 1970) under the title 'Am Fuss der blauen Berge' (In the Foothills of the Blue Mountains). Fuller was voted by *Bravo* readers three years in succession (between 1964 and 1967) as the best-loved TV star.[25]

The popularity of American and British TV formats and stars among teenagers was in all likelihood triggered by their 'transgressive' appeal, particularly within a domestic context. Discussing American western TV formats of the 1950s and 1960s, Martin McLoone has argued that series such as 'Laramie', 'Wagon Train', 'Bonanza', and 'Gunsmoke' (German title: 'Rauchende Colts') domesticated the Hollywood western through its family-oriented storylines: 'Many of the series of the 1950s and 1960s were generic replays of *Rebel Without A Cause* (1955), and worked around the opposition of a 'contemporary' male hero, embodying elements of youth sub-cultural attitudes, and an older, wiser counsellor who represented the mythic value systems of the genre'.[26] Unlike in the United States, however, where series such as 'Bonanza' or 'Gunsmoke' generated cross-generational appeal, in 1960s Germany, American TV westerns are more likely to have caused, at least initially, generational differences. What becomes evident in the 1960s issues of *Bravo* is that German teenagers preferred the indigenous Karl May films in the cinema to Hollywood westerns. Among television genres, however, American western shows were the most popular. The crucial distinction here may have been the different viewing environments and the different restrictions imposed on teenagers with regard both to these genres and to their respective viewing spaces. The Karl May films, as I shall elaborate in a later chapter, were able to diffuse generational tensions through their reliance on the iconic, and 'timeless', status of their literary source, with which parents could still identify even when the films themselves might have significantly differed from their childhood memories. The Karl May films were thus unthreatening to the older generation, and yet at the same time exciting for its younger audiences. The cinema experience of the May films furthermore provided teenagers with a welcome escape from the family home. The generational dynamic with regard to American TV shows, however, was different.

Since the 1950s, there had been public debates in Germany on the 'corrupting' and potentially dangerous influence of television, particularly on children and adolescents. The psychological and social effects of popular genres such as westerns and crime thrillers were widely discussed, both in pedagogical journals and in the tabloid press. Moreover, this critical discourse was frequently underlined by a deep-rooted suspicion, particularly of American popular genres. Thus, fears of 'foreign cultural infiltration' became linked to the discourse of social disintegration and youth corruption. Complaining about the inherent 'sadism' (but implicitly, equally about the representation of women) of the British show 'The Avengers', the listings magazine *Hör Zu* noted in 1968 that 'in the 13 episodes shown in this country so far, there were 47 corpses, some of them dying in the most outrageous ways … And the charming Emma Peel was also actually a rather violent girl; she engaged in 39 brawls, and in three of them she fought other women'.[27]

One argument, still fairly familiar today, was to link increased crime figures among adolescents with violent images on television and to trace copycat crimes to particular television formats. In an article entitled 'Jugendliche und Krimis' (Adolescents and Crime Thrillers), author Günther Quabus noted that 'even classical and well-made crime thrillers often do not allow adolescents to distinguish between right and wrong, good and evil, and between a villain and the forces of law and order, particularly when scenes follow in rapid succession.[28] Similar concerns were raised against the western. In the early 1960s, a number of West German teachers had publicly burnt American western novels and toys, protesting against the genre's allegedly brutalising tendencies.[29]

Importantly, distinctions were being made with respect to differences in viewing environments and exhibition contexts. Thus, what was perceived as dangerous in television, could be more leniently viewed in the context of the cinematic experience, presumably on account of cinema's capability to enforce stricter controls of access:

Television may transmit a film such as André Cayatte's *Nous sommes tous les assassins*, but hardly a film such as *Anatomy of a Murder*, which includes an explicit description of a rape. Jack the Ripper and prostitute killers, and any-thing that comes under the rubric 'crime and sex' may be appropriate for the cinema. Massive aggression, alongside the idolisation of 'super-gangsters' and appealing villains, should also remain the prerogative of the cinema.[30]

Undoubtedly such discourses filtered down to parental decisions on what television formats children and adolescents were allowed to watch at home. However, even when parents were not influenced by the discourses outlined above, middle-class households in particular were still likely to belong to the audience segment the introduction to *Red River* characterised as those 'who would not normally watch a western'. *Bravo* frequently gave its readers advice on how to persuade parents to allow them access to series such as 'Laramie'. Teen favourite Robert Fuller addressed German parents directly in an open letter published in *Bravo*, in which he assured them that he stood for good moral values.[31] Overall, then, the domestic environment became the space where the respective values of 'national' or indigenous culture versus American mass entertainment were contested along generational lines.

By the end of the 1960s, foreign films and TV series had become firmly established in the schedules of ARD and ZDF. For most of the decade, the balance between Hollywood imports and other foreign films was rela-tively even – American productions constituted 25 per cent at the most. This balance would only begin to shift more in Hollywood's favour from the late 1960s onwards.[32] The most prestigious Saturday evening slot, however, had become reserved for feature films with action and suspense, which increasingly meant a Hollywood film. In this respect, one can see how television's strategy of screening 'classic' American films and youth-oriented TV series complemented each other. While the latter formats had gradually cultivated a new audience up to the early 1970s, when this audi-ence became almost exclusively oriented towards these formats, the screenings of 'classic' Hollywood films such as *Red River* had worked towards a cultural legitimisation of popular American genres, particularly among those segments of the audience that had previously preferred indigenous entertainment.

The internationalisation of television programmes had a fundamental impact, not only in view of the changes in audience preferences it initiated, but also on the overall organisation of the German film industry. While television may have contributed to, but was certainly not exclusively responsible for, the crisis in German cinema, it did transform the circula-tion and distribution of feature films. By 1972, feature films constituted roughly a quarter of the output by West German television channels.[33] As a consequence, German distributors in particular, who throughout the decade had linked their fortunes to the declining indigenous exhibition sector, had to rethink their relationship to television. The career trajectory of Leo Kirch is characteristic of this changed distribution context.

Kirch, initially an outsider within the German distribution sector, had invested since the mid-1950s in the acquisition of television rights of Hollywood and other foreign films.[34] His sale of the Franco-Italian co-production *Amici per la pelle* (1955, German title: *Freunde fürs Leben*) to ARD in 1958 created the precedent of the first foreign film being screened on West German television before it had been released in the cinema.[35] By the mid-1960s Kirch's company Sirius had secured a vast number of titles, which it sold to television stations in profitable packages (including both attractive cinema blockbusters and cheaply acquired B films). In sharp contrast to the fate of most traditional distributors, Kirch's fortunes grew throughout the 1960s and 1970s, by which time most of German television's foreign imports were leased from him. In the 1980s and 1990s, Kirch's empire expanded into commercial TV stations and pay-TV channels, which still capitalised on his impressive film library, until the spectacular collapse of Kirch's empire in 2002. Among the many films for which Kirch held the German television rights, *Casablanca* (1942), originally bought by him in 1959 for 3000 DM, became a consistent source of income. In 1975, a restored and newly dubbed version had its première on ARD. It was the first time German audiences were able to see *Casablanca* in a version that was faithful to its original. According to Irmela Schneider, the 1975 transmission was watched by half of all German television viewers.[36] This indicates how far, by that time, German audiences had accepted Hollywood's generic conventions. Since 1975, *Casablanca* has, as in other countries, attained the status of a 'cult film' in Germany and has been repeated more than a dozen times on West German television.

In conclusion, then, one has to characterise the relationship between West German cinema and television in the 1960s as an ambivalent one. Unlike in America, where, according to Martin McLoone, 'the institutions of television and cinema had, by the mid-1950s, arrived at a perfectly equitable level of co-existence',[37] in West Germany, this coexistence was marked by intense competition during the same period. The West German film industry, lacking substantial production facilities and distribution networks comparable to those of Hollywood's major studios, remained financially dependent on cinema exhibition and could therefore not easily shift from one medium to another. This structural weakness accelerated the reliance of television stations on foreign imports.

In terms of stylistic, technological, and aesthetic principles, however, it was the model of cinema that began to determine the formats and structural organisation of television and which increasingly sidelined the medium's original ethos of 'immediacy'. While a number of differences in technological capabilities, and spectatorial address remained, the narratives of film and television were marked by a number of intertextual correspondences. In this respect, an understanding of the development of popular genres in both television and film remains insufficient if it does not take into account their interaction.

The problem of the German film industry in the 1960s thus rested not, as has often been argued, on a lack of attractive productions, but more on the industry's reliance on one exclusive exhibition context. One could argue that television, rather than destroying the indigenous film culture, actually cultivated a new, more knowledgeable, and certainly more internationally minded audience for feature films. German broadcasters' programming of foreign films and TV series created divergent expectations and preferences. Television certainly aided an increased acceptance of American generic conventions, stars, and narratives, which would lead, in the following decades, to an increased Hollywood dominance, both in television and in the cinema, but also to the emergence of an alternative, cine-literate, cosmopolitan, and film-historically informed audience.

Notes

1. Charles Barr, 'They Think It's All Over. The Dramatic Legacy of Live Television', in *Big Picture, Small Screen. The Relationship between Film and Television*, ed. John Hill and Martin McLoone, Luton 1996, pp. 50–51.
2. Karl Prümm, 'Film und Fernsehen. Ambivalenz und Identität', in *Geschichte des deutschen Films*, ed. Wolfgang Jacobsen, Anton Kaes, and Hans-Helmut Prinzler, Stuttgart and Weimar 1993, p. 502.
3. Knut Hickethier, 'Vom Ende des Kinos und vom Anfang des Fernsehens', in *Zwischen Gestern und Morgen. Westdeutscher Nachkriegsfilm, 1946–1962*, ed. Jürgen Berger, Hans-Peter Reichmann, and Rudolf Worschech, Frankfurt 1989, p. 283.
4. Prümm, in Jacobsen et al., *Geschichte des deutschen Films*, p. 502.
5. Hickethier, in Berger et al., *Zwischen Gestern und Morgen*, p. 284.
6. Peter J. Humphreys, *Media and Media Policy in Germany. The Press and Broadcasting since 1945*, Oxford and Providence, Second Edition 1994, p. 148.
7. Hickethier, in Berger et al., *Zwischen Gestern und Morgen*, p. 300.
8. Claudia Dillmann-Kühn, *Artur Brauner und die CCC. Filmgeschäft, Produktionsalltag, Studiogeschichte 1946–1990*, Frankfurt 1990, p. 151.
9. Klaus Kreimeier, *Die UFA Story*, Munich 1992, pp. 451–452.
10. Dillmann-Kühn, *Artur Brauner und die CCC*, p. 158.
11. Prümm, in Jacobsen et al., *Geschichte des deutschen Films*, p. 506.
12. Siegfried Zielinski, 'Aspekte des Fernsehens in den fünfziger Jahren', in *Bikini. Die fünfziger Jahre. Kalter Krieg und Capri Sonne*, ed. Eckhard Siepmann and Irene Lusk, Reinbek 1983, p. 359.
13. Ibid., p. 353.
14. Quoted in Hickethier, in Berger et al., *Zwischen Gestern und Morgen*, p. 298.
15. *Am Fuss der blauen Berge. Die Flimmerkiste in den sechziger Jahren*, ed. Bernd Müllender and Achim Nollenheidt, Essen 1994, p. 113.
16. Werner Skrentny, 'Soweit die Füsse tragen. Vergangenheitsbewältigung im deutschen Wohnzimmer', in Müllender and Nollenheidt, *Am Fuss der blauen Berge*, p.100.
17. Ibid., pp. 99–100.
18. Matthias Bröckers, 'Vom Sprechen über das Schreiben zum Schweigen. Wolfgang Neuss, Halstuchverräter und Kabarettist', in Müllender and Nollenheidt, *Am Fuss der blauen Berge*, p. 90.
19. Knut Hickethier, 'Die Zugewinngemeinschaft', in *Abschied von Gestern. Bundesdeutscher Film der sechziger und siebziger Jahre*, ed. Hans-Peter Reimann and Rudolf Worschech, Frankfurt 1991, p. 190.

20. Quoted in Irmela Schneider, 'Grosse Bilder -Kleiner Schirm', in Müllender and Nollenheidt *Am Fuss der blauen Berge*, p. 142.
21. Ibid.
22. Cf. Irmela Schneider, 'Ein Weg zur Alltäglichkeit. Spielfilme im Fernsehen', in *Das Fernsehen und die Künste*, ed. Helmut Schanze and Bernhard Zimmermann, Munich 1994, pp. 227–301.
23. The British version of this show format, 'It's a Knock-Out', was less 'European' than its French and German counterparts. Instead of competing teams from different nations, it featured competitors from different British cities.
24. Zielinski, in Siepmann and Lusk, *Bikini*, p. 350.
25. Thommi Herrwerth, *Partys, Pop, und Petting. Die Sixties im Spiegel der Bravo*, Marburg 1997, p. 109.
26. Martin McLoone, 'Boxed In? The Aesthetics of Film and Television', in Hill and Loone, *Big Picture, Small Screen*, p. 90.
27. Bernd Müllender, 'Das rabiate Mädchen Emma', in Müllender and Nollenheidt, *Am Fuss der blauen Berge*, pp. 181–182.
28. Erich Wasem, 'Der Erzieher und der Wildwestfilm', *Jugend-Film-Fernsehen*, vol. 6, no. 1, 1962, p. 28.
29. Cf. Erich Wasem, 'Kriminalspiele und Kriminalfilme im Fernsehen', *Jugend-Film-Fernsehen*, vol. 8, no.1, 1964, pp. 10–11.
30. Ibid.
31. Herrwerth, *Partys, Pop, und Petting*, p. 32.
32. Knut Hickethier, *Geschichte des deutschen Fernsehens*, Stuttgart and Weimar 1998, p. 254.
33. Hickethier, *Geschichte des deutschen Fernsehens*, p. 221.
34. Thomas Clark, *Der Filmpate. Der Fall des Leo Kirch*, Munich 2002.
35. Hickethier, *Geschichte des deutschen Fernsehens*, p.148.
36. Schneider, in Müllender and Nollenheidt, *Am Fuss der blauen Berge*, p. 143.
37. McLoone, in Hill and Loone, *Big Picture, Small Screen*, p. 85.

PART II
Case-Studies

Chapter 6

ARTUR BRAUNER'S CCC: REMIGRATION, POPULAR GENRES, AND INTERNATIONAL ASPIRATIONS

An analysis of the popular genres of the 1960s requires not only an understanding of contemporary modes of production and distribution but also an acknowledgement of how these genres draw on and reformulate established cultural traditions. My case-studies of specific film companies, genres, and biographical trajectories in the following chapters are meant to illustrate how specifically national cultural expectations and a more transnational imagination could interact and how such 'international' narrative formulae were received in different markets. What becomes apparent in the following chapters is that the West German popular cinema of the 1950s and 1960s was coordinated by a network of cosmopolitan filmmakers and producers, frequently former exiles, a network that spanned across Europe, and also included transatlantic connections. My case-studies also interlink with other developments in consumer culture. During the 1960s West Germany, like many other Western societies, experienced the contradictory influences of a proliferating youth culture (often patterned after American role models) and, on a more general level, shifting leisure habits, which included greater mobility and increased spare time. These general shifts in social behaviour significantly informed the stylistic and promotional patterns and the reception of popular film genres.

One of the major players among producers in the postwar West German film industry was Artur Brauner's CCC (Central Cinema Company). Unlike other companies from this period where business strategies have to be deduced primarily from second-hand sources and anecdotal evidence, the Artur Brauner Archive at the Deutsches Filmmuseum in Frankfurt, provides a unique opportunity to study in detail the aspirations and motivations of an internationally minded West German film company in the 1960s. Brauner donated his business archive in 1989 to the Frankfurt-based institution, encompassing about 3,500 folders. These include personal correspondence, budget plans, invoices, press releases, and in-house memoranda. Under the supervision of Claudia Dillmann, the archive has been sorted and catalogued and has become an indispensable source of research for anyone interested in the history of postwar German cinema and its international connections. Moreover, Dillmann's book-length study of Brauner remains one of the few serious analyses of postwar German film producers.[1]

As a figurehead of the West German commercial film industry, Artur 'Atze' Brauner has often featured in histories of New German Cinema as the quintessential antagonist, exemplifying everything that was wrong with and derivative about German film culture of the 1950s and 1960s. There is a distinctive irony in the fact that Brauner, the establishment figure, is simultaneously very much a cultural outsider, and indeed very vocally so. Brauner was born in 1918 in the Polish town of Lodz into an orthodox, upper-middle-class Jewish family. Uprooted by the German invasion of Poland, Brauner's family fled, the exact details of which Brauner has never discussed in public, and managed to survive the Holocaust. Close to the Zionist movement since before the war, most of the family relocated to what was then Palestine, with the exception of Artur, who moved to Berlin. In a cultural context marked by the legacy of the Nazi period, Brauner defiantly remained an outsider, combining entrepreneurial shrewdness and flamboyant self-promotion with an acute sense of his Polish roots and his Jewish identity. As an active member of national and international Jewish organisations, he frequently intervened in public debates about Jewish issues, the Holocaust, and the state of Israel, and has continued to do so to the present day. Brauner's status simultaneously as the 'Jewish conscience' within the West German film industry and as an unashamedly capitalist entrepreneur, however, has made him a disquieting and controversial figure in German cultural life, irritating to both sides of the political spectrum.

Artur Brauner's Central Cinema Company (CCC-Film GmbH) was the first film company to be issued with a licence by the French authorities in the postwar years. Founded in 1946, the company initially ventured into producing films in West Berlin's remaining studios in Tempelhof, before acquiring, in 1949, studio facilities in the Berlin suburb of Spandau. These, by a macabre irony given Brauner's personal background, had formerly housed a poison-gas factory. Already in the first postwar years, CCC's output was characterised by stylistic and ideological eclecticism. Next to comedies such as *Herzkönig* (1947, King of Hearts) and melodramas such as *Mädchen hinter Gittern* (1949, Girls Behind Bars), Brauner also produced more ambitious projects. *Morituri* (1947/8), for example, which Brauner not only produced, but for which he also co-wrote the screenplay, was a drama about a group of concentration-camp inmates (and, indeed, the first German film after the war to visually represent a concentration camp). The film, broadly belonging to the postwar 'rubble cycle' and directed by Eugen York (who started his career in the Nazi film industry), was rejected by the critics for its over-conciliatory political agenda and the way in which the film addressed the issue of the Holocaust. As Robert Shandley has argued, the film 'takes pains to show' that its central group of characters 'do not necessarily belong to the European Jewish population ... but to a multi-ethnic group of prisoners whose reasons for internment remain undefined. In fact, the very point of the film is that a universalist mix of *morituri*, those condemned to death, has become an ethnic category unto itself'.[2] Meanwhile, the film's intended audience was taken aback by the fact that the film dealt at all with German aggression and the victimisation of a kaleidoscope of foreign nationals by Nazis. In fact, press reports told of numerous cinema-goers demanding their money back for being confronted with Nazi victims in an evening's entertainment.[3]

Brauner would create similar commotions several decades later with his production of *Hitlerjunge Salomon / Europa, Europa* (1990), the true story of a young Jew passing as a Hitler Youth during the Second World War. On its first release only moderately successful at the German box office, the film achieved notoriety after German officials rejected it as a German Academy Award nomination in the category for best foreign film, on the grounds that the film had been directed by a Pole, Agnieszka Holland. Several German critics, on the other hand, had criticised the film for its alleged political naïvety and artistic mediocrity. Brauner countered with an international and highly effective publicity campaign, accusing the German officials' stance of being anti-Semitic. As a result of the ensuing international controversy, the film became one of the biggest export hits of the German film industry of its year.

Already in the 1950s, Brauner had pursued commercially risky ventures that were likely to cause political controversies, but which also carried the potential of enormous publicity beyond German borders. *Osmy dzien tygodnia/Der achte Wochentag* (1957, The Eighth Day of the Week), one of Brauner's 'political' projects, was a grim portrait of life in postwar Poland, directed by Polish director Aleksander Ford and co-produced by CCC, and banned by the Communist authorities in Poland. Another project was the semi-documentary drama *Der 20. Juli* (1955, The 20th of July), which was based on the failed assassination attempt on Hitler in 1944. As the film's release coincided with West Germany's postwar rearmament, it performed an ambivalent ideological function. On the one hand, the project continued Brauner's commitment with at least some of his films in the 1950s towards remembering the frequently repressed Nazi past. In the case of *Der 20. Juli* specifically, it was Brauner's and the film director's (Falk Harnack) aim to redress a still widely held perception of the conspirators of 1944 as traitors against the 'fatherland'. On the other hand, the film's portrait of a heroic élite aristocratic officer class in the figure of the failed assassin Count Stauffenberg (Wolfgang Preiss) not only served as a retrospective exculpation of the *Wehrmacht* for the German atrocities during the Second World War, but also provided legitimation and a model lineage for the newly formed *Bundeswehr*, which in reality, of course, hardly recruited its initial élite from former Resistance fighters but precisely from the remnants of an army that had helped to sustain Hitler and Goebbels' total war. What followed in the wake of films such as *Der 20. Juli* and *Canaris* (1954, a biopic of the legendary leader of the German intelligence service, and another of the conspirators of July 1944) was a whole cycle of Second World War films (such as Frank Wisbar's Stalingrad epic *Hunde, wollt ihr ewig leben*, 1958), which, in a similar spirit of exculpation and rehabilitation but also as a means of addressing a new generation of army conscripts, dealt with the tribulations of 'ordinary' German soldiers.

In the main, however, CCC specialised in popular genres such as the *Heimatfilm*, melodramas, and musical comedies. Brauner always retained something of a childhood passion for the popular genres of Weimar cinema, and most of CCC's output in the 1950s and into the 1960s can be seen as a consistent attempt to continue where the popular German film culture of the 1920s and early 1930s had been interrupted. What is striking about Brauner's output in the 1950s is the number of remakes of Weimar films, among them classics such as *Die Privatsekretärin* (1931, The Private Secretary, remade 1953), and *Mädchen in Uniform* (1931, Girls in Uniform, remade 1958).

Brauner and Remigrants

Motivated partly by his apparent desire to reinvent the culture of Weimar cinema and partly by his own biographical background, Brauner became the driving force in persuading Hollywood exiles to return to Germany. The list of the remigrant directors working for Brauner in the 1950s and 1960s is indeed impressive. This group included Fritz Lang, Robert Siodmak, William Dieterle, and Wilhelm Thiele. Also working in CCC studios in the 1950s and early 1960s were the émigrés Steve Sekely, Ernst Neubach, Leonhard Steckel, and Max Nosseck. Gottfried Reinhardt and Gerd Oswald who had started their careers in America, were, respectively, the sons of exiled directors Max Reinhardt and Richard Oswald. Ladislao Vajda, who had started his career in German and Hungarian films of the 1930s as a screenwriter and editor and later became a director in Spain (and occasionally Britain), was the son of Weimar scriptwriter Ladislaus (László) Vajda, a close collaborator of G.W. Pabst in the 1920s and early 1930s. Many in this group had crossed each other's paths before, either at Ufa during the Weimar years or later in exile. Neubach had previously collaborated with both Siodmak and Richard Oswald; Siodmak had also worked with Nosseck; Thiele and Vajda Senior had been former collaborators, as were Sekely and Vajda Jr., while Gottfried Reinhardt had adapted one of Vajda Jr's screenplays in Hollywood (*The Story of Three Loves* 1953). Meanwhile, Steckel and Dieterle had started their career as actors under Lang and Max Reinhardt. Given these complex intertwined histories and such a resultant cluster of former exiles or descendants of Weimar luminaries working for CCC in the 1950s and 1960s, it is hard to accept Jan-Christopher Horak's claim that 'a remigration of German film artists practically did not happen',[4] and his argument that within the context of popular postwar West German cinema 'there was apparently no place for those who had left Germany'.[5] In fact, it was precisely remigrants such as the above, in addition to returning scriptwriters (see, for example, the role of Egon Eis in the creation of the Edgar Wallace series, as discussed in chapter 7), composers, and actors, who helped to reshape the popular genres of the 1950s and 1960s.

Horak's assessment, however, is true in so far as critical evaluations of remigratory trajectories and Brauner's role in this process have been decidedly ambivalent. The West German productions of Lang, Siodmak et al. were often rejected as outmoded and anachronistic copies of Weimar genres, and yet at the same time the exiles were accused of having succumbed to Hollywood's populism. They were portrayed as the victims of an exploitative production system, epitomised in turn by Hollywood and by Brauner. For a younger generation of critics and film-makers who had cultivated themselves as a 'fatherless' generation, the exiled directors did not quite fit their stereotype concept of the enemy. Either they were dismissed as relics of the past whose continuing presence in West German cinema obstructed the rejuvenation and 'national' reorientation of West German film culture, or their return to a system that was seen as being a natural inheritor of the Nazi past was perceived as at best a disappointment or at worst a betrayal. From a conservative perspective, on the other hand, the remigrants' biographical background provided an uneasy reminder of the ethnic-cleansing policies of the Nazis. In other words, the remigrant film-makers, at least where they were identified as such, faced critical expectations and political sensibilities in West Germany which they could hardly live up to, especially if they had a highly public profile.

The former exiles working for Brauner adapted in different ways to the context of 1950s and 1960s West German cinema and its international dimensions. Wilhelm Thiele, who had directed one of the most successful German musical comedies of the early sound period, *Die Drei von der Tankstelle* (1930, The Three of the Filling Station), filmed for Brauner *Sabine und die 100 Männer* (1960, Sabine and the 100 Men). Starring teenage actress Sabine Sinjen and featuring a guest appearance by violinist Yehudi Menuhin, the film centred on a young girl's attempt to get her unemployed conductor father a new job. The film was a remake of the Hollywood musical comedy *100 Men and a Girl* (1938), which had been based on a film script by the German author Hanns Kräly and directed by fellow émigré Henry Koster (Hermann Kosterlitz).[6] Like other former exiles, Thiele thus returned full circle and back to his origins, after years of having worked as an expert for Hollywood adventure films, such as the *Tarzan* series. Thiele's only other postwar West German film, *Der letzte Fussgänger* (1960, The Last Pedestrian) was a vehicle for comedian Heinz Erhardt.

While a film such as *Sabine und die 100 Männer* does not give any indication in terms of style of the director's previous career in Hollywood, Gottfried Reinhardt's West German films betrayed much more of an 'American' influence. Reinhardt had worked as a scriptwriter and producer for M-G-M since the early 1940s. In the early 1950s, he had directed a number of women's melodramas, including *Invitation* (1952), starring Dorothy McGuire, the portmanteau film *Story of Three Loves* (1953, co-directed by Vincente Minnelli), and the Lana Turner vehicle *Betrayed* (1954). Initially reluctant to film in West Germany (he later commented, 'I wanted to return to Europe, not to Germany'[7]), Reinhardt was contracted by Brauner to film Gerhart Hauptmann's naturalist drama *Vor Sonnenuntergang* (1956, Before Sunset), the story of an ageing industrialist's affair with his young secretary. The fact that Reinhardt's father Max had been the most important and prestigious stage director in Germany prior to his enforced exile in 1933 certainly contributed to Brauner's invitation.

The film starred former Ufa idol Hans Albers, a choice Brauner was initially not happy with as he preferred a culturally more respectable actor for this role.[8] Literary adaptations in the West German cinema of the 1950s were on the whole characterised by stilted stage acting, ponderous narration, and a cinematically static *mise en scène*, functioning like picture-book illustrations to their source texts (perhaps the best example for this type of film is Alfred Weidenmann's 1959 Thomas Mann adaptation *Die Buddenbrooks*). Preserving the cultural prestige of the literary work was a major criterion of quality, particularly in the case of an author such as Gerhart Hauptmann (1862–1946), Nobel prize winner for literature and regarded by one of the major German literature encyclopaedias as 'the most important German author of the twentieth Century and the greatest playwright of the last 100 years'.[9] Reinhardt, however, transformed Hauptmann's play into a 1950s Hollywood melodrama. Albers, at the end of his career and cast against his usual swashbuckling screen persona, performed the leading role in an uncharacteristically non-theatrical style. The film further camouflaged the source's stage origins through surprisingly fluid cinematography, an emotionally charged musical score, and a contemporary setting. Reinhardt later argued, 'I have made *Vor Sonnenuntergang* just like an American film (I could not do it any different, because I have learnt my profession in America, and not in Germany). I have made a German film, with German actors, in a German setting, with German themes, in the German (but not Nazi) language, but technically, the film is American'.[10]

Vor Sonnenuntergang was a critical disaster in West Germany and was denied any official accolades and prizes, but it also became a box-office success. Reinhardt's subsequent films for CCC continued to blend German and Hollywood influences. *Abschied von den Wolken* (1959, Farewell to the Clouds) was an airborne disaster movie, following the international success of William Wellman's *The High and the Mighty* (1954), and prefiguring the *Airport* series of the late 1960s and 1970s. Again a box-office success, the film was dismissed by critics as 'an airborne pulp novel based on foreign film formulae'.[11] Drawing on Reinhardt's Hollywood connections, CCC managed to sell the film in America, where it was released as *Rebel Flight to Cuba*. *Menschen im Hotel/Grand Hôtel* (1959), Reinhardt's next assignment, was a Franco-West German remake of the Hollywood film *Grand Hotel* (1932), itself based on the Weimar-era best seller by Vicki Baum.

Reinhardt's last film for Brauner, *Liebling der Götter* (1960, Darling of the Gods), merits a closer look. The film tells the story of real-life Ufa star Renate Müller, who after a meteoric rise to fame in the early 1930s was increasingly sidelined by the film industry after the Nazis came to power.[12] Although Müller's death in 1937, at the age of 31, was officially declared to have been caused by a cerebral haemorrhage, it was widely rumoured that the actress, under pressure from the Nazis due to her affair with a Jewish man, had committed suicide while being sectioned in a private clinic. During the Second World War, even wilder speculations, very possibly tools in the propaganda war between the Allies and Germany, about an alleged affair of Müller with Hitler emerged, combined with the theory that Müller had been murdered.[13] It is easy to see why Müller's biography, mysterious, unresolved, and with its sensational mix of sex and politics, attracted Brauner, while the story's melodramatic potential may have appealed to Reinhardt. Georg Hurdalek's script adopted the suicide theory and invented the figure of Jewish diplomat Dr Simon (played by Peter van Eyck), based on the figure of Georg Deutsch, allegedly a real-life lover of Müller. *Liebling der Götter* promptly caused a legal commotion behind the scenes, as Müller's surviving relatives objected in court to the portrayal of the late actress, principally owing to the film's suggestion that Müller had committed suicide, and, seemingly an even greater *faux pas*, that Müller was portrayed as an alcoholic and is seen to be admitted in the end to a psychiatric sanatorium.[14] Possibly as a result of these objections, the ending of the film is extremely vague about the exact circumstances of Müller's death. The camera follows her running along a corridor, ostensibly trying to escape her confinement, but an abrupt cut leaves it open how she actually dies. In the following scene, Müller's lover, who has come back from his exile in London, is informed about her death, again without being given any details.

In terms of genre, *Liebling der Götter* is a curious and, at times, even jarring hybrid between a women's melodrama (in its motifs of female suffering and self-sacrifice) and a homage to late Weimar musical comedy, while its theme of Nazi oppression places it closer to Brauner's politically more ambitious projects such as *Morituri* and *Der 20. Juli* than to his remakes of Weimar light entertainment classics. Sabine Hake has argued that Brauner and Reinhardt 'used the behind-the-scenes recreation of the film world to reflect on their own precarious position in the German film industry after the war' and, given the biographical background not only of Brauner and Reinhardt but also of the leading actor van Eyck (a former émigré) this reading is certainly suggestive.[15] On the other hand, the film's casting, in the lead, of Ruth Leuwerik, one of the foremost stars of 1950s women's melodramas, was aimed at a predominantly female audience. This particular target audience, however, did not react too well to the film's downbeat narrative, which, unlike a more typical melodrama, offered its viewers very little in terms of redemption. Even audiences previously unfamiliar with Müller's fate would have known not to expect a happy ending after an introductory, and rather didactic, caption at the beginning of the film informed them that the narrative would 'portray the life and death of an artist in unfree times'. Claudia Dillmann suggests that 'the older cinemagoers could not bear to accept the fact that their former screen favourite had been pressured by the Gestapo. The younger ones were not interested'.[16] While this is a plausible interpretation of the film's only moderate success with West German audiences, it is equally likely that the film's ambivalent reception had to do with its narrative and performative incongruities.

These incongruities begin first and foremost with the highly disparate star images of Renate Müller and Ruth Leuwerik. At the height of her popularity in the early 1930s, Müller represented an energetic, 'girl-next-door' type with her athletic, androgynous appearance, and her greatest successes had been in comedies that centred on the ambiguities of Müller's characters in terms of class (e.g., in *Die Privatsekretärin*, 1931, and *Die englische Heirat*, 1934) and gender (*Viktor und Viktoria*, 1933). Leuwerik's star image, in contrast, was defined by the her poised stillness, by a mild, well-modulated voice, by an unambiguously feminine appearance, and by her graceful and aristocratic demeanour. Indeed, one of the star's epithets during the period was *die Dame* – the lady, and she had portrayed a fair share of aristocratic and royal figures (e.g. *Ludwig II*, 1955, and *Königin Luise/Queen Luise*, 1957). The discrepancies in performance style, star image, and generic register in *Liebling der Götter* are particularly evident in those scenes where Leuwerik is taking on Müller's old comedy and musical roles. There are two scenes where Leuwerik is required to perform a song-and-dance routine. The first is at the beginning of *Liebling der Götter*, where Müller and her partner attend the première of *Die Privatsekretärin* and where the film cuts to selected moments of the latter film, in particular the musical number 'Ich bin ja heut so glücklich' (I am so happy today), Müller's greatest hit. The scene follows the composition and choreography of the equivalent scene from the original film (where Müller and Felix Bressart charge frenetically through an office and engage in a burlesque battle with inanimate objects, from typewriters to filing cabinets) relatively closely. Compared with Müller's energy, however, Leuwerik's elegance, which lends itself more to the melodramatic than to the comedic register, seems out of sync with the exuberance and speed the song's lyrics and the choreography demand. Instead, the number comes across as a highly self-conscious and, at times, awkward generic parody, which accentuates Leuwerik's physical inhibitions. Even more incongruent is the film's second musical scene, the revue number 'Ich brauch zum Leben nur die Liebe' (I need only love for living), where Leuwerik is supported by a group of male dancers in top hats and tails, but where the sound of tap-dancing shoes does not match Leuwerik's dance routine. Moreover, while the song may have been an original from the 1930s, its orchestration and arrangement is distinctly from the late 1950s. However, while Leuwerik's performance does not match the far more kinetic and self-confident image the real Renate Müller projected in her films, it none the less fits the persona *Liebling der Götter* wants to get across in that the character's shyness and anxiety are understood to be expressions of sincerity and modesty.

The indeterminacy in generic register and in historical positioning that is so clearly evident in the musical numbers is symptomatic of the film as a whole. Thus, the film's opening credit sequence offers vistas of different parts of Berlin, interestingly many of them in the eastern part of town, which at the time of the film's release was not yet separated by the Wall but was nevertheless part of a different political regime. As the film is in black and white and as these vistas do not relate to the subsequent narrative in any way apart from stating where the film's story is primarily set,

Figure 6.1. Remaking Weimar Cinema: Ruth Leuwerik as Renate Müller in *Liebling der Götter* (1960, Darling of the Gods). Deutsches Filminstitut (DIF), Frankfurt-on-Main.

it is not clear whether these images consist of footage from the 1930s or from the 1950s. This may be precisely the intention of using this footage, in the sense that the problems associated with each period (the 'Third Reich' in the first case, the increasing political division of Germany in the second) cancel each other out in the historical indeterminacy of these images, leaving only the timelessness of archetypal Berlin locations.

The rest of the film continues in this vein of indeterminacy. For example, at no moment is there any attempt at authenticity in re-creating the 1930s in terms of the decade's fashion, hairstyles, architecture, or interior design. Even the more typical paraphernalia of the Nazi years, such as swastikas, etc., are used relatively sparingly, as, for example, in a scene where Müller encounters a group of SA men in a train station or when one of Müller's entourage (Robert Graf) is shown suddenly wearing a swastika badge. Mostly, at least as far as its *mise en scène* is concerned, *Liebling der Götter* is resolutely set in the late 1950s, exemplified by Leuwerik's exquisitely coiffed bouffant hairstyle (as opposed to the cropped *Bubikopf* frequently sported by Müller) and her Dior-influenced dresses. Another significant aspect of the *mise en scène* is a distinct emphasis on emptiness, which effectively underscores the film's themes of isolation and alienation. Thus, there are few extras in this film, its cast consisting of a small group of main protagonists. Consequently, spaces are characterised primarily by the absence of other people, as in Leuwerik's and van Eyck's favourite wine bar, in which they always appear to be the only customers, but also the absence of much else, as in Müller's spacious but at the same time spartanly furnished home. In terms of absence, it is moreover surprising that *Liebling der Götter* does not exploit its film-industry context in any detail. Müller's everyday studio work features sparsely and, apart from Müller herself, two brief dialogue references to Hans Albers and Lilian Harvey, and the shadowy presence of Joseph Goebbels (Willy Krause) as Müller's nemesis, there are no other real-life characters from the film industry in evidence, nor are there any explicit references, with the exception of *Die Privatsekretärin*, to any of Müller's other films. As for the film people who do appear, on the other hand, such as Renate's friends played by Willy Fritsch (who adds a certain authenticity to this role, as he was twice a screen partner of the real Renate Müller[17]) and Hannelore Schroth, it is unclear what functions in the film industry they have, as they are always shown in a social rather than professional capacity.

It is evident that *Liebling der Götter* is hardly a realist interpretation even of the uncertain and unreliable versions of Müller's biography that circulated in the postwar years, nor is there much mileage, irrespective of Brauner's and Reinhardt's intentions, in viewing the film as a serious representation of the 'Third Reich'. If anything, the film's evasive *mise en scène* may indicate just how repressed the Nazi years still were in West Germany in 1960. What the film does offer instead, and in this it uses a similar aesthetic and narrational strategy to the *Heimatfilme* of the 1950s and subsequently the Edgar Wallace films of the 1960s, is to follow a parallel time line that is neither in the past nor in the present, but in a virtual space in between. It is in this space, then, that the film can articulate its main generic (in this case melodramatic) and ideological concerns – female self-determination between work, romantic fulfilment, and matrimonial duty – which are phrased within the parameters of West German society's reconstitution of 'appropriate' gender roles. On the other hand, the bleakness with which Reinhardt represents not only his main protagonist's workplace but also her romantic life results in a disconcertingly gloomy portrait of the life choices available for women in the late 1950s, which may be one of the reasons why audiences, who expected a confirmation, not a negation, of their own life choices from popular cinema, were less than impressed with *Liebling der Götter*. In other words, the failure of *Liebling der Götter* may have had less to do, as Dillmann and other critics have suggested, with the film's depiction of fascism, than with its representation of gender.

In the early 1960s Reinhardt made two further films in West Germany. The German-American co-production *Town without Pity/Stadt ohne Mitleid* (1960), starring Kirk Douglas, was set during the American occupation period and centred on a trial in which three American GIs were accused of raping a German girl (Christine Kaufmann). This narrative, even bleaker than that of *Liebling der Götter*, which ends with the girl committing suicide after being rejected by her own community, was more or less ignored on its first release, but has since been regarded as Reinhardt's most ambitious West German production and as a devastating portrait of postwar West German society. Werner Sudendorf has argued that the film thematises 'in what is for the German cinema of the time an unusually factual way, the cowardly violence of voyeurism, the loss of trust between the generations, and the end of the family idyll'.[18]

Reinhardt directed another women's melodrama, *Elf Jahre und ein Tag* (1963, Eleven Years and One Day), again starring Ruth Leuwerik, before returning to Hollywood. His last film, *Situation Hopeless – But Not Serious* (1965), continued his interest in German themes with a comedy about a German clerk, played by Alec Guinness, who holds two American soldiers prisoner for years after the end of the Second World War. The film's cast included former Ufa stars Paul Dahlke and Mady Rahl, but it was rejected on its West German release as 'implausible and overblown'.[19] Internationally too, the film was a complete flop, and barely released.

While not all of Reinhardt's CCC films may be rehabilitated as forgotten masterpieces, they certainly deserve a place among the more interesting West German productions of the postwar years. As melodramas they hold their own with equivalent contemporary Hollywood examples, indeed, Reinhardt shares a number of stylistic characteristics with Douglas Sirk, such as a sense of Brechtian irony, as well as a proclivity for female protagonists, although perhaps tinged in Reinhardt's case with a certain amount of sadism towards his heroines. Moreover, as can be seen in

Liebling der Götter, Reinhardt's West German films negotiate in sometimes fascinating ways the conventions of Hollywood melodrama, the legacy of Weimar, and the aesthetics as well as ideologies of the late Adenauer years. Reinhardt's intermezzo in the West German film industry of the 1950s and 1960s has, in retrospect, a somewhat tragic dimension. His career trajectory may seem to provide incontrovertible evidence of Horak's verdict that the West German film industry was incapable of accommodating former exiles. At closer inspection, however, Reinhardt's case may illustrate less a rejection of former exiles by the film industry or cinema audiences as such, but more of the ingrained hostility towards popular genres among the West German critical establishment of the time. In the 1950s and 1960s, the conservative critique of Reinhardt centred on him being too 'American' and not 'German' enough, while for critics associated with the New German Cinema he came to embody the typical faceless professional of the despised indigenous industry. Perhaps tellingly, only a handful of pages in Reinhardt's memoirs are devoted to his career in postwar West German cinema, though he finds time to express his respect for Brauner's idealism, albeit modified by ironical asides on the producer's miserliness.[20] Reinhardt summarised his West German experience, perhaps slightly disingenuously in his self-deprecation, as follows: 'I have never been the darling of German critics. They found me suspect not only because of my parents, but also because I did not fit in their worldview. I am no cineaste, no film ideologue, and I don't believe in stylistic corsets. I don't want to prove anything'.[21]

Someone who had arguably less to prove to West German critics, partly because of a lesser-known public profile, was Ernst Neubach. Neubach, a prolific director, scriptwriter, and song-lyricist in the German cinema of the late 1920s and early 1930s, had survived the war years not in Hollywood, but in French exile under the pseudonym of Ernest Neuville, under the protection of Hermann Göring's brother Albert.[22] In 1938 he had co-written the screenplay for *Pièges*, directed by another émigré, Robert Siodmak. After 1945, Neubach re-established himself in postwar French cinema with writing credits on *Le Signal rouge* (1948), which starred Erich von Stroheim, and as the writer-director of *Les Mémoires de la vache Yolande* (1950). Neubach was one of the first film-makers in the postwar years to actively pursue transnational modes of production, in his case primarily between West Germany and France. He boasted that 'I'm one of very few who can write and direct in both languages, and since I have detailed knowledge about both mentalities, my propositions appeal. To combine French *ésprit* with German efficiency is a fruitful endeavour'.[23]

The contact between Neubach and Brauner dates back to the late 1940s when Brauner bought from Neubach the synopsis of a dark comedy in which a man hires a killer to end his life but has a change of heart. The prehistory and subsequent developments of this transaction are indicative not only of how both Neubach and Brauner perceived transnational interaction, but also of how Neubach capitalised on his own past. The synopsis Neubach sold to Brauner was neither new nor original. In the 1920s Neubach had written a stage play with the same plot line, and the play itself was already an adaptation of a lesser-known Jules Verne story, *Les Tribulations d'un chinois en Chine*, originally published in France in 1879. In the early 1930s, Neubach had sold the story to Ufa, where it was adapted as *Der Mann, der seinen Mörder sucht* (The Man who Searches for His Murderer, 1931), directed by Robert Siodmak, and starring Heinz Rühmann.

In 1949 and 1952, the story resurfaced again in two more versions. Neubach, seemingly ignoring his contract with Brauner, adapted it into a screenplay for the French film *On demande un assassin* (1949), a vehicle for French comedian Fernandel, which Neubach also directed. In 1952, Neubach directed for Brauner's CCC another remake of the same material, *Man lebt nur einmal* (You Only Live Once), this time starring German comedian Theo Lingen.[24] According to Claudia Dillmann, 'in 1949, Neubach obviously deemed it impossible that the French version would ever be distributed in Germany'.[25] It was, and the multiple remake resulted in a series of legal wrangles, not least with the Ufa trustees, who argued that the rights to the story had been with the company since the film version of 1931. Neubach's defence, which he later also attempted to pursue through the courts with Brauner's support, rested on the immorality and illegality of Ufa's (and more generally the German state's) policy of disowning Jewish copyrights during the 1930s and 1940s, which had deprived him of his rightful royalties.[26]

Neubach's career as a director and writer in France and West Germany in the 1950s remained associated with his attempts to recycle his earlier successes from the Weimar years. In the *Heimatfilm* musical *Ich hab mein Herz in Heidelberg verloren* (1952, I've Lost My Heart in Heidelberg), Neubach capitalised on the popularity of a song of the same title the lyrics of which he had penned in the 1920s. *Ein Lied geht um die Welt* (1958, A Song Goes Around the World), on the other hand, was a sentimental biopic of the famous Jewish tenor Joseph Schmidt, who had died penniless in Swiss exile in 1942 at the age of 38. Schmidt once starred in a Neubach-scripted film called – *Ein Lied geht um die Welt* (1933).[27]

As above examples indicate, Neubach's binational career was dependent on a situation where markets were sufficiently independent to use the same material repeatedly. Furthermore, while Neubach's West German films tapped into distinctly indigenous popular traditions (he wrote the screenplays for several *Heimatfilme* and nostalgic confections such as *Die Prinzessin von St. Wolfgang*, 1957, and *Der Kaiser und das Wäschermädel*, 1957), his French films always emphasised what Neubach presumably understood as 'French *ésprit*'. His script for *Tourbillon* (1952), for example, closely followed the conventions of the French *policier* genre and drew on the local atmosphere of its setting in the port of Marseille.

Robert Siodmak, another of Brauner's émigré imports, had collaborated with Neubach both in Weimar cinema and in France. After a prestigious career in Hollywood in the 1940s and early 1950s, he had already returned to European cinema with the Franco-Italian co-production *Le Grand Jeu* (1953) when Brauner contracted him for CCC. While Siodmak had carved himself a niche in Hollywood with moody and visually stylish *film noir* classics such as *The Spiral Staircase* (1945), *The Killers* (1945) and *Cry of the City* (1948), his postwar European films were on the whole big-budget star vehicles and literary adaptations that recalled the *Kammerspielfilme* he had directed in Germany in the early 1930s, relatively static, and dialogue-oriented chamber plays. In the 1950s and 1960s Siodmak directed for Brauner's CCC six films in total, including *Die Ratten* (1955, The Rats), based, like Reinhardt's *Vor Sonnenuntergang*, on a drama by Gerhart Hauptmann; and *Mein Vater, der Schauspieler* (1956, My Father the Actor). In a rather different generic register were Siodmak's three Karl May assignments in the early to mid-1960s and the historical epic *Kampf um Rom* (1968, The Battle of Rome), a sprawling saga about the end of the Roman empire and the dynastic battles among the Gothic invaders and the Byzantine rulers. Both literally and aesthetically, the film turned out to be Byzantine, a swansong to the genre, with an eccentric cast that included Laurence Harvey, Swedish actress Harriet Andersson, and Orson Welles.

In his posthumously published autobiography, Siodmak devoted a whole chapter to Brauner, entitled 'My friend Atze' (Brauner's nickname), and referred to him as a 'genius'.[28] Claudia Dillmann, drawing on Brauner's correspondence, however, has documented a less harmonious professional relationship between the two men, characterised by a decreasing artistic independence on Siodmak's part.[29] Among the critical establishment in West Germany, Siodmak had quickly forfeited the reputation and advance publicity that accompanied his return from the United States. While *Die Ratten* and *Nachts wenn der Teufel kam* (1957, The Devil Struck at Night) were prestigious critical successes, Siodmak's other West German productions had proved to be either expensive flops or critical disasters. Siodmak's attempts to find work elsewhere in Europe, for example, on the Franco-German Romy Schneider vehicle *Katia* (1959) and the British production *The Rough and the Smooth* (1959), did not result in further offers.

By the early 1960s, the relationship between Brauner and Siodmak had changed from that of a famous international star director and his West German producer to the more prosaic one of contract employee and demanding studio head. Seen from a different angle, Siodmak was one of the few remigrants who did not recycle his earlier successes in Weimar cinema and who relatively successfully adapted to the specific generic and production context of the postwar film industry. Critical evaluations, however, have not been kind to Siodmak's professional flexibility and his conversion to what was effectively an even more formulaic mode of production than the one Siodmak had served in Hollywood. Karl Prümm suggests that 'the Karl May films are the negation of his work, the contradiction of his best work. They stand for a naive pictorialism, for simplistic structures, coarse effects, and moral certainties'.[30]

Arguably the most publicised and the most disastrous return of a former exile, however, was the case of Fritz Lang. By the time he was contracted by Brauner to return to West German studios, Lang had reached the end of his career in Hollywood. *Cahiers du Cinéma* in France and later *Movie* in Britain by this time had already initiated the canonisation of Lang as an *auteur* precisely on the evidence of his Hollywood films. In contrast, Lang's critical reputation in West Germany at this time rested almost entirely on his German films of the 1920s and early 1930s, while films canonised today as classics, such as *The Woman in the Window* (1945) or *The Big Heat* (1953), were regularly dismissed. The inability to conceive of popular Hollywood genres in positive terms is evident in the following summation of Lang's American work in the weekly *Der Spiegel*: 'Lang did not manage to establish himself as an artistically ambitious Hollywood director. He had to be content to manufacture adventure and crime films'.[31] Like other remigrants, Lang, under the guidance of Brauner's populist agenda, returned to the generic formulae of his early career, the exotic melodrama of *Der Tiger von Eschnapur* (1958, The Tiger of Eschnapur) and *Das indische Grabmal* (1959, The Indian Tomb) which adapted an original story Lang once intended to make, but never did; and the arch-villain Dr Mabuse in *Die tausend Augen des Dr Mabuse* (1960, The Thousand Eyes of Dr Mabuse). While Lang's CCC productions were, commercially speaking, neither more nor less successful than comparable productions made by other directors, his perceived cultural status engendered a particularly hostile critical reception for his West German films, which Joe Hembus likened to 'barbaric executions'.[32]

Lang's return to West Germany was originally motivated by Brauner's strategy to translate the exoticist adventure serials of the Weimar period into the new context of Franco-German co-productions. Lang's 1958/9 two-part spectacular *Der Tiger von Eschnapur* and its sequel *Das Indische Grabmal*, each part nearly two hours long, were shot on location in India with a largely German crew and a cast that starred the Hollywood actress Debra Paget in the female lead (her main male partner was played by the Swiss Paul Hubschmid in the German version, and by Henri Mercier in the French version). After Richard Eichberg's versions made in 1937 and 1938, Lang's spectacle was already the second remake of Joe May's silent German films made in 1921 (written by Thea von Harbou), attesting to a continued fascination of German film-makers and audiences with all things Indian. Indeed, Lang's two films, like their predecessors, provide a compendium of the sub-genre's preferred iconographical elements, from snake-charmers to mystical holy men (yogis) and cruel despots residing in magnificent palaces and luring young (frequently European) women into their lairs, while subterfuge and court intrigue always threatens social stability. The plot of *Der Tiger von Eschnapur* and *Das indische Grabmal* remains surprisingly similar in all three versions. Lang's version goes like this: An architect in India, invited by a seemingly kind and liberal maharaja to build hospitals and orphanages, incurs the wrath of his patron by falling in love with a Eurasian temple dancer the maharaja himself is in love with. The maharaja forces the architect into a fight with a tiger (which the architect wins) and subsequently commissions the building of a monumental tomb in which he intends to bury alive the unfaithful dancer/wife and her lover. The two escape, but are recaptured and thrown into the cavernous underbelly of the palace, which houses a colony of lepers. The lovers' fortunes are eventually reversed when the maharaja is toppled in a palace coup by his sinister adviser.

Despite basic similarities, there are different narrative nuances between the various versions. In the films of 1921 and 1937, the story was supposedly set in the present, in other words, in the colonial India of the late Raj. Indeed, in Joe May's version, the affair the maharaja's wife is having is with a British officer, not with the architect whose own wife is pursued by the maharaja (Conrad Veidt). The ending leaves the interracial lovers dead and the maharaja mad; only the architect and his wife survive what is, of all three adaptations, the most tragic and Gothic version. Eichberg's 1930s version eliminates most of the British characters, strengthens the role of the now German architect, and uniquely introduces humorous elements (largely through the participation of comedians Theo Lingen and Gisela Schlüter). By the time of Lang's 1950s version, the architect and romantic

Figure 6.2. Artur Brauner (right) in 1958 with Fritz Lang and actress Debra Paget. Deutsches Filminstitut (DIF), Frankfurt-on-Main.

lover roles have largely been merged, while a subsidiary architect couple hover in the background of the story – by this time the nationalities of the relevant characters have become difficult to decipher, and become interchangeable in the different language versions. Lang and his co-screenwriter Werner Jörg Lüdecke made no attempt to update the material to a new postwar and postcolonial India even though the costumes and technology seem to suggest a contemporary setting. In most other aspects, however, Lang's film invokes a pre-colonial, and entirely mythical India of legends and fairytales (after all, the narrative's central conceit of the tomb recalls the stories that surround the building of the Taj Mahal), while revising the tragic gloom of May's film's conclusion into a more upbeat ending.

Although Germany never had any colonial involvement in the Indian subcontinent, its culture had captured the German imagination since the late eighteenth century.[33] An imaginary India was perceived to be the reverse of Germanness, the rationality and modernity of the latter being either mirrored or complemented by the former's 'mysteriousness', ancient heritage, and perplexing complexity of cultural manifestations and traditions. This discourse is manifest in all film versions of the Eschnapur story, where rationality, technology, science and modernity are embodied in the figure of the architect, while the Indian characters are guided by instinct, passions, religion, and superstition. In these imagined cultural contrasts, Germans could either confirm their supposed cultural superiority, or else use the imagined India for a critique or rejection of German and, by extension, Western, values and inhibitions. The way in which the German fascination with India is frequently narrativised, either in exoticist fictional films such as the Eschnapur films through the tropes of adventure, romance, and sexuality, or in *Kulturfilme* through the mode of ethnographical research (which aims at controlling the other through surveys and classification), recalls a discourse of appropriation that Edward Said has identified as typical for the Western imagination of the Orient.[34] Moreover, over all three Eschnapur films, but particularly over May's version, hovers a deep fear of miscegenation, which expresses itself not only in the persistent discourse of contagion in the narrative (e.g., the lepers), but also in the drastic and fatal punishment it assigns to the transgressive cross-racial lovers.

On the other hand, one should be cautious in interpreting the ideological content of these narratives too literally. As in the later Karl May and Edgar Wallace films, Lang's Indian spectacles are characterised by a mode of historical and cultural camouflage and a concomitant rejection of authenticity, which Thomas Brandlmeier sees as typical for exoticism in general:

> Exotic images are influenced by the past, but are not part of that past, they correspond to contemporary styles and topoi, yet are themselves not contemporary, and they formulate what has never been without pointing towards the future. They are inventions in space and time, a parallel world … Exoticist worlds are not physical reality, not even inner worlds, but spaces for fantasy and expectation.[35]

These expectations and fantasies can be identified in the positioning of India as a site of escape from the constraints of national identity, which finds its expression in the Indian films' ethnic masquerade, where white actors in colourful costumes and with brown face paint represent highly fetishised role models and icons. Thus, particularly in Joe May's and Lang's films (but decidedly less so in Eichberg's 1930s version), the figure of the maharaja (played by Conrad Veidt in the 1921 version of *Das indische Grabmal*, and by Walter Reyer in Lang's film) is seen as the central protagonist and (albeit highly problematic) hero of the narrative, providing an exotic, dangerous, but also sexually attractive version of masculinity. Debra Paget's exotic attraction, meanwhile, consists of her being not only a racial hybrid in the narrative of the film but also a Hollywood star appearing in a European production.

At about the same time as Lang's Indian films, Brauner invested in the three-hour-long Franco–German–Italian *Herrin der Welt* (1959/60, Mistress of the World). For this film Brauner had contracted yet another Weimar veteran and Hollywood émigré, William Dieterle, although the film's cinematographer, Richard Angst, had to take over the director's chair in Indochina after Dieterle walked off following a row with Brauner (seemingly a not too infrequent occurrence between Brauner and his directors). *Herrin der Welt* was a remake of Joe May's eight-part German adventure-film serial from 1919, which centred on a woman's world wide quest to find her abducted scientist father. The search ends in the temple ruins of Cambodia's Angkor-Vat. Like Lang's co-production, the film was originally shown in West Germany in two parts, but was edited into a single release version in Italy and France. As with Lang's film, *Herrin der Welt* had a largely German crew and a multinational cast, which included Martha Hyer and Sabu from Hollywood, Carlos Thompson from Argentina, Gino Cervi from Italy, Micheline Presle and Lino Ventura from France, and German actors such as Wolfgang Preiss.

Both Lang's and Dieterle's films were critically mauled in West Germany. One newspaper printed a mock obituary which read: 'Here lies Fritz Lang, once the creator of important films such as *Metropolis* and *M*. *The Indian Tomb* is his own'.[36] In France and Britain, in contrast, Lang's film found acclaim particularly among the critics of *Cahiers du cinema* and *Movie*, both of which found much to admire in Lang's exotic adventure. A distinct division in evaluation has persisted with regard to Lang's Indian films between German and foreign critics. Enno Patalas, for example, notes 'a direction that refrains from any spectacle' and provides 'ideas of images instead of images'.[37] Patalas also declares that 'it is possible to talk about the Indian films without wasting time on how the German cinema of the Adenauer years has influenced them'.[38]

For Tom Gunning, in contrast, the Indian films constitute a natural progression and conclusion of Lang's oeuvre as an *auteur*. Gunning rejects the criticism of the films as anachronistic relics of a more primitive era of film-making, citing as specifically modern 'Lang's control of colour photography (particularly the ways the colours and hues of costumes relate to the colour values in the various decors)' and the films' 'non-realistic, semi-abstract plot and characters'.[39] What Patalas and other critics perceive as signs of amateurism and artistic failure, Gunning sees as a supreme expression and realisation of Lang's aesthetic principles: 'Lang insisted on the constructedness and artificiality of his archetypal fantasy worlds, and did not try to endow them either with emotional immediacy or even believability'.[40] Gunning acknowledges here the self-reflectivity with which Lang (and Brauner) approached not only a venerable classic of silent German cinema, but also a more complex tradition of popular genres, which extends (and here Gunning's analysis is ultimately too limiting despite his generosity and sympathy for the films) beyond the *auteurist* framework of the Indian films, and precisely into the arena that Patalas thought not worth going into, namely the hierarchies, structures, and strategies of the popular West German cinema of the late 1950s and 1960s. The exoticism of Lang's Indian films is in this respect an extension of the escapist mode of the *Heimatfilm* and it anticipates the Karl May and Edgar Wallace films of the 1960s.

At the time, despite reasonable box-office results (both *Der Tiger von Eschnapur* and *Das indische Grabmal* were among the ten best-grossing films in West Germany in 1958/9), however, neither Lang's nor Dieterle's film could fully recuperate their substantial production costs. While Lang's and Dieterle's attempts had proven that there was a demand for exotic adventure films, their particular mode of production had been too expensive and too excessive to be financed by European money alone. Co-produced epics such as these continued to be made intermittently throughout the 1960s, but only with substantial American backing and frequently with only minimal West German involvement. Both *Herrin der Welt* and Lang's Indian two-parter were conceived as unique, one-off events. In their monumentalism (both in terms of production values and length) and in their multi-part format, these films had tried to revive a mode of production that had characterised the inflation period in Weimar cinema, of which both Lang and Dieterle were veterans. For future project, however, Brauner looked for more affordable prototypes.

Like Siodmak, Lang became primarily a pawn in Brauner's strategy to develop popular generic series franchises. Following the success of the Edgar Wallace series, Brauner envisaged that a series of Dr Mabuse films would have the potential to partake in the crime-film boom of the time. Lang later acknowledged that the idea of a new Mabuse film had originated with Brauner.[41] The mentally unstable arch-villain, a master of disguise, deception, and mass hypnosis, and a Nietzschean superman with erotic powers over women, was a creation of the Luxemburg-born journalist, globe-trotting adventurer, and pulp novelist Norbert Jacques (1880-1954).[42] First published in serial instalments in the *Berliner Illustrirte*

Zeitung in 1921, Jacques' novel, conceptualised both as an action thriller and as a critique of the urban lifestyle and culture of the Weimar republic, became an almost immediate best seller. Mabuse had been brought to the screen in 1922 by Lang in *Dr Mabuse, der Spieler* (Dr Mabuse, The Gambler). Following the best-selling success of Jacques' novel, the film was both a box-office hit and critically acclaimed as a milestone of expressionist cinema, which is ironic given that Jacques' original novel had explicitly polemicised against the 'unnaturalness' of expressionist art.

For Siegfried Kracauer the figure of Mabuse as created by Lang's film and Jacques' novel became a prime example for his archetypal Weimar screen tyrants, 'an omnipresent threat which cannot be localized, and thus reflects society under a tyrannical regime – that kind of society in which one fears everybody because anybody may be the tyrant's ear or arm'.[43] This political association was brought to the fore in Lang's sequel ten years later, *Das Testament des Dr Mabuse* (1932, The Testament of Dr Mabuse), widely perceived as Lang's critique of the Nazis and consequently banned by the authorities in 1933. *Die tausend Augen des Dr Mabuse* (1960) continues in these political analogies, in many ways even more explicitly than the earlier Mabuse films. In this film, set in a restored, newly confident West Germany, Mabuse (Wolfgang Preiss) operates in an international hotel, the rooms of which are monitored by an extensive system of surveillance cameras. Television technology, and its aiding function in gaining knowledge and creating paranoia, has thus replaced Mabuse's earlier tools, telepathy and hypnosis. This has an effect on the appearance of Mabuse himself; no longer Rudolf Klein-Rogge's mad, explosive genius whose piercing eyes would always betray any disguise, in Preiss' interpretation of the role the master criminal becomes a self-effacing bureaucrat, while the façade of his public profession is no longer the society psychoanalyst of Jacques' novel, but a clairvoyant astrologer. The film makes clear that the hotel that doubles as a panopticum is a legacy of the Nazis, who built it in order to spy on foreign diplomats and that Mabuse, the opportunist criminal, has appropriated this inheritance in order to undermine the consumerist society of the *Wirtschaftswunder* to his own ends. Tom Gunning has argued that:

> although Lang's film has rarely been treated in terms of the postwar processing of the Nazi trauma in Germany, Lang proposes a vision of German history which sees continuity rather than rupture and which refuses to either memorialise or forget the past ... The Nazi past pervades *The Thousand Eyes of Dr. Mabuse* without needing to be rendered visible. Like Mabuse's technology, it's embedded in the structure of things, powerful because it lacks a spectacular presence.[44]

For Brauner, the appeal of Mabuse rested probably less with the political symbolism of the earlier adaptations and more with the material's blend of Gothic horror, crime, and technological gadgetry, and its potential to become a series franchise. However, the personal correspondence between Lang and Brauner, compiled by Claudia Dillmann, documents that Lang was neither willing to become another of Brauner's series directors nor prepared to continuously recycle his earlier films. After Brauner suggested to Lang a remake of his *Nibelungen* (1924), Lang refused.[45] *Die Tausend Augen des Dr. Mabuse* marked the end of Lang's collaboration with Brauner, and, indeed, the end of Lang's career. Brauner, meanwhile, would realise a new Mabuse series with other directors. It is easy to see in retrospect how the revived Mabuse corresponded to the Wallace series, but also how he prefigured similar icons in European cinema of the 1960s, from the James Bond villains to Dr Fu Manchu and Fantômas (the latter two, of course, like Mabuse, revived from earlier incarnations in the silent and early sound period). Like the Wallace films would do subsequently, the narrative of Lang's Adenauer-Mabuse film emphasises the deceptiveness and *trompe l'oeil* effects of its architecture, particularly in the panoptic hotel in *Die tausend Augen des Dr. Mabuse*. The narrative and stylistic proximity of Lang's last film to the Wallace series is not too surprising. While Lang was reunited in this film with erstwhile collaborator Erich Kettelhut (who had been one of the production designers of the first Mabuse film in 1922), his cinematographer was Karl Löb, who would become one of the most prolific cameramen on the Wallace cycle.

What the individual career trajectories of former exiles at CCC illustrate is that their employment was overall part of Brauner's wider strategy to internationalise West German film production, and to react to domestic as well as international competition. Apart from their status as 'star directors', figures such as Lang, Siodmak, and Reinhardt also functioned for Brauner as mediators, providing useful contacts and connections with the American film market or, in the case of Neubach, with the French film industry. The Hungarian-born Steve Sekely (István Székely), meanwhile, who had directed *Die Kaiserin von China* (1953, The Empress of China) for Brauner, was one of CCC's unofficial agents in Hollywood and helped arrange distribution deals with U.S. companies.[46]

International Networks and the Rise and Fall of CCC-London

Brauner had expanded into European co-production since the mid-1950s. *Stern von Rio/Stella di Rio* (1954/5, The Star of Rio), the remake of a Tobis melodrama from 1940, was simultaneously shot in Brazil in a German and an Italian language version. On the French film *Les Héros sont fatigués* (1955) CCC provided financial support in return for the inclusion of West German actors Curd Jürgens and Gert Fröbe, who acted opposite Yves Montand and the Mexican film star Maria Félix. A similar arrangement was achieved in the case of the Italian 'white telephone' melodrama

Suprema confessione (1956), which had the West German *Heimatfilm* star Sonja Ziemann as the female lead.

By the late 1950s CCC had, in addition to its collaborations with Italian and French partners, also entered into co-production deals with Brazil (*Tumulto de paixoes/Tom Dooley – Der Held der grünen Hölle*, 1958), Spain (*Es geschah am hellichten Tag/El Cebo*, 1958, directed by Ladislao Vajda, who had worked in Spanish exile throughout the 1940s and 1950s) and Finland (*…und immer ruft das Herz/Avaruusraketilla Rakauteen*, 1959). Notably, most of these films were small-scale and low-budget productions with rather obscure production partners and, where they went beyond these limitations, CCC often featured only as a minority partner. In the case of Fritz Lang's Indian epics and William Dieterle's *Herrin der Welt* (1959), on the other hand, CCC was the initiator, providing most of the production budget and crew. The trade paper *Film-Echo* outlined CCC's policies with regard to co-productions:

> Co-productions, particularly when they are shot in foreign studios, are in danger of not being recognised, for a variety of reasons, as German films by the German audience. This occasionally results in such a drastic slump in domestic revenues that the advantages of co-production agreements become illusory. CCC takes care that their co-productions appear as fully German films. Experience has shown that the German audience does not necessarily perceive a film as non-German if it has an international cast. If a film is no longer recognised as a specifically German product by its German audience, it has more to do with the script and the way in which it is filmed.[47]

The dilemma Brauner's CCC thus had to face by the late 1950s was that exportable big-budget productions were financially viable only through co-production agreements. The problem, however, was to find narrative formulae that were accepted by different national audiences as being part of an 'indigenous' cultural framework. Rialto's Edgar Wallace cycle had proven that a 'foreign' cultural source could be successfully adapted into a recognisably 'German' film series, while the Karl May films simultaneously fitted into a German cultural context and into international expectations of the Western genre. CCC attempted to get a foothold in both cycles, as I will document in the next two chapters.

CCC's international connections manifested themselves as a fairly loose network of personal contacts. In the early 1960s, however, Brauner attempted to formalise these contacts by launching his own company subsidiary abroad. The idea had been suggested by Gene Gutowski, Brauner's contact in London. Brauner had established contacts in Britain since the late 1950s, with the two principal aims of negotiating distribution rights for his films in the anglophone markets and acquiring literary material to fill the gap in his production output. Brauner had personal and professional contacts with former exiles, such as the producers Marcel Hellmann (whose brother Carol was the head of the West German Export-Union and a producer with his own subsidiaries in Italy) and Steven Pallos, a former collaborator of Alexander Korda. Brauner's main talent-scout and negotiator in Britain, however, was fellow-Pole Eugene (Gene) Gutowski, who had worked in the American film and television industry in the 1950s and had co-produced Brauner's Polish-West German venture *Der achte Wochentag*. In 1961, Brauner appointed Gutowski as the director of a new British-based company. 'CCC-Film London Limited' was launched and legally incorporated in 1961 with the stated aim to 'produce British films for the international market, and to supply talent and properties to CCC Berlin not available in Germany'.[48] CCC-London's most significant British partner was British Lion, which provided up to two-thirds of the production costs, with CCC-Berlin supplying the rest. British Lion was to organise distribution in the U.K. and America, while Brauner looked after the continental European market. For tax reasons, a CCC subsidiary in Liechtenstein channelled funds to Gutowski.

Among a long list of rather highbrow projects initially announced by CCC-London were film adaptations of Shakespeare (*The Merchant of Venice*), Thomas Mann (*The Magic Mountain*) and Aldous Huxley (*The Genius and the Goddess*), as well as a film about the life of Janusz Korczak, a Polish paediatrician who, during the German occupation, had accompanied a group of orphaned Jewish children into the gas chamber. On a rather different cultural level, Gutowski also negotiated with Hammer about a possible co-production of a 'Jack The Ripper' film, and he tried to secure the West German film rights for Agatha Christie novels.[49] Of all these plans, the Korczak story was in terms of personal passions probably closest to Brauner, and yet he ultimately realised it not with CCC-London but as a West German-Israeli co-production in 1974. The *Magic Mountain* idea was for a while considered as a West German-based production with a British director (Guy Green) and British crew, but most of CCC-London's other projects were abandoned or fell through at an early stage.

What CCC-London achieved from 1961 until Gutowski's resignation in 1963, comes across in the surviving documents in the Artur Brauner archive as a series of production disasters, an accumulation of debts, an increasingly hostile correspondence between Berlin and London, and ultimately a complete breakdown of trust in Brauner and his representatives by the British film industry. However, it is precisely in its economic failure and its mutual misunderstandings that this saga provides fascinating insights. As the business correspondence of CCC-London indicates, British industry circles viewed Brauner's activities with trepidation and suspicion from very early on. The reason for this had to do with Brauner's previous involvement in an ill-fated Anglo-West German production, *The Devil's Agent* (1961), a Cold-War thriller based on a novel by the exiled author Hans Habe (the pseudonym of Hungarian writer János Békessy), and directed by John Paddy Carstairs, which predated the launch of CCC-London. Nominally co-produced by Emmet Dalton and the West German company Eichberg, the film went into production without properly signed contracts and financial guarantees, leaving several of the production crew without payment.[50] Although Brauner's involvement in this film was relatively minimal (he had supplied the services of his contract actor Peter van Eyck), his association with *The Devil's Agent* was seen as a less than auspicious sign.

To a certain extent, CCC-London's subsequent activities would confirm these suspicions. After all its initial ambitions and despite a vast number of projects in the pipeline, CCC-London completed in the end just two films, *Station Six-Sahara* (1962, directed by Seth Holt) and *Sherlock Holmes und das Halsband des Todes* (*Sherlock Holmes and the Deadly Necklace*, 1962, directed by Terence Fisher). With additional financial backing from Italian and French companies, the latter did not qualify as a British quota film and was registered as a foreign production. In addition CCC-London collaborated on the CCC-Berlin and Raymond Stross co-production *Vengeance* (1962, directed by Freddie Francis).

In terms of both box-office success and style, this output comprises a rather mixed bag. *Station Six-Sahara* is a taut, well-made melodrama, shot at Shepperton and on location in the Libyan desert. The film tells a torrid story, set among a disparate, all-male group at an isolated desert outpost, which culminates in sexual jealousy, madness, and murder after the arrival of a woman in the camp. Leading the film's multinational cast were Hollywood star Carroll Baker,[51] British actors Ian Bannen and Denholm Elliott, and Peter van Eyck, by that time an established star in West Germany. Before production began, however, CCC-London became entangled in a legal dilemma concerning the ownership of the story, the details of which shed a poignant light on the personal and institutional legacies of Germany's recent history and the guilty entanglement of the German film industry in that history.

In 1960, Brauner had acquired the film rights of *Men Without a Past*, a stage play by Jean Maret, which was later turned into a screenplay by Bryan Forbes and Brian Clemens. It transpired that Maret, a French Jew who had emigrated to Brazil at the outbreak of war, had written an earlier synopsis of the same material in the late 1930s, which was used for the 1938 film *SOS Sahara*, produced by Alliance Cinématographique Européenne (A.C.E.), a French subsidiary of Ufa. As in the case of Ernst Neubach, Maret had been effectively stripped of his rights during the Occupation period and his name deleted from the film's credits. The question was therefore whether the ownership of the story had returned to Maret after the war or whether it remained with the caretakers of the former Ufa.[52] The matter was finally settled in favour of Maret and Brauner, though this was followed by further disagreements about the new script. Bryan Forbes and director Seth Holt threatened to resign after Brauner suggested spicing up the plot by adding a number of prostitute characters.[53] Forbes and Holt finally won the argument, partly by pointing out that the suggested changes would not pass the British censors.

Considering the film's setting, its multinational cast, and the personal biographies of many involved, including Maret, Brauner, Gutowski, van Eyck, and Seth Holt (who was born in Palestine), it may be suggestive to read *Station Six-Sahara* as an existentialist parable about being 'alien' and the quest for identity. The film's clashing acting styles and its narrative emphasis on exile and displacement also recalls the kind of international film the 'Film Europe' movement of the late 1920s and 1930s produced, while its narrative is reminiscent not only the plot of the 1938 French film, but also of G.W. Pabst's earlier multilingual desert adventure *Die Herrin von Atlantis/The Mistress of Atlantis* of 1932. In its review, the *Monthly Film Bulletin* characterised Holt's directing style as 'filming with the courage of its own clichés' and summed up the film's claustrophobic atmosphere by noting its 'amount of sweating faces in close-up, snarled dialogue and brooding Teutonic silences'.[54]

Today unjustly forgotten and underrated, *Station Six-Sahara* was reasonably successful on its initial release in West Germany and Britain, though British Lion struggled to secure a distribution deal in the United States. The promotional campaign attempted to exploit the film's multinational cast. According to the stars' status and familiarity in each market, different poster and credit listings were designed.[55] For the film's release in the U.S. and Canada, Baker's name was the only one above the title, followed by Ian Bannen and Denholm Elliott below. For U.K. and Commonwealth distribution purposes, Baker, Bannen and Elliott were all above the title. In West Germany, Continental Europe and the Far East, Baker, van Eyck and Hansjörg Felmy came first, with Bannen and Elliott billed as 'also starring' below the title.

Vengeance/Ein Toter sucht seinen Mörder (also known as *Over My Dead Body*, and under its American release title *The Brain*), directed by Freddie Francis and shot simultaneously in two language versions in Twickenam and CCC's Spandau studios, was based on the novel *Donovan's Brain* by Robert Siodmak's brother Curt, in which a scientist becomes possessed by a dead man's brain kept alive in a jar. In all likelihood, Robert Siodmak, by that time working for CCC, brought the novel to Brauner's attention and initiated the contacts to his brother. Curt Siodmak, a prolific author, journalist, and scriptwriter (e.g. *F.P.1 antwortet nicht*, 1932) in Weimar Germany, had established himself in Hollywood after a stopover in the 1930s in France and Britain, as an expert for horror and science-fiction films, mostly B-films produced by Universal (e.g. *The Wolf Man*, 1941) and Republic.

Donovan's Brain, originally written in 1942, had been filmed four times before in Hollywood, as *The Lady and the Monster* (1943), *The Phantom Speaks* (1944), and *Donovan's Brain* (1953), and as a TV film in 1955, again under the novel's original title.[56] Although Curt Siodmak was not directly involved in the filming of *Vengeance* (his novel had been adapted by Robert Stewart and Philip Mackie), he was contracted by Brauner to write the script for CCC-London's Sherlock Holmes project.

As in the case of *Station Six-Sahara*, the production of *Vengeance* was fraught with disagreements between Brauner and his British production partners, particularly with regard to the film's cast. Dieter Borsche, who played a supporting role in the German version, was replaced in the British version by Miles Malleson, presumably because both actors were seen to represent specifically 'German' or 'British' types. While the male lead (Peter van Eyck as the scientist) went undisputed by both sides, Raymond Stross, the film's British producer, was interested in upgrading the part of the female lead, played by his actress wife Anne Heywood. For Brauner, on the other hand, it was Ellen Schwiers, who played what was essentially a supporting role, who would be recognised by German audiences.[57] The wrangles about star status and screen time are evident in the final film, in which the narrative function of the two respective female characters played by Schwiers and Heywood remains somewhat unclear.

Unlike *The Lady and the Monster*, which had emphasised the novel's Gothic horror aspects, and *Donovan's Brain*, which had dealt more with the story's science-fiction elements, *Vengeance* functioned more like a traditional whodunnit crime thriller, with the main emphasis on unmasking a killer. This emphasis comes across particularly in the film's German title, *Ein Toter sucht seinen Mörder* (A Dead Man is Searching for His Murderer). Peter van Eyck's hero was thus no longer either the sinister or obsessed scientist of previous adaptations, but more of a sleuth who exploits the unusual assistance of the murder victim's living brain. As a crime story with a bizarre twist, it is clear why Brauner was interested in *Donovan's Brain* and how it fitted into CCC's generic framework – it matched the current vogue among West German audiences for slightly macabre crime narratives as epitomised by the Wallace series. Unfortunately, *Vengeance* sank almost without trace in West Germany, where it was dismissed as a 'routine horror film'.[58] In Britain, the *Monthly Film Bulletin* noted the film as an interesting directorial effort for former cinematographer Freddie Francis, and concluded that the film's 'preposterous mixture of crime, horror and science fiction, with a dash or two of neurosis, art and medical ethics stirred in, comes off unexpectedly well'.[59]

Of all CCC-London's films, *Sherlock Holmes und das Halsband des Todes* (1962) had the most turbulent history in terms of production and reception. Starring Christopher Lee as Holmes, Thorley Walters as Dr Watson, and German actor Hans Söhnker as Professor Moriarty, it was a highly formulaic adaptation, close in spirit and style to the 1940s American Sherlock Holmes B-film series starring Basil Rathbone. As in the case of CCC's Dr Mabuse films, Brauner originally conceived the film as a pilot for a prospective series of Sherlock Holmes adaptations. As in *Station Six-Sahara*, however, complications arose concerning the literary ownership of the material.

CCC-London had signed a contract with the Conan Doyle estate which stipulated in detail the degree of faithfulness to Doyle's work the film had to fulfil. During production the estate and its representative Henry Lester indignantly rejected suggestions by Brauner and Siodmak to update the story to a more contemporary setting, to dress the female actresses in mini skirts, and to cast the role of Dr Watson with Heinz Erhardt, a popular comedian.[60] The plan of bringing in a comedian suggests that Brauner intended the film to be similar to the Wallace series, which equally combined comedy with horror and crime. Moreover, in the 1940s American series, too, Nigel Bruce had portrayed the character of Watson essentially as a lovable buffoon. Being caught between desperate attempts at making the material more marketable and a strict adherence to the literary source contractually required by the Conan Doyle estate, however, left the film with nowhere to go. Rushes, presented to and vetoed by the estate, had to be reshot on a regular basis. The script, frequently criticised by the principal director Terence Fisher (who was assigned Frank Winterstein as a pro forma co-director for the purposes of qualifying the project as a bona fide co-production) in personal memos to Brauner as too static and not cinematic enough, underwent numerous revisions, not only by Siodmak but also by a number of uncredited authors, and was still being rewritten during filming, leading to stylistic and narrative inconsistencies.[61] Shot partly in CCC's Berlin studios and partly on location in Ireland (resulting in additional continuity errors), the film's production was riddled with setbacks and disasters.

In West Germany, *Sherlock Holmes und das Halsband des Todes* was released in 1962 and was modestly successful at the box office. One contemporary critic referred to the film without much enthusiasm as 'an amusing detective game, approximating the spirit of Conan Doyle'.[62] In France and Italy, the film disappeared without much notice after a brief and limited release in 1964. In Britain, the film was shelved, undoubtedly due to the lack of confidence distributors had in the film's box-office potential, until, eventually, the company Golden Era picked it up in 1968. Compared with the much more explicit British crime and horror films of the time, *Sherlock Holmes and the Deadly Necklace* must have appeared quaint and antiquated to British audiences. When the film finally came out in a severely cut and dubbed version with a jazzy electronic score (similar to the musical soundtracks used in the Wallace series, and later imitated by Italian horror films), the critical response was disastrous. The *Monthly Film Bulletin* called it 'plodding and colourless' and found the photography 'reminiscent of an early German silent film' (this was indeed a perceptive observation, as the film's cinematographer was Richard Angst, a veteran of Weimar cinema).[63] In his memoirs, Christopher Lee nominated the film as among the greatest disappointments of his career and claimed that the project had been sabotaged by the West German production crew.[lxiv] Wheeler Winston Dixon, author of a critical study of Terence Fisher's life and work, argues that the film is 'one of the very worst productions Fisher was ever associated with, and is impossible to watch for more than a few hundred feet'[65], while a more recent study on Fisher concludes that the film 'feels more like an extended episode of a rather mediocre television series than it does a piece of cinema'.[66]

Apart from documenting a history of misfortunes and bad business decisions, CCC-London's archived business correspondence suggests that Brauner, who remained in overall charge of his subsidiary's activities from Berlin, seriously underestimated the costs the company would need to achieve its aims in Britain as a bona fide British enterprise. It is likely that Brauner saw as the company's main priorities the arrangement of distribution deals for CCC's West German films in the British market; the acquisition of literary rights; the negotiation of employment for actors and personnel under contract with Brauner; and conversely the negotiations with British personnel to be used for West German productions. Brauner's interest in producing 'British' films in Britain, on the other hand, was at best half-hearted. There is also evidence of significant differences in business and production practices between Brauner and his British partners. Gutowski wrote in 1962 to Brauner that Anglo-Amalgamated refused to cooperate further with either CCC or CCC-London, citing outstanding payments and delays in production as its main reasons.[67] In the same letter Gutowski also reported that Hammer studios had been warned off by other, unnamed, British industry insiders from entering into deals with CCC.

Accustomed to a management style that was answerable only to financial backers and distributors, Brauner's dealings with casts and crews and his ad hoc decisions appear to have antagonised British film personnel and unions. Between 1961 and 1963 several complaints were lodged against CCC-London by screenwriters, directors, and other personnel to the Federation of British Filmmakers and the Association of Cinema and Television Technicians (ACTT), leading to the company' being blacklisted by the middle of the decade. Through the case of one of the complainants, the director Seth Holt, CCC-London incurred additional blacklisting from the Writers Guild of America, of which Holt was a member. Holt had signed a contract with CCC-London for two films, the second of which (a project called 'Seven Men at Daybreak') never materialised. Even after CCC-London was virtually defunct, these boycott measures continued to affect Brauner's dealings with American and British business partners.[68]

In 1963, Brauner conceded defeat, and, following acrimonious accusations and counter-accusations, Gutowski resigned. While not abandoning joint ventures with British companies altogether, Brauner increasingly saw the future of the international film not in direct intervention in other film industries, but in projects that were secured either through co-production agreements (which Britain did not properly ratify until the early 1970s) or through the backing of American or other European distributors. Examples of such productions included *Die Hölle von Macao/The Peking Medallion* (1966), an exotic adventure thriller with Hollywood's Robert Stack, Elke Sommer, and Nancy Kwan headlining an international cast. Shot in English on location in Asia and in the CCC studios, the film was co-financed by Brauner with French and Italian partners, but directed and written by British contractees (James Hill and Brian Clemens, respectively).[69] Brauner thus returned to the standard co-production deals with France, Italy, and Spain, following emergent genre trends such as spy thrillers and soft porn. He also continued to pursue more personal projects, such as *Zeugin aus der Hölle* (1965, Witness out of Hell), a film about a former concentration-camp inmate who commits suicide rather than confront her former torturer in court, and the West German-Israeli co-production *Tevye und seine sieben Töchter* (1967/8, Tevye and His Seven Daughters), based on the novel by Sholem Aleichem, later to be turned into the musical *Fiddler on the Roof*.

Following the CCC-London débâcle, Brauner's involvement in British films was primarily as a minority partner, supplying financial support and access to West German distribution. This applies to *Genghis Khan* (1964/5, a co-production between CCC, Irving Allen Enterprises, and the Yugoslav company Avala), the horror film *Frozen Alive* (1964, directed by former cinematographer Bernard Knowles), *The Boy Cried Murder* (1965/6, a mainly British-Yugoslav remake of the Hollywood film *The Window*, 1949), and the Euro-western *Shalako* (1968, directed by Edward Dmytryk and starring Brigitte Bardot, Sean Connery, and Peter van Eyck). CCC-London had no direct involvement in any of these productions, and all contractual negotiations were made directly with Berlin.

After Gutowski's departure, CCC-London meanwhile led a ghostly existence, with a board of caretaking lawyers managing the company's deficits, though some correspondence after 1963 suggests that negotiations about literary rights were still being pursued. There is also the possibility that CCC-London may have helped Brauner in establishing contacts with British distributors and thus getting access to British screens for his West German productions. In the main, however, after 1963 CCC-London appears to have dealt primarily with financial and legal claims by its former business partners, including Gutowski, Raymond Stross, and Henry Lester. In a letter from March 1964, CCC's Berlin head office noted somewhat exasperatedly:

> In May 1961, a sad date for us, CCC-London was founded on the suggestion of Mr Gutowski; and naturally from that date all his actions were to serve the interests of CCC, for which he was given a salary … In return we have received eleven books which we could throw in the dustbin, contracts for which we still have to pay but which weren't fulfilled by the other side, expenses which went into the hundreds of thousands – and on top of all that a bad reputation.[70]

Suggestions by the British board of CCC-London to revitalise the company's production profile in the mid- to late 1960s met with silence from Berlin. In 1970, what were left of CCC-London's assets were finally liquidated or transferred into CCC property. Rosalind Erskine's novel *The Pas-*

sion Flower Hotel, one of CCC-London's literary acquisitions, was finally produced in 1977 by CCC as *Leidenschaftliche Blümchen* (Passionate Flowers), a soft-porn film starring the young Nastassja Kinski. In the meantime, Gutowski, on the other hand, had continued his international operations in Britain. In 1965, he teamed up with Brauner's other nemesis, Henry Lester, to produce a second, partly Swiss-financed Sherlock Holmes film, *Study in Terror*, one of CCC-London's aborted projects.

More famously, however, Gutowski collaborated with another West German-based producer of Polish origins, Sam Waynberg,[71] to launch the British career of Roman Polanski with *Repulsion* (1965) and *Cul-de-sac* (1966). Incidentally, Polanski had been a graduate from the prestigious Lodz film school in Poland, which was run by Aleksander Ford, who had worked with both Gutowski and Brauner. A Polish theme seems to characterise a number of Gutowskis's assignments. During the latter half of the 1960s, Gutowski fostered the career of the exiled director Jerzy Skolimowski, and produced Abraham Polonsky's Polish-set Yugoslav–Franco-Italian–British co-production *Romance of a Horsethief* (1971). In addition to these 'Polish' films, he also worked with director/photographer David Bailey and collaborated on yet another Conan Doyle adaptation, Billy Wilder's *The Private Lives of Sherlock Holmes* (1970).

While the history of CCC-London may appear to be merely a curious footnote in the history of both British and German cinema, it provides some interesting insights into the strategies and ambitions of international film producers in the 1960s. It documents difficulties in coordinating different production practices, conventions, and audience expectations, obstacles that did not help in the already precarious financial situation most European industries faced at the time. In this respect one could dismiss CCC-London's achievements as one among many failed attempts to challenge Hollywood's dominance, particularly within the British market with its traditionally closer ties to the American film industry.

Viewed from another perspective, and taking into account Brauner's and Gutowski's prior and subsequent activities, the history of CCC and CCC-London suggests a different mode of international interaction. It becomes part of a transnational cinema history with a dispersed but close-knit diasporic film community at its mobile centre. This community negotiated national regulations and conventions within an increasingly global film market, operating across Europe and also entering into liaisons with American companies, and encompassing both popular genres and art cinema. Few of CCC's films may be characterised in retrospect as great artistic achievements, although some, such as *Station Six-Sahara*, several of Lang's, Siodmak's, and Reinhardt's films, Brauner's Jewish projects, or Gutowski's later Anglo-Polish endeavours, thematised very interestingly the experience of being rootless or of being an outsider.

This, however, reflected not just the personal backgrounds of a select group of film-makers, but also corresponded to the widespread social, political and cultural mobility in postwar Europe, including Britain. Brauner and Gutowski were not isolated figures in the British film industry of the 1960s. They belonged to a group of globe-trotting producers, which included the Polish-born Sam Spiegel (*Lawrence of Arabia*, 1962), the Romanian Samuel Bronston (producing Hollywood spectacles in Spain with British personnel), the Italian Carlo Ponti (*Operation Crossbow*, 1965, and *Blow Up*, 1966), 'Cubby' Broccoli of the James Bond series, and Harry Alan Towers, whom I shall discuss in more detail in chapter 9. In its own right, CCC-London may have had a limited impact, but within the context of this wider transnational network its history provides a useful reminder of the internationalism in and conjunctions of postwar European cinema.

Notes

1. Claudia Dillmann-Kühn, *Artur Brauner und die CCC. Filmgeschäft, Produktionsalltag, Studiogeschichte 1946–1990*, Frankfurt 1990.
2. Robert R. Shandley, *Rubble Films. German Cinema in the Shadow of the Third Reich*, Philadelphia 2001, p. 91.
3. Dillmann-Kühn, *Artur Brauner und die CCC*, p. 19.
4. Jan-Christopher Horak, *Fluchtpunkt Hollywood. Eine Dokumentation zur Filmemigration nach 1933*; Münster 1986, p. 36.
5. Ibid., p. 37.
6. Cf. Helmut G. Asper and Jan-Christopher Horak, 'Three Smart Guys: How a Few Penniless German émigrés saved Universal Studios', *Film History*, vol. 11, 1999, pp. 134–153.
7. Werner Sudendorf, 'Ich wollte nach Europa, nicht nach Deutschland', *Film-Exil*, no. 3, November 1993, p. 39.
8. Claudia Dillmann, 'Treffpunkt Berlin, Artur Brauners Zusammenarbeit mit Emigranten', *Film-Exil*, no. 3, November 1993, p. 20.
9. Gero von Wilpert, *Lexikon der Weltliteratur, Band I: Autoren*; Stuttgart 1975, p. 675.
10. Dillmann,'Treffpunkt Berlin', p. 21.
11. Anon., 'Abschied von den Wolken' in *Filmdienst*, no. 8616, 1959.
12. Brauner had remade one of Müller's best-known films, *Die Privatsekretärin* (1931) only a few years earlier, in 1953, with Sonja Ziemann in Müller's old role.
13. For further theories and for another fictionalisation of the Müller case, see Katja Wolf's novel, *Ich bin ja heut so glücklich*, Munich 2001.
14. Anon., 'Film: Renate Müller: Liebling der Götter', *Der Spiegel*, no. 13, 30 March 1960.
15. Sabine Hake, *Popular Cinema of the Third Reich*, Austin 2002, p. 218.
16. Dillmann-Kühn, *Artur Brauner und die CCC*, p. 141.
17. The two appeared together in *Saison in Kairo* (1933) and *Walzerkrieg* (1933).
18. Sudendorf, 'Ich wollte nach Europa', p. 42.
19. Anon., 'Lage hoffnungslos – aber nicht ernst', *Filmdienst*, no.13844, 1966.
20. Gottfried Reinhardt, *Der Apfel fiel vom Stamm. Anekdoten und andere Wahrheiten aus meinem Leben*; Munich 1992, pp. 435–439.
21. Sudendorf, 'Ich wollte nach Europa', pp. 39–40.
22. *Aufbruch ins Ungewisse. Band 2: Lexikon, Tributes, Selbstzeugnisse*, ed. Christian Cargnelli and Michael Omasta, Vienna 1993, p. 102.
23. Dillmann, 'Treffpunkt Berlin', p. 19.

24. The story of the man who hires his own killer has retained its fascination for filmmakers long after Neubach's death in 1968. Very close to Neubach's original scenario is Aki Kaurismäki's Finnish-French-British co-production *I Hired a Contract Killer* (1990), while the premise of someone ordering his own murder also plays a part in Warren Beatty's *Bulworth* (1998). Both of these films claim original authorship for what essentially is a very old narrative ploy, and although Kaurismäki's film did engender legal challenges about its originality, no one seemed to remember Neubach's previous rights to the material.

25. Dillmann, 'Treffpunkt Berlin', p. 19.

26. Ibid., p. 20.

27. A British version of this film, *My Song Goes Round the World*, produced for British International Pictures, was released in 1934.

28. Robert Siodmak, *Zwischen Berlin und Hollywood. Erinnerungen eines grossen Filmregisseurs*, ed. Hans C. Blumenberg, Berlin 1980, p. 229.

29. Dillmann-Kühn, *Artur Brauner und die CCC*, pp. 121–130.

30. Karl Prümm, 'Universeller Erzähler. Realist des Unmittelbaren', in *Siodmak Bros. Berlin-Paris-London-Hollywood*, ed. Wolfgang Jacobsen and Hans Helmut Prinzler, Berlin 1998, p. 180.

31. Quoted in Dillmann-Kühn, *Artur Brauner und die CCC*, p. 107.

32. Joe Hembus, *Der deutsche Film kann gar nicht beser sein. Ein Pamphlet von gestern. Eine Abrechnung von heute*, Munich 1981, p. 33.

33. Brigitte Schulze, 'Land des Grauens und der Wunder. Indien im deutschen Kino', in *Triviale Tropen. Exotische Reise- und Abenteuerfilme aus Deutschland 1919–1939*, ed. Jörg Schöning, Munich 1997, pp. 72–83.

34. Edward W. Said, *Orientalism*, London 1978.

35. Ibid., p. 44.

36. Quoted in Hembus, *Der deutsche Film kann gar nicht besser sein*, p. 31.

37. Enno Patalas, 'Der Tiger von Eschnapur/Das Indische Grabmal, 1958/1959', in *Fritz Lang*, ed. Peter W. Jansen and Wolfram Schütte, Munich and Vienna 1976, p. 140.

38. Ibid.

39. Tom Gunning, *The Films of Fritz Lang. Allegories of Vision and Modernity*, London 2000, p. 459.

40. Ibid., p. 392.

41. Ilona Brennicke and Joe Hembus, *Klassiker des deutschen Stummfilms, 1910–1930*; Munich 1983, p. 98.

42. For an edition comprising Jacques' novels and detailed dossiers about the film adaptations, see *Dr Mabuse – Medium des Bösen*, ed. Michael Farin and Günter Scholdt, 3 vols, Hamburg 1994.

43. Siegfried Kracauer, *From Caligari to Hitler*, Princeton 1947, p. 83.

44. Gunning, *The Films of Fritz Lang*, pp. 472–473.

45. Brauner realised this project in 1966; the film was eventually directed by Harald Reinl.

46. Letter CCC-Berlin to Gene Gutowski, London, 15 May 1962; Artur Brauner Archiv, Deutsches Filmmuseum Frankfurt, thereafter ABA.

47. Anon., 'Thema Coproduktionen. Ein Filmkapitel unterschiedlicher Wertschätzung', *Film-Echo*, no. 49, 21 June 1961, p. 689.

48. Anon., 'CCC Films of London in Reciprocal Coin, Distrib Deal with German Co', *Variety*, 12 September 1962, p. 20.

49. Letter CCC-London to Edna Tromans, Shepperton Studios, undated 1961, ABA.

50. Letter Gene Gutowski to Artur Brauner, 23 February 1962, ABA.

51. The business correspondence indicates that several other actresses were approached first, among them Anita Ekberg, Joan Collins, Melina Mercouri, Jean Seberg, and Pier Angeli. After these names had been rejected by Brauner's American contacts, Baker was chosen.

52. Letter CCC Berlin to Transit Filmvertrieb GmbH, 24 February 1960, ABA.

53. Letter Gene Gutowski to Artur Brauner, 11 May 1962, ABA.

54. Anon., 'Station Six Sahara', *Monthly Film Bulletin*, vol. 30, no. 357, October 1963, p. 148.

55. Letter Gene Gutowski to Harry Friedman, 13 April 1962, ABA.
56. Jacobsen and Prinzler, *Siodmak Bros*, pp. 387–394.
57. Letter Artur Brauner to Gene Gutowski, 28 March 1962, ABA.
58. Anon., 'Ein Toter sucht seinen Mörder', *Filmdienst*, no.11473, 1962.
59. Anon., 'Vengeance' *Monthly Film Bulletin*, vol. 30, no. 359, December 1963, p. 174.
60. Letter Henry Lester to Artur Brauner, 16 May 1962, ABA.
61. Letter Henry Lester to Michael Hardwick, 30 May 1962, ABA.
62. Anon., 'Sherlock Holmes und das Halsband des Todes', *Filmdienst*, no.11619, 1962.
63. Anon., 'Sherlock Holmes and the Deadly Necklace', *Monthly Film Bulletin*, vol. 35, no. 410, March 1968, p. 44.
64. Christopher Lee, *Tall, Dark, and Gruesome. An Autobiography*, London 1977, pp. 233–234.
65. Wheeler Winston Dixon, *The Charm of Evil. The Life and Films of Terence Fisher*, New York 1991, pp. 363–364.
66. Peter Hutchings, *Terence Fisher*; Manchester 2001, p. 125.
67. Letter Gene Gutowski to Artur Brauner, 11 June 1962, ABA.
68. Memorandum Peter Hahne (CCC production dept.) to Artur Brauner, 21 July 1970, ABA.
69. The fact that, in Germany, assistant director Frank Winterstein is credited as the film's director is likely to have been motivated by co-production requirements and national quota regulations. Winterstein had been used in a similar way during the filming of *Sherlock Holmes und das Halsband des Todes*. Equally difficult in retrospect to determine is who was responsible for the script. Depending on the source, Clemes and Ladislas Fodor are credited. One can presume though that Clemes wrote the original script and that Fodor wrote the German version.
70. Letter CCC Berlin to Otto Joseph (Gutowski's German solicitor), 26 March 1964, ABA.
71. In the late 1970s, Waynberg had a phenomenal, Europe-wide box-office success with his *Lemon Popsicle* films, a series of teen comedies set in the 1950s (patterned after the international success of George Lucas' *American Graffiti*, 1973), which were shot by a largely Israeli crew and cast in Israel. In Germany, the series was called *Eis am Stiel*.

Chapter 7

IMAGINING ENGLAND: THE WEST GERMAN EDGAR WALLACE SERIES

Artur Brauner's main rival in the 1960s was Horst Wendlandt, and the latter's company Rialto. Wendlandt, son of a Russian father and a German mother, had started out in the 'Third Reich' as an apprentice for Tobis in the late 1930s, and after the Second World War had gradually worked his way up before becoming executive producer for Brauner's CCC in 1956.[1] Wendlandt had gained expertise in almost every conceivable domestic genre and film trend of the 1950s, ranging from musical comedies and *Heimatfilme* to William Dieterle's monumentalist production *Herrin der Welt* (1959). In 1961 Wendlandt moved to Rialto, the company of Danish producer and Constantin co-founder Preben Phillipsen. In the previous two years, Rialto had established its West German reputation with a handful of highly successful Danish-German Edgar Wallace adaptations, to which Wendlandt added in 1962 a second franchise, a series of westerns based on the novels by German adventure author Karl May. In the following decade, Rialto, increasingly under Wendlandt's sole creative direction, became the major success story of the West German film industry, even outperforming his former employer Brauner. Moreover, Wendlandt's economic, generic, and transcultural strategies defined the strategies of the decade as a whole.

The Edgar Wallace series adapted the work of an early twentieth century British crime novelist and reformulated it according to contemporary West German perceptions of Britain. The Karl May films adapted the novels of a German author of the late nineteenth century and represented, for its audiences, a specifically indigenous imagination of the American Wild West. In Britain and America, in contrast, the Karl May series was received according to the parameters of the Hollywood western, while the Edgar Wallace films largely conformed to Anglo-American expectations of a crime-thriller. Both cycles thus could be seen at first glance to relate to 'classical' Hollywood genres, and thus provided West German producers with internationally recognisable formulae. In their historical, geographical, and cultural setting, Rialto's Karl May and Edgar Wallace series were clearly escapist, and more specifically articulated an evasion of the country's present situation and recent past. At the same time, it was precisely the series' strategy of blurring cultural distinctions and historical specificities that made these cultural forms internationally viable. In the following two chapters, I shall place the two series in relation to their literary sources, and will analyse them in the context of contemporary cultural trends and modes of reception.

Edgar Wallace, Crime Fiction and the German Market

The international currency enjoyed by the detective novel is related both to the internationalism of its representation of society, and to an absence of national specificity in the genre's structure and principal themes – an absence that is reflected in the uniformity of the detective novel in different national contexts. There is, however, a national specificity in the detective novel's differing shades and tones, and it is certainly no coincidence that it is the highly civilised Anglo-Saxons who have defined the genre's typology and produced its clearest models.[2]

In the above quote from his 1925 study of the detective novel, Siegfried Kracauer conceives of an international circulation of thematic motifs and genres, which are reinterpreted in different nuances according to specific cultural needs and historical contexts. This suggests a rather different methodology – and a less fixed notion of national cultures – from the one that Kracauer is commonly known for. It was, after all, Kracauer, in his *From Caligari to Hitler* (1947), who saw German cinema as temperamentally incapable of producing a properly native version of the crime genre, aping Anglo-Saxon conventions instead.[3] By now, this is a well-worn verdict frequently levelled at many other European-made popular genres, seen as inferior copies of their Hollywood counterparts and often castigated for eschewing their duty of properly reflecting their national context. As my discussion will show, the German crime film was indeed frequently an extraterritorial genre, centred on a transnational imaginary or fantasy world (very often featuring Britain, or a particular version thereof, as its emblematic location or reference point). Rather than dismissing such fantasies for their stereotypes, their inauthenticity, or their escapism, I propose that these fantasies provide clues as to not only how constructed and constantly shifting any notions of national identity are, but, more specifically, how identity formations are negotiated through an engagement and sometimes identification with an imaginary idea of the foreign. After all, what, if not also a projective fantasy of the foreign, informs Kracauer's comment above about those 'highly civilised Anglo-Saxons'?

Observers of the German Wallace phenomenon have always been puzzled as to why, at a time when American hard-boiled crime fiction (both in its literary and cinematic variants) had become the dominant form of the genre in most other countries, postwar German cinema audiences and readers still remained attached to rather old-fashioned tales about sinister castles, foggy and gas-lit London streets, and incorruptible Scotland Yard inspectors. Elsewhere, the former global best-selling phenomenon Edgar Wallace had been superseded in terms of literary style and imagination by authors such as Raymond Chandler, whose work emphasised social realism and moral ambivalence whereas Wallace's had been sensationalist and committed to an uncomplicated, Manichean, worldview. In literary criticism, Edgar Wallace (1875–1932) has not received much attention either over the years. In surveys of the history of British crime fiction, he is mostly remembered alongside Sax Rohmer as a prolific author of pulp novels in the 1910s and 1920s, interesting for the evolution of the genre only in so far as his novels marked a move away from the intellectual puzzles of Victorian crime fiction towards a blend of traditional conventions and elements of adventure or tough masculine action: 'Wallace was one of the first crime-story writers to break away from the old tradition of the private detective and make his central figure a Scotland Yard official … his own ideal was the detective inspector who catches criminals not because he is intellectually brilliant but because he is part of an all-powerful organisation'.[4]

As far as Wallace's literary value is concerned, the overriding critical opinion follows Colin Watson's damning verdict that 'trying to assess Wallace's work in literary terms would be as pointless as applying sculptural evaluation to gravel'.[5] From an ideological perspective, Wallace already attracted criticism when he was still alive. His staunch and uncompromising endorsement of British colonial rule, including the use of concentration camps in Africa (expanded in his stories *Sanders of the River*, first published in 1911), led one critic to reflect in the 1920s that 'from his days as a war correspondent Wallace has retained an amazing degree of contentment with colonial rule and its methods. And he reserves strong words for sentimental humanitarians who protest against slavery'.[6] In Wallace's later crime thrillers of the 1920s, set in London, critics have identified a strong undercurrent of xenophobia. Jens Peter Becker has argued that 'Wallace and his contemporary Sax Rohmer deserve the dubious merit of having popularised the stereotype of the evil Chinese'.[7] Critics have moreover attested in Wallace's work sentiments of misogyny, homophobia, and contempt for the working class. Writing in the 1940s, George Orwell found Wallace's work to 'exhibit a fearful intellectual sadism' and its support of almost totalitarian police power as 'pure bully-worship'.[8] It is not my intention here to contribute further to a discussion of Wallace's literary merits or the ideological problems his work may pose. Nor do I believe that an investigation of the ideologically problematic aspects of Wallace's fiction, or of his personal political beliefs, ultimately help explain his success with German readers and audiences. Indeed, as I shall argue below, the German reception of Wallace's work always had more to do with democratising and progressive aspirations of his readers than with the potentially reactionary textual features of the novels themselves. A further reason to object against a traditional author-centred approach, or one that aims to determine an original textual meaning with regard to Wallace's work is Wallace's assembly-line writing practice (which often involved substantial rewritings from ghost-writers, secretaries, and editors), as well as the additional processes of adaptation to which his novels were subjected by stage producers and screenwriters.

One feature of Wallace's life and work remains instructive, however, namely how it shaped and intersected with the history of popular culture and media and their consumers in the first half of the twentieth century. One of the reasons why Wallace's work elicited strong reactions and controversies was that (unlike some of his contemporaries who shared both his narrative strategies and his political views) Wallace was an extremely public as well as successful figure. Indeed, Wallace, in his tireless self-promotion and through his diversification into journalism, theatre, cinema, and politics, provides the very prototype of the twentieth century's bestseller author *cum* media celebrity.[9] Wallace's success and popularity in the 1920s reflected the development of international entertainment industries, increasing media intertextuality, and strategies of industrial manufacturing within the sphere of cultural production, and it coincided with similar aspirations of international film industries towards ever-greater vertical and horizontal integration. M.J. Birch, for instance, has pointed out that 'the case of Edgar Wallace provides a perfect example of the transition of authors from relatively free producers in the period before the war to mere author-functions producing a rigidly codified product at high speed'.[10]

Wallace's career began as a war correspondent for the *Daily Mail* during the Boer War.[11] His first major crime novel, *The Four Just Men*, was serialised in 1905, accompanied by a promotion scheme, which promised £500 to the reader who could predict the story's outcome.[12] In the following years Wallace expanded his repertoire to colonial adventure stories, stage plays, and newspaper articles on horseracing. During the First World War Wallace made his first contact with the film industry, writing the screenplay for a propaganda feature, *Nurse and Martyr* (1915), on the life of Nurse Edith Cavell, who had been executed as a spy by the Germans.[13] A year later, the first film based on a Wallace novel reached the screen, *The Man Who Bought London* (1916), followed by several other British adaptations, which were mostly produced by Sir Oswald Stoll.[14]

By 1928 every fourth book sold in Britain was a new or reprinted Wallace title. In America, 250,000 copies of Wallace titles were sold annually. In Germany, where Wallace's success took off in the mid-1920s, the figures were estimated at half a million copies.[15] Part of this success was due to a significant shift in publishing practices, initiated by Wallace's main British publisher, Hodder and Stoughton: 'Until about 1923 all major publishers produced 2 shillings novels for the reprint end of the market in coloured wrappers of increasing sophistication. In 1923, though, Hodder and Stoughton changed the nature of the 2-shilling product. Instead of reprints, Hodder customers could buy cheap copies of new books'.[16] Both Wallace and his publisher gained from this strategy: Wallace expanded his readership and Hodder and Stoughton gradually achieved a top position among British publishers of popular fiction. However, Wallace's contract had another consequence – his literary output became generically much more restrictive. One of Hodder and Stoughton's prime publishing objectives was the drive towards an increasing formularisation of literary genres. Since it saw its top author primarily as a supplier of crime fiction, stories that fell outside this framework were given far less promotion and were sold more cheaply.[17] Wallace books were made easily identifiable through specifically coloured spines and covers, using distinctive fonts and the symbol of a crimson circle (the title of one of Wallace's best-known novels). Wallace accelerated his already impressive writing speed by relying on the modern technology of the Dictaphone and a staff of secretaries and editors. Wallace's stories were recycled several times over, first in serialised form in newspapers, then as published books, and later as stage plays (some of which Wallace also produced and directed) and as sources or screenplays for films. Since 1919 Edgar Wallace adaptations had become regular features of British cinema, and Wallace himself joined the Board of Directors of British Lion in 1927. As Robin Smyth has argued, 'the advertisement was the product, and the trailer carried the film'.[18]

By the late 1920s, Edgar Wallace could best be described as an international media celebrity. Drawing on his experience as a tabloid journalist, Wallace designed promotional slogans for himself ('The King of Thrillers') and for his work ('It is impossible not to be thrilled by Edgar Wallace'), which were used as marketing ploys worldwide to sell his books and films. Newspapers reported on his extravagant lifestyle, his expensive cars, houses, and clothes, the ubiquitous long cigarette-holder, his gambling and horse-racing obsessions, his personal contacts with and insights into the workings of Scotland Yard, and his legendary productivity. After Wallace died of pneumonia in 1932, during a three-month stay in Hollywood to write the screenplay for *King Kong* (1933), his body was returned on the warship *Berengaria* to a large mourners' gathering in Southampton.

In his heyday, Edgar Wallace was often perceived as a quintessentially British phenomenon, and yet a great part of his success, both during his lifetime and even more after his death, depended on his works' distribution in other national markets, including Europe and the United States. During his later years, Wallace recognised the German market as crucial and he considered the German public as more loyal than the British, despite the fact that, during the First World War, he had referred to them in his journalism as 'decadent apes' and 'beasts without courage or brains'.[19] According to Florian Pauer, enthusiastic German fans regularly mobbed Wallace on his visits to Germany.[20] In order to understand Wallace's German success, and particularly its longevity, it is necessary to look more generally at the development of the crime genre in Germany and how Wallace fitted into this context.

Detective novels, in both indigenous and foreign variants, in book form or as dime novels, had been published widely in Germany since the turn of the century. British crime fiction, particularly Sir Arthur Conan Doyle's Sherlock Holmes stories, provided the main model for and influence on the genre, and German crime authors frequently imitated the style of British novels. German cinema had already adopted the crime-film formula in the early 1910s, resulting in serials featuring fictional detective heroes with English names, such as 'Stuart Webbs' or 'Joe Deebs'.[21] Sebastian Hesse and Heide Schlüpmann, among others, have argued that these early detective serials were instrumental not only in establishing a commercially powerful symbiosis between the film industry and mass publishing, but also in providing, through their narratives' enlightened rationality, emancipatory fictional alternatives to the repressive class and gender hierarchies of Wilhelmine society.[22] Kracauer suggested in similar vein that the Germans' 'deep-founded susceptibilities to life abroad enabled them … to enjoy the lovely myth of the English detective'.[23]

An English influence, however, was not only evident in what were commonly perceived as lowbrow cultural forms. Indeed, an iconography of crime, as Maria Tatar has documented, became pervasive after the end of the First World War, cross-fertilising commercial entertainment and the artistic avant-garde.[24] Central to this iconography was the figure of Jack the Ripper. Bertolt Brecht, for example, refashioned the seventeenth century London of John Gay's *Beggar's Opera* into the Victorian underworld of *Die Dreigroschenoper*, which was famously adapted for the screen by G.W. Pabst in 1931, and whose anti-hero Mackie Messer (Mack the Knife) was at least in part modelled on Jack the Ripper folklore. Frank Wedekind's stage tragedy *Erdgeist*, filmed in the Weimar period twice, first under its original title by Leopold Jessner in 1922/23 with Asta Nielsen, then as *Pandora's Box* (1929) by Pabst with Louise Brooks, featured Jack the Ripper as a lethal avenger of male insecurities, a figure, at least in Pabst's version, that seems to suggest a German masculinity torn apart by the social and psychological legacies of the First World War. Jack the Ripper mythology, moreover, provided the template through which the Weimar period's real-life serial killers (for example, Hanover-based Fritz Haarmann,[25] who dismembered and drank the blood of his young male victims, or Peter Kürten from Düsseldorf, who killed over thirty-five women and children) were framed and sensationalised in the tabloid press. This discourse in turn resurfaced in the disturbingly ubiquitous and frequently misogynist representations of mutilation, murder, and sexual aggression in Weimar pictorial art (George Grosz, Otto Dix), as well as in films such as Fritz Lang's *M* (1931), which documented not only the psychopathology of a paedophile killer (given great pathos by Peter Lorre's performance), but also the paranoid public and media response to such individuals.[26]

Compulsive serial criminals can of course be prominently found elsewhere in Weimar cinema, albeit in more fantastical guises: thus films such
as *Das Cabinet des Dr Caligari* (1919, The Cabinet of Dr Caligari), *Nosferatu*
(1921), or *Dr Mabuse der Spieler* (1922, Dr Mabuse the Gambler) can be seen
as both drawing on and subverting the conventions of the detective formula, in that the genre's traditional agents of order are either rendered
unreliable, implicated in the crimes, or turn out to be passive and ineffec-
tual bystanders, giving full rein to the urges and drives of pathological
criminals. One should be careful not to arrive too quickly (as Kracauer
famously did) at neat explanations as to how this diverse array of serial
killers, sex crimes, and subverted narrative formulae reflects a perceived
collective German psychology. Thomas Elsaesser has suggested with
regard to the expressionist classics mentioned above that these texts functioned to some extent as highly self-reflective and almost proto-post-mod-
ernist commentaries on the formulae and conventions they were using,
and should therefore not be seen as an unmediated reflection of Weimar
social realities.[27] Similarly one could argue that the popular detective serials of the 1910s and 1920s invited a pleasurable recognition less of psychological or social motivations than of (often internationally circulating)
generic attractions and familiar visual, performance, and narrative codes
that were often imported wholesale from British literary conventions. That
German audiences were well versed in these codes is evident in the success of numerous crime parodies of the time on stage and in film and book
form, which crucially relied on the audience's generic foreknowledge.
Already in the 1920s, for example, Edgar Wallace's narratives could be
consumed with ironic detachment, as the following contemporary report
about a Wallace stage première indicates: 'At the opening night of Wallace's play *The Man Who Changed His Name* in Berlin, the audience mistak-
enly thought it was a parody, and they laughed throughout. Despite this,
the play had enormous suspense and became a huge hit'.[28]

Largely responsible for Wallace's success in Germany was its German
publisher, the Jewish-owned house of Goldmann, which, alongside Ullstein with its major star author Vicki Baum (*Menschen im Hotel/Grand
Hotel*), had gained major prominence in the German market through promotional strategies similar to those of Hodder and Stoughton in Britain.[29]
Among these measures were the introduction of inexpensive book editions and advertising campaigns in newspapers and magazines, which
were often affiliated with or run by the publishing houses themselves. As
in Britain, the Wallace boom in Germany branched out into theatre and
cinema. Max Reinhardt staged *The Ringer* as *Der Hexer* in Berlin in 1926 –
this was followed by several other stage adaptations of Wallace's work in
German theatres.[30]

Between 1927 and 1934 five German or German co-produced Wallace
adaptations were filmed. The first was *Der grosse Unbekannte* (1927, The
Great Unknown), directed and produced by Manfred Noa, and starring
British actor John Loder in the leading role. Loder's casting indicates that

the film was intended from its very inception to appeal to both German and British audiences. Particularly in the latter market the film was well received and was eventually re-released in 1931 with added soundtrack under the title of the original novel, *The Sinister Man*. Subsequent Wallace adaptations in the early 1930s, too, can best be understood as transnational productions within the wider framework of the 'Film Europe' project of the time. *The Crimson Circle/Der rote Kreis* (1929) was shot in an English and a German-language version by Friedrich Zelnik, made through a production agreement with British International Film Distributors. Again, the film's casting aimed at both national constituencies: the female lead was Latvian-born German star Lya Mara, and the male lead Stewart Rome, who had previously starred in British Lion's Wallace adaptation *The Man Who Changed His Mind* (1928). In 1931 and 1932, respectively, Ondra-Lamac-Film (the company of actress Anny Ondra and director Carl Lamac) produced two Austrian-German co-productions, *Der Zinker* (1931, based on Wallace's *The Squeaker*), starring Lissy Arna and Carl Ludwig Diehl, and *Der Hexer* (1932, based on *The Ringer*), starring Paul Richter (Siegfried in Fritz Lang's Nibelungen epic of 1924) and Maria Solveg. For *Der Zinker*, the screenplay was written by the brothers Egon and Otto Eis and by Rudolf Katscher, who would later change his name in British exile to Rudolph Cartier and become a major producer of postwar British television. Katscher would also write the screenplay for a later West German Wallace film, *Der Rächer* (1960). Egon Eis, meanwhile, became one of the major creative influences on the Wallace films of the West German company Rialto. There are further continuities between Lamac's films of the early 1930s and the later Wallace series of the 1960s. Lamac, Katscher and Eis, for example, developed the narrative balance between suspense and slapstick humour that would become so characteristic of the 1960s films, and which in *Der Zinker* (1931) is centred on comedian Paul Hörbiger, playing the reporter Joshua Harras (a role that would in the 1960s be played by Rialto regular Eddi Arent).[31] Fritz Rasp, meanwhile, playing the villain in both of Lamac's films, reappeared in numerous Wallace films in the 1960s.

The last German Wallace adaptation before the Second World War was Ondra-Lamac's *Der Doppelgänger* (1934, The Double, directed by E.W. Emo). Unlike the previous films, this was no longer a 'straight' crime thriller, but rather a light-hearted farce of mistaken identities and primarily a vehicle for the comedian Theo Lingen, co-starring alongside Georg Alexander as a timid businessman torn between Camilla Horn and Gerda Maurus. There were no more German Wallace adaptations until the late 1950s. By the late 1930s, British Wallace adaptations, in contrast, actively mobilised anti-German sentiments, as they had done before and during the First World War.[32]

There are a number of reasons why the end of the Weimar crime boom in publishing, theatre, and cinema was a direct result of the political take-over by the Nazis. The internationalist ethos of the 'Film Europe' movement of the late 1920s and early 1930s, which at least in part motivated the production of co-produced Wallace films, was one the first casualties of the Nazis' policies of cultural re-nationalisation, alongside the spirit of cosmopolitanism more generally. Most of the personnel involved in the making of the Wallace films of the late 1920s and early 1930s went into exile. Jewish publishing houses, meanwhile, such as Goldmann, found themselves the target of the Nazis' policy of 'Aryanisation'; their management and owners were disowned and had to flee persecution. Alongside theatre and the film industry, publishing came under the control of Nazi ideological directives. Dime novels were banned, possibly because their circulation was difficult to control.[33] While a number of foreign crime novels continued to be published in Germany at least until the late 1930s, the main priority of publishers now rested with promoting a new nationalist literature. Similarly, crime thrillers became an almost insignificant aspect of German film production after 1933 and, where they were made at all, any potentially disturbing social comment was avoided through the format of the crime comedy, for example, in the case of the Wallace adaptation *Der Doppelgänger*, or, more famously, *Der Mann, der Sherlock Holmes war* (1937, The Man Who Was Sherlock Holmes), which tells the story of two impostors impersonating Holmes and Watson. The Nazis' ideological hostility towards crime fiction is well documented. Acknowledging the fact that crime thrillers continued to be read surreptitiously by a large number of Germans, Nazi academic Erich Thier perceived this situation as 'not without danger',[34] since:

> the detective novel is a specific product of a bourgeois society in its capitalist, Western and Anglo-Saxon variant ... Bourgeois societies are, by their very nature, susceptible to crime ... They thus differ from other forms of national communities that are based on power and honour, faith and loyalty, labour and achievement ... The prevalence of the detective novel in Germany is therefore comparable to the invasion of an alien mentality.[35]

Interestingly, Thier offers here a similar argument, albeit from a very different ideological perspective, to Kracauer's 1925 analysis of the genre, namely that the figure of the detective and the emergence of a crime genre more generally are dependent on the social context of a liberal democracy, exemplified primarily by Great Britain. Although the United States equally qualifies as a capitalist Anglo-Saxon society, American generic conventions (e.g. the iconography of the urban gangster, emerging out of the confines of immigrant ghettoes, which Hollywood disseminated in the early 1930s in films such as *Scarface*, 1931, or *Little Caesar*, 1931) appear to have influenced the German understanding of the genre to a lesser extent during this period. Having thus established an explicit connection between Britishness and crime fiction, it is not surprising that one of the few German crime films produced during the war, *Dr. Crippen an Bord* (1942, Dr

Crippen On Board), was conceived as a vehicle for anti-British propaganda. What is clear, however, and what even Thier's study has to admit rather grudgingly is that the appeal of crime fiction was and remained widespread even in totalitarian Germany, despite a shortage of supply during the Nazi years and despite ideological attempts to discredit the genre and to discourage its distribution.

After 1945 the boom in crime fiction (though initially not in crime-film genres) resumed in West Germany, and the number of crime novels in circulation rose rapidly throughout the 1950s.[36] By the mid-1950s, Edgar Wallace had once again become one of the most widely read and distributed novelists in West Germany. Goldmann resumed its pre-war promotional strategies by reissuing Wallace novels in paperback, in its series *Rote Krimis* (Red Crime Thrillers). As in the pre-war period, the books had distinctive scarlet spines and lurid cover illustrations, and Wallace novels often also carried a photograph of the author. The old slogan 'It's impossible not to be thrilled by Edgar Wallace' was revived as well,[37] and Goldmann invested in bookshop window displays and newspaper advertisements. Series such as the *Rote Krimis* helped reintegrate popular literature within a framework of consumer culture, and Goldmann's aggressive and unashamedly populist marketing was chiefly responsible for the renewed crime boom in the 1950s. It attracted not only readers already familiar with Wallace from the 1920s, but also, and perhaps more importantly, a younger generation. As an easily available and inexpensive consumer product, the *Rote Krimis* were not only a sign of increased consumer choice, but more generally they provided confirmation of West Germany's new confidence and worldliness.

Robin Smyth has suggested some of the reasons why Wallace increasingly fell out of favour with postwar British tastes and why he could appeal in particular to non-British readers: 'what is chiefly disappointing on rereading the books is that there is so little authentic London atmosphere ... Perhaps that is one reason why he comes over better in translation where readers are less exacting about such details ... Despite the obvious efforts to be modern his plots are comfortably old-fashioned and Gothic and steeped in wish-fulfilment'.[38] Wallace's nostalgia for the past (from a German perspective, significantly, a pre-Nazi past), his disregard for authenticity, and his eagerly proclaimed modernity certainly fitted existing patterns of cultural production and reception in West Germany. It was precisely the duality of tradition and social progress (seen in contrast to the stagnation of social achievements in Germany) with which German Wallace readers had connected in the 1920s, and which finds an echo in Kracauer's previously noted pronouncements about the Germans' 'deep-founded susceptibilities' for the 'highly civilised Anglo-Saxons'. It was the same susceptibilities that Nazi ideologues worried about and tried to suppress. By the 1950s, however, West Germany was promoting a new sense of a national identity as cosmopolitan (i.e. European), and of the country's normality *vis-à-vis* other nations as a bona fide social democracy. In this context, Wallace came to epitomise the 'classic crime novelist' and the guarantor of essentially nostalgic pleasures. His public persona (circulated through book-cover photographs of the author in a wide-brimmed hat and with a long cigarette holder) was marketed in Germany as embodying qualities of quintessential Englishness. While this notion of Englishness did not carry the same associations of longing for social progress as it had before the war, it still carried aspirational connotations in the sense that English individuality and eccentricity could be seen to provide alternative behavioural models to the conformism of West Germany's postwar reconstruction ethos.

Despite the popularity of 'classic' crime fiction in the 1950s, the West German film industry rarely ventured into this genre until the late 1950s. In the early postwar years, there had been a few attempts to revive the format, including *Mordprozess Dr Jordan* (1949, The Murder Trial of Dr Jordan), *Fünf unter Verdacht* (1949, Five Suspects), *Epilog – Das Geheimnis der Orplid* (1949/50, Epilogue – The Orplid Mystery), or *Der Fall Rabanser* (1950, The Rabanser Case), but these films remained exceptions among indigenous productions increasingly dominated by the *Heimatfilm*. For a return to Weimar's obsession with sex crimes and serial killers one has to look even harder in the cinematic output of the 1950s: both Peter Lorre's *Der Verlorene* (1951, The Lost One) and Robert Siodmak's *Nachts wenn der Teufel kam* (1957, The Devil Strikes At Night) featured serial killers, and indeed reminded contemporary critics of Lang's *M*. This reminder, however, may have proved too uncomfortable, not least because both films suggested analogies between their pathological protagonists and the collectively condoned or perpetrated crimes of the Nazi period. They thus explicitly challenged West Germany's ideology of a political 'zero hour' – of a national reinvention after 1945. While Siodmak's film at least found some critical acclaim, former *M* star Lorre's only directorial effort, a stylish and melancholy film set in a bleak postwar wasteland, was almost completely ignored. The only other serial-killer film of any impact was *Es geschah am hellichten Tag* (1959, It Happened in Broad Daylight), directed by Ladislao Vajda, who, like Siodmak and Lorre, had a personal connection to Weimar's crime-film tradition – Vajda's father had written the screenplay for Pabst's *Die Büchse der Pandora* and *Die 3-Groschenoper*.

The Wallace Films of the 1960s

The lack of indigenous crime films in the 1950s is surprising in view of the fact that foreign crime films were regularly shown on West German screens, and with great success. Under the headline 'Is the German crime film dead?' one newspaper reported that 'a great many foreign crime films have appeared in German cinemas … In the English examples, good old Scotland Yard has made a welcome reappearance. In recent years these foreign films have attracted an increasing number of admirers'.[39] The apparent appeal of 'good old Scotland Yard', the success of crime films on television, and changing cinema audience demographics by the late 1950s made Edgar Wallace and his reassuringly formulaic and 'foreign' interpretation of crime-film conventions an obvious choice for the West German film industry.

In 1959, the Edgar Wallace estate sold the film rights to novels, plays, and stories simultaneously to two companies. The British producers Merton Park acquired the rights to produce adaptations for the anglophone market,[40] while the Danish producer Preben Phillipsen's company Rialto secured a deal to make Wallace films for the German market. Horst Wendlandt, later argued that 'in England, there was not much interest in Wallace. That is why it was not very difficult to get the film rights. In Germany, however, the people were mad about him'.[41] Until 1964, when Merton Park discontinued its Wallace series, the German and British Wallace series ran in parallel, neither proving to be much of a competition to the other in their respective markets. Rank's attempts to distribute the Merton Park products in Germany met with no significant box-office response, and only five of Rialto's thirty-two Wallace films, three of which were Anglo-German co-productions, were released in cinemas in Britain. Contemporary British reviews of the few German Wallace films that were distributed in the U.K. found the films not so much reminiscent of Wallace novels, but more of silent melodrama, and of Weimar expressionism. But even positive reviews were slightly puzzled by the films' topography of Britain, as this comment on *Der rote Kreis* (1959, released in Britain in 1965 as *The Crimson Circle*) indicates, 'the trappings of the involved, murder-crammed plot … are surprisingly enjoyable – as is the spectacle of Fritz Rasp ambling up to a suburban railway booking-office and asking for a ticket to Toulouse, as if it were three stops from Ealing'.[42]

Rialto's first two Wallace films, *Der Frosch mit der Maske/Frøen* (1959, The Masked Frog) and *Der rote Kreis/Den blodrøde cirkel* (1959, The Crimson Circle) were nominally Danish-German co-productions, shot largely in Danish studios with an almost exclusively German cast and crew. After the success of the two films, Phillipsen relocated his production base, first to Hamburg where *Die Bande des Schreckens* (1960, The Terrible People) and *Der grüne Bogenschütze* (1960, The Green Archer) were shot and then to Berlin. Under Wendlandt's management, the Wallace series developed into a highly formalised (and formulaic), cost-effective, and extremely successful mode of production. The average shooting schedule was just over a month, with an average budget of 1.4 million DM. Most of the shooting took place in Berlin studios, such as Spandau and Tempelhof, though the films also used footage of London locations (frequently this footage was reused in other films of the series). The production team remained fairly constant throughout most of the series. Alfred Vohrer, a former dubbing director, alone directed fourteen Wallace films, followed by Harald Reinl with five entries. The majority of the film scripts up to 1963 were penned or co-written, under the pseudonym Trygve Larsen, by Egon Eis, who had spent most of the Nazi years in Mexico.[43] Other frequently employed writers included Hanns Wiedmann, also known as Johannes Kai, and later on in the decade Herbert Reinecker, whose writing career spans forty years, from war films in the 1950s to TV crime series in the 1970s, 1980s, and 1990s. Perhaps even more influential were those technicians assigned to give the series its distinctive visual style. Regular cinematographers included Karl Löb, Ernst W. Kalinke, and Richard Angst – all veterans from Weimar and Nazi cinema – who, between them, defined the series' combination of low-key lighting, wipes, zooms, canted angles, and extreme close-ups, while the production designers Erik Aaes and, later on, Wilhelm Vorwerg and Walter Kutz created the series' disorientating, deceptive, and treacherous locations, from foggy streets to labyrinthine mansions. The musical scores were almost invariably provided by Peter Thomas and Martin Böttcher, who created a musical patchwork of distorted electronic sound effects, orchestral interludes, and nightclub music. Most of the films were shot in black and white until 1965, after which they were made in colour.

Gross returns of the Wallace series at the German box-office averaged at 5 million DM each, with added export revenues (mostly from Austria, France, and Italy) of 500.000 DM per film. Given that the films' production budgets rarely exceeded 2 million DM, the Wallace series' box-office per-

Figure 7.1. Producer Horst Wendlandt (left); director Alfred Vohrer is second from the right. Deutsches Filminstitut (DIF), Frankfurt-on-Main.

formance, both in the indigenous market and through exports, was unusually healthy and stable compared with German film production in general. Many of the Wallace films, particularly in the early and mid-1960s, were among the top-grossing films in Germany, outperforming Hollywood blockbusters such as *The Longest Day* (1962), *Cleopatra* (1962), and even James Bond films, such as *From Russia With Love* (1962).[44]

The Rialto Series and Its Domestic Competitors

Between 1959 and 1972 Rialto produced thirty-two Wallace films, eleven of which were co-productions. During the same period six further Wallace adaptations were produced by Kurt Ulrich (*Der Rächer*, 1960), CCC (*Der Fluch der gelben Schlange*, 1963; *Der Teufel kam aus Akasawa*, 1970), and the British producer Harry Alan Towers, who adapted some of Wallace's African adventures (*Death Drums Along the River/Todestrommeln am grossen Fluss*, 1963; *Coast of Skeltons/Sanders und das Schiff des Todes*, 1964) and one crime thriller (*Circus of Fear/Das Rätsel des silbernen Dreiecks*, 1966). The latter films are discussed in greater detail in chapter 9. In the wake of the Wallace boom, other classic British crime novelists were adapted by German producers as well, among them Victor Gunn, James Hadley Chase, and Francis Durbridge.

Effectively barred from the Wallace franchise through Rialto's exclusive rights to the literary sources, Artur Brauner developed a number of generic formulae which were close enough in style to the Wallace films, yet sufficiently independent not to incur prohibitive court claims of plagiarism or copyright infringement. Following Fritz Lang's Mabuse film of 1959 and despite copyright problems with Norbert Jacques' estate, CCC produced nonetheless five more sequels between 1961 and 1964. Only one of these, however, *Das Testament des Dr Mabuse* (1962, The Testament of Dr Mabuse), a remake of Lang's film from 1932 and directed by Werner Klingler, had any direct relation to Lang's earlier films, let alone Jacques' original creation; instead they were meant to resemble the contemporaneous Wallace cycle.

Harald Reinl's West German-Franco-Italian co-production *Im Stahlnetz des Dr. Mabuse/ F.B.I. contro Dr Mabuse/Le retour du Docteur Mabuse* (1961, In the Steel Net of Dr Mabuse) is typical of CCC's approach to the franchise. It introduced an American FBI agent as the main hero (portrayed by Lex Barker as a James Bond prototype), where all the previous Mabuse films had had an austere and rather unglamorous middle-aged public prosecutor as Mabuse's antagonist. It also transposed the setting from a recognisably German environment to Britain or to unspecified metropolitan locations. As the series progressed, the Mabuse films became increasingly international, featuring actors such as the Israeli Daliah Lavi, Yvonne Fourneaux from France, and Yoko Tani from Japan, as well as Anglo-American supporting actors, such as Leo Genn and Robert Beatty. Where

Norbert Jacques' original narratives and Lang's earlier adaptations had centred on its central villain's personal charisma and demonic genius, CCC's series emphasised fantastic technologies and gadgetry and elements of the supernatural. In the last entry of the series, *Die Todesstrahlen des Dr Mabuse/Les rayons mortels du Docteur Mabuse* (1964, The Death Rays of Dr Mabuse) Mabuse was no longer human, but an entirely supernatural apparition. While the films retained Dr Mabuse as a central character, they deviated more and more from the original sourc, and introduced elements 'borrowed' from other generic formulae or narrative sources. *Die unsichtbaren Krallen des Dr Mabuse* (1962, The Invisible Claws of Dr Mabuse), for example, again directed by Reinl, combined elements of the Mabuse mythology with H.G. Wells' *The Invisible Man*. *Scotland Yard jagt Dr. Mabuse* (1963), on the other hand, was based on a fairly traditional crime novel *The Device*, written by Wallace's son Bryan Edgar Wallace.

Brauner also established talks with the British Wallace franchise holders, Merton Park, and arranged a distribution deal for their films for the West German market, thus circumventing Rialto's exclusive film rights for West Germany.[45] That the Merton Park Wallace series itself aimed not just at national but also at continental markets is evident in their casting, frequently using West German and other European actors, who were suggested and negotiated through Brauner. West German actors who appeared in Merton Park's Wallace series included Erika Remberg, Hans von Borsody, Ivan Desny, and Margit Saad. None of these were admittedly in the premier league of West German film stars (and they were therefore cheaply available to Merton Park), and yet they were familiar enough to be recognised by West German audiences. None the less, at the West German box office the British Wallace films fared badly.

Brauner's strategy to contract Edgar Wallace's son was perhaps the most ingenious in gaining a foothold in the Wallace boom. Brauner secured the film rights of Bryan Edgar Wallace's novels, which were more or less indistinguishable pastiches and imitations of his father's style. Between 1962 and 1972 CCC produced ten Bryan Edgar Wallace films, which were stylistically exact replicas of the 'genuine' Rialto productions, proclaiming the author's name in bold letters on posters, though with the Bryan part in distinctly smaller letters. In *Der Würger von Schloss Blackmoor* (1963, The Strangler of Blackmoor Castle), Bryan Edgar Wallace even appeared in the film's credit sequence, dressed identically to his father. Brauner's productions adapted the iconography of the Rialto series almost slavishly by employing directors such as Harald Reinl and Franz Josef Gottlieb, cinematographers Ernst W. Kalinke and Richard Angst, and Wallace 'stars' such as Karin Dor, Barbara Rütting, and Elisabeth Flickenschildt. They also emulated Rialto's particular blend of comedy and horror, with guest appearances by well-known comedians, such as Chris Howland. Despite a temporary court injunction initiated by Rialto, the deception seems to have worked, as CCC's Wallace variations managed to cash in on the West German Wallace phenomenon.

Marketing and Narrative Differentiation

Given this flood of fairly similar products, marketing and targeted publicity campaigns became crucial. In order to counter the efforts of an increasing competition from other producers, Constantin sold the Rialto films as 'genuine' Wallace films.[46] In order to differentiate his franchise from the increasingly popular crime series on German television, Wendlandt also devised the slogan 'A feature-length Wallace is better than television crime thrillers in instalments'.[47] To avoid further confusions among cinema audiences between 'genuine' Wallace films and their imitations, Wendlandt signed actors such as Joachim Fuchsberger, Heinz Drache, and Karin Dor on exclusive contracts. There were more predictable pre-publicity stunts. During the filming of *Der Hexer* (1965, The Ringer), *Film-Echo/Filmwoche* breathlessly informed its readers that 'not even the people on the set know the outcome of the story ... the last pages of the script have not been released yet, and are kept in a safe until the last day of shooting'.[48] One of the most elaborate and spectacular promotion stunts was a gala première in Munich in 1968, celebrating the twenty-fifth film and simultaneously the last financial success of the series, *Der Hund von Blackwood Castle* (1968, The Hound of Blackwood Castle).[49] At the cinema in the evening, a battalion of extras, dressed up as London 'bobbies', patrolled the entrance. A genuine police inspector from the Metropolitan Police Force was flown in as a special guest and welcomed by a German counterpart and the mayor of Munich. During the gala, Horst Wendlandt received a *Goldene Leinwand* award for the success of his previous Wallace productions, and a ballet company performed a dance on a theme about London's criminal underworld. After the screening, several regular Wallace actors appeared on stage, handcuffed to each other, and the series' most prolific director, Alfred Vohrer, was presented with a live dachshund puppy, named Edgar.

Like the original Wallace novels themselves, Rialto's Wallace films relied on distinctive trademarks for instant recognition by their audiences. After the first few films, by which time the series had settled into a recognisable narrative and stylistic pattern, every film began with a pre-credit sequence (usually presenting an elaborately staged murder) that was interrupted by the off-screen sound of gunshots. Blood-red (even in otherwise black and white films) bullet holes emerged on the screen out of which the letters Edgar Wallace appeared. A metallic off-screen voice with a faintly Anglo-American accent announced 'Hallo, hier spricht Edgar Wallace' (Hello, this is Edgar Wallace), after which the credits began to roll.[50] Edgar Wallace remained a main reference point for the series, even at a time when the films' plots bore only minimal, if any, resemblance to the novels on which they were supposedly based. In-joke references to the Goldmann paperbacks, Wallace as a star author, and even the Rialto series itself and its creators littered the films' narratives, which became increasingly knowing and self-parodic, so much so that for a contemporary viewer the films may appear almost post-modern in their self-reflexivity.

Thus, in *Der grüne Bogenschütze* (1960, The Green Archer) the apparent happy end is interrupted by the sound of gunshots, after which one of the characters explains that a new Wallace film is being shot nearby. In the denouement of *Das indische Tuch* (1963, The Indian Scarf) it transpires that the mystery beneficiary of a large inheritance is 'the greatest man of this century', who turns out to be none other than Edgar Wallace. And in *Der Hexer* (1965, The Ringer) and its sequel *Neues vom Hexer* (1966, Again the Ringer) characters are seen reading the Goldmann paperback of the Wallace novel on which the film is based. Needless to say, the Wallace film posters, trailers, and credits never failed to refer back to the Goldmann series, while later editions of Goldmann's paperback used photographs from the Rialto series on their covers. Both Rialto and Goldmann evidently profited from this symbiotic relationship. In 1959, as previously mentioned, forty of Wallace's novels had been available in translation in West Germany. Ten years later, the number had risen to over a hundred.

Figure 7.2. Klaus Kinski in *Die toten Augen von London* (1962, The Dead Eyes of London). Deutsches Filminstitut (DIF), Frankfurt-on-Main.

While the Wallace series, unlike the detective serials of the 1910s and 1920s, never had one consistent main hero, there were nevertheless a number of continuities. Almost all the crimes depicted in the series had financial motives and were frequently linked to internecine family feuds over inheritance. These feuds were fought out in labyrinthine settings, such as country mansions with hidden doors, mazes, or traps or subterranean hide-outs in London's underworld, all of which could equally have featured as backdrops for the detective serials of the 1910s. Thus, in *Der Hexer* a white-slavery ring uses a submarine to dispose of corpses in the Thames, while the villains in *Die toten Augen von London* (1961, The Dead Eyes of London) operate from the crypt of a derelict church that is connected via labyrinthine networks of tunnels to the London sewers. The British nether world of the German Wallace films was inhabited, respectively, by crude stereotypes of the British working and upper classes (the latter portrayed with their tongues firmly in cheek by a gallery of eminent German stage actors, including Elisabeth Flickenschildt, Charles Regnier, and Wolfgang Kieling). Modernity, on the other hand, was invariably associated with a white-collar middle class, embodied by an efficient, upwardly mobile, and morally unambiguous young Scotland Yard detective (frequently portrayed by either Joachim Fuchsberger or Heinz Drache), who solved the cases, despite regular obstruction from pompous

Figure 7.3. Eddi Arent in a publicity still for *Der Hexer* (1965, The Ringer). Deutsches Filminstitut (DIF), Frankfurt-on-Main.

and senile superiors (mostly portrayed by Siegfried Schürenberg). The hero's sidekick (invariably portrayed by Eddi Arent up to the late 1960s) provided the typical comic touch for the series, making Arent one of the best-loved actors of the series. Female protagonists were divided into three main categories, the innocent 'woman in peril' (usually an heiress), morally dubious 'call-girls', and monstrous matriarchs. The use of such stereotypes is particularly revealing in what it can tell us about German perceptions of Britishness at the time and what the appeal of this imagined Britishness may have been. It displays a great deal of incomprehension of the real dynamics of the British class system, but it also points to a pre-ferred version of Britishness that cherishes its most idiosyncratic, irrever-ent, and non-conformist qualities, exemplified by the films' roll-call of eccentric aristocrats, dotty old ladies, and Dickensian rogues, all of whom represented qualities which stood in sharp contrast to the strait-laced norms and values of the Adenauerian work ethic of the postwar West Ger-man *Wirtschaftswunder*.

In terms of narrative conventions, methodical crime detection played a subordinate, almost irrelevant, part in the Wallace series. The films spe-cialised in convoluted subplots, while the final uncovering of the criminal mastermind seemed to happen by mere coincidence. Many films ended abruptly without providing sufficient explanations or motivations. While the basic narrative set-up of the series rarely changed, differentiation man-ifested itself in increasingly bizarre villains, technological gadgets, and methods of killing. Victims harpooned by killers in diving-suits, drug-ped-dling nuns, and homicidal gorillas (a nod less to Wallace than to Edgar Allan Poe's *The Murders of the Rue Morgue*) were among the more surreal inventions of the series. Perhaps the most iconic presence of the cycle, however, was, in his pre-Herzog incarnation, the actor Klaus Kinski, whose manic portrayals of deranged characters not only provided a sinis-ter counterpart to Arent's clownish antics, but also represented a virtually unique reinvention of Weimar performance style in postwar German cin-ema, an articulation of the otherwise repressed legacy of Peter Lorre's child killer, Conrad Veidt's somnambulist, and Haarmann's real-life vam-pire. As if to underline its referentiality to and reverence for the Weimar period, the Wallace films also frequently featured veteran stars such as Lil Dagover, playing the title character in *Die seltsame Gräfin* (1961, The Strange Countess), Fritz Rasp, and Rudolf Forster, the Mackie Messer of Pabst's *Die 3-Groschenoper*.

Wallace Co-Productions

While Rialto produced the core of the Wallace series in Berlin, there were a number of co-productions, which sometimes deviated from the formula established in the series as a whole. Fairly indistinguishable from the 'purely' German Wallace films were those that Rialto realised with French cooperation, such as *Die Tür mit den sieben Schlössern* (1962, The Door with Seven Locks), *Der Zinker* (1963, The Squeaker), and *Zimmer 13* (1963, Room 13). French involvement in these cases appears to have been limited to financial aid in return for distribution rights, while Rialto's incentive for such cooperations was to get access to French subsidy money. In co-productions with Britain and Italy, however, the Wallace series underwent sometimes significant stylistic and narrative transformations.

The first Anglo-German Wallace venture in the 1960s was *Das Geheimnis der gelben Narzissen/The Devil's Daffodil* (1961), directed by Akos von Rathony and co-produced by Rialto and the British companies Omnia Pictures (Steven Pallos) and Donald Taylor. Unlike the majority of Rialto's Wallace productions, the film was shot in London with a predominantly British crew and it was written by a British screenwriter, Basil Dawson. As in the heyday of pan-European co-productions in the early sound period, the film was shot simultaneously in two language versions, tailored to their respective markets.[51] The German version had a typical German Wallace cast that included Joachim Fuchsberger as the hero and Klaus Kinski as a villain. The cast also featured Christopher Lee (a fluent speaker of German) as a Chinese detective and Albert Lieven, a German émigré actor who had established himself in British cinema from the late 1930s but who managed to balance a bi-national career after the war. In the British version Fuchsberger, Kinski, and the female lead Sabine Sesselmann were replaced by, respectively, William Lucas, Colin Jeavons, and Penelope Horner, while Lee and Lieven appeared in both versions. The basic plot of the film, which included a serial killer leaving daffodils at the scene of the crime, intricate conspiracies, and kinky Soho nightclubs, was fairly similar to that of previous German Wallace films produced by Rialto. In contrast to the German Wallaces, however, the film provided little comic relief, and it also lacked other 'typical' trademarks, such as the quirky musical soundtrack (Keith Papworth's score provided mainly routine background music). *The Devil's Daffodil* used a great amount of real London locations and Desmond Dickinson's style of cinematography was more realistic and less effects-oriented and expressionistic than the camera-work of his German counterparts Löb or Kalinke. This difference in aesthetic approach has not helped the film's evaluation among German critics, which has ranged from indifference to outright rejection: 'Production design, direction, music, everything in this film is simply third-rate. The daffodil killer, disguised simply by a balaclava, is so awkwardly introduced and so unimaginatively presented that one rarely becomes interested in his identity'.[52] Unfortunately, *The Devil's Daffodil* fared little better in Britain. While German critics mainly complained about the film's lack of visual imagination, however, British criticism centred more on the narrative's lack of plausibility, labelling it a 'preposterous and involved shocker with a plot that goes back to *The Clutching Hand*'.[53]

Like *Das Geheimnis der gelben Narzissen* (1961), *Das Verrätertor/Traitor's Gate* (1964) was released in two language versions and registered as German and British films in their respective markets. The production was initiated and largely financed by Rialto, but a nominal British partner, Summit Films, ensured that the film was eligible for British quota regulations. Freddie Francis, who had gained his reputation as a cinematographer and as a director of Hammer horror films, was the film's director.[54] The crew was predominantly British, with the notable exception of composer Martin Böttcher who provided a 'typical' German Wallace score. In terms of visual style and in narrative construction, however, *Das Verrätertor* was even further removed from the standard German Wallace productions than *Das Geheimnis der gelben Narzissen*. The film's plot centred on an elaborate plan to steal the crown jewels from the Tower of London by replacing one of the guardsmen with a double. Instead of the quirky blend of horror, comedy, and expressionist flamboyance the German Wallace films by that time were known for, *Traitor's Gate* was more of a 'heist film' in the tradition of Jules Dassin's *Du Rififi chez les hommes* (1956) or Basil Dearden's *The League of Gentlemen* (1960). Unlike in the German Wallace films, the criminal mastermind (played by Albert Lieven) was known to the audience from the beginning, and the narrative charted the methodical and professional preparation and execution of the plot. As a concession to Rialto's house style, the film gave Eddi Arent and Klaus Kinski their usual roles of clown and madman, respectively, but their characters fit in uneasily with the rest of the protagonists. Furthermore, unlike in the German Wallaces, the film had no central detective hero, as the film ends with the criminals betraying and killing each other. The narrative's semi-documentary tone and pacing has its visual equivalent in the film's rather muted, although certainly not un-atmospheric, *mise en scène*. Production design and visual style more generally in *Das Verrätertor* are resolutely realist, emphasised by Denys Coop's predominantly outdoor photography, which also includes some spectacular aerial shots from a helicopter. Instead of a Gothic and foggy East End, the film is mostly based in the bright and modern surroundings of London's City district, and the glittering world of Soho by night. Of all the Wallace films *Das Verrätertor* comes closest to conveying a relatively 'authentic' contemporary impression of London. This is perhaps not surprising, as both Denys Coop and Freddie Francis had significantly contributed as cinematographers to the visual aesthetics of the British new wave.

Like *Das Geheimnis der gelben Narzissen*, *Das Verrätertor* elicited quite different reactions in West Germany and Britain. The *Monthly Film Bulletin* rated it as a 'lively thriller, presented with speed and panache' and argued that, 'despite a little modernisation, the intricate, yet crystal-clear, plot remains characteristic of Edgar Wallace's thriller writing at its best'.[55] Florian Pauer has summed up the prevalent German view by describing it as 'the most boring and uninspired of all the Rialto productions' and by arguing that the British production team 'clearly had no understanding of how to dramatise an Edgar Wallace thriller'.[56] What this comment indicates is how far the notion of an 'Edgar Wallace thriller' had become conflated in a German perception with the specific iconography of the Rialto series.

Rialto's last Anglo-German Wallace venture was *The Trygon Factor/Das Geheimnis der weissen Nonne* (1966), with a budget of 4 million DM the most expensive entry of the series. The film was shot at Shepperton studios by a British crew, again in two language versions with minimally different casts,[57] and directed by the British Cyril Frankel. *The Trygon Factor* had a convoluted plot reminiscent of earlier German Wallaces, which included an order of criminal nuns, a Gothic mansion inhabited by an insane aristocratic family, and characters being killed with poison gas, or drowned in molten gold. Apart from its convoluted plot, however, the film had very little in common with the established Rialto style, and even Eddi Arent, in his last Wallace film, was cast against type as a cold-blooded cat burglar. Stewart Granger, by this time popular with German audiences through his appearances in German westerns, starred as a Scotland Yard detective, supported by British character actors, such as Susan Hampshire, Cathleen Nesbitt, Terry-Thomas, and Robert Morley. Significantly, only in Germany was *The Trygon Factor* marketed as a Wallace film, and the promotional poster featured a sinister nun against a red backdrop. In fact, the story was not based on any identifiable Wallace source, and the German credits more cautiously phrased it as being 'inspired by Edgar Wallace'. The British promotional material, on the other hand, highlighted the film's action elements, as poster illustrations featured fist fights and speed boats, but avoided any Gothic imagery, and there was no mention whatsoever of Wallace. Despite these attempts to tailor the film to their respective markets, *The Trygon Factor* flopped both in West Germany and in Britain. The film's liberal use of gas as a murder weapon caused particular irritation among West German critics, who found this, in the wake of the Holocaust, 'the height of bad taste, and inappropriate for an entertainment film'.[58] Despite negative critical responses and a less enthusiastic feedback for the Anglo-German Wallace films, however, this mode of production none the less proved profitable:

> Wendlandt's productions in Britain save him money, as he gets back 49 per cent of his investment through British tax relief. It is simply not worth it to produce a film in Germany with an international cast and crew, which could at best earn export revenues of $20,000. If, however, he films the same script with the same crew in London, he may end up with $250,000.[59]

Despite their critical – if not necessarily, as above quote outlines, financial – failure, Rialto's three Anglo-German Wallace productions highlight different production practices in the two countries at the time and reveal significant differences in national expectations and aesthetic preferences. The dominant aesthetic paradigm for British cinema in the early 1960s was realism, exemplified perhaps most prominently by the films of new wave directors such as Lindsay Anderson, Karel Reisz, and Tony Richardson.

However, as Peter Hutchings has argued, even the popular British cinema of the time – e.g. Hammer's horror films, or Merton Park's own Edgar Wallace films – often has a restrained quality in terms of narration, and with respect of visual and performance style. At the same time, British cinema of the early 1960s, for example in the James Bond series, can also convey a heightened sense of realism in the depiction of violence, sexuality, and class, which sets this kind of cinema apart from the nestled narratives and the visual and performative flamboyance of contemporary popular German productions.[60] The difference in critical reception of the three Wallace films thus indicates different national preferences. For British critics, the typical German Wallace style is at best amusingly anachronistic and old-fashioned, at worst convoluted and over the top. Conversely, it is precisely the elements of realism, modernisation and streamlined, tight narratives which British critics welcome that become the source of disappointment and rejection for German Wallace fans.

A different cross-cultural dynamic was at work in those Wallace films Rialto co-produced with Italian partners. By the late 1960s, the cycle showed signs of exhaustion domestically. While still relatively profitable (mainly due to a remaining loyal core audience), Wallace films after 1966 were no longer in the league of top-grossing indigenous productions. Cinema attendance in general had gone down, and the competition from both indigenous and imported television crime series had increased. Regular Wallace actors, such as Joachim Fuchsberger, Heinz Drache, Eddi Arent, Siegfried Schürenberg, and Klaus Kinski, who had clearly assigned narrative functions in the cycle and provided an important recognition value for audiences, had left the series. Moreover, after *The Trygon Factor*, few films in the cycle were explicitly based any more on Wallace novels, taking away the tie-in relationship with the Goldmann paperbacks on which the Rialto series had thrived. The only foreign market in which the Wallace films still exported reasonably well and where they had done so since the early 1960s was Italy. This inevitably led the Wallace series to phase out with Italian co-productions by the end of the decade.

The Italian film industry in the early 1960s had also reacted to the widespread popularity of crime novels at home by creating a new cinematic genre, the '*giallo*', named after a crime-novel series of the 1950s and 1960s with distinctive yellow covers.[61] Like the Wallace films, the *giallos* directed by Mario Bava, Umberto Lenzi, or Massimo Dallamano had deliriously convoluted plots featuring masked killers and elaborately staged murders, and an excessive visual aesthetics, characterised by a highly mannered cinematographic style and flamboyant *mise en scène*. Unlike the Wallace films, their depiction of violence was quite graphic. They were also fairly sexually explicit where the Wallace films had been comparatively prudish, and they lacked the comic distractions that were such an integral element of the Wallace films' appeal. Finally, the *giallo* was mostly set in a contemporary Italian context, instead of a Gothic London.

Rialto's first Italian co-produced Wallace film, *Das Gesicht im Dunkeln/A doppia faccia* (1969) was shot in Rome and co-financed by an American distributor who later released it in the United States under the title *Puzzle of Horror*.[62] The resulting film is clearly modelled more on the conventions of the Italian *giallo* than on Rialto's previous productions, despite the presence of Klaus Kinski in the unusual role of the film's hero. The international cast also included Sydney Chaplin, Christiane Krüger, and Margaret Lee. Similar to other Italian *giallos* of the time the narrative included a mysterious stalker, highly stylised sadistic murder scenes, characters plagued by premonitions and amnesia, disorientating flashbacks, and a gratuitous amount of sex and nudity. Although the film is allegedly based on the Wallace novel *The Face in the Night*, the narrative bears little resemblance to this source. In West Germany the film carried the promotional slogan 'a psycho-thriller of international dimensions', without capitalising much on the supposed Wallace connection.[63] Wendlandt, and the marketing team at Constantin, clearly intended the film to cater both to loyal Wallace fans, and to new and possibly younger audiences, but in the end failed to attract either constituency. The trade paper *Film-Echo/Filmwoche*, traditionally rather generous in its reviews, noted with some trepidation that the film was 'a Wallace thriller without the comic elements, so well-liked by the German fans of the genre', and criticised the film's 'careless dubbing'.[64] Florian Pauer later argued that *Das Gesicht im Dunkeln* 'irrevocably ruined the established Wallace style'.[65] Wendlandt's other two Italo-German Wallaces, *Cosa avete fatto a Solange?/Das Geheimnis der grünen Stecknadel* (1972)[66] and *Das Rätsel des silbernen Halbmonds/Sette orchidee macchiate di rosso* (1972), were successful in Italy but fared little better than *Das Gesicht im Dunkeln* at the German box office. The West German response to *Das Rätsel des silbernen Halbmonds* was particularly devastating. The Berlin newspaper *Tagesspiegel* argued that 'the comforting conventionality of the German Wallace films is missing in this German-Italian co-production. The spaghetti western and the sex film have left their traces and have created a terrible combination of horror, porn and tabloid kitsch',[67] while the review in the Munich paper *Abendzeitung* read more like a prescient obituary of the Wallace series:

> Already when the Edgar Wallace films turned to colour, this most popular film series of the 1960s lost much of its atmosphere. Now Horst Wendlandt has done away with looming shadows, the murky waters of the Thames, and with the London fog. In this German-Italian co-production the murder mystery is set in sunny Rome. But this shade-loving genre is not well suited to a different climate. One has to believe in Edgar Wallace's old-fashioned horror fairy-tales, otherwise one destroys them.[68]

Unlike the Anglo-German Wallace films, which had attempted to combine the realism of British productions with the more expressionist Wallace house style and which had largely failed in both of their target markets, the Italo-German Wallace films managed to be successful, albeit only in Italy, by abandoning the established German Wallace style altogether, and by becoming indistinguishable from the already pre-existing Italian *giallos*. As with Rialto's Wallace films, CCC realised its later Bryan Edgar Wallace films as Italian co-productions. Two of these co-productions, *L'uccello dalle piume di cristallo/Das Geheimnis der schwarzen Handschuhe* (1969, The Bird with the Crystal Plumage) and *Il gatto a nove code/Die neunschwänzige Katze* (1971, The Cat- o-Nine Tails) were among the early directorial efforts of the Italian horror director Dario Argento, though later discussions of these films have rarely acknowledged their origins in Brauner's CCC series, or even Bryan Edgar Wallace as the literary source.

Unlike the earlier Anglo-German ventures that had mostly originated with Wendlandt, Rialto had very little actual involvement in the later Italo-German Wallace films, which were, apart from the participation of a number of German actors, largely Italian productions. *Das Rätsel des silbernen Halbmonds* was the last Rialto Wallace film released in cinemas in West Germany, after which the series' back catalogue was sold off to television. There, the series appears to have found its permanent home, since the Rialto films are nearly constantly repeated on various channels. As a result, several generations have grown up since the demise of the original series with memories of the cycle on television. As Malte Hagener has pointed out, even today the German film industry holds up the Wallace cycle of the 1960s as a model producers should emulate.[69] As recently as the mid-1990s, the German TV station RTL commissioned and transmitted a new series of Wallace adaptations. As in the 1960s, the new series was produced by Wendlandt's Rialto, this time shot exclusively on London locations and starring British guest actors, such as Leslie Phillips.

Reading the Wallace Cycle

In critical writing on the genre, the predominant strategy to explain the German Wallace phenomenon has been the recourse to postwar Germany's political landscape and its textual manifestations in the films themselves. Jack Edmund Nolan, one of the first anglophone critics to take note of the Wallace film series in 1963, commented that 'the Wallace films evidently displace the tensions in a country which has only a wall between it and the People's police'.[70] Nolan saw the Wallace films as promoting 'the socially dangerous idea that successful enterprises are conducted by likeable master criminals who can be stopped only by other criminals. And running through them is a faint tone of Anti-Americanism and a heavier rumble of anti-British feeling'.[71] While Nolan does not expand on what exactly constitutes anti-Americanism and anti-British feelings in the Wallace films, his Kracauer-inspired link between narrative patterns and national history has nevertheless stuck. Robin Smyth, writing on the German Wallace phenomenon in the *Observer* in 1982, equally concluded: 'Why has Germany kept the Edgar Wallace flame alive? Probably because Germany is, as it ever-more insistently proclaims, an Angst-ridden society'.[72]

Other critics have offered different analogies between the Wallace films and their perceived national and social context. Norbert Grob has inter-preted the films as expressing the conservative political consensus of the early to mid-1960s, an evaluation shared by other German film critics.[73] In Grob's reading, which is diametrically opposed to Nolan's perception of 'likeable master criminals', the violence with which the forces of law and order in the Wallace films dispatch their criminal adversaries anticipates and mirrors the repressive actions by the state authorities against non-conformist elements in German society by the end of the decade.

What is problematic in the interpretative approaches above is the way in which narrative (defined almost exclusively in terms of plot and char-acter development) is prioritised over the genre's visual characteristics, its *mise en scène*, the formal traditions it draws on, and its actual mode of cir-culation and reception. Tassilo Schneider has rightly suggested that 'the key to an understanding of the popular German cinema after World War II is not to be found in sociological content analysis'.[75] For Schneider, pop-ular genres such as the Wallace series provided 'imaginary solutions to ideological contradictions',[75] and he argues that 'the moving in and out of popularity of particular genres, and the displacement of one genre by oth-ers at particular points in history, can give access to changes in the terms through which audiences related to and understood the social relations and positions that structured the environment in which they found them-selves'.[76]

Unlike Nolan, Smyth, and Grob, Schneider sees the Wallace films as the cultural product of a society precisely characterised not by consensus or homogeneity, but instead by social tensions and conflicting ideological discourses. Like Nolan, Smyth, and Grob, however, Schneider locates the interaction between the genre and its social context primarily at the level of plot and character development. Thus, the series' 'ruthless speculators, power- and money-hungry entrepreneurs, and corrupt officials' represent the conflict in 1960s German society between a new economic élite and a disenfranchised underclass, while the cycle's 'sexually aggressive, revengeful and greedy female protagonists' are seen to reflect fraught gen-der relations and, more specifically, German women's uncertain position in the 1960s between 'liberation and instrumentalisation'.[77] In such char-acterisations, the Wallace films enact 'a concerted return of the repressed',[78] resulting in 'violent but helpless expressions of paranoia'.[79]

Schneider's methodology here is heavily informed by Anglo-American genre criticism, which has traditionally focused on Hollywood genres and their dominant narrational paradigms, and his analysis is couched in an explicit comparison between the Wallace series and American *film noir*. In terms of the Wallace films' *mise en scène* and cinematography, one can cer-tainly identify continuities not just from *film noir* but perhaps more directly from Weimar cinema. The well-known devices of chiaroscuro lighting, angled compositions, emblematic sets, and stylised performances are all frequently employed in the Wallace films (which may be due, at least in part, to a continuity of studio personnel and production practices from the late 1920s to the 1960s). Perhaps more questionable, however, are the reading strategies Schneider imports from *film noir* criticism in reading the Wallace films' narrative patterns and characters, and how such patterns relate to social formations of the time. David Bordwell has argued that despite its distinctive stylistic and narrative characteristics, *film noir* can still be seen to conform overall to the principles of a classical narrative cinema, based on the notion of character-centred causality: 'formally and technically these noir films remained codified: a minority practice, but a unified one. These films blend causal unity with a new realistic and generic motivation, and the result no more subverts the classical film than crime fiction undercuts the orthodox novel'.[80]

If one accepts Bordwell's premise that *film noir* remains essentially a form indebted to the principles of narrative coherence, causality, and psychological verisimilitude and that these principles equally delineate the genre's critical assessment, then the problem with the Wallace films is that they seem to eschew the normative parameters of such a 'narrative cinema'. In this respect, a reading of the Wallace films as texts of social paranoia, as is proposed with differing emphases by the aforementioned critics and film historians, only works after exercising some fundamental omissions. What is striking about most of the above readings, for example, is the deliberate downplaying of the series' endemically self-reflexive, parodic, or comic elements and characters, which were frequently foregrounded in contemporary German reviews. Similarly, the films' shamelessly blatant product placements of the Goldmann paperbacks and the series' constant self-referentiality hardly lend support to interpretations, which render the films' textual and ideological operations much more coherent than they appear on screen. Thus, reflectionist approaches often succumb to the fallacy that Thomas Elsaesser identified in Kracauer's analysis of Weimar cinema in *From Caligari to Hitler*: 'it is only with considerable violence that the visual and narrative organization of the films he discusses can be made to submit to his reading which is actually derived from an altogether paradigm: that of the classical narrative film'.[81]

Commenting on the films' eclectic blend of horror, crime, comedy, and advertising, German critic Joe Hembus once quipped that the Wallace series 'presented itself with a certain self-ironic pride as if it had succeeded in growing bananas in a Prussian allotment'.[82] This analogy sums up neatly the incongruity of the series' aesthetic and narrational strategies. Like *film noir*, the Wallace films feature narratives that bordered on incomprehensibility, but, unlike *film noir*, this incomprehensibility is not motivated by protagonists' social or psychological disempowerment. Unlike *film noir*, with its fatalism, its relentless narrative drive towards a predetermined ending, and its consistently pessimistic outlook, the Wallace films are the cinematic equivalent of a 'House of Horrors' theme-park ride. In this respect, then, the Wallace films very much remind one of a silent 'cinema of attractions'.[83] More specifically, and this may ultimately be both a historically and culturally more fitting comparison than a reference to *film noir*, the Wallace series conforms to and replays early German cinema's 'sensationalist' detective serials, where generic conventions and character stereotypes were blatantly foregrounded, with only minimal investment in psychological realism or cause-and-effect chains to drive the narratives; instead a much higher priority is given to a spectacular aesthetics of amazement, fairground magic, and technological gadgetry.

In the Wallace series, technology nearly always functions narratively as a tool for misdirecting perception – of the audience as well as of the characters in the films themselves. A good example is the opening of *Neues vom Hexer*, which, while preposterously complex in its narrative set-up, remains an extraordinarily choreographed cinematic *tour de force*, which, at least in part, is expected to be enjoyed at the level of continuous amazement. The scene begins with a close-up of a pair of hands playing a harmonious tune on a harp – as the camera zooms out, the player turns out to be a menacingly staring Klaus Kinski, who appears to be a manservant in an upper-class household. A 180-degree pan across a lushly over-furnished room presents four other characters – two middle-aged women and a young man playing cards at a table, and a boy, playing with his toys on the floor, who seems to be watched over by both the butler, and one of the two women at the table. After having finished playing the harp, the butler is about to leave the room to get more tea when the grandfather's clock chimes 10.30. The sound of the clock is deliberately exaggerated, reverberating, and making Kinski turn and stare at the clock. Having left the room, the butler then proceeds swiftly through another door into what appears to be a subterranean room, where an elderly man in a wheelchair is shooting a gun at a target. This target is connected to the other end of the room by parallel tracks on which the wheelchair can supposedly be moved. Meanwhile, in the lounge, the young man excuses himself, followed by the ominous comment by one of the women that "it shouldn't take too long". The young man turns and smiles, then leaves the room and goes to the cellar where he shoots the old man. The butler, an accomplice to the crime, pulls a lever which opens up a secret passageway behind the shooting target. As disharmonious, echoing music wells up on the soundtrack, the wheelchair with the dead man is pushed forwards, and as it hits a pair of sliding doors, an abrupt cut brings us back to the lounge and to a close-up of two mechanical toy monkeys applauding. While the killer returns to the lounge, the butler has brought the wheelchair-bound corpse via an internal lift to an upstairs room, and there activates a tape recorder, hidden in a secret drawer, which will play the sound of a death yell once the butler has come down again to join the others.

What this brief description conveys is that the scene presents the execution of a ludicrously complicated murder plot, predicated on a perfectly coordinated manipulation of time, space, and technology. That the scene is not meant to be read as a realistic representation of narrative facts is perhaps best illustrated by the narratively gratuitous insert of the two applauding mechanic monkeys, which can only be read as a self-reflexive gesture. Instead the perfect timing of the murder shown in the sequence is replicated by the cinematic rendering of the act, making use of the same elements of deception and disorientation the killers are reliant on for their crime to succeed. Thus, the scene is densely compacting a number of different camera angles and sound effects, rapidly changing points of view, and different modes of lighting through imaginative editing. The scene also productively uses narrative ellipsis (the audience is left completely in the dark throughout about the relations between the characters, and more significantly, about the wider topography of the space where the scene is set). Atmospheric effectiveness resides moreover in the enigmatic performances of the actors, frequently deliberately undermining principles of psychological verisimilitude (e.g., the friendly young man turns out to be killer, whereas the butler changes from artistic activity – his musical performance – and subservient attitude towards callous criminality).

Sabine Hake has recently argued that the performative and representational excess and the ironic self-awareness in the Edgar Wallace films have contributed to their enduring status as (postmodern) cult movies'.[84] While this may explain the enduring success of the series into the twenty-first century, it does not fully account for the initial reason for the series' emergence, a reason, which extends beyond the purely economic motivations that I have outlined previously. For German audiences in the 1960s, I would suggest the Wallace series articulated a very particular fantasy about England and London, a fantasy grounded both in established generic expectations (which in some cases reach back to, as I have argued, as early as the 1910s), and in the interrelationship with other forms of cultural consumption. The Wallace cycle envisaged Britain as a site of escape, distraction, and adventure – to the point where location and settings became one of the series' main attractions, and may have accounted for more meaning than the superficial machinations of the cycle's increasingly absurd narratives. The Wallace films constructed a topography of Britain, and more specifically of London, which fragmented urban space into distinct units, such as a Gothic underworld, and famous tourist landmarks (Big Ben, the Tower, Tower Bridge), as well as more contemporary and seedy attractions (such as Soho strip clubs, which, like many other ingredients of the German Wallace cycle, do not feature in the original novels). Very often it was Eddi Arent's comic characters who in seemingly gratuitous narrative subplots explored London's 'real' tourist attractions. In *Das Gasthaus an der Themse* (1962, The Inn on the Thames) Arent frantically trains for and vainly tries to join the annual Oxford and Cambridge boat race, his attempts thwarted not least by the fact that his training locations become crime scenes. In *Das Verrätertor/Traitor's Gate* (1964) Arent is a camera-happy German tourist with language problems, who, while searching for a museum, is directed instead to a strip club, where he stumbles into a murder scene. In *Neues vom Hexer* (1965), he is a tourist from Australia, a travel guide always in hand.

Arent's eccentric mass cultural *flânerie* finds its aural equivalent in the films' psychedelic soundtracks, liberally plundering any conceivable international musical style, from weirdly overdubbed mambos to rock 'n' roll and Stockhausen. In this respect, the Wallace cycle creates visual and aural hierarchies and dichotomies between a 'hip' and attractively modern metropolis ('swinging London') and a dark British netherworld that is locked in a distant past, exemplified alternatively by a Jack the Ripper East End or by Gothic mansions of the 'haunted-house' variety. However, as my analysis of the opening scene from *Neues vom Hexer* suggested, even Gothic country mansions are intrinsically tied up with, and defined by modern technology. In *Neues vom Hexer*, the house literally becomes a deadly theme park ride – the old façade nothing more than a superficial deception to hide the technology that keeps the illusion running. How much this particular topography solidified for audiences into a distinctive imaginary space can be gauged from the fact that the very few films in the series that were actually shot on real locations in Britain were perversely rejected by West German audiences for their 'inauthenticity', i.e., for their deviation from the genre's established visual codes and (largely fake) settings.

The cultural imagination shared by the films and their audiences appears to have been characterised simultaneously by an obsession with a more distant past and by forward-looking aspirations, a strange form of progressive nostalgia that bracketed the white spot of an absent present and recent past. I would argue that this skewed temporality might well explain the phenomenal success of these cultural forms. The Wallace series was able to provide distractive pleasures at least in part because its historical and cultural reference point was a period untainted by German national guilt and, more generally, by memories of the Second World War. Twenty years after the German bombing of London and the subsequent destruction of German cities by the RAF, the Wallace cycle promoted not so much, as Nolan assumed, anti-British feelings than a new, if rather forced, normality in international relations, which drew equally on pre-war cultural interactions and on the changing socio-political landscape of postwar Europe. The simultaneously modern and quaintly old-fashioned Britain the Wallace cycle portrayed was reassuringly a place in which the Second World War had never happened. As the failure of crime films with a more recognisably German setting in this period suggests, it was the imaginary as well as codified space of the Wallace films that provided its audiences a temporary and pleasurable escape from the constrictions of a troublesome and often repressed national identity through the processes of impersonating and identifying with a largely fictitious cultural other. The series' eagerly proclaimed cosmopolitanism and its fantasy Britain created in German studios inhabited by German actors masquerading as British characters transformed national identity into a generically coded commodity. In other words, the Wallace cycle disavowed its contemporary national context, and yet reified it within the parameters of an internationally proliferating consumer culture.

That the pleasures of the 'anglophile' German crime film thus depended ultimately not on a reflection or consolidation of a real or stable national referent (whether German or British), but precisely on its loss, diffusion, and generic reinvention was noticed even abroad. Puzzled by a German cinema that mostly bypassed German contemporary reality altogether, Robin Bean in the British journal *Films and Filming* commented on Germany's genre patterns in the 1960s: 'West German filmmakers are almost succeeding … in destroying German nationalism. So far as many of them are concerned these days, no such race seems to exist'.[85]

Notes

1. Cf. Tim Bergfelder, 'Horst Wendlandt', in ed. Hans-Michael Bock, *CineGraph. Lexikon zum deutschsprachigen Film*, Munich 1984–.
2. Siegfried Kracauer, 'Der Detektivroman. Ein philosophischer Traktat, 1922–1925', reprinted in *Schriften 1*, Frankfurt 1971, pp. 103–104 (translation: Erica Carter).
3. Siegfried Kracauer, *From Caligari to Hitler. A Psychological History of the German Film*, Princeton 1947, pp. 20–21.
4. George Orwell, 'Raffles and Miss Blandish' (1944), in *The Collected Essays, Journalism, and Letters of George Orwell, vol .III, As I Please, 1943–1945*, London 1968, pp. 220–221. See also David Glover, 'The Stuff that Dreams Are Made of', in *Gender, Genre, and Narrative Pleasure*, ed. Derek Longhurst, London, Boston, and Sydney 1989, p. 73; Jens-Peter Becker, *Sherlock Holmes und Co. Essays zur englischen und amerikanischen Detektivliteratur*, Munich 1975, pp. 15–27.
5. Colin Watson, *Snobbery and Violence. Crime Stories and their Audience*, London 1971, p. 79.
6. Wolf Zucker, 'Edgar Wallace', *Die Weltbühne*, vol. 23, no. 49, 6 December 1927, pp. 877–878.
7. Becker, *Sherlock Holmes und Co.*, p. 24.
8. Orwell in *The Collected Essays*, p. 221.
9. Margaret Lane, *Edgar Wallace. The Biography of a Phenomenon*, London 1938 (2nd, revised, ed. 1964). See also Becker, *Sherlock Holmes und Co.*, pp. 15–27.
10. M.J. Birch, 'The Popular Fiction Industry. Market, Formula, Ideology', *Journal of Popular Culture*, vol. 21, part 3, 1987, p. 85.
11. For further biographical details on Wallace, see Lane, *Edgar Wallace*.
12. See David Glover, 'Introduction' to Edgar Wallace, *The Four Just Men*, Oxford 1995, pp. ix–xxiii.
13. The film's original title *The Martyrdom of Nurse Edith Cavell* was rejected by the British Board of Film Censors: see Richard Falcon, 'No Politics! German Affairs im Spionage- und Kostümfilm', in *London Calling. Deutsche im britischen Film der dreissiger Jahre*, ed. Jörg Schöning, Munich 1993, p. 80.
14. For (sometimes conflicting) filmographies of Edgar Wallace adaptations, see Jack Edmund Nolan, 'Edgar Wallace: His Literary Pop-eries, Unread for Decades, Are Being Revived on Film', *Films in Review*, vol. 18, no. 2, 1967, pp. 71–85; Denis Gifford, 'Nolan's Edgar Wallace', *Films in Review*, vol. 18, no. 5, 1967, pp. 313–316; Florian Pauer, *Die Edgar Wallace Filme*, Munich 1982; Michael R. Pitts, 'The Cinema of Edgar Wallace',*Classic Images*, nos. 126–128, December 1985-February 1986; Joachim Kramp, *Hallo! Hier spricht Edgar Wallace. Die Geschichte der deutschen Kriminalfilmserie von 1959–1972*, Berlin 1998; Christos Tses, *Der Hexer, der Zinker, und andere Mörder. Hinter den Kulissen der Edgar Wallace Filme*, Essen 2002.

15. Pauer, *Die Edgar Wallace Filme*, p. 14.
16. Birch, 'The Popular Fiction Industry', p. 87.
17. Ibid., p. 85.
18. Robin Smyth, 'Wurst Wallace',*Observer*, 14 February 1982.
19. Quoted in Rudolf W. Leonhardt, 'Mit Schreiben Millionen verdient', *Die Zeit*, no.15, 4 April 1975, p. 51.
20. Pauer, *Die Edgar Wallace Filme*, p. 14.
21. See, e.g., Karen Pehla, 'Joe May und seine Detektive. Der Serienfilm als Kinoerlebnis', in *Joe May. Regisseur und Produzent*, ed. Hans-Michael Bock and Claudia Lenssen, Munich 1991, pp. 61–73; Tilo Knops, 'Cinema From The Writing Desk: Detective Film in Imperial Germany', in *A Second Life. German Cinema's First Decades*, ed. Thomas Elsaesser and Michael Wedel, Amsterdam 1996, pp.132–142; Sebastian Hesse, 'Kult der Aufklärung. Zur Attraktion der Detektivfilm-Serien im frühen deutschen Kino (1908–1918), in *Die Modellierung des Kinofilms*, ed. Corinna Müller and Harro Segeberg, Munich 1998, pp. 125–153.
22. Hesse in Müller and Segeberg, *Die Modellierung des Kinofilms*, pp. 127–129. For a similar argument on the emancipatory qualities of early German genre cinema, see also Heide Schlüpmann, *Die Unheimlichkeit des Blicks. Das Drama des frühen deutschen Kinos*, Frankfurt-on-Main 1990; Robert J. Kiss, 'The Doppelgänger in Wilhelmine Cinema (1895–1914): Modernity, Audiences and Identity in Turn-of-the-Century Germany', (PhD diss., University of Warwick, 2000).
23. Kracauer, *From Caligari To Hitler*, p. 20
24. Maria Tatar, *Lustmord. Sexual Murder in Weimar Germany*, Princeton 1995.
25. Haarmann's story has been filmed twice in recent decades: Ulli Lommel's *Die Zärtlichkeit der Wölfe* (1973, The Tenderness of Wolves), and Romuald Karmakar's *Der Totmacher* (1995, Deathmaker).
26. Anton Kaes, *M*, London 2000.
27. Thomas Elsaesser, 'Social Mobility and the Fantastic: German Silent Cinema', in *Fantasy and the Cinema*, ed. James Donald, London 1989, pp. 23–38; see also Thomas Elsaesser, *Weimar Cinema and After. Germany's Historical Imaginary*, London and New York 2000.
28 Willy Haas, 'Die Theologie im Kriminalroman', 1929, reprinted in *Der Kriminalroman. Band I*, ed. Jochen Vogt, Munich 1971, p. 116.
29. For a study of best sellers and publishing houses in Weimar Germany, see Lynda J. King, *Bestsellers By Design. Vicki Baum and the House of Ullstein*, Detroit 1988.
30. Smyth, 'Wurst Wallace'.
31. Since Wallace's *The Squeaker* was such a well-known story at the time, Lamac and his screenwriters devised a different ending for the film: see Pauer, *Die Edgar Wallace Filme*, p. 91.
32. For example, *The Gaunt Stranger* (1938) and *The Four Just Men* (1939), discussed in Charles Barr, *Ealing Studios*, London 1977 (2nd ed. 1993), pp. 15–16.
33. Peter Nusser, *Der Kriminalroman*, Stuttgart 1980, p. 118.
34. Erich Thier, 'Über den Detektivroman', 1940, reprinted in *Der Kriminalroman. Band II*, ed. Jochen Vogt, Munich 1971, p. 483.
35. Ibid., pp. 484–485.
36. Nusser, *Der Kriminalroman*, p. 9.
37. The slogan has also frequently been used by Wallace detractors, for example Ernst Bloch, who wrote that 'it is very easy not to be thrilled by Edgar Wallace', in 'Philosophische Ansicht des Detektivromans', in *Verfremdungen I*, Frankfurt 1963, p. 41.
38. Smyth, 'Wurst Wallace'.
39. Ralph G. Bender, 'Ist der deutsche Kriminalfilm tot?', *Westfälische Rundschau*, 30 January 1960.
40. Unlike the full-length feature films of the German Wallace series, Merton Park's productions were sixty-minute long supporting films, distributed by Anglo Amalgamated for the purpose of double bill programmes.
41. Martin Morlock, 'May-Regen', *Der Spiegel*, 23 September 1964.

42. Anon., 'The Crimson Circle', *Monthly Film Bulletin*, vol. 32, no. 373, February 1965, p. 26.
43. Interview with Egon Eis: 'Was soll ich im Ausland? In Mexiko hätte ich ja keine Zukunft gehabt', in *Aufbruch ins Ungewisse. Bd.1: Österreichische Filmschaffende in der Emigration vor 1945*, ed. Christian Cargnelli and Michael Omasta, Vienna 1993, pp. 63–75.
44. Joseph Garncarz, 'Hollywood in Germany. The Role of American Films in Germany', in *Hollywood in Europe. Experiences of a Cultural Hegemony*, ed. David Ellwood and Rob Kroes, Amsterdam 1994, pp. 126–127.
45. Letter Merton Park to CCC Berlin, 4.1.1962, ABA.
46. Anon., 'Edgar Wallace ohne Ende', *Frankfurter Rundschau*, 16 September 1963.
47. Anon., 'Goldene Leinwand für den 25. Wallace-Krimi', *Film-Echo/Filmwoche*, 17 January 1968, p. 4.
48. Anon., 'Besuch bei Dreharbeiten: Der Hexer', *Film-Echo/Filmwoche*, 19 June 1964, p. 20.
49. Anon., 'Goldene Leinwand für Wendlandt und Wallace', in *Film-Echo/Filmwoche*, 26 January 1968, pp. 10–11.
50. The British Merton Park series used a similar, though less flamboyant, strategy by inserting Edgar Wallace's bust underneath the films' main titles.
51. See Kramp, *Hallo! Hier spricht Edgar Wallace*, p. 63. Kramp's claim that this film was the first Anglo-German co-production since E.A. Dupont's *Atlantic* in 1929 is factually incorrect. *The Devil's Daffodil* is, however, one of the few postwar experiments with filming two language versions of the same film simultaneously, a production practice that is generally understood to have been superseded by dubbing technology in the mid-1930s. Rialto used the same production method in *Traitor's Gate* (1965). Equally incorrect is Kramp's claim that Alfred Hitchcock worked as assistant director on Dupont's film.
52. Pauer, *Die Edgar Wallace Filme*, p. 157.
53. Anon., 'The Devil's Daffodil', *Monthly Film Bulletin*, vol. 29, no. 340, May 1962, p. 67.
54. Francis had previously been involved in another Anglo-German co-production, *Vengeance/Ein Toter sucht seinen Mörder* (1962), produced by Artur Brauner's CCC and Raymond Stross. For more details on this film, see chapter 8.
55. Anon., 'Traitor's Gate', *Monthly Film Bulletin*, vol. 32, no. 379, August 1965, p. 126.
56. Pauer, *Die Edgar Wallace Filme*, p. 95.
57. In the British version Sir John, head of Scotland Yard, was played by James Robertson Justice and in the German version by Siegfried Schürenberg.
58. Anon., 'Das Geheimnis der weissen Nonne', *Filmkritik*, no. 3, 1967, p. 18.
59. Kurt Joachim Fischer, 'Relationen wie bei einem Eisberg', *Film-Echo/Filmwoche*, 23 December 1966, p. 6.
60. See, e.g., Peter Hutchings, 'Beyond the New Wave: Realism in British Cinema, 1959–1963', in *The British Cinema Book*, 2nd edn, ed. Robert Murphy, London 2001, pp. 146–152.
61. Kim Newman, 'Thirty Years in Another Town: The History of Italian Exploitation', *Monthly Film Bulletin*, vol. 53, no. 624, January 1986, p. 23.
62. The film was initially made in English, and both the Italian and German release versions were dubbed, see H.H., 'Unternehmungslust Marke Wendlandt', *Saarbrücker Zeitung*, 7 March 1969.
63. Pauer, *Die Edgar Wallace Filme*, p. 51.
64. Georg Herzberg, 'Das Gesicht im Dunkeln', *Film-Echo/Filmwoche*, 25 July 1969, p. 11.
65. Pauer, *Die Edgar Wallace Filme*, p. 51.
66. Released on video in Britain in the 1990s by Redemption under the title *What Have You Done To Solange?*.
67. kn, 'Das Rätsel des silbernen Halbmonds', *Der Tagesspiegel*, 9 August 1972.
68. R.H., 'Der düstere Rächer im sonnigen Rom', *Abendzeitung München*, 1 July 1972.
69. Malte Hagener, 'German Stars of the 1990s', in *The German Cinema Book*, ed. Tim Bergfelder, Erica Carter, and Deniz Göktürk, London 2002, p. 103.
70. Jack Edmund Nolan, 'West Germany's Edgar Wallace Wave', *Films in Review*, vol. 14, part 6, 1963, p. 378.
71. Ibid., p. 379.

72. Smyth, 'Wurst Wallace'.
73. Norbert Grob, 'Das Geheimnis der toten Augen. 13 Aspekte zum deutschen Kriminalfilm der sechziger Jahre', in *Abschied von Gestern. Bundesdeutscher Film der sechziger und siebziger Jahre*, ed. Hans-Peter Reimann and Rudolf Worschech, Frankfurt 1991, pp. 72–97. See also Georg Seesslen, 'Edgar Wallace. Made in Germany', in *epd film*, vol. 6, June 1986, pp. 31–35.
74. Tassilo Schneider, 'Somewhere Else: The Popular German Cinema of the 1960s', *Yearbook of Comparative and General Literature*, no. 40, Bloomington 1992, pp. 81–82.
75. Tassilo Schneider, 'Finding a New Heimat in the Wild West: Karl May and the German Western of the 1960s', in *Back in the Saddle Again. New Essays on the Western*, ed. Edward Buscombe and Roberta E. Pearson, London 1998, p. 157.
76. Ibid., p. 153.
77. Ibid., pp. 153–154.
78. Ibid., p. 153.
79. Ibid., p. 155.
80. David Bordwell, 'The Bounds of Difference', in David Bordwell, Janet Staiger, and Kristin Thompson, *The Classical Hollywood Cinema. Film Style and Mode of Production to 1960*, London and New York 1985, p. 77.
81. Elsaesser in Donald, *Fantasy and the Cinema*, p. 25.
82. Robert Fischer and Joe Hembus, *Der neue deutsche Film 1960–1980*, Munich 1981, p. 196.
83. Tom Gunning's famous term accounts for a pre-narrative-centred mode of filmic production, representation, and – crucially – spectatorship position, which according to Gunning became superseded by the classical narrative cinema exemplified by Hollywood. See, e.g. 'An Aesthetic of Astonishment: Early Film and the (In)credulous Spectator' in *Art and Text*, vol. 34, Spring 1989.
84. Sabine Hake, *German National Cinema*, London and New York 2002, p. 153.
85. Robin Bean, 'Sex, Guns and May', *Films and Filming*, vol. 11, part 6, 1965, p. 52.

Chapter 8

FROM SOHO TO SILVERLAKE:
THE KARL MAY WESTERNS

Labelled 'sauerkraut' westerns (the terminology following similar culinary epithets found for Italian and Spanish westerns, spaghetti and paella variants, respectively), West German excursions into the genre have often been dismissed as particularly bland and derivative imitations. Yet during the 1960s, the Karl May westerns, produced like the Edgar Wallace films by Horst Wendlandt's Rialto, were among the most popular films in the domestic market and were among the few West German genres in the 1960s that exported well into other countries. More importantly, they completely outperformed, at least in West Germany, any 'original' western produced by Hollywood. Indeed, there was no precedent, prior to the 1960s and at least since the war, that could have given any indication for the phenomenal success the western as a genre would have with West German audiences, particularly during a decade that is generally seen as one of decline of the genre in the United States itself.

In the immediate postwar years, Hollywood's big-budget and 'mature' westerns (for example, the postwar films of John Ford, Anthony Mann, George Stevens, or Henry King) were largely ignored by West German cinema audiences, while B-film serials were relegated to children's matinées. The 'western' of the 1960s thus emerged primarily not in response to current manifestations of the genre produced in Hollywood, even though it was clearly aware of them. Instead, like the contemporaneous Edgar Wallace thrillers, the West German westerns capitalised on an indigenous literary phenomenon that had its origins in the early part of the century and adapted this tradition to changing demographics and preferences of consumption in West Germany, most notably by targeting a young audience. Like the Wallace films, the West German westerns marked a significant shift in generic patterns from the predominant models of the 1950s. They combined a nostalgic revival of older traditions of popular culture with modern cinematic attractions (in the case of the westerns, Cinemascope, colour, exotic locations, and special effects) and an internationalist agenda. They were characterised by a mode of production that fostered recognition through constant crews and casts, visual and narrative distinctiveness, and sequelisation.

Both cycles diversified into tie-ins with other culture and leisure industries. Unlike the Wallace films, however, the point of reference or trademark of authenticity for the westerns was not a foreign author but a home-grown icon of popular culture, the adventure novelist Karl May (1842–1912). The Karl May adaptations (seventeen in total between 1962 and 1968, eleven of which had a western setting) were thus ostensibly rooted in an indigenous literary context, and they relied, at least in West Germany, to a great degree on the familiarity of successive generations with May's work. Yet at the same time they were, in their mode of production, even more international than the Wallace series – shot on location in Yugoslavia, co-financed by French and Italian production partners, and starring actors from different countries. As with the Wallace films, the international, rather than simply indigenous, impact of the Karl May films has often been underestimated. The films sold well in France and Spain and, again, particularly well in Italy. The Italian film industry, motivated by the success of the Karl May films in Italy, in turn formulated its own version, the spaghetti western. The May films were also widely distributed throughout the Eastern bloc states, Scandinavia, and, unusually for productions originating in either East or West Germany at the time, even in Britain and America.

As I have argued previously, popular European film genres of the 1960s have not only frequently been dismissed as pale imitations of established Hollywood models, but their very emergence has been seen as the more or less futile attempt by European film producers to capitalise on and compete with the dominance of American genres in their own markets. Nowhere is this critical perception as strong as in the case of the western, which, in its iconography, settings, and mythology, is seen as the quintessentially American genre, as one of America's genuinely indigenous and authentic cultural forms, and yet also one of its universally popular cultural exports. I would counter that the Karl May films of the 1960s, and also the Italian spaghetti westerns,[1] should not be regarded as imitations but as manifestations of an alternative tradition of imagining the Wild West that ran parallel to the aesthetic codes and ideological concerns of the Hollywood western. To understand the emergence of this tradition and its resonances as late as the 1960s, it is necessary to consider the literary, cultural, and, not least, commercial prehistory and tradition of the German film western across different periods.

Karl May and the German Wild West

Immensely popular already during his lifetime, Karl May remains to this day the most widely read or, perhaps more accurately, most widely published German-language author. Since its foundation in 1913, shortly after

May's death, the Karl-May-Verlag has dominantly, though not exclusively, handled the publication of May's entire works (amounting to over seventy volumes). The Karl-May-Verlag's edition, with its distinctive dark green covers, has been, similarly to the scarlet-spined Wallace paperbacks, an instantly recognisable literary product for ninety years. Handed down from successive parent generations to their children, May's novels, however anachronistic they may appear in style and language, remain for many adolescents in Germany a significant initiation into reading literature, although in the new millennium increasingly being superseded by the Harry Potter phenomenon. In any case, it is certainly no exaggeration to argue that May's portrayal of the Wild West has profoundly shaped the German perception of America for most of the twentieth century.

A list of self-professed May fans would comprise a roll-call of some of the most influential cultural and political figures in German life in the twentieth century, ranging from Albert Einstein to Bertolt Brecht, from Fritz Lang and his wife Thea von Harbou to Ernst Bloch, and from, infamously, Adolf Hitler to, more acceptably, West German presidents Theodor Heuss and Roman Herzog. By 1995, an estimated 100 million copies of his books had been sold, and his work has been translated into twenty-eight languages.[2] Hyperbole has been a frequent characteristic in the public evaluation of May. In 1962, the year the first postwar Karl May western film was released, the Hamburg-based weekly *Der Spiegel* declared that 'May has become a kind of *praeceptor Germaniae*, whose influence is undoubtedly greater than that of any other author between Goethe and Thomas Mann'.[3] More than thirty years later, May's German publisher stated that 'May's appeal is timeless. His creations are better known than many Disney characters or Helmut Kohl'.[4] Indeed, even in the new millennium, German audiences remain so familiar with Karl May iconography that a film spoof of this specific genre, Michael Herbig's *Der Schuh des Manitu* (2001, Manitou's Shoe), became a runaway box-office hit. While May's public reception in Germany has exhibited signs of almost cultist reverence and hero-worship, however, critical and academic evaluations of his work have been less unified. Within a German context, May had, for decades, fallen victim to German academia's blanket dismissal of what is commonly termed *Schundliteratur* (trash literature). As such, May's work was condemned for exerting a bad and even corrupting influence on his predominantly adolescent readers.[5] In the German Democratic Republic, meanwhile, May was rejected as an exemplar of bourgeois escapism. Colleen Cook has argued that 'the bulk of literature on May was written with an axe to grind. While May was alive, over a thousand articles were written in either savage condemnation or overwhelming praise of the author'.[6] A more serious, though still partisan, Karl May scholarship in West Germany commenced in the early 1970s, triggered to some extent by Arno Schmidt's psychoanalytical reassessment of May[7] and the foundation in 1969 of the Karl-May-Gesellschaft (Karl May Association). May's publisher, the Karl-May-Verlag, has encouraged research activity through its yearbooks, while the Karl-May-Gesellschaft has expanded into a critical and enormously productive academic industry, exploring the author's work in yearbooks, newsletters, specialised publications, conferences, journals, and, more recently, on the Internet.

Outside Germany, the academic reception of May has overall accepted a critical consensus that tends to view his work as the expression of a particularly Germanic mind-set, and his novels are frequently seen to promote an imperialist, racist, and proto-fascist ideology. Heribert von Feilitzsch, for example wonders 'whether May's widely read stories contributed to Germany's overly nationalistic and chauvinistic fervour during the first half of the century'.[8] This perception has undoubtedly been helped by Hitler's reputed admiration for May and the continued, though selective, promotion of his work throughout the Nazi period.[9] In 'Karl May: Hitler's Literary Mentor', a polemic written in exile in 1940, Klaus Mann argued that 'the Third Reich is Karl May's final triumph, the terrible realisation of his dreams'.[10] Mann's eminently quotable reading of May's Indians and cowboys prefiguring the homosocial order of the Nazi hierarchy by several decades has been reiterated with some regularity ever since in Anglo-American studies on the western,[11] and it has also been used more generally to explain the psychosocial and gender dynamics of the "Third Reich".[12]

In order to understand such divergent modes of critical reception, which have also significantly shaped the interpretation of the May films of the 1960s, it is necessary to revisit the cultural and social context out of which May originally emerged.[13] To briefly sketch the essential elements of his biography, May was born in 1842 into a poor, working-class Lutheran weaver family in rural Saxony, at that time part of the Prussian empire, and was trained as a schoolteacher. For most of his early life, May was in conflict with the law, and he spent nine years in prison for offences ranging from petty theft and insurance fraud, to medical quackery and imposition of false titles. An avid reader of Gothic novels and adventure stories since childhood, May used his appointment as prison librarian to read a large number of travel diaries, ethnographic and anthropological textbooks, and novels which included the 'Leatherstocking' tales of James Fenimore Cooper, popular among German readers at the time.[14] Cooper's work had a profound impact on May's later conception of the Wild West, alongside the influence of authors such as Friedrich Gerstäcker and Charles Sealsfield, who, in the wake of a German emigration wave since the late eighteenth century, had written about their travels to and firsthand experiences in early nineteenth century America. As Deniz Göktürk has argued, these writings were 'directed as realistic descriptions at potential immigrants, and they were in sharp contrast to the hostile attitude towards America running through the élitist German high literature'.[15] After his release from prison, May embarked on a literary career, writing village tales, exotic travelogues set in America and the Middle East, and historical adventure stories, comprising the most popular literary genres of the time. May's work was published and serialised in the dominant medium for popular literature, periodical publications such as *Der Deutsche Hausschatz* (The German Homely Treasure) and *Feierstunden am häuslichen Herde* (Festive Hours at the Homely Hearth).[16]

By the early 1880s, May had established himself as a prolific writer, and ten years later he had attained the status of a best-seller author. Crucially, May's rise in popularity coincided with an increasing industrialisation of literary and, more generally, cultural production. This shift in cultural production ran parallel to developments in the social sphere. Colleen Cook has pointed out that 'the peak of the *Kolportage*[17] genre aided significantly in forming a literate population among the lower classes in German society'.[18] It was not just May's work but May himself who became a marketable commodity through a carefully constructed public persona. By the 1890s, May had reinvented himself and his past, eradicating his criminal background from his biography, claiming instead that during the years he had actually spent in prison he had travelled the world. This myth was further enhanced by the fact that most of May's stories merged author, narrator, and hero into one singular voice, giving the impression of auto-biographical, firsthand experience and authenticity.

In May's oriental tales, the main hero was the German traveller Kara Ben Nemsi ('Karl, Son of Germany'), who fights, with the help of his Arab sidekick, oppressive Ottoman despots and desert bandits. In May's Wild West stories, his alter ego was 'Old Shatterhand', an educated German immigrant with strong Christian beliefs and nearly superhuman powers. He graduates over several novels from being a 'greenhorn' to a widely respected westerner and, through his emotionally intense relationship with the Apache chief Winnetou, he becomes the honoured and revered friend of the native Indians whose various dialects he learns to speak fluently. Like Shatterhand, May also claimed to have mastered more than twenty-six languages. The conflation between May's fictional world and his own life was further promoted by May posing for publicity photographs in western or oriental costumes. From the early 1890s May established his home in the Saxon town of Radebeul in a house he named 'Villa Shatterhand', filled with exotic memorabilia and souvenirs he claimed he had collected during his trips abroad. In fact, most of these artefacts had been made for him on his own specifications in German workshops, as May had rarely ventured outside Germany. When he finally did, his experiences were either traumatic or deeply disappointing. During a trip to the Middle East and Asia in 1899, May suffered a nervous breakdown he himself termed a 'creative crisis',[19] and his impression of America was confined to a short stay in 1908 in New York and a tourist excursion to Niagara Falls, where he briefly visited a carefully monitored Indian reservation. Towards the end of his life, May's past caught up with him, and tabloid journalists began to expose his frauds, criminal past, and biographical inventions. While his popularity among his readers and his publishing success remained relatively untarnished, May was constantly involved in libel suits and subjected to increasingly hostile attacks from right- and left-wing journalists until his death in 1912.

May's literary imagination is difficult to pin down in ideological terms, or, as Colleen Cook has argued, 'while nearly everyone can find something endearing in Karl May, so can nearly everyone find something distasteful'.[20] Despite detailed descriptions of local customs and a fairly accurate sense of geography, May's Wild West is essentially a projective fantasy rooted in the symbolism of Protestant sectarianism, betraying a cultural formation May shared with a great number of his readers. Following the failed revolution of 1848 and widespread disillusionment about political change (which led to a massive emigration wave to America), churches and Christian fellowships in Germany had experienced a surge in membership, particularly among the lower classes.[21] The almost complete absence in May's novels of sexual romance, or indeed any significant female characters, and their heroes' hypertrophic masculinity and intense homosocial bonds have frequently been interpreted as misogynist, as a sign of May's latent homosexuality, and more generally as articulating the militarised gender hierarchies of imperial Germany. Not surprisingly, May's fiction features as a reference in Klaus Theweleit's famous study on the intersections of German militarism and masculinity, *Männerphantasien*.[22] Another line of interpretation, however, might equally explain the sexual politics of May's fiction by the puritan Protestantism of May's upbringing and perhaps also by May's traumatic experience of his first marriage.

May's America is an allegoric landscape, in which a spiritual battle between good and evil is fought against the background of a *Götterdämmerung* of the native Indian race. Unlike in the American tradition of the western, May's stories do not develop the dichotomies between 'desert' and 'garden', nor are they particularly concerned with the notion of the 'frontier'. Instead they present an enclosed utopian Arcadia, the value of which is determined precisely by its 'untouched' nature and the fact that it lies outside the parameters of urban civilisation and capitalism and modern culture more generally. May's work (like Cooper's before him) exhibits an acute awareness that this Arcadia is ultimately doomed, and there is a consistently elegiac and mournful romanticism in his descriptions of the American wilderness and Indian culture. Unlike the American western, May's work opposes the commercial cultivation of the West, and its villains are therefore frequently white land prospectors, railway engineers, cowboys, and oil barons. May's sympathies were clearly directed towards the plight of the Native American, who is envisaged as the morally uncorrupted and innocent noble savage. His novels also include positive, though equally stereotyped, portraits of black people, and he condemned the activities of the Ku-Klux-Klan.

However, as many commentators have pointed out, May's concerns for ecology and interracial understanding were underlined by a curiously Germanocentric perspective, which frequently slipped into nostalgic regressions. Richard Cracroft has noted that 'all of his heroes are Germans

– and his villains Americans ... May's Western heroes drink German beer, hear German music, sing German songs and read (authentic) German newspapers'.[23] Cracroft's criticism is reductive, however, in so far as he equates with and therefore naturalises American identity as Anglo-Saxon-ness, and he ignores the fact that Germanness has also been a significant constitutive part of American ethnicity over the past centuries. Thus, at closer inspection, the villains in May's novels are not Americans as such, as Cracroft claims, but more specifically Anglo-Saxon Americans. What makes May's America distinctive as a cultural space is the way in which German, and Christian, values and Indian traditions coalesce to create a new utopian and homely community in union with nature, which is set against the encroaching dominance of Anglo-Saxon settlers and Western capitalism and technology. America is portrayed as the paradise that awaits German immigrants as their reward for having endured economic hardship, spiritual deprivation, and political persecution at home. It is a place of both religious and national redemption. However, May's Ger-mans in America are far from being the Kaiser's loyal colonisers. Indeed, one character, Klekih-Petra, the 'white teacher' of the Apache Indians, is explicitly introduced as a political refugee from Germany. There is still, though, something particularly missionary about the way May envisages the German role in America. The native population is required to adopt German customs, or at least to conform to a set of Christian ethical values that are imported wholesale from imperial Germany. As Cracroft has argued, May's Indian hero Winnetou 'is noble because of his willingness to embrace the best of European culture and blend it with the finest traits of his own nation'.[24] Thus, Winnetou is not only a formidably brave chief and an Indian messiah with a 'Roman' physiognomy, but he is also an avid reader of poetry, he appreciates German beer and learns German Christ-mas carols, and, shortly before his death (sacrificing himself to save Old Shatterhand), he converts to Christianity. Martin Kuester has argued that, while May realised 'that the Indians' miserable future is the Europeans' fault, he continues preaching his European religion to them'.[25]

May's work, and this may ultimately account for his popularity across such a wide political and social spectrum, is riddled with ideological con-tradictions and thus extremely polysemic. On the one hand, his anti-capi-talism, his anti-bourgeois and anti-modern attitude, and his notion of masculinity may be seen to conform to the state ideology of Wilhelmine Germany and its military hierarchy and to have its later resonances in 1930s fascism. May's conception of Germans abroad as peacemakers, Christian missionaries, cultural educators, and arbiters of justice can be seen to support imperial Germany's nationalist and colonialist aspirations, played out in the dichotomy between 'good' German and 'bad' Anglo-Saxon settlers. That May's novels were read in that way is evident in his later appropriation by the Nazis, who even distributed May's works to army recruits as guidelines for heroic and moral conduct.[26]

On the other hand, these same characteristics may also indicate the exact opposite, namely a deep resentment of the prevailing political, militarist, and social structures of imperial Germany. May's idea of 'race' may have been informed by the theories of social Darwinism, but he was also an outspoken pacifist and a strong critic of German colonialism and anti-Semitism. During his trip to America, May condemned in a public lecture 'the horrendous amount of money and blood' wasted by 'German greed for power' and he encouraged his audience of predominantly German immigrants to work towards a 'humanist' country in the United States, based on Christian principles.[27] Significantly, however, despite May's proclaimed anti-bourgeois stance and all the exotic trappings of his novels, the humanist utopia he had to offer in his writings was both reassuringly familiar and surprisingly stolid. Considering the fact that the publication of May's novels followed and, to some extent, still coincided with a period of intensive migration from Germany to America, May's vision of the Wild West can be seen to have addressed two particular constituencies and mediated their reciprocal imaginings. For those readers who yearned to escape the social constraints of Imperial Germany, May's novels represented both a distractive fantasy and an encouragement to build a new life elsewhere. This new life, however, was still comfortably cushioned in cultural familiarities. For those who had already emigrated, on the other hand, May's novels established nostalgic links to the lost homeland. In the later Karl May film adaptations, this escapist and transnational imagination would be substantially redefined and adapted to its new cultural contexts.

Karl May and German Cinema before the 1960s

As in the case of the Edgar Wallace film boom in the 1960s, it is notable that, despite their literary popularity, it took several decades before Karl May's stories made a noticeable impact in the cinema. There had been previous German film adaptations; significantly, however, none of these films had been based on May's Wild West tales. The earliest adaptations date back to the early Weimar period. In 1920 Dr Adolf Droop, an academic who had written a study of May's work in 1909, and his wife Marie Luise founded the company Ustad (the name derived from a character in May's novels) in Berlin with the aim to bring May's work to the screen.[28] Marie Luise had been an ardent May fan since childhood and had actually met and befriended her idol. In May's last years, she had vehemently defended him in public against his enemies, and earned herself in the tabloid press the nickname 'Karl May's beautiful spy'.[29] During the First World War, Marie Luise Droop had relocated to Copenhagen, where she worked for the film company Nordisk as a scriptwriter and director of exotic melodramas and managed the company's public relations department. The production team that the Droops assembled at Ustad was certainly colourful and cosmopolitan. It included May's widow Klara and his illustrator

Sascha Schneider as artistic advisers, the Turkish director Ertogrul Musshin-Bey, and the Hungarian actors Bela Lugosi and Meinhart Maur. Between 1920 and 1921 Ustad produced three May films, based on his oriental adventure tales, and shot in the Brandenburg plains near Berlin. Released in quick succession were *Auf den Trümmern des Paradieses* (In the Ruins of Paradise), *Die Todeskarawane* (Caravan of Death), and *Die Teufelsanbeter* (The Devil-Worshippers). While no prints of these films have survived, contemporary press reviews indicate that they were received favourably.[30] Despite this, however, Ustad went bankrupt shortly after, and before the Droops could embark on their most ambitious projects, namely the adaptations of May's Wild West adventures.

It would be a mistake to deduce from Ustad's ill-fated venture that stories of the Wild West were uncommon or unpopular in German cinema at the time. As Deniz Göktürk has documented, not only had American films starring William S. Hart and 'Broncho' Billy Anderson been shown to German audiences since the early years of the century, but there were also a large number of home-grown films set in the Wild West. Around the same time as the Ustad films, production companies in southern Germany ventured into the genre with fictional heroes such as 'Bull Arizona', and there had been 'horse operas' in German cinema since the early 1910s. Significantly, many of the early German 'westerns', like May's novels before, were less about the taming and civilisation of the wild frontier than about escape, travel, migration, and displacement. Furthermore, in many of these films, America was frequently just one location among others, as the films' travelling protagonists often moved on to other continents or returned home as prodigal sons or daughters. As Göktürk has suggested, the social referent for these narratives was no longer, or exclusively, a 'real' migratory experience; instead, 'the Wild West shrunk to a facet in a kaleidoscope of adventures, and was incorporated as an integral element into the episodic structure of international chase stories ... In their rapid succession of exotic locations these films enacted what Kracauer called the "shrinking of the world" for the tourist gaze'.[31]

This shift in spectatorial perspective from potential migrant to (cinematic or real) tourist, and the change in perception of an 'authentic' elsewhere to an exotic commodity is also evident in most of the Karl May film adaptations, and it will later become important in determining the 'national' properties of the 1960s May films. *Durch die Wüste* (1935/6, Across the Desert) was the next attempt after the Ustad films to film May's work. Shot on location in Egypt by the B-film production company of Lothar Stark, the film resembled the international adventure films of the silent period, both in its restless episodic structure and in its explicitly tourist perspective.[32] Rather than integrating settings and narrative into a coherent causal whole, the film presented instead a series of famous tourist vistas and digressed into displays of indigenous folklore. As I have argued elsewhere, the film's German hero and the spectator in the audience were cinematically 'positioned similar to a package tourist on an Orient trip whose evening entertainment includes a performance of "authentic" local customs in the Hotel lobby'.[33] *Durch die Wüste* was criticised by contemporary reviewers for its perceived lack of heroic determination and national sentiment, and it remained the only May film adaptation during the Nazi period, although the press reported on a number of other May projects that never materialised. These included a mooted Wien-Film production starring Hans Albers in 1936, a project in 1938 with Luis Trenker, and a possible Tobis film with Harry Piel. It took another fourteen years, however, before Karl May's oriental stories resurfaced as the source of two Spanish-Austrian co-productions of the late 1950s, *Die Sklavenkarawane/ Caravana de esclavos* (1958, Caravan of Slaves) and its sequel *Der Löwe von Babylon/Las ruinas de Babilonia* (1959, The Lion of Babylon). Shot in Spain under the direction of *Heimatfilm* expert Georg Marischka, the films were conceived largely as parodies and functioned mainly as vehicles for their stars, comedians Georg Thomalla and Theo Lingen. Following the financial failure of Marischka's films, producers and distributors came to the conclusion that May represented a bad proposition at the box-office.

The Karl May Westerns of the 1960s

Anecdotes, legends, and myths abound as to why Horst Wendlandt's Rialto, following its success with the Edgar Wallace series, decided in 1962 to embark on an adaptation of May's Wild West novel *Der Schatz im Silbersee* (The Treasure of Silver Lake), the most often told being that Wendlandt's eleven-year-old son, an avid May reader, encouraged his father.[34] Although such an explanation may justifiably be dismissed as folklore, the anecdote points to one of the major motivations to embark on the series. While May's 'Winnetou and Old Shatterhand' stories had never been filmed before, they certainly constituted his most popular tales, particularly among children and teenagers. Moreover, while there may have been no Karl May westerns until Wendlandt's venture, Karl May's American novels had been adapted since 1952, with increasingly phenomenal success, in annual open-air stage spectacles at the Karl May festival at Bad Segeberg, which combined the attractions of acrobatic stunts, narrative, and ethnographic display, and in this respect were and remain a post-Second World War remnant of the *Völkerschauen* or ethnic shows that had been so popular with German audiences since the Wilhelmine period.[35] Wendlandt's venture into the Karl May western can be seen to have been motivated by a number of considerations: the increased importance of the youth segment among cinema audiences, the attempt to tap into the childhood memories of an older audience, and as a strategy to provide an internationally viable genre formula with box-office potential in export markets. One factor that certainly facilitated Rialto's venture was that, in 1962, fifty years after May's death, royalty rights over his work ceased and May's novels thus entered the public domain. This also meant that the

Figure 8.1. West German cinema's 'dream couple' Pierre Brice (left) and Lex Barker (right) in a publicity still from *Der Schatz im Silbersee* (1962, The Treasure of Silver Lake). Deutsches Filminstitut (DIF), Frankfurt-on-Main.

Karl-May-Verlag's publishing monopoly was faced with new competition, which resulted in a war of rival May editions in the bookshops and consequently in an increased availability and visibility of May's work.

There were a number of problems in adapting May's novels for the screen. Partly owing to their originally serialised format, the books tend to be episodic and digressive, crammed with narrative subplots, secondary characters, and developments that extend not only over a number of different locations but also over several novels. Moreover, May's religious symbolism, his antiquated dialogues, his description of flamboyant and flagrantly inauthentic costumes, and his dream of a German utopia in America may still have been digestible in writing. It is unlikely, however, that mainstream cinema audiences in the early 1960s, and particularly those outside Germany, would have warmed to the on-screen spectacle of Indian tribesmen with beehive hairdos singing German carols under a Christmas tree. Rialto's approach to May's Wild West thus had to balance the demands of an internationally oriented popular genre cinema with the established expectations of May's loyal readers.

As with the Edgar Wallace cycle, Wendlandt's Karl May films drew on the familiarity of May as a cultural icon, while at the same time devising a distinctive and, to some extent, independent generic iconography. Significantly, they de-Germanised and internationalised May's America. Rialto's films still occasionally featured German characters, but their nationality was merely incidental. Rialto's strategy is most prominently exemplified in the filmic reinterpretation and casting of May's main heroes. For the role of 'Old Shatterhand', Wendlandt chose the American actor Lex Barker.[36] In Hollywood, Barker's career had floundered after brief stardom as 'Tarzan' in five RKO films in the late 1940s and early 1950s. These films, however, had been successful at the German box office and had familiarised West German audiences with Barker. Following a number of fairly undistinguished B westerns, Barker became one of many American tax exiles to relocate to Europe in the 1950s and 1960s. He came to Italy in 1958, where he starred for the next couple of years in swashbuckling and pirate adventure films, which were frequently Franco-Italian co-productions. Prior to the Karl May films, Barker had also appeared in other West German films, two Dr Mabuse thrillers and a melodrama, produced by Wendlandt's rival Artur Brauner.

Manfred Barthel claimed that the major problem of earlier May adaptations had been that their German stars had given them a 'stale, provincial stench instead of the international flair of Karl May's world'.[37] Barker brought to the Karl May films not only the looks of a matinée idol, celebrity status (he had been briefly married to Hollywood star Lana Turner), and an established European box-office appeal, but also a laconic, casual style of acting, which was very much in line with the Hollywood western but distinctly different from the performance style of West German stars at the time. At the same time, Barker's physiognomy (his blondness, blue eyes, and athletic body) still conformed to the kind of Teutonic racial stereotype that had informed the character's description in May's novels. Old Shatterhand's Indian 'blood-brother' Winnetou, on the other hand, was portrayed by the French actor Pierre Brice, a former dancer with handsome, almost feminine, features.[38] In Brice's interpretation, Winnetou became a sad and dreamy beauty icon, which had little in common with Hollywood's Indians, or, in fact with May's 'noble savage'. As in May's novels' intensely emotional relationship between the two main characters (bordering on the homoerotic), the on-screen rapport between Barker and Brice was crucial, and they were frequently referred to, and without any apparent irony or innuendo, as the 'dream couple' of 1960s West German cinema.[39]

Like the Wallace cycle, the 1960s May adaptations emphasised continuity in terms of production personnel and protagonists. Brice and Barker were obviously the main star attractions. While Brice's Winnetou, however, appeared in all of the films, in later entries of the series Barker was on occasion replaced by Stewart Granger as 'Old Surehand' and, less successfully, by another Hollywood B-film actor, Rod Cameron, as 'Old Firehand'. Like the Wallace series, the Karl May cycle had its *buffo* parts for popular German comedians. Regulars included the Berlin comedian Ralf Wolter as the heroes' eccentric sidekick Sam Hawkens, Eddi Arent as the butterfly-hunting English tourist Lord Castlepool (the casting of Arent was clearly meant as a cross-reference to the Wallace series), Chris Howland, the British DJ and presenter of television's 'Candid Camera', as a photographer for *The Times*, and Heinz Erhardt as a choir-master. May villains included international character actors such as Herbert Lom, Anthony Steel, Mario Adorf, and Rik Battaglia.

Of the eleven May westerns produced between 1962 and 1968, five were directed by Harald Reinl and three by Alfred Vohrer. Reinl in particular shaped the visual and narrative characteristics of the series. His expertise for outdoor shoots had been trained in the mountain films of Arnold Fanck in the late 1920s, on which Reinl had worked as an actor and assistant director. He later became one of the most prolific directors of the *Heimatfilm* genre in the 1950s. Reinl himself summed up the main ingredients of his May films as 'sensations, action, beautiful images, beautiful landscapes, lots of Indians, and a suspenseful story'.[40] Hailed by his producer Wendlandt as 'the German Cecil B. de Mille',[41] Reinl worked with an established team of collaborators which included the writer Harald G. Petersson, the cinematographer Ernst W. Kalinke, the composer Martin Böttcher, and the special-effects supervisor Erwin Lange, an expert in pyrotechnics and explosions, which were a particularly significant element of nearly all of Rialto's May films.

Unlike the Edgar Wallace series, with its low-cost mode of production, the Karl May films were conceived from the beginning as spectacular events. Rialto's first venture, *Der Schatz im Silbersee* (1962), like all subsequent May films shot in Eastmancolor and CinemaScope, was, with a budget of 3.5 million DM, the most expensive West German production up to this point, and could only be financed as a co-production. As in most subsequent May films, Rialto had Italian and French production partners, with Rialto and its distributor and backer Constantin providing the majority of the money. An acceleration of production cost could be avoided by filming in a low-cost country, such as Yugoslavia. The state-owned Yugoslav company Jadran contributed technical staff, production equipment, and extras in exchange for distribution rights in the Eastern bloc. On *Der Schatz im Silbersee* alone, 3,000 Yugoslav extras and 2,500 horses were used.[42] Given that outside West Germany *Der Schatz im Silbersee* was perceived as merely a B western, the attention to detail by the production team was extraordinary and may justify to some extent Wendlandt's comparison of Harald Reinl with Cecil B. de Mille: 'For weeks the team toured Yugoslavia in search of the wildest landscapes. For a single scene entire pueblos and western towns were built, without thought for future use, each costume was hand-made, each prop lovingly crafted, and not a single take of any significance was left to the second unit'.[43]

The Rialto films' 'international flair' was clearly underlined by their beautiful Yugoslav scenery (all films were shot on location in the karst mountains and lakes north of the Adriatic coast of Croatia), by their pedantic attention to props and *mise en scène* more generally, and by the series' heightened use of clichés from American western repertoires. Martin Böttcher's epic scores in particular, mixing symphonic grandeur with whimsical, 'typically western' touches (banjo riffs, out-of-tune bar pianos, fiddles, harmonica, etc.), not only provided the series with perhaps the single most recognisable element apart from the natural scenery, but also anticipated the operatic use of music in many subsequent Italian spaghetti westerns. As in the later Italian productions, the May films constructed an American West that was overburdened with Hollywood clichés but, at the same time, was so original and imaginative in its combination of stereotypical constitutive parts that a distinctive version of the western emerged in the process. While Rialto's May adaptations kept the basic story lines of the novels on which they were based, they reduced May's narrative digressions and secondary characters to a minimum. All of the films followed a fairly simple narrative formula: peace between Indians and white settlers is threatened by the evildoing of white racketeers (railway engineers, corrupt cavalry officers, oil barons, bounty hunters). Innocent settlers (often, but not exclusively, German) are threatened and often taken hostage. Old Shatterhand and Winnetou intervene and rescue the victims, often with the help of friendly Indians. The villains meet a horrible death (however, in order to preserve the heroes' saintly and pacifist credentials, villains usually perish in convenient accidents or kill themselves), and fire or explosions destroy their hide-outs. Old Shatterhand and Winnetou pontificate about the values of nature, peace, and friendship and then ride into the sunset.

Der Schatz im Silbersee is in many ways the prototype of the series' formula, and the film's opening illustrates its combined use of Hollywood clichés and divergent styles very nicely. The film's first ten minutes almost provide an audiovisual compendium of the genre's familiar attractions and narrative elements. As the opening credits appear in a dark red 'western'-type font, the camera pans slowly across a barren and dusty valley, interspersed only by the occasional saguaro cactus, nestled in the foothills of dramatically craggy mountains. A lonely stagecoach traverses the valley and, once the credits have come to an end, is promptly ambushed by bandits. The coach driver and one of the two passengers are killed (the other passenger turns out to be the leader of the bandits). The narrative then abruptly moves with a dissolve to a different location, a stereotypical frontier town with a 'prairie saloon' and a post office. A drunk staggers through the swinging doors of the saloon, where the camera quickly introduces the audience in a slow 180 degree pan to familiar western stock characters: a few 'loose women', the slightly older landlady of the saloon (there is the clear implication that this saloon might well be a brothel and the woman in the scarlet dress its madam), an Indian scout, cowboys, a couple of eccentric-looking trappers, a quack selling dubious medicines, the saloon's piano player. A jolly mood prevails among the saloon's inebriated guests. Eventually the camera settles on a small group of drinkers, one of whom (a young German settler named Fred Engel) will shortly after emerge as one of the film's central characters. As there is little, and mostly incidental, dialogue during these opening minutes, Böttcher's score provides the main cues of changing tone and mood, as well as providing links and contrast between disparate locations, from the solemn and wistful opening music that accompanies the shots of the snow-capped mountains to the folksy, vaguely country-and-western polka melody that is played on the piano (and a non-diegetic violin) in the saloon sequence. The latter scene maintains its comedic and raucous tone for a further few minutes with the appearance of an incongruously dressed 'greenhorn', a British tourist who is made fun of by the more seasoned westerners and who will provide periodic comic relief for the rest of the film. The arrival of the unmanned stagecoach at the saloon, harbouring the dead body of, as we now learn, the young German settler's father, dramatically reverses the tone of the film. The music, both diegetic and non-diegetic, and the other raucous noise from the saloon stop, while Fred Engel vows to avenge his father's death, thus setting in motion one of the film's two central quests (the other one being the search for the treasure of the film's title, while a third plot strand involves the romance of Fred Engel with a young farmer's daughter). It is at this stage that the film's two main heroes, Old Shatterhand and Winnetou, enter the narrative. Fred Engel's vow of vengeance is followed by a cut back to the mountain landscape of the film's opening and, to the melody of what will become the two heroes' musical leitmotif throughout the film, Shatterhand and Winnetou ride into the scene.

What I aim to emphasise with these descriptions is that the opening sequences establish a pattern of alternation of polar opposites in both location and tone (e.g., from dramatic to comedic register, from open landscapes to town life, from stillness to action, from silence to loudness, etc.) that the film will largely adhere to for its remainder, a pattern, moreover, that is characteristic of the series as a whole. What is particularly noticeable, and what I would argue distinguishes the style of the May westerns from the tight and economic narration of most contemporary American westerns, is the, in parts almost 'primitive', conception of narrative progression the film employs, which makes *Der Schatz im Silbersee* look at times more like a Griffith short from the 1910s than a contemporaneous Hollywood western. Unlike in the latter, which would aim to align its heroes and villains and the narrative's central quest as early as possible, it takes *Der Schatz im Silbersee* the best part of the film's first half to finally bring all its various narrative strands together; indeed, it is only at the very end of the sequence described above that the film's main heroes are introduced. Thus, rather than creating the protagonist-centred cause-and-effect chain that David Bordwell has identified as characteristic of classical Hollywood narration, the opening scenes of Reinl's film function more like spectacular set pieces, showing off the elements of the genre it uses rather than being committed to the most functional way of telling a story or linking the separate scenes together. Also, while the relatively abrupt change in register from the dramatic to the comedic from one scene to another is a not unusual feature of a number of West German popular film genres (the contemporaneous Edgar Wallace films have similar alternations in tone and style), it is a fairly uncommon mode of narration in classical cinema, particularly where such alternations are seen to undermine the generic verisimilitude of either or both registers. The impression of a pre-classical aesthetic in the May films is further underlined by the crucial narrative function Böttcher's emblematic score assumes, which, particularly in its use of leitmotifs and mimetic sound, has many similarities with the score for a silent film. Where *Der Schatz im Silbersee* and the May westerns that followed further deviate from the classical Hollywood western is in their conception of the American Wild West itself. While the film appears on the one hand committed to an 'authentic' representation of saloons, landscapes, and so on, there are a number of incongruities that cannot simply be dismissed as faulty continuity or as an example of the film-makers' ignorance of geographical facts. The landscape of the opening scene, including the presence of cacti, for example, seems to suggest that the film is set in the American South-west, most probably somewhere in the high deserts of Arizona, California, or New Mexico. Yet the saloon in the frontier town is called a 'prairie saloon' (despite the absence of any prairie in the surroundings) and there is a reference in the dialogue to supposedly nearby Tulsa, which in reality, of course, is to be found in Oklahoma in the flatlands (including prairies, but not the mountains the film shows) of the Great Plains, a considerable distance from the South-west. In other words, the landscape that *Der Schatz im Silbersee* constructs is less the authentic representation of a real America than a condensed image of a European idea of the Wild West.

Der Schatz im Silbersee was released in December 1962 during the Christmas holidays, a release date traditionally reserved for blockbuster events. All of the subsequent May films would follow a similar release pattern, coinciding with Christmas or other holidays. More than thirty years later, television programmers still regularly schedule Rialto's productions as Christmas specials. Both the films' release patterns and their FSK certification of 12 aimed at a family audience, rather than exclusively male adolescents or loyal May readers. Not only did *Der Schatz im Silbersee* become by far the most successful film at the West German box office in 1962 and

1963, but within months of its release, the film had been sold in sixty coun-tries.[44] Rialto repeated the success the following year with *Winnetou I* (1963), again the top-grossing film at the West German box office. Between 1962 and 1965 Rialto's Karl May westerns were in West Germany consis-tently among the top five box-office hits of their year, and received a total of six *Goldene Leinwand* awards.

The intense popularity of the Karl May series was supported by a highly diverse merchandising industry. Martin Böttcher's soundtracks were released on records, went straight into the West German album charts, and triggered off a series of 'western'-themed hits. Both Barker and Brice recorded songs in German.[45] May-related collectables included Karl May film calendars, coffee-table books, star postcards, board and card games, toy figures and guns, and May-themed teacups.[46] Youth and fashion mag-azines propagated a 'western-Lady' and 'Indian' look of denim and leather dresses and fake Indian jewellery. During the 1960s, the Karl May open-air shows at Bad Segeberg, which modelled themselves increasingly on the Rialto productions, attracted about 100,000 visitors each season.[47]

As with the Wallace films, the Karl May series quickly found its imita-tors. Since Wendlandt had acquired the rights to all of May's western nov-els, Artur Brauner's CCC responded with *Old Shatterhand* (1964), which had an original script not based on an identifiable May source. Despite the presence of Pierre Brice and Lex Barker in their established roles, the film differed significantly from Rialto's productions. Brauner had contracted the Argentinian Hugo Fregonese as the film's director, who brought to bear his expertise in Hollywood westerns on the production. *Old Shatter-hand* remained the only Karl May adaptation of the 1960s that featured a hostile Indian attack, and it also introduced an unusual romantic interest in the form of Israeli actress Daliah Lavi.

With a budget of 6 million DM the most expensive of all the May films of the 1960s, the film's eventual box-office success in West Germany was in all likelihood less due to its 'American' style than to its established cast. Given the film's high production costs, however, it is also very likely that Brauner speculated on the export potential of a more Hollywood-style western, particularly in markets such as Britain and the United States. Brauner was unable to repeat this strategy, however, as Pierre Brice had signed an exclusive contract with Rialto and was therefore unavailable as Winnetou in further CCC projects. Brauner signed up Barker and Marie Versini instead for *Der Schut* (1964, The Shoot), an adaptation of one of May's oriental tales, and directed by Robert Siodmak. This production turned out to be CCC's last successful attempt to participate in the May boom. *Der Schatz der Azteken* (1964, The Treasure of the Aztecs) and *Die Pyramide des Sonnengottes* (1964, The Pyramid of the Sun God), based on May's South American stories, failed to have a box-office impact, despite the presence of Barker. Equally unremarkable were two further attempts at May's oriental adventures, *Durchs wilde Kurdistan* (1965, Wild Kurdistan) and *Im Reiche des silbernen Löwen* (1965, In the Empire of the Silver Lion).

By 1966, the cinematic May boom had generally exhausted itself. Production costs had gone up in Yugoslavia, as had the wage demands by Brice and Barker. The change of managerial control at Rialto's distributor Constantin, meanwhile, meant that Wendlandt could no longer rely on unconditional support and seemingly unlimited funds. Much to its detriment, the series began to cut down costs, and thus production values. *Winnetou und das Halbblut Apanatschi* (1966, Winnetou and the Half-breed Apanatschi) was no longer based on a May novel and no longer a top box-office success, although it launched the career of the popular West German film and TV star Uschi Glas. After another disappointing box-office result with *Winnetou und sein Freund Old Firehand* (1966, Winnetou and His Friend Old Firehand), which had been co-produced by Columbia, Wendlandt announced the end of the series. Brauner's CCC produced one last entry, *Winnetou und Old Shatterhand im Tal der Toten* (1968, Winnetou and Old Shatterhand in the Valley of Death), which was in all but name a remake of *Der Schatz im Silbersee*. Brauner's distributor Constantin, however, did not have enough confidence in the film and it lacked a consistent promotion campaign and, without sufficient copies, appeared in West German cinemas over a drawn-out period.[48]

Selling May Abroad: Transformations of Genre

While Rialto's May films in 1960s West Germany functioned as cultural 'events' and there was a high degree of interaction with other media and leisure industries, entirely different distribution and reception patterns for the series can be observed in other countries. Between 1965 and 1969, seven of Rialto's May films were released in cinemas in Britain, initially by the British companies British Lion and Planet, and later by the American distributors Columbia and Warner-Pathé. Columbia also handled the films' distribution in the United States. At the time when the Karl May films were released in Britain, Karl May himself was virtually unknown in anglophone countries. Until the 1970s his works were not even translated into English, which explains the factually inaccurate references to him in British reviews. In the British trade paper *Kinematograph Weekly*, Karl May was credited as the producer of the Rialto cycle.[49] Another review described May as a German author 'who died in 1920' (May died in 1912) and who was 'passionately devoted to the works of Zane Grey'.[50] There is in fact no evidence for such an assumption; indeed, there could not be any influence of the western novelist Grey (1873–1939) on May's work since most of the latter actually predates Grey's.

Without the recognition value and cultural prestige associated with May as a literary figure, the main point of reference for the Rialto series in Britain and in the United States was obviously the Hollywood western, with which the films were compared and accordingly judged. Unlike in West Germany, where the films' titles were taken from the original books (particularly obvious in the titles of *Winnetou I, II,* and *III*), British release titles sounded much more like standard US westerns. *Old Shatterhand* (1964), for example became *Apaches Last Battle, Winnetou II* became *Last of the Renegades, Der Ölprinz* (1965, The Oil Prince) became *Rampage at Apache Wells,* and *Old Surehand* (1965) became *Flaming Frontier.* Furthermore, whereas in West Germany the principle of serialisation and sequels was paramount, in Britain the films were released in no particular order. *Winnetou III,* for example, released as *The Desperado Trail* and climaxing with Winnetou's death, preceded *Winnetou II* in British cinemas by two years, although neither critics nor audiences seem to have noticed the main protagonist's miraculous resurrection.

The fact that the Karl May westerns were overall labelled as B films in Britain had to do not only with their content but also with their specific exhibition context. Unlike their high-profile releases in West Germany, marked by lavish and highly publicised premières, in Britain and the United States the Rialto films were marketed as supporting features in double-bill programmes and were frequently cut to fit this format. The British release version of *Der Schatz im Silbersee* (*The Treasure of Silver Lake*), for example, was more than half an hour shorter than the original, while *Winnetou the Warrior,* the British release version of *Winnetou I,* was cut by ten minutes. Judging by a print of *The Treasure of Silver Lake* held by the British National Film and Television Archive, attempts were made to trim the film in all those aspects that had attracted West German audiences. This interpretation is largely speculative; it is equally, perhaps even more, plausible that the cuts were made arbitrarily to have the film's length comply with that of a supporting feature. Nevertheless, it is notable that what are edited out in the British version (in a rather botched and careless manner) are most of the long and digressive landscape pans, and gone as well are the emotionally charged encounters between Winnetou and Old Shatterhand. As a result, *The Treasure of Silver Lake* has a much quicker pace, and indeed resembles more a standard Hollywood B western in its series of mass battle tableaux and relentless action. Without the mythical relationship and emotional melodrama between the two heroes, however, and without much character motivation left generally, *The Treasure of Silver Lake*'s narrative would have made little sense to West German audiences, and contemporary reviewers in Britain also noted that 'the story line does little more than jerk along'.[51] *Kinematograph Weekly* found *The Treasure of Silver Lake* 'useful for undemanding audiences'.[52]

British critics regularly mentioned narrative incomprehensibility and dreadful dubbing in connection with the Rialto films. Given their multinational cast, the Karl May films had also been dubbed for their West German release. Barker, Brice, and other regular foreign actors had been assigned German voices, which remained constant throughout the series, while the films' German actors recorded their own voices. A small number of foreign actors (for example, Czech-born Herbert Lom) also recorded their own voices in German. This dubbing process created a more natural and authentic impression, and a greater diversity of sounds than the English-language versions (distributed both in the United Kingdom and the United States), which relied on a rather primitive dubbing technology and on often untrained and monotonous voices.

Despite the technical inferiority of the British release versions the Rialto films nevertheless appear to have found in their re-edited format at least some admirers in 1960s Britain. After the first releases, reviews referred to 'new Old Shatterhand and Winnetou adventures', which indicates at least some recognition of these characters. The Rialto films found their most ardent British champions among the writers of the journal *Films and Filming*, who not only redefined the international status of the May series, but also that of the European western more generally. While the contemporary reviews in the *Monthly Film Bulletin* frequently compared the May series unfavourably with the artistically more worthwhile Hollywood westerns of Howard Hawks, John Ford or Delmer Daves, the critics in *Films and Filming*, particularly Allen Eyles and Robin Bean, were more inclined to view the Rialto productions as valuable contributions in the development of the western genre. This interpretation was based on the British release versions of the May films and was articulated against what was perceived as the Hollywood western's malaise and aesthetic stagnation in the early 1960s. Thus Allen Eyles argued in his review of *Winnetou I* (*Winnetou the Warrior*), the first of the Rialto films released in Britain: 'It's taken the Germans to really bring back the straight western, unstunted by low budgets, the emphasis firmly on action and not on psychological overtones … I shed years as I lapped it all up with a rejuvenating relish'.[53] Robin Bean, who in 1965 was invited to visit the set of the Rialto production *Unter Geiern* (*Among Vultures*), reiterated Eyles' stance: 'It's ironical but looking at recent American westerns, it seems that maybe the Germans just have the edge on them. Whereas the Americans have become too slick, humorous, or message conscious about the West, the Germans have taken the boyhood glamorous image where villains are villains and the good guys are supermen'.[54]

Such comments indicate that the May films were successful in Britain (and, arguably, for similar reasons, in the United States as well) precisely because they could be accommodated (notably after substantial re-editing) to the expectations and nostalgic memories of the 'straight' or classical Hollywood western of earlier decades. The Rialto productions were perceived not so much as culturally distinctive German forms but as, albeit enjoyable, imitations of a Hollywood formula. While the Karl May films were appreciated as naïve entertainment, their dominance within the context of German film production, however, was perceived as problematic: 'Until there is an attempt to find an individual identity for the German film, there is not much chance of any original creative ideas emerging. Like much of German life itself, the film world has allowed itself to be dominated by influences from other countries'.[55]

Christopher Frayling has made similar comments about the Karl May westerns in his comparison of the Italian spaghetti western and its West German antecedents. Frayling acknowledges that the West German Karl May adaptations 'created a commercial context which made the Italian westerns possible'.[56] *Der Schatz im Silbersee* (1962) and *Winnetou I* (1963), co-financed with Italian money, had indeed been very successful at the Italian box office, and encouraged Italian producers and directors to venture into the genre. Horst Wendlandt had advised Sergio Leone on production conditions in Yugoslavia, although Leone (and the spaghetti westerns that followed) decided in the end to film elsewhere.[57] Like Germany, Italy had a long tradition of literary adventure fiction, which had been adapted for cinema since the early silent period. A good example is Emilio Salgari and his pirate novels (Lex Barker had appeared in several Salgari adaptations in the late 1950s). Like the Karl May films, the spaghetti westerns had a distinctively operatic quality (indeed Martin Böttcher's haunting use of the harmonica in the Winnetou films foreshadows Ennio Morricone's score for *Once Upon a Time in the West*, 1968), but they replaced the morally unambiguous, almost Manichean, universe of the Rialto series with a much more ambivalent and cynical world-view.

Frayling argues that, from early on, 'the best spaghettis were to demonstrate that, even within a co-production context, it was possible to retain some vestiges of a cultural identity'.[58] The Karl May films, in contrast, are perceived as 'bland' and 'non-committal' and as a 'key factor militating against the development of a legitimate German film culture'.[59] Frayling suggests that the Rialto series forfeited its national-cultural roots by abandoning Karl May's particularly mournful brand of romanticism in favour of an emphasis on physical action, presumably on account of the rather stereotypical view that German culture at its most acceptable is supposed to be tragically romantic, rather than featuring physical action. Nevertheless this, for Frayling, is evidence of the commercial West German film production's complete dependence on an American-dominated industry and on Hollywood's generic formulae. It would be interesting to know whether Frayling's analysis is based on the original West German or the British release versions, as his textual readings seem to suggest the latter. His claim, for example, that the Rialto films de-emphasised the figure of Winnetou certainly cannot be supported by watching the original versions. For Frayling, 'an authentic, critical form of German cinema' is inevitably exemplified by the New German Cinema, rather than by the populist genres Rialto produced in the 1960s, which seems a somewhat odd and less than convincing argument in a book that seems otherwise strongly committed to and makes such an eloquent case for popular traditions in European cinema.

In the following pages I shall challenge Frayling's conclusions by studying firstly, the series' most loyal fan base (West German adolescents), secondly, the relation of the series to discourses of tourism, and thirdly, the reasons for West German Indianophilia that forms a significant background for the success of the Karl May films. While the series may well have presented an 'inauthentic' version of the Wild West (arguably, the films' very intention) and never appeared to represent recognisably German cultural themes and places, they do none the less provide a thoroughly legitimate expression of a German film culture in the 1960s, precisely because they articulate and reflect an ambivalence regarding identity formations (particularly, but not exclusively, of national identity) among its audiences.

Karl May, *Bravo*, and Teenage Fan Culture

Like May's original novels, the Rialto productions fostered a loyal fan following in West Germany, which expressed an almost cultish reverence for the films and their stars. In a 1965 survey of ten- fourteen-year-old boys by a Munich children's book publisher, Pierre Brice was cited in second place after John F. Kennedy as a role model, followed by Albert Schweitzer and James Bond.[60] But it was not only male adolescents that idolised Barker and Brice. Christian Unucka quotes a twenty-year-old female student as saying, 'Lex Barker is for me the ideal of a man. He is strong, intelligent, but also a calm, and fatherly type',[61] while an eighteen-year old female pupil described her admiration for Pierre Brice thus: 'what I particularly like about him is his genuineness, his love for nature, and his attitude to life. He is more than a brilliant actor, he has personality and unusual charisma'.[62] Clearly evident in most of these responses is a high degree of identification, expressed in the conflation between star persona and fictional character that characterises a particularly intense form of star-fan relationship. Perhaps more importantly, these responses suggest that Winnetou and Shatterhand did not function as transgressive rebel icons (as, for example, James Dean or Elvis Presley had been in the 1950s). Indeed, none of the comments, despite their evident intensity of attachment, suggests anything remotely like sexual attraction or passion; instead, Barker and Brice (in their fictional guises) are seen as consensual role models of moral values and civic duties. Crucially, these include charity and a greater international and ecological awareness, rather than a simple collusion with consumerist principles as with previous popular genres.

The series' reception among younger cinema audiences can be documented particularly well in the way West German youth magazines featured the May phenomenon. The weekly teen publication *Bravo* accompanied the Rialto series with regular articles, star photographs, posters, and competitions, the first prize of which was a meeting with the stars, or a visit to the film-set.[63] In line with the magazine's editorial policy, *Bravo* reached its readers by blurring their featured stars' on-screen personae and their 'private' lives. The magazine also clearly understood its pedagogical remit in shaping its readers' ideological attitudes and values. The discursive framework for *Bravo*'s reports was couched in normative contemporary notions regarding general issues of morality, but most specifically regarding marriage and, even more contentiously, sexual identity.

A recurrent motif that emerges from many of *Bravo*'s reports of the May series is its frantic attempt to counter and keep at bay any potential homoerotic interpretation of the two heroes' on-screen relationship and, indeed, any question mark over the actors' sexuality. Salacious scandal mongering of the kind that *Confidential* magazine had pioneered in America in the 1950s, or even the faintest innuendo, never found their way into the pages of *Bravo*. Indeed, when American actor George Nader left Hollywood and subsequently found a new career in the West German crime-film series Jerry Cotton, rumours about his alleged homosexuality were well enough known in West Germany to be alluded to in a number of reviews – not so in the pages of *Bravo*.[64] The general strategy, where the paper did cover more intimate or private details, tended to be not to probe in great depth. It is worth noting, however, that while gay stars, or even speculations about stars' sexuality, were off-limits, homosexuality was not generally a taboo subject in *Bravo*; indeed, it featured quite frequently on its 'life advice' pages, although editorial policy throughout the 1960s was to regard it as a tragic infliction or illness. What seems initially puzzling about *Bravo*'s curious attempt to deflect any homoerotic interpretation of May's heroes and the actors who portray them is that, unlike with Nader, there is no evidence for any actual rumours about either Barker or Brice at the time or any suggestion that either actor was anything but heterosexual. However, in 1963/4 the weekly *Der Spiegel* did cause some furore by suggesting a homosexual subtext in May's original novels. The reason for *Bravo*'s reaction thus has to be found less in extratextual information about Barker or Brice but in the films themselves and their source. In other words, what instigated *Bravo*'s concerted campaign appears to have been motivated by what, on the one hand, made the May films such a hit with adolescents and initially such a safe proposition from the perspective of concerned parents, and by what, on second thoughts rendered them rather dubious, namely the films' (and the novels' before them) complete lack of heterosexual romance. The fact that both the films and subsequently the magazine itself fetishised the two principal male actors in exquisite costumes and make-up, on posters and glamour postcards, only contributed to and even accentuated their somewhat contested masculinity.

As a result, rather contrived and contradictory reports about the May films abounded in the pages of *Bravo*. Thus, in 'No Wife for Pierre Brice', *Bravo* investigated why the actor taking the part of Winnetou was still unmarried, despite the many love-letters sent to him by West German fans (the answer provided was that Brice was simply too busy working, although he very much liked German women, and that he would of course eventually answer all personal letters sent to him by *Bravo* readers).[65] In the feature 'Old Shatterhand triumphs', Old Shatterhand's doomed love story (on screen a rather brief and marginal episode, and completely overshadowed by the character's 'blood-bond' with Winnetou) in *Winnetou I*

(1963) was combined with a brief discussion of Barker's failed marriages.[66] In a more radical step to balance out Barker's and Brice's on-screen homosocial ideal of male friendship, *Bravo* also construed an entirely fictive romantic, and yet curiously chaste, bond between Brice and fellow French actress Marie Versini, who became an identification figure for female readers and a kind of mediator between them and their idol Brice. Versini had played Winnetou's sister Ntscho-Tschi in *Winnetou I* (1963), who, despite her on-screen death in that film was, as a result of her popularity with teen audiences, resurrected in *Winnetou und sein Freund Old Firehand* (1966). As Thommi Herrwerth has argued in his semi-autobiographical and ironic memoir of the magazine, 'The two, neither engaged nor married to each other, appeared as a film dream couple, and almost symbiotically linked. Every day they had to be apart from each other was for the *Bravo* readers a day of sorrow and pity'.[67]

Bravo's annual reader polls and prizes (an Indian figurine called Otto) for the most popular film and pop music stars are a further indication of the enormous success of the Rialto films with a teen audience.[68] Until the early 1960s, the *Bravo* polls were invariably headed by indigenous stars such as O.W. Fischer, Hardy Krüger, and Ruth Leuwerik. Foreign stars, on the other hand, featured more erratically. In the 1950s only James Dean and Brigitte Bardot had experienced temporary popularity. In the 1960s, Rock Hudson, Anthony Perkins, and Sean Connery were the only popular foreign male stars. Non-German female stars had even less of an impact (from 1960 to 1970 only Doris Day and Sophia Loren ever reached the top three). Pierre Brice and Marie Versini, however, gained top position as best male and female film star in five consecutive years between 1964 and 1969, significantly outclassing Barker, who only once, in 1965, managed to reach third place. This corresponds to the way in which *Bravo* centred its features about the May films predominantly around Brice and Winnetou, rather than on Barker and Shatterhand.

There were two occasions where the demands of the teenage fans and Rialto's intentions clashed very publicly. In the pre-production phase of *Winnetou III* (1965), Horst Wendlandt had reassured May readers in newspaper interviews that the film would be faithful to its literary source, namely that it would end with Winnetou's death. Director Harald Reinl was initially more cautious: 'I don't think it is as easy as that. We get numerous letters that plead: Winnetou must not die. If he does, we won't see the film'.[69] *Winnetou III* eventually did end with a long and drawn-out death scene, full of pathos and sentiment and one of the few scenes in the whole series where May's original romanticism came to the fore. *Bravo* prepared its readers for the inevitable. Prior to the film's release, it printed production stills depicting Winnetou's last moments (according to *Bravo* the 'photo scoop of the year') and serialised excerpts of the original novel. It also provided a teaser for the film with captions such as: 'Who shot Winnetou? What were his last words? Is Old Shatterhand able to avenge his friend's death?'.[70] By the time *Winnetou III* was released, the distributor's promotional material declared in bold headlines: 'Winnetou is dead! Winnetou is immortal! Winnetou lives on!', before reassuring both teen audiences and faithful May readers: 'One consolation remains. Karl May wrote after *Winnetou III* earlier adventures of the noble Apache chief, and the film-makers will follow in May's footsteps'.[71] Contemporary reviews, however, reported devastated audience reactions at the film's tragic ending: 'the pain felt in the stalls was real and audible'.[72]

Wendlandt's decision to discontinue the Karl May series altogether one and a half years after *Winnetou III* elicited an unprecedented and well-publicised public outcry among fans, which was carefully orchestrated and fanned by *Bravo*. Over several issues, *Bravo* printed articles attacking Wendlandt with headlines such as 'Winnetou must not die like this', 'Who saves Winnetou?', and 'Aren't you ashamed, Herr Wendlandt?' and published over a hundred letters, significantly mostly from female fans. In an open letter to Wendlandt, an anonymous Berlin housewife wrote, 'We want to see Pierre Brice as Winnetou, a man we unfortunately don't have in real life',[73] while another letter stated 'We are eighty girls in the first year of a commercial college and we are outraged by Horst Wendlandt's infamy'.[74] While Wendlandt's decision remained final, expressions of loyalty for the May films and their stars continued to appear in the pages of *Bravo* for years after the series had ended, and explain the enduring popularity of Pierre Brice and Marie Versini at a time when neither of them had appeared in any significant film production since the Rialto series.[75]

Bravo's coverage of the Karl May phenomenon of the early to mid-1960s is instructive in that it provides an, albeit highly mediated, insight not only into the profiles of the series' most ardent fans (which, unlike most other westerns, included female as well as male spectators), but, more specifically, into these fans' identificatory preferences, and fantasies, the ideological parameters that underpinned them, and, most crucially, how popular mass journalism of the time reflected upon, negotiated, and reformulated the desires of its readers through its engagement with the separate mass medium of cinema.

In the Footsteps of Winnetou: Karl May and Mass Tourism

While the fan discourse of *Bravo* helps one to understand the relationship between a younger audience and the Rialto series' stars, publications such as the *Illustrierter Film-Kurier*[76], reveal another appeal of the series. From very early on, these promotional ephemera foregrounded the series' production values. It included maps of the locations and fact sheets that list the props in use in the minutest detail: 'unwieldy goods, such as one locomotive (built in 1860), 200 metres of rail tracks including points, five stagecoaches, one kitchen van, 40 canoes, and 20 telegraph poles'.[77] The lists continue by detailing the number of guns (down to their exact specification), boots, bracelets, and belts. The *Illustrierter Film-Kurier* presented the films' production as an adventure in its own right, and frequently focused on stunt work and Erwin Lange's pyrotechnic special effects. Thus, the issue on *Winnetou II* (1964) highlights the film's main attractions as 'grottoes filmed for the first time in colour; Winnetou's fight with a grizzly bear; explosions and fire in the oilfields; the destruction of an Indian village through fire; a catapulted Wild West bomb; and numerous individual fights and mass battles'.[78] Subsequent issues document the difficulties the production team encountered in, for example, filming canoe rides on rapids, and usually note how bravely actors and production personnel master these situations. The *Illustrierter Film-Kurier* reported production disasters with the same factual tone it used for lists of props. Thus, the issue on *Old Surehand* (1965) catalogues a series of mishaps, atrocious weather conditions, and, finally, a tragic bus accident. This reads almost like a report from a battlefield: 'The end result: three serious casualties in intensive care among the Yugoslav crew, one of whom has died in the meantime, one other serious injury, and twelve slight injuries'.[79]

Apart from such morbid sensationalism, however, the *Illustrierter Film-Kurier* also emphasised the scenic beauty and tourist qualities of the films' Yugoslav locations (in fact, even the most horrendous location reports are still presented as if it were a kind of extreme adventure tourism). The issue on *Winnetou II* mentions 'the bizarre, and beautiful grottoes, a widespread system of caves near the village of Postojna, better known under its old name from the time of the Austrian empire: the Adelsberg grottoes'.[80] Even more specifically addressed at a tourist audience – in fact, reading more like a tourist brochure – is the following passage in the issue on *Winnetou III* (1965):

> One can hardly find a more romantic landscape than the cobalt blue and emerald-green Plitvice lakes in Yugoslavia … The water is clear and transparent for several metres in depth. On the bottom of the lakes are tree branches covered in lime scale, producing an effect of glittering silver … The Yugoslavs are aware of the uniqueness of this natural beauty. The lakes and surrounding forests have been given the status of a protected natural park. The forests are more like jungles, and are the habitat for bears, wolves, wild cats, eagles, and vultures. During the summer months, many tourists explore this region on designated tracks, though they will rarely encounter these elusive animals.[81]

Of course, the films' textual organisation in many ways encouraged such modes of reception. Particularly in the films directed by Harald Reinl (following in the footsteps of Arnold Fanck's mountain films of the 1920s) scenery becomes an attraction in its own right. As in the *Heimatfilm* of the 1950s, the narratives of the May films frequently come to a standstill at certain moments, in order to adequately capture the colours of the lakes, the shapes of the mountain ranges, and the romantic beauty of waterfalls, rapids, and grottoes. There is clear evidence that audiences saw the Rialto films' landscape images not just as a cinematic attraction but also as a potential tourist destination (Yugoslavia, and especially the Croatian coast, slowly emerged during these years as one of the prime foreign holiday destinations for West German tourists after Austria and Italy). According to Lutz Helm, both Rialto and its distributor Constantin were inundated with letters, asking for the exact locations of the May films: 'A "European Arizona" was discovered in Yugoslavia, and one can hardly imagine a more beautiful and photogenic place. Consequently the tourist boom in this region has become much stronger. Between Ljubljana and Zadar, and from Rijeka to Sibenik numerous Karl May fans are searching for the real landscapes of their childhood dreams, recreated on the cinema screen'.[82]

Bravo's coverage also exploited the tourist angle of the May series. Following her winning a *Bravo* competition, a seventeen-year-old female May fan was sent to Yugoslavia to meet Pierre Brice and Lex Barker on location. The two-page spread documenting her trip includes photos of the lucky winner visiting the filmset, buying water melons at the local fruit market, going to the beach, dining at a local restaurant (the young woman's verdict of Yugoslav cuisine: spicy, but tasty), and enjoying a dance with Pierre Brice, while the text captions fills in more information about the 'beautiful spa town of Opatija', its sights, and the comfortable hotel accommodation.[83]

Significantly, none of the promotional material ever claimed any American authenticity for the Croatian locations of the Karl May westerns. While the America of May's original novels was an imagined and idealised place, it still claimed a certain authenticity as a migratory destination. America was for May a utopian refuge for disenchanted and socially disenfranchised Germans, where a better and benevolently patriarchal German community could be built on the principles of a Christian-informed ecological and pacifist way of life. This particular way of life was seen by May as a resistance to the ongoing progress of modernity and industrialisation. The Rialto films, on the other hand, replaced the context of migration with tourism and leisure and, although they carry some of May's themes (e.g. ecological awareness, pacifism), the America they portray is as unashamedly fake and at the same time as hyper-real as the Alpine theme parks of the *Heimatfilm* were in the 1950s. The scenery is not perceived as second-choice, but is presented with a certain pride that wild landscapes are in fact not confined to America, but can be found in Europe as well. While the Rialto films may faithfully re-create recognisable props from the American western repertoire (border towns, saloons, saguaro cacti, stagecoaches), the main visual emphasis, highlighted in the panoramic CinemaScope images, is on the scale and distinct emptiness (in terms of human presence) of their decidedly un-American landscape. As I argued earlier with respect to the rather incongruous locations of *Der Schatz im Silbersee*, the films are concerned with generic rather than with geographical verisimilitude.

Tassilo Schneider has argued that the Karl May films offered a 'neatly organised narrative and social utopia where everything is out in the open, plain to see, and under control'.[84] In his reading of the series, the reassuring and comforting conventions of the Rialto films and the reasons for their success are to be found in their evasion of the prevalent sexual and social conflicts in West German society and their postulation of moral certainties. For similar reasons, West German tourists temporarily escaped their constrictions, identities, and moralities in their annual pilgrimages to Southern European beach resorts. The controlling gaze that Schneider detects in the May films is essentially the same impulse that determines tourists' selective appropriation and collection of vistas, sights, and signs. In other words, tourism and popular cinema in the 1960s provided very similar functions and, as in the case of the *Heimatfilm* and the domestic tourist industry in the 1950s, supported each other. John Urry has pointed out that 'generally places are chosen to be gazed upon because there is an anticipation, especially through daydreaming and fantasy, of intense pleasures … Such anticipation is constructed and sustained through non-tourist practices, such as film, TV, literature … which construct and reinforce that gaze'.[85]

The Karl May films and their function for audiences in the 1960s lend support to Urry's argument. The series constructed a tourist gaze for its audiences that could be satisfied in the cinema itself (audiences could experience the 'journey' to the karst mountains and silver lakes 'virtually' from their seat, enjoying the CinemaScope colour spectacle). Alternatively, the films, and in particular the promotional literature surrounding them, could hold out the promise and potential for a real journey, made possible by West German tour operators. Conversely, tour operators offering holidays in Yugoslavia could draw on the images and iconography of the May films in their own promotional campaigns and discourses. Tourists themselves, meanwhile, could enter a previously entirely fictional on-screen world, the films' 'real' landscapes of their 'childhood dreams'. The psychological processes involved in this juggling of real, virtual, imagined, and remembered places are quite complex: a real Yugoslavia that becomes an imagined America, which becomes a virtual reality in the cinema, the impression of which may then feed back into the experience of the real location. What this blurring of real, virtual, and imagined places does ultimately achieve, though, is a concomitant dispersal and increasing irrelevance of any sense of 'essential' or 'real' national signifiers. A number of critics of the May films have noted that, despite their magnificent scenery, they do seem to lack a sense of place, partly because the films, like the products of the tourist industry, subscribe to a definition of space that is linked exclusively to their function *vis-à-vis* individual desires, dreams, needs, and expectations:

> In a May film, the landscape… is never a malignant, subversive force, to be subdued/conquered by the agents of a social order. In fact, what precisely constitutes such a social order…is in the May films altogether hard to iden-

tify. Social communities, farms, ranches, towns, play decidedly minor roles in these films, and despite the prominence of Indian tribes and characters, there is little concern for their social organization and the cultural and ideological structures that govern their existence.[86]

In this respect, the Karl May films can be seen to have updated May's own 'escapism' to the parameters of a new social and cultural context, in which new moralities and identities are being forged either alongside or against the demands of a consumerist society. The resulting ambivalences are evident in the films themselves, as well as in the promotional strategies and reception patterns I described earlier. Narratively the films extolled the virtues of male friendship (to such an excessive extent that a publication such as *Bravo* felt the need to police this element extra-textually) and the values of an untouched nature. Yet the films' very mode of production, as described in the location reports in the *Illustrierter Film-Kurier*, participated in the exploitation of a 'real' natural idyll and paved the way for subsequent tourist invasions in the 1970s and 1980s. Following the bloody disintegration of Yugoslavia in the 1990s, the battles of which reached the same locations that had been used in the Rialto films and left scars on the landscape in the form of unexploded mines, Karl May tourism to the region appears to have tentatively recommenced in recent years, and has led to at least one publication specifically designed to identify and introduce Rialto's film locations to potential fan travellers.[87] In the 1960s, the Rialto films may have tried to capture the nostalgic and old-fashioned appeal of May's works, but they also represented a state-of-the-art and modern cinematic attraction, replete with colour, CinemaScope, and special effects, which effectively negated the novels in their old-fashioned quaintness. Moreover, while the appeal of May's heroes with West German audiences still focused to a certain extent on their moral values and their concern for nature and peace, these characteristics were no longer couched in terms of either German identity or Christianity.

National Identity and Special Affinities

What the reception of the Rialto series had in common with that of other popular genres of the 1960s (such as the Edgar Wallace films) and, more generally, with the political discourses in West Germany of the time was an underlying uneasiness with and diffusion of the notion of national identity and a concomitant emergence of a cosmopolitan, consumer-oriented, and individualist identity. Like the Edgar Wallace films, the Karl May series enabled its German audiences to experience a feeling of cultural nostalgia, while at the same time evading references to Germany's more recent past. Like the Wallace films, the Karl May films were set in what Tassilo Schneider has referred to as a 'utopia of the adventure', a pleasurable fantasy of loss of identity. At the same time, the series also catered to a craving, particularly among the younger generation, for a 'universal', largely secular 'humanist', and 'modern' identity. In this context it is particularly interesting to see how May's partisanship towards the American Indian, which remained largely intact in Rialto's productions, could be functionalised and appropriated in the postwar decades.

Even before Karl May, identificatory fantasies had existed in Germany that proclaimed special affinities between Germans and Indians, although, as Hartmut Lutz has sarcastically pointed out, 'few Native Americans are aware of this supposedly special relationship'.[88] As Lutz documents, from the Wilhelmine period into the Nazi era, this imagined bond was frequently conceptualised around notions of racial purity and exclusivity, of segregated tribal social organisation, and of an anti-modernist and anti-Enlightenment perspective Germans and Indians supposedly shared.[89] Couched in these terms, anti-Semitism and a romantic attachment towards the plight of the American Indian could easily be negotiated alongside each other and posed no real contradictions, and the fact that there was hardly any real contact between Germans and Indians on German soil and that the relationship was thus largely imaginary surely helped.

The perception of a special affinity and the form of adulation that Lutz has termed German 'Indianthusiasm' persisted well into the postwar period and, to a certain extent, is still relevant today, although the ideological parameters for this identification have clearly changed. Contemporaneously with the first postwar Karl May festivals and stage shows in Bad Segeberg in the 1950s, amateur societies of Indianthusiasts (referred to as 'hobbyists' or 'Indianists') were founded in both East and West Germany, whose main pastime was (and remains) to study and collect native American culture and, most importantly, to dress up in Indian clothes and imitate native American social and cultural practices, behaviour, and crafts. This curious practice of ethnic impersonation (which recalls of course Karl May's own ethnic masquerade and which is replicated in the Rialto productions with their French Indian Pierre Brice) could well be, and has been, interpreted as a form of offensive 'caricature', as 'ethnic drag', and as a neocolonial, racist reflex.[90] However, Katrin Sieg, who has studied a number of hobbyist and Indianist groups, notes that there are highly diverse political and individual motivations for these ethnic performances:

> Some (primarily within the younger generation) identify with American Indians as a way of practicing an alternative, 'green' lifestyle marked by ecological awareness and a rejection of the trappings of consumer culture and the class distinctions it fosters. By contrast, others (who first took up hobbyism in the postwar years) appear to have been impelled by a sense of victimization, national defeat, and emasculation feelings that they were able to symbolically redress through the ritual of ethnic masquerade.[91]

Sieg goes on to argue that particularly during the early postwar years, the oppression of American Indians by white Americans could aid German hobbyists' identification in the sense of a shared experience of occupation.

While Sieg's subject is clearly demarcated and highly distinctive groups, it is tempting none the less to apply her findings to the concerns of this chapter, namely to the audiences of the Rialto films and the reasons why they were so successful. In any case, it is reasonable to assume that the German hobbyists constituted a loyal audience segment of the Karl May westerns, since hobbyism and an appreciation of Karl May's novels often appear to go together, or the former is triggered off by the latter. Similarly, the identification by Sieg's younger generation of hobbyists along the lines of alternative, ecologically aware lifestyles tallies with some of the comments made by May fans in publications such as *Bravo*. Although Tassilo Schneider's previously quoted comment that in the Rialto films there is 'little concern' for the 'social organisation' of Indian tribes and the 'cultural and ideological structures that govern their existence' may largely hold true, there are aspects of the films' *mise en scène*, in particular the attention to and elaborate detail of Indian costumes and handicrafts, that do suggest the films' ambitions of authenticity. Moreover, apart from the films themselves, evidence for a more ethnographic angle to the series can again be found in the promotional ephemera of the phenomenon, such as the *Illustrierter Film-Kurier*, which regularly published articles on Indian history, culture, and crafts, as well as reports on how the series' art directors incorporated authentic Indian designs in the films. Finally, it is worth speculating as to whether the widespread rejection of Hollywood westerns in the postwar years in West Germany can also be traced back to the special identification of Germans with Indians that Lutz, Sieg, and others have identified. After all, it is only in the 1950s that Hollywood, and then only gradually, revised its version of Indians from largely negative portrayals to more complex representations (e.g., in Delmer Daves' *Broken Arrow*, 1950, or John Ford's *Cheyenne Autumn*, 1963). It is notable that American westerns with positive Indian characters have often fared better with West German audiences than Hollywood's more traditional tales of Indian ambush and cavalry rescue (the latter element, following Katrin Sieg's argument, perhaps providing an uncomfortable reminder of U.S. military occupation). What seems clear, however, and what is supported by Sieg's studies is that the German Indianophilia that expresses itself in the postwar period with such force in the Bad Segeberg festivals and the literary and ultimately cinematic revival of Karl May provided an opportunity for West Germans to negotiate questions of identity and otherness without having to return to the tainted and compromised ideology of otherness the Nazi period had instilled. In this respect, Rialto's Karl May films provided a similar function to the Edgar Wallace films, even if their generic, visual, and narrative constructions were significantly different from each other.

It is no coincidence that during the second half of the 1960s East Germany's national film company DEFA also produced its own version of westerns (the *Indianerfilm*), their emergence being at least partly a response to the enormous success of the Karl May films in the West and certainly conceived as a corrective to the escapist romanticism of May's novels, which were denounced as inappropriately bourgeois throughout the GDR period.[92] Like their western counterpart, the *Indianerfilme* were planned on an international scale; many of the films were also shot in Yugoslavia, and their leading 'Indian' was the Yugoslav actor Gojko Mitic, who had previously appeared as a supporting actor in the Rialto films. However, where the Rialto productions emphasised spectacle and adventure, the East German *Indianerfilme* aimed more for ethnographic authenticity and the depiction of social realities. Although certainly more subdued and politically didactic than their Western counterparts, these films proved highly popular in East Germany, and they made Mitic a star. They also continued to be made long after the May series in the West had reached its end – a later example being *Blauvogel* (1978), directed by Ulrich Weiß, which tells the story of a young English settler's son being raised by an Indian tribe in the late eighteenth century. In the DEFA western, as in the Karl May films, questions of identity and personal morality were paramount. In the *Indianerfilm*, of course, Karl Marx rather than May, the international solidarity of the oppressed, and anti-imperialist sentiments provided the answer to the quest for identity. Nevertheless, in films such as *Blauvogel*, with its expression of an at times desperate yearning to be someone else, to shed one's national identity, escapist fantasy often wins out over serious ethnographic intentions and didactic concerns. Moreover, as Katrin Sieg has pointed out, evidence among East German hobbyists (or Indianists) suggest that identification in the GDR with American Indians could indicate resistance against socialism as a 'form of alien domination', which suggests that the *Indianerfilme* too may have been open to multiple and even resistant, ideological readings.[93]

In the context of 1960s West German popular culture, in contrast, a new form of a cosmopolitan identity was articulated within the framework of global consumerism and increasing leisure opportunities. The May phenomenon thus provides an interesting example of how social utopianism, consumer culture, and the erosion of national identity interlinked in the early to mid-1960s in very unusual and almost paradoxical combinations. In its address of issues of individual rather than national identity and morality, the Karl May series was able to tap into general anxieties and uncertainties that would find a more pronounced outlet several years later. Given the youth profile of the May series' audience, it is interesting to note that the subsequent student movements of the late 1960s and 1970s would equally define themselves against established notions of German identity, and emphasise issues of pacifism, ecological concern, and international solidarity (issues that are strongly addressed by May's work). I am not suggesting that all of the teenage May fans of the early 1960s matured into the left-wing student protesters of the 1970s (though some of them might have), or that either May's novels or the Rialto adaptations somehow paved the way for civil disobedience through some textually immanent layers of subversion. Indeed, as I have argued above, the May phenomenon of the 1960s was in many ways both conformist and strongly consumerist, though not without the potential of divergent interpretations. Rather, what I want to suggest is that the early to mid-1960s and its cultural products possess a greater degree of ideological complexity than they are generally given credit for. Many of the discourses that surface in seemingly innocuous popular phenomena such as the May media frenzy indicate the beginnings of a significant revision of the interrelationship between social ideals, capitalism, and national identity that dominated debates in the West and East German societies over the next two decades.

Notes

1. For studies of the spaghetti western, see Christopher Frayling, *Spaghetti Westerns*, London and New York 1981; and Christopher Wagstaff, 'A Forkful of Westerns: Industry, Audiences and the Italian Western', in *Popular European Cinema*; ed. Richard Dyer and Ginette Vincendeau, London and New York 1992, pp. 245–263.
2. Rudolf Augstein, 'Weiter Weg zu Winnetou', *Der Spiegel*, 1 May 1995, p. 130.
3. Anon., 'Karl der Deutsche', *Der Spiegel*, 12 September 1962, p. 154.
4. Quoted by Augstein, 'Weiter Weg zu Winnetou', p. 141.
5. Colleen Cook, 'Germany's Wild West Author: A Researcher's Guide to Karl May', *German Studies Review*, vol. 5, part 1, 1982, p. 79.
6. Ibid., p. 71.
7. Arno Schmidt, *Sitara und der Weg dorthin: Eine Studie über Wesen, Werk, & Wirkung KARL MAY'S*; Karlsruhe 1963.
8. Heribert von Feilitzsch, 'Karl May: the Wild West as Seen in Germany', *Journal of Popular Culture*, vol. 27, part 3, 1993, p. 185.
9. An exception was made for May's later novels, which were deemed to exhibit a pacifist tendency and were therefore kept out of print: see Cook, 'Germany's Wild West Author', p. 75.
10. Klaus Mann, 'Karl May: Hitler's Literary Mentor', *Kenyon Review*, no. 2, 1940, pp. 391–400.
11. Cf., for example, Richard H. Cracroft, 'The American West of Karl May', *American Quarterly*, vol. 19, no. 2, Summer 1967, pp. 249–258; Christopher Frayling, 'Karl May and the Noble Savage', in Frayling, *Spaghetti Westerns*, pp. 103–117.
12. Cf. Glenn Infield, 'The Führer and the Cowboys', in Infield, *Hitler's Secret Life: The Mysteries of the Eagle's Nest*, New York 1979.
13. For comprehensive biographical studies of May, cf. Hans Wollschläger, *Karl May: Grundriss eines gebrochenen Lebens*, Zurich 1976; *Karl May. Biographie in Dokumenten und Bildern*, ed. Gerhard Klussmeier and Heiner Paul, Hildesheim 1987; Hermann Wohlgschaft, *Große Karl-May-Biographie: Leben und Werk*, Paderborn 1994.
14. Deniz Göktürk, *Künstler, Cowboys, Ingenieure. Kultur- und mediengeschichtliche Studien zu deutschen Amerika-Texten 1912–1920*, Munich 1998, p. 158.
15. Ibid., pp. 158–159.
16. Jörg Kastner, *Das grosse Karl May Buch*; Bergisch-Gladbach 1992, pp. 308–309.
17. Term for nineteenth-century German pulp novels.
18. Cook, 'Germany's Wild West Author', p. 85.

19. Cf. Tim Bergfelder, 'Im wilden Orient. Die Karl May-Verfilmung Durch die Wüste 1935/6', in *Triviale Tropen. Exotische Reise- und Abenteuerfilme aus Deutschland 1919–1939*, ed. Jörg Schöning, Munich 1997, p. 184.
20. Cook, 'Germany's Wild West Author', p. 75.
21. Von Feilitzsch, 'Karl May: the Wild West as seen in Germany', p. 182.
22. Klaus Theweleit, *Männerphantasien*, Frankfurt-on-Main 1978.
23. Cracroft, 'The American West of Karl May', p. 257.
24. Ibid., p. 255.
25. Martin Kuester, 'American Indians and German Indians. Perspectives of Doom in Cooper and May', *Western American Literature*, vol. 23, part 3, 1988, p. 220.
26. Augstein, 'Weiter Weg zu Winnetou', p. 138.
27. Quoted in ibid., p. 133.
28. Kastner, *Das grosse Karl May Buch*, p. 106.
29. Wolfgang Jacobsen and Heike Klapdor, 'Merhameh – Karl Mays schöne Spionin', in Schöning, *Triviale Tropen*, pp. 124–141.
30. Kastner, *Das grosse Karl May Buch*, pp. 110–111.
31. Göktürk, *Künstler, Cowboys, Ingenieure*, pp. 175 and 181.
32. Bergfelder in Schöning, *Triviale Tropen*, pp. 185–186.
33. Ibid., p. 186.
34. Kastner, *Das grosse Karl May Buch*, p. 133.
35. Cf., e.g., Hilke Thode-Arora, *Für fünfzig Pfennig um die Welt. Die Hagenbeckschen Völkerschauen*, Frankfurt-on-Main and New York 1989.
36. Cf. Manfred Christ, *Von Tarzan bis Old Shatterhand. Lex Barker und seine Filme*, Tuningen 1995.
37. Manfred Barthel, *So war es wirklich. Der deutsche Nachkriegsfilm*, Berlin 1986, p. 165.
38. Brice's previous career in France had consisted predominantly of supporting roles; among these were minor parts in Claude Chabrol's *Les Cousins* (1958) and Marcel Carné's *Les Tricheurs* (1958). Cf. *Karl May im Film*, ed. Christian Unucka, Hebertshausen 1991, p. 298.
39. Tassilo Schneider, 'Finding a Heimat in the Wild West: Karl May and the German Western of the 1960s', in *Back in the Saddle Again. New Essays on the Western*, ed. Edward Buscombe and Roberta E. Pearson, London 1998, p. 150.
40. Rüdiger Koschnitzki, 'Harald Reinl', in *CineGraph. Lexikon zum deutschsprachigen Film*, ed. Hans–Michael Bock, Munich 1984– .
41. Ibid.
42. Kastner, *Das grosse Karl May Buch*, p. 141.
43. Joe Hembus, *Der deutsche Film kann gar nicht beser sein. Ein Pamphlet von gestern. Eine Abrechnung von heute*, Munich 1981, p. 200.
44. hkf, 'Exporterfolg für Karl May', *Film-Echo/Filmwoche*, 17 August 1963, p. 11.
45. Anon., 'Singend auf Kriegspfad', *Bravo*, no. 48, 22 November 1965, pp. 4–5.
46. Anon., 'Karl May Sensationen – aber nicht nur für Filmproduzenten', *Ringpress-feature* 1964.
47. Kastner, *Das grosse Karl May Buch*, p. 280.
48. Ibid., p. 263.
49. Anon., 'The Treasure of Silver Lake'. *Kine-Weekly*, 3 March 1966.
50. David Austen, 'Continental Westerns', *Films and Filming*, vol. 17, 1971, p. 36.
51. Anon., 'The Treasure of Silver Lake', *Monthly Film Bulletin*, vol. 33, no. 387, April 1966.
52. Anon., 'The Treasure of Silver Lake'. *Kine-Weekly*, 3 March 1966.
53. Allen Eyles, 'Winnetou the Warrior', *Films and Filming*, vol. 11, part 7, 1965, p. 29.
54. Robin Bean, 'Way Out West in Yugoslavia', *Films and Filming*, vol. 11, 1965, p. 51.
55. Robin Bean, 'Sex, Guns, and May', in *Films and Filming*, vol. 11, part 6, p. 56.
56. Frayling, *Spaghetti Westerns*, p. 115.
57. Interview by the author with Horst Wendlandt, January 1993, in Berlin.
58. Frayling, *Spaghetti Westerns*, p. 115.
59. Ibid., p. 114.

60. Anon., 'Pierre Brice als Vorbild', *Film-Echo/Filmwoche*, 5 November1965, p. 18.
61. Unucka, *Karl May im Film*, p. 291.
62. Ibid., p. 299.
63. Anon., 'Reise zu Winnetou', *Bravo*, no. 38, 22 September 1963, pp. 8–9.
64. Cf., e.g., Ulrich Hoppe, 'Interview mit George Nader: Jerry Cotton tut mir leid', *Bravo*, no. 24, 6 June 1966, pp. 8–9.
65. Anon., 'Keine Frau für Pierre Brice', *Bravo*, no. 42, 20 October 1963.
66. Anon., 'Old Shatterhand triumphiert', *Bravo*, no. 40, 6 October 1963, p. 9.
67. Thommi Herrwerth, *Partys, Pop und Petting. Die Sixties im Spiegel der Bravo*, Marburg 1997, p. 36.
68. Ibid., p. 108.
69. Hans Höhn, 'Teenagers Leinwandwunsch: Winnetou darf nicht sterben', *Der Kurier/Der Tag*, 30 July 1964.
70. Anon., 'Winnetous Tod', *Bravo*, no. 30, 25 July 1965, p. 8.
71. Anon., 'Winnetou III', *Illustrierter Film-Kurier*, no. 66, 1965, p. 9.
72. R.F., 'Winnetou ist tot', *Münchner Merkur*, 19 October 1965.
73. Anon., 'Leserbrief', *Bravo*, no. 14, 27 March 1967, p. 17.
74. Anon., ''Leserbrief', *Bravo*, no. 18, 24 April 1967, p. 82.
75. Brice's career came to a halt, in fact, with the end of the Karl May series and was only revived in 1975 when he again took on the role of Winnetou in the Karl May open-air shows at Elspe, a rival festival to the longer-established one at Bad Segeberg. Brice portrayed Winnetou at Elspe until 1986. Cf. Unucka, *Karl May im Film*, p. 17.
76. The *Illustrierter Film-Kurier* has accompanied German cinema releases (both indigenous and foreign films) since the 1920s, and it is still being published today. Usually on sale at the box office, it focused on one film in a glossy, 12- to 16-page pamphlet, and included synopsis, production information, star portraits, production stills, and features, as well as adverts for tie-in products, such as books, toys, etc.
77. *Illustrierter Film-Kurier*, 'Winnetou I', no. 22, 1964, p. 9.
78. *Illustrierter Film-Kurier*, 'Winnetou II', no. 15, 1965, p. 4.
79. *Illustrierter Film-Kurier*, 'Old Surehand', no. 76, 1965, p. 6.
80. *Illustrierter Film-Kurier*, 'Winnetou II', no. 15, 1965, p. 4.
81. Paul Gnuva, 'Hinter den Wasserschleiern von Plitvice', *Illustrierter Film-Kurier*, 'Winnetou III', no. 66, 1965, p. 7.
82. Lutz Helm, 'Land der Urlaubs-Sehnsucht: Winnetous Jagdgründe', in 'Winnetou und das Halbblut Apanatschi', *Ringpress-feature*, 1966, p. 6.
83. Anon., 'Reise zu Winnetou', *Bravo*, no. 38, 22 September 1963, pp. 8–9.
84. Schneider, in Buscombe and Pearson, *Back in the Saddle Again*, p. 155.
85. John Urry, *The Tourist Gaze. Leisure and Travel in Contemporary Societies*, London 1990, p. 3.
86. Tassilo Schneider, 'Genre and Ideology in the Popular German Cinema 1950–1972' (PhD diss., University of Southern California 1994), p. 278.
87. Michael Petzel, *Der Weg zum Silbersee. Dreharbeiten und Drehorte der Karl May Filme*, Berlin 2001.
88. Hartmut Lutz, 'German Indianthusiasm. A Socially Constructed German National(ist) Myth', in *Germans and Indians. Fantasies, Encounters, Projections*, ed. Colin G. Calloway, Gerd Gemünden, and Susanne Zantop, Lincoln and London, 2002, p. 169.
89. Ibid., pp. 167–180.
90. Cf., e.g., Marta Carlson, 'Germans Playing Indians', in Calloway et al, *Germans and Indians*, pp. 213–216.
91. Katrin Sieg, 'Indian Impersonation as Historical Surrogation', in Calloway et al, *Germans and Indians*, p. 218.
92. Cf. Gerd Gemünden, 'Between Karl May and Karl Marx: The DEFA *Indianerfilme*', in Calloway et al, *Germans and Indians*, pp. 243–256.
93. Sieg, in Calloway et al, *Germans and Indians*, pp. 218–219.

Chapter 9

BEYOND RESPECTABILITY: B-FILM PRODUCTION IN THE 1960s

On an international scale and particularly compared with a major Holly-wood studio, Rialto and CCC were minor outlets, producing the equivalent of American B films, and they remained overall dependent on distributors such as Gloria and Constantin (see chapter 4). To distinguish them in this chapter from smaller production companies, therefore, requires a definition of the concept of the B film that is in proportional relation to the context of the West German film industry in the 1960s. Within this context, Rialto and CCC constituted the established mainstream and their films represented the best in production values the national industry as a whole could muster. In other words, Brauner and Wendlandt constituted the top of the hierarchy in West German film production of the 1960s. The producers I am dealing with in this chapter, on the other hand, frequently operated from the fringes of mainstream production. They specialised in low-budget and disreputable film genres (such as sex and horror) and gained notoriety rather than acceptance within the West German film establishment. Partly owing to cash shortage and partly motivated by unexplored production and market possibilities, these producers embraced multinational co-production even more enthusiastically than their established counterparts. For smaller companies, frequently lacking consistent backing by indigenous distributors, the spreading of profits across different national markets was vital.

As discussed in the previous chapters, Rialto and CCC largely concentrated on established European co-production partners, such as Italy and France, and on low-cost production bases in Spain or Yugoslavia. The West German B-film sector in the mid-1960s, reacting to an international demand for exotic adventure films and cosmopolitan spy thrillers in the vein of the James Bond series, ventured into co-productions with countries as far away as Thailand, South Africa, and Hong Kong. That this international mode of production was closely linked to generic preferences is evident in the reorientation that occurred by the late 1960s, when the B film refocused on the home-grown sex film.

From *Sittenfilme* to Exotic Adventures

Among West German B-film producers, Wolf C. Hartwig is possibly the best known and most reviled. Attacked equally by the film establishment and by the emerging protagonists of the New German Cinema, his Munich-based company Rapid was labelled a 'filth factory', occupying 'the basement of German film production'.[1] Hartwig's regular clashes and disputes with the West German film industry's self-regulating censorship board (FSK) were widely reported in the national press. In conservative newspapers of the late 1950s Hartwig was seen as a producer who corrupted moral values, and who could tarnish West German respectability abroad.

What enraged critics in particular was that Hartwig made no effort at all to disguise the exploitative nature and motivations of his productions. On the contrary, notoriety and scandal were skilfully employed by Hartwig in publicising his films even further.[2] In a press interview Hartwig was disarmingly frank about his ambitions and limitations: 'I am a sober businessman. You won't hear me using phrases such as artistic endeavour and humanistic problem film. I have researched the market situation, tested the audience demands, while always remaining realistic about the possibilities of my company'.[3] On a less moralistic note than his conservative counterparts, the film critic Joe Hembus, a strong supporter of the up-and-coming New German Cinema, wrote about Hartwig in the early 1960s: 'It is not that terrible that there is someone like Mr Hartwig. It is terrible that we don't have a Resnais, a Kubrick, or a Bolognini. You can't blame Mr Hartwig for that'.[4]

It must have been galling for conservative and left-wing critics alike that by the end of the 1960s Hartwig's special brand of disreputable B film had not only moved from the 'basement' to the centre of West German film production, but that he was one of very few West German producers who made a highly successful and profitable transition to the 1970s, outperforming his former rivals such as Brauner and Wendlandt.

A look at Hartwig's output and the gradual movement towards soft porn in the 1960s is instructive for understanding the changing production strategies, generic formulae, and audience expectations of the decade. Hartwig, born in 1921 in Düsseldorf, studied law, publishing, and sociology before entering the West German film industry in the early 1950s.[5] He began as an independent distributor, specialising in the acquisition of only a handful of carefully selected films. Among these were F.W. Murnau's classic ethnographic fable *Tabu* (1931) and Christian-Jaque's French-Italian co-production *Lucrèce Borgia* (1952), causing Hartwig's first encounter with the censors. After a public prosecutor in Munich had objected to the plunging neckline of the film's star, Martine Carol, *Lucrèce Borgia* was temporarily confiscated, providing its subsequent re-release with invaluable publicity.

Hartwig's first production, *Bis fünf nach zwölf* (1953, Until Five Past Twelve), a documentary compiled mainly from newsreel footage, about the private lives of Adolf Hitler and Eva Braun, caused a political storm after Konrad Adenauer, the West German Chancellor, publicly intervened, and the film was briefly banned by the Ministry of the Interior.[6] After his distribution outlet Tempo went bankrupt in 1954, Hartwig concentrated his efforts fully on his production company Rapid. Between 1957 and 1960 Hartwig established his position as West Germany's foremost producer of *Sittenfilme* or 'vice films'. The term had first been coined in the aftermath of the First World War for a number of sensationalist melodramas dealing with issues such as prostitution, venereal diseases, and homosexuality. The most prominent exponent of the early Weimar *Sittenfilm* was the director Richard Oswald and his *sozialhygienische Filmwerke* (socio-hygienic film productions).[7]

Hartwig revived this tradition, albeit within a very different social context. Generically speaking his films were difficult to define, the only common denominator being a gratuitous amount of female nudity, often amply provided by the 'West German Jayne Mansfield', Hartwig's discovery Barbara Valentin, who in the 1970s would resurface again as a character actress in the films of, among others, Rainer Werner Fassbinder. Valentin's image in the late 1950s and 1960s was that of a buxom, peroxide-blonde, and dangerous vamp from the wrong side of town. In Hartwig's films she was often required to engage in wrestling matches or violent cat fights with other women, and her low-class status was further underlined by her broad southern dialect.

Valentin's screen persona in Hartwig's films is interesting in so far as it stood in sharp contrast to the demure, desexualised, and middle-class ideal of womanhood West German mainstream films projected at the time. Indeed, she remains to this day one of the very few genuine sex icons postwar German cinema has produced. The Karl May westerns and Edgar Wallace thrillers were mostly male-centred affairs, while more typical female stars of the time were prim bourgeois actresses, such as Ruth Leuwerik, tearful tragediennes, such as Maria Schell, teenage waifs, such as Christine Kaufmann and Conny Froboess, or tomboy comedians, such as Lieselotte Pulver. Only Nadja Tiller and Elke Sommer occasionally approximated the impact of Valentin's sexualised persona, though Tiller's 'bad girl' roles (for example in *Das Mädchen Rosemarie/The Girl Rosemarie*, 1958) were far too refined, while Sommer, whose career at any rate was launched primarily through French and Italian productions, lacked Valentin's menacing dimension. In its uncomfortably raw vulgarity, Valentin's screen image, on the other hand, and particular in Hartwig's productions, articulated and elicited class and gender anxieties to a degree that amounted to public scandal.

Hartwig's films in the late 1950s and early 1960s can be subsumed under the definition of 'exploitation cinema', as suggested by Pam Cook: 'schematic, minimal narratives, comic book stereotypes, "bad" acting, and brief film cycles which disappear as soon as their audience appeal is exhausted'.[8] *Die Nackte und der Satan* (1959, international title: *The Head*) and *Ein Toter hing im Netz* (1959, international title *Horrors of Spider Island*) are horror films. The former, a combination of *Frankenstein*, *Das Cabinet des Dr Caligari*, and Georges Franju's *Les Yeux sans visage*, stars Horst Frank as a somnambulist scientist who transplants the head of a physically deformed nurse on to the body of a striptease dancer. A contemporary reviewer criticised the film's cheap effects and Frank's 'Conrad Veidt pos-

Figure 9.1. The West German Jayne Mansfield: Barbara Valentin in the early 1960s. Deutsches Filminstitut (DIF), Frankfurt-on-Main.

turing', both interesting comments when one learns that the art director of the film is Hermann Warm, one of the pioneering art directors of *Das Cabinet des Dr Caligari* (1919).[9] *Ein Toter hing im Netz* meanwhile, has witnessed a revival as a cult film since the late 1980s. The film concerns a group of go-go dancers who, together with their manager (Alex D'Arcy), are stranded on an uninhabited, radioactively contaminated, jungle island. The manager gets bitten by a mutant giant spider, turns into a werewolf, and eventually drowns in a swamp, while the women are rescued. This skeletal narrative is regularly interrupted and delayed as the film's main aim appears to be to present its female cast in various stages of undress and engaged in cat fights with each other (Barbara Valentin is chiefly responsible for these).

Apart from these forays into horror, Rapid plundered other genres as well. Thus *Endstation Rote Laterne* (1959, Final Destination: Red Lantern) belongs in the 'white slavery' genre, another long-standing tradition in German cinema, which had its heyday in the 1910s with the productions of the Danish company Nordisk.[10] *Der Satan lockt mit Liebe* (1959, Satan Tempts with Love) is a torrid gangster melodrama, replete with noirish *femmes fatales*, while *Insel der Amazonen* (1960, Amazon Island) is an exotic adventure story, again set on a desert island inhabited by scantily clad women. While all these films encountered regular problems with the censors and were frequently attacked in the press, they did not elicit widespread public outrage. Interestingly, it was imported high-profile art films, such as Ingmar Bergman's *Tystnaden* (1963, The Silence) and Vilgot Sjöman's *491* (1964) that caused church leaders and conservative politicians to demand film bans and led to the picketing of cinemas and the disruption of screenings by pressure groups.

Hartwig liberally exploited not only the repertoire of earlier German genres, but also elements from Hollywood B serials and drive-in movies and from other European genre traditions. What made and still makes these generic hybrids so refreshing, is less their unashamed cannibalisation of established genres, but the sheer ingenuity in creating these incongruous concoctions. Pam Cook has argued that a 'contradiction is generated by the exploitation film's schematic form and its appeal to audiences who are assumed to care little about style'.[11] This, as Cook has shown for the American context (and for Roger Corman's productions in particular), paradoxically gave exploitation film-makers a sometimes greater scope for stylistic experimentation than their mainstream generic counterparts. Many of Hartwig's films bear out this argument.

Until 1962, Hartwig produced without the financial backing of a major distributor, which required cost-cutting measures in terms of production values, such as sets and costumes, and tight shooting schedules. Like other European producers at the time, Hartwig frequently used the tax loophole of registering his productions in Liechtenstein, which officially functioned as a co-production partner. All of the fifteen Rapid films produced between 1957 and 1962 were based on 'original' (though clearly derivative) scripts to avoid expensive copyright acquisitions. Hartwig's production teams consisted mostly of inexperienced newcomers, the industry's second or third league, and tax exiles from Hollywood (for example, Alex D'Arcy, who had played opposite Marilyn Monroe in *How to Marry a Millionaire*, 1954) and Britain (the Rank starlet Belinda Lee). Yet it also included veterans from Weimar days who had slipped through the net of the postwar industry (for example, the director of *Die Nackte und der Satan*, Victor Trivas) and occasionally technicians of international calibre, such as the cinematographer Georg Krause, who in 1957 had shot Stanley Kubrick's *Paths of Glory*. In this respect, Rapid (like Roger Corman's film factory) provided a fertile training ground for younger commercial filmmakers, many of whom would later move into television.

In 1962, Rapid changed its corporate strategy in a number of ways. Firstly, Hartwig distanced himself from the *Sittenfilm* and publicly announced a new cinematic trend: 'As a genuine counterpart and competition to the small television screen I envisage the widescreen adventure film in colour, where suspense and exoticism are effectively combined, and where the beauty of foreign countries can be realistically captured in images'.[12] This, of course, meant location shooting in these countries, and consequently cooperation and co-production agreements, about which Hartwig was confident: 'These days I can produce more cheaply in Spain, Bangkok, Rangoon, Hong Kong, or Manila than in Germany where the costs have gone through the roof. In various trips around the world I have acquired detailed knowledge about the technical aspects and personnel issues of film production in these countries'.[13]

In the following years, Hartwig gained the reputation of an expert in coordinating the production of adventure films and, later, spy thrillers in the Far East, particularly in Hong Kong and Thailand. His know-how and established contacts overseas frequently attracted French and Italian co-production partners. In 1962, Hartwig also finally gained the support of major West German distributors, such as Constantin and Gloria, by offering his products for a fixed rate.[14] Most agreements between distributors and producers were made under guarantee conditions, where both parties shared profits but also possible losses. Under a fixed-rate agreement, distributors invested a certain amount and benefited from all eventual box-office profits exceeding this amount. Hartwig could operate in this way by undercutting the initial budget during shooting and by pocketing the remainder. Between 1962 to 1969, Rapid almost exclusively concentrated on the exotic-adventure genre, providing Constantin with a steady stream of inexpensive, and yet highly marketable products both for the domestic market and for European export. Hartwig's sporadic ventures into other genres during this time were less successful, such as his attempts to capitalise on the Karl May boom with three French-Italian-West German westerns, shot in Czechoslovakia.

Rapid's first 'colourful adventure film', made in Hong Kong and sold to Constantin for a fixed rate, was *Heisser Hafen Hong Kong* (1962, The Hot

Port of Hong Kong), directed – ironically, given Hartwig's previous comments on the limitations of television – by television director Jürgen Roland. Among Hartwig's regular collaborators in this period, apart from Roland, were TV director Fritz Umgelter, the former dubbing director Manfred R. Köhler, the actor Horst Frank, and the cinematographer Rolf Kästel. The stories for Rapid's East Asian films frequently came from a multi-authored pulp-novel series featuring the adventures of private agent Rolf Torring. Torring conveniently provided Hartwig with a home-grown version of James Bond. By this time, the Bond series had become one of the most successful imports in the West German market, and imitation series mushroomed in many European countries. Hartwig had an almost unlimited supply of Torring material, and he could safely rely on its indigenous box-office appeal: an estimated 1,000 novels had been published in Germany since the 1930s, with, on average, 100,000 to 200,000 copies per print run. In other European countries, Rapid's Torring films could pass as standard Bond imitations.

Like Hartwig's earlier exploitation pictures, his East Asian adventure films were formulaic and yet flexible enough to respond to topical issues and incorporate a number of different generic discourses. Typical in this respect is *Die jungen Tiger von Hongkong* (1969, The Young Tigers of Hong Kong, directed by Ernst Hofbauer), a curious mixture of pseudo-documentary, thriller, Hong Kong tourist vistas, and moralistic tirades against hedonistic and rebellious youth. Over the opening credits an off-screen voice announces that the film is going to be 'tough, as tough as the story that actually happened. Even if some details may seem unbelievable, they are facts, shocking facts, based on the files of the Hong Kong police'. This spurious recourse to authenticity, a common cliché of many exploitation films, is further stressed in the film's credits, which thank the Hong Kong police and the Royal Air Force. The film's narrative divides into two not always clearly connected plot strands – one concerns an American pilot (played by U.S. actor Robert Woods) who is searching for his disappeared wife, while the other concerns a gang of youths, led by psychopathic Walter Hinrichs (Werner Pochath), whose pastimes include Russian roulette, petty crime, and frequenting the 'Shocker' nightclub which provides drugs, drinks, topless dancing, and striptease entertainment. The latter two attractions in particular take up a considerable amount of screen time, with the camera zooming in on naked flesh and pole-dancing performances. The narrative proceeds to include a series of murders, perpetrated by a drug-smuggling white-slavery syndicate. The film closes with Walter being convicted of the manslaughter of a friend, and leaving the prison after two years as a more mature person, with his girlfriend waiting for him.

Apart from the contemporary settings and the psychedelic musical score, much of this narrative recalls the conventions of a white-slavery film of the early 1910s or alternatively a juvenile-delinquency film from the 1950s. Indeed, Pochath does his best to imitate the style and mannerisms of the 1950s star Horst Buchholz in *Die Halbstarken* (1956, The Hooligans).

However some of Pochath's character's railings against 'the establishment' and 'bourgeois values' appear to invoke the late 1960s student movement in West Germany, which the film – through the portrayal of Pochath and his gang and through the framing commentary – seemingly denounces as morally corrupt. At least the very end of the film seems to suggest that gangs such as Pochath's may not be beyond the potential of redemption and reintegration into society. At the same time as the film purportedly subscribes to a moralistic stance, however, it voyeuristically revels in the dissolute lifestyle of its young hooligans, in particular their sexual behaviour and the gang's sadomasochistic group dynamic. The latter finds its most disturbing expressions in a scene at the beginning where Pochath pressures a gang member into a game of Russian roulette, which ends in an accidental suicide, and in a scene later on in the film where the gang torture a fellow member to death. The film's emphasis on Pochath's gang, however, skews the narrative balance of the film and relegates the ostensible hero of the story (the American pilot) and his quest (the search for his wife), as well as the main criminal story line (the activities of the white-slavery ring), to the sidelines. *Die jungen Tiger von Hongkong* is thus a juvenile-delinquency film, with all the ambivalences towards its protagonists this exploitation subgenre entails, which merely masquerades as an exotic adventure. Indeed, although the film uses Hong Kong locations quite extensively, the scenery is in many ways incidental to the main concerns of the story. Asian characters appear only as background figures, while Pochath's gang and their rich families appear to belong to a vaguely defined international community. While one assumes that Walter is German, national identities are never mentioned in the film, with the sole exception of the pilot's Americanness. In this respect, Hong Kong, like many other exotic locations in 1960s popular cinema, becomes de-ethnified into an international playground of adventure and leisure.

Hartwig was not the only B-film producer operating on this international scale during this period. From the late 1950s onwards the aristocratic Ernst Ritter von Theumer (also known under the pseudonyms Mel Welles and Richard Jackson) produced and directed, with his Munich-based company Tefi, a number of exotic-adventure and white-slavery films, frequently set in and co-financed by South American countries and Turkey. By the mid-1960s nearly all Tefi films were largely Italian-financed.

Like Rapid, Theo Maria Werner's Munich-based company Parnass established connections in South-East Asia, after its first indigenous productions (such as the comedy *Erzähl mir nichts*, 1964, Don't Tell Me) had flopped at the box office. Following Hartwig's example, Werner discovered another German cousin of James Bond in *Kommissar X*, a pulp-novel series about a secret agent that had spawned about 500 novels. The series resulted in seven films between 1965 and 1971, filmed by a mostly Italian crew and frequently directed by Gianfranco Parolini, who adopted the more international-sounding pseudonym of Frank Kramer. The series starred Tony Kendall (real name: Luciano Stella) and former Hollywood stunt man Brad Harris, supported by German film starlets and TV actors.

Clearly modelled on James Bond and infused with Cold War ideology and rhetoric, the films' narratives centred on foreign villains threatening world peace with, among other weapons, mass hypnosis, deadly bacteria, laser rays, and LSD, and they focused on fast-paced action and pyrotechnic special effects. The *Kommissar X* films were co-productions between Italy, West Germany, and Austria, while other countries providing exotic locations, technical support, and associate production partners. The series was widely distributed in German-speaking markets, as well as in France and Italy, but had next to no impact in Britain and the U.S.[15] Like Hartwig, Werner had researched the possibilities of collaboration with countries beyond Europe during business trips to India, Pakistan, Ceylon, Thailand, and Lebanon, all of which featured in or financially contributed to individual entries of the series.[16] Subsequent films in the *Kommissar X* series were co-financed by Hungarian, Yugoslav, Turkish, Canadian, and Austrian production partners, often supported by the tourist boards in these countries.

The main competition for the *Kommissar X* series in the cinemas came from yet another German pulp-novel hero, the FBI agent Jerry Cotton, described by one literary critic as a 'well-behaved James Bond',[17] and by Manfred Barthel as an 'Old Shatterhand of the big city'.[18] Since 1956 the adventures of the incorruptible and brave G-man Cotton against New York gangsters had been published in weekly instalments, written (like the *Kommissar X* and *Rolf Torring* novels) by mostly non-professional and anonymous authors. A team of editors at the publishing house Bastei ensured that the series' formula and ethical values were upheld: 'sadism', 'realistic descriptions of murder and sexual activities', 'psychological causes of crime', and 'corrupt authority figures' were strictly forbidden.[19] The Bundesprüfstelle für jugendgefährdende Schriften (Federal Examining Board for Youth Endangering Publications) recommended the series for its model character. By the early 1960s, the readership of the Jerry Cotton novels was estimated in West Germany at 2.8 million.[20]

Given this profile and success with West German readers, a film series became almost inevitable. Financially backed by Constantin, the series was brought to the screen in 1965 by the small company Allianz, although Bastei retained significant control over its franchise and the right to veto script and casting choices. Although starring a Hollywood actor (George Nader) in the leading role, in terms of overall production values, the eight Jerry Cotton films made between 1965 and 1969 very much retained the low-budget aesthetic of their literary sources. Manfred Barthel has described, for example, how the films used surreptitious location shooting in New York in order to circumvent the salary rates set by American screen trade unions. However, while practices such as these may have helped to keep costs down, this mode of production often resulted in a patchwork of studio scenes, location stock shots, and archive footage.[21] Despite French and Italian investment, the series firmly catered to the West German market and appears to have made little impact elsewhere. In Britain, only the first film of the series, *Schüsse aus dem Geigenkasten* (1965), had a limited release under the title *Tread Softly*. Unlike Hartwig's and Werner's pulp series, which tried to emulate the James Bond films, the Jerry Cotton series oriented itself on American television formats, such as 'The Untouchables' and 'FBI', which were highly popular with West German television audiences at the time. As in the case of Hartwig's and Werner's productions, the Jerry Cotton films were released in quick succession, and they responded to the boom of spy thrillers with a production strategy that focused on quantity rather than quality.

Harry Alan Towers and the Anglo-German B Film

Harry Alan Towers and his company Towers of London provide an interesting variation on the previously discussed producers.[22] His films, though nominally British (at least until 1965), were specifically designed to appeal to West German audiences and were substantially motivated by West German distributors' (in particular, Constantin's) demands. Throughout the

Figure 9.2. A well-behaved James Bond? George Nader as Jerry Cotton in *Schüsse aus dem Geigenkasten* (1965, *Tread Softly*). Deutsches Filminstitut (DIF), Frankfurt-on-Main.

1960s, Towers catered explicitly to European rather than exclusively British markets, where his films faced much stronger competition from Hollywood and other indigenous productions. Many of Towers' films, especially those that were co-financed by Constantin, premièred in West Germany, predating their British release by sometimes over a year, and West German revenues far exceeded British profits.

Towers, born in 1920 in London, established himself in the 1950s as a TV producer in the United States. Back in Britain by the late 1950s, he produced, among other series, the TV detective series 'The New Adventures of Martin Kane' (thirty-nine episodes in 1957), before moving into British film production in the early 1960s. Following his first two feature films, *High Adventure* (1962) and *Secret Cities* (1962), Towers emulated continental genre patterns, frequently filming in Spain, Africa, the Middle East, and South-East Asia. Towers once boasted that 'I can walk in almost any city in the world where films are made and have a co-production before the cameras within a month'.[23] While most of Towers' films qualified for British quota regulations, they were substantially financed through European co-production arrangements.

Set in Central, South and West Africa, Towers' first European films, *Death Drums Along the River/Todestrommeln am grossen Fluss* (1963) and *Coast of Skeletons/Sanders und das Schiff des Todes* (1964) were based on Edgar Wallace's stories from the turn of the century, which had centred on the figure of the colonial Commissioner Sanders and his fight against unruly African tribes and diamond smugglers. Alexander Korda had previously filmed the material as *Sanders of the River* (1935). Towers' adaptations were commissioned and partly financed by Constantin, and the two films were marketed in West Germany as entries in the home-grown Wallace series, with the additional attraction of being the first Wallace films to be released in West Germany in colour and in a widescreen format.[24] Apart from British star Richard Todd as Sanders, the films included many actors familiar from Rialto's Wallace and Karl May productions, and yet the films were shot on African locations and in British studios by predominantly British crews. Towers' production team included both established, if not exactly top-rank, professionals, such as the directors Lawrence Huntington, Peter Bezencenet (a former editor at Ealing Studios), and Robert Lynn, and talented newcomers, such as the young cinematographer and scriptwriter (and later director) Nicholas Roeg. Towers himself frequently collaborated on the scripts under the pseudonym Peter Welbeck. British and West German release versions differed in detail and length, especially where the FSK demanded cuts in material depicting violence.[25] In terms of the films' narratives, Towers and his co-screenwriters attempted to update the material from Wallace's unadulterated glorification of British imperialism, a tone that was still remarkably intact in Korda's 1930s film (despite the presence of the black icon Paul Robeson), to a more contemporary setting. The differences between Wallace's original imperialist tales and Towers' attempts to render the narratives more postcolonial, however, led to considerable textual and ideological incongruities.

Death Drums Along the River is set in a fictitious African colony, and although the film's main hero, Sanders, and his assistant, Hamilton, are clearly meant to be British, there is uncertainty not only about who is in charge of this colony, but also where exactly the colony is supposed to be. Thus, apart from Sanders and his assistant, there are no other British characters; instead, the nationality most prominently represented is German and the only airline represented at the local airport is Lufthansa. Although the film's actual outdoor locations were in South Africa, the film is careful not to be pinned down to an identifiable country or even region. Thus the river of the title is meant to be the Congo, while parts of the dialogue imply that the colony borders on Senegal, several thousand miles both from the film's actual location and the Congo. As in the Karl May westerns, the idea is to construct a condensed and generic image of and not to represent a 'real' Africa. Although the film clearly attempts to avoid any political comment, various references are made in the film to the fact that independence for this colony is imminent and that the country will be returned to the native population. For example, responding to the question as to what he will do when the country becomes independent, Sanders replies that he will 'stay as long as he is asked to'. Later on in the film, benevolent Dr Schneider (Walter Rilla) – a humanist in the Albert Schweitzer mould – decides to hand over his property to the indigenous people. Yet, despite these nods towards a more postcolonial perspective, most black characters in *Death Drums Along the River* remain extras and background figures, primarily present to authenticate the film's African setting. The only scene that features black characters more prominently is a supposedly Zulu tribal funeral ceremony. In its 'de-ethnification' of a foreign location, Towers' production is, of course, not unique among the exoticist genres of the 1960s, as I have previously argued.

Circumventing much engagement with African culture beyond faked folkloristic-ethnographic vistas, the film is more concerned with Sanders' fights against white adversaries. Given the film's aspirations to be an adventure film, the narrative is surprisingly devoid of physical action. Most of the story takes place in the confines of a jungle hospital, which looks more like a luxury tourist complex, where Sanders and the heroic German doctor and World Health Organisation representative Inge Jung (Marianne Koch) uncover a series of murders and diamond smuggling. Apart from the relatively perfunctory whodunnit structure, which offers few surprises, the film's main emphasis is on African flora and fauna. Early on in *Death Drums Along the River*, Sanders travels with newly arrived Dr Jung on the river, providing the spectator with lengthy views of crocodiles, hippos, and flocks of wild birds, while Sanders offers brief explanations of the animals' behaviour. Scenes like these, in which the film's register shifts into the semi-documentary mode of a *Kulturfilm*, occur throughout the narrative until the very end, when Dr Jung and

Sanders, now a couple, return to the river, while the Lufthansa plane flies overhead back to the homeland, thus sealing the film's fantasy of tourism, adventure, and escape. Unsurprisingly, the *Film-Echo/Filmwoche* highlighted in its review less the films' formulaic narratives than attractions such as 'interesting underwater photography' and 'fascinating images of wild African animals'.[26]

Coast of Skeletons, Towers' follow-up to *Death Drums Along the River*, offers a variation on the first film only in so far as the location this time is a 'real' country, namely South-West Africa (today's Namibia). Again, the breathtaking desert, coastal, and underwater scenery provide the film with its main attractions. Given the country's history as a former German colony, it is interesting that this time around most German actors are portraying Dutch or Afrikaans characters or are at least less easy to identify as Germans than in the previous Sanders adventure. In a similar style of cultural and ethnic camouflage, Towers' mode of production of filming in exotic locations with a British crew, German casts and international stars continued with *Victim Five* (1964, a crime thriller set in Cape Town, starring Lex Barker), *Mozambique* (1964, a white-slavery film with Steve Cochran and Hildegard Knef) and *24 Hours To Kill* (1965, a crime thriller set in Beirut, starring Lex Barker and Mickey Rooney).

In 1965 Towers inevitably ventured into the series format with the oriental arch-villain Fu Manchu, a creation of Wallace's near-contemporary Sax Rohmer (1883–1959).[27] In over thirteen novels and several short stories between 1913 and 1959, Rohmer's 'evil yellow doctor' had attempted to gain world supremacy, his fiendish conspiracies invariably thwarted by upright Scotland Yard inspector Nayland-Smith. A Fu Manchu series clearly had trans-European box-office potential in the 1960s. First, there was a long tradition of similar arch-criminals in other European popular cultures, such as Germany's Dr Mabuse and Fantômas in France (both of whom had their own 1960s film incarnations). Secondly, Rohmer's crime novels had been exported into many European countries since the 1920s, although in West Germany their distribution was restricted by the Federal Examining Board for Youth-Endangering Publications which objected in principle to villains as heroes.[28] However, since the board's power at the time only extended to printed material, a prospective film series was safe from intervention.

There had been several previous film adaptations in Britain in the 1920s, in Hollywood in the 1930s and 1940s, and in Spain (*El Otro Fu Manchu*, 1945). Republic's Fu Manchu serials had been distributed in West Germany by Gloria throughout the 1950s. Moreover, Rohmer's emphasis on the 'yellow peril', exotic locations, global crime conspiracies, master criminals, and bizarre inventions and technologies fitted in with popular contemporaneous genre cycles, such as the James Bond series (a figure such as Dr No, for example, is likely to have been modelled on Fu Manchu) and its numerous European imitations. As with Rialto's and Towers' own Wallace adaptations, Towers' Fu Manchu films on the whole toned down the robustly pro-colonial and racist elements of the original novels and avoided any specific political references. They also refrained from following Rohmer's own post-war reworking of his most famous creation, whom Rohmer sent out in his later novels 'to fight communism and help democracy'.[29] Towers' Fu Manchu, in contrast, remained an unreconstructed pantomime villain, based in an exotic fantasy environment with no clear historical or geopolitical context. In this respect, Towers' series perfectly fitted the historical evasiveness of the popular genres in European cinema of the time.

Towers' first three films in the series (*The Face of Fu Manchu*, 1965, *The Brides of Fu Manchu*, 1966, and *Vengeance of Fu Manchu*, 1967) were made by largely British crews on location in Ireland and Hong Kong. After that, the series became increasingly multinational. Imitating similar campaigns for the James Bond series (such as the widely publicised searches for 'Bond girls'), Towers initiated a considerable amount of international promotional activity surrounding the films, as Christopher Lee, who played Fu Manchu, remembers in his autobiography:

> *Brides of Fu Manchu* was tosh, in which an extravagant publicity stunt almost sank the picture. At the instigation of Harry Alan Towers ... I toured European countries, choosing from each the winner of a national beauty competition whose prize was a part in the film ... But they could not show themselves off to best advantage because they were not members of Equity and therefore they had not a line to speak between the whole dozen ...[30]

As far as the West German market was concerned, Towers and his distributor and co-financier Constantin were eager to encourage connections and correspondences between the Fu Manchu series and Rialto's Wallace films. Already the first entry in the series, *The Face of Fu Manchu* (1965, *Ich, Dr. Fu Manchu*), was compared by West German reviewers with the Wallace series, undoubtedly triggered by the presence of a number of Wallace regulars in the film (Joachim Fuchsberger, Karin Dor, Walter Rilla).[31] In fact, apart from Christopher Lee and the Chinese-British actress Tsai Chin as Fu Manchu's daughter, all of Towers' Fu Manchu films had a significant number of German names in their cast lists, in all likelihood required by Constantin.[32] Between 1965 and 1968 Towers produced five Fu Manchu films and two further Rohmer adaptations featuring the villainess Su-Muru (*The Million Eyes of Su-Muru*, 1967, and the Spanish-West German co-production *Ciudad Sin Hombres*, 1968), in which a group of modern Amazons (led by the actress Shirley Eaton of *Goldfinger* fame) plot the creation of a female-only world order.

While the Fu Manchu series was still running, Towers returned once more to Edgar Wallace in 1966 with *Circus of Fear/Das Rätsel des silbernen Dreiecks*. The film was an attempt to blend the generic conventions of the Rialto and Merton Park series and thus to cater to both the British and the West German market. An influence of the British Wallace films was perhaps inevitable, given that not only the film's director, John Moxey, but also several of its actors had been closely associated with the Merton Park series.[33] Significantly, while the West German release version explicitly capitalised on the name of Wallace, the British film credits did not mention him at all. In Britain, the main star attraction was Christopher Lee, though his role in *Circus of Fear* as a sinister lion-tamer was rather a thankless one, as he wore a mask for most of the film's duration.

Circus of Fear opens with a spectacular heist on Tower Bridge, recalling Rialto's *Traitor's Gate* (1964), followed by a car chase, reminiscent of contemporary British TV crime series. After the first ten minutes, however, the narrative switches from a straightforward gangster-film plot to the tale of a hooded killer hiding among an international group of circus performers. The circus environment, with its garishly lit arena and its dim backstage scenes provided the film with the bizarre props and characters the West German audience of the Rialto series would have been familiar with.[34] As in the Rialto series, the narrative features hidden family secrets and crime conspiracies motivated by personal revenge. Towers' production certainly displays an acute awareness of Rialto's established narrative and casting conventions. Thus, apart from Heinz Drache as the film's hero, Klaus Kinski is cast as an enigmatic German gangster, while Eddi Arent is responsi-

Figure 9.3. Tsai Chin and Christopher Lee in the Spanish-West German-British-Italian co-production *The Castle of Fu Manchu* (1968). Deutsches Filminstitut (DIF), Frankfurt-on-Main.

ble for the film's comic relief (although the narrative makes him the surprise villain in the end). Even the British actors assume roles that were modelled on regular characters from the West German films. For the role of Sir John, the pompous and irritable head of Scotland Yard, Towers cast Cecil Parker, whose established screen persona in British cinema as a bewildered figure of authority was very similar to the image Siegfried Schürenberg had created in the West German films.

In 1967, Towers relocated his production base to low-cost countries, such as Spain and Italy, and began a long-lasting partnership with the Spanish director Jesús Franco (also known as Jess Franco and by at least twenty other pseudonyms). Franco shifted the emphasis of the Fu Manchu series from old-fashioned adventure yarns to kinky sadism. Franco was also a low-budget specialist and, if not much else, phenomenally productive (during the 1960s his output of primarily European co-productions averaged about four films per year). Case-studies in ingenious cost-cutting methods rather than shining examples of artistic integrity, Franco's Fu Manchu films frequently recycled material from earlier entries. Since all of his films used post-production sound, these patchworks of newly shot and 'borrowed' scenes were re-edited into seemingly new narratives. With the fifth entry, *The Castle of Fu Manchu* (1968), the franchise was finally exhausted. The film flopped at the West German box office, and it took four years before it had a brief and limited release in Britain.

One reason for the temporary success of the Fu Manchu series and the exotic films produced by Hartwig, Theumer, and Werner may have had to do with their generic adaptability. Chameleon-like and composed of various generic influences, they could fit a number of current European subgenres in circulation. West German reviews of the Fu Manchu films, for example, alternatively referred to them as crime films, exotic spectacles, horror films, spy thrillers, adventure films, and even as science fiction.[35] The strategy of casting actors from other established genre cycles (such as James Bond films, Edgar Wallace adaptations, and Hammer horrors) fostered a mutual referentiality between different genres and a blurring of generic distinctions. While the Fu Manchu, *Kommissar X*, Jerry Cotton, and Torring films may not have been able to compete with the James Bond series in terms of production values, they could easily be adapted in terms of narratives or casting and marketed according to changing audience preferences in different countries. By 1966, however, the various spy and exotic-adventure cycles showed early signs of exhaustion, and the trade press became increasingly concerned about the variety of films on offer.[36]

The Sex-Film Boom of the Late 1960s

From the late 1960s, the West German B-film sector changed its generic focus from exotic adventure film to the production of soft porn. Costume sex romps, such as the Franco-Italian-West German co-productions *Lady*

Hamilton (1968) and *Der Turm der verbotenen Liebe* (1968, The Tower of Forbidden Love, allegedly based on an Alexandre Dumas novel), indicated a shift in Rapid's generic output and a return to its origins in the *Sittenfilm*, but now in a far more sexually explicit format. Hartwig's East Asian adventure series, which increasingly displayed a greater interest in Asian sex industries and strip clubs than in suspense, faded out after *Die jungen Tiger von Hong Kong*. Theumer, with an American co-production partner, produced a Munich-based sex film in 1970 (*Cream – Schwabing-Report*) before relocating to Italy, where he specialised in directing spaghetti westerns and horror films. Werner's company Parnass ceased business in 1968, though Constantin commissioned two further *Kommissar X* sequels from other producers. Towers continued with his Spanish- and Italian-based productions and his close collaboration with Jesus Franco, specialising in soft-porn-horror hybrids with a marked emphasis on sexual sadism (in fact, some of his films were supposedly based on Marquis de Sade's novels).

One significant trigger for this change in direction in the West German production sector was the unexpected European box-office success of the sex-education documentary *Helga* in 1967, produced by the small company Rinco and distributed by Hanns Eckelkamp's Atlas. The film, which documented the story of a young woman from the first stages of pregnancy to a graphically shown birth, had been commissioned by the West

Figure 9.4. Ruth Gassmann as *Helga* (1967). Deutsches Filminstitut (DIF), Frankfurt-on-Main.

German Ministry of Health, and was originally intended to be shown in educational contexts. Instead, it went straight on to general release and became the biggest indigenous box-office success of the year, surrounded by widespread public debate, and inevitable protests by religious organisations and right-wing lobbying groups such as the *Aktion Saubere Leinwand* (Action for a Clean Screen). *Helga* was eventually followed by *Helga und Michael* (1968), which counterpointed information on sexual hygiene with a thin story of the titular heroine's marriage. In the second sequel, *Helga und die Männer – Die sexuelle Revolution* (1969, Helga and Men – The Sexual Revolution) an educational pretence was abandoned altogether, dealing instead with the heroine's extramarital escapades on a trip to Brazil. Taken together, the three *Helga* films had a box-office turnover of 150 million DM in just two years.

Apart from breaking box-office records in West Germany, *Helga* also proved to be an export hit in several European countries, particularly in Italy, leading the trade paper *Film-Echo/Filmwoche* to proclaim rather grandly that 'Germany has begun to educate Italy about sex'.[37] The same article also noted pointedly that none of the culturally more prestigious recent films of the New Cinema (the directorial débuts of Volker Schlöndorff and Alexander Kluge among them) had found their way into Italian distribution, the clear implication being that sex sold better abroad than art. Georg Seesslen speculates that the Italian success of *Helga* was possibly helped by the Nordic name and appearance of the film's main protagonist.[38] In subsequent years, West German-made sex films recorded the highest box-office figures among films imported into Italy, which explains why Italian companies increasingly invested in co-productions of these films. Owing to Italian censorship regulations, however, Italian and West German release versions often differed significantly in their sexual explicitness.

In the following years, sex-education cycles mushroomed, combining scenes of 'scientific' information with feature film narratives or episodic sketches. Like the *Helga* films, other sex film cycles gradually transformed from educational documentaries into titillating soft-porn narratives, while still claiming to be based on serious research. The most prominent education cycle was written by and named after the journalist, and sometime film critic, Oswalt Kolle. Kolle had originally published his ideas about sexual reform and liberation (strongly influenced by the Kinsey reports) in West Germany's tabloid press, acquiring a reputation as the country's foremost sex guru. In this function he introduced and narrated a series of eight films between 1968 and 1972, where, again, 'exemplary' narratives were commented on by academic experts (in later years these were frequently played by actors).

After the first three films, *Das Wunder der Liebe* (1968, The Miracle of Love), *Sexuelle Partnerschaft* (1968, Sexual Partnership), and *Deine Frau – das unbekannte Wesen* (1968, Your Wife – the Unknown Being), Kolle made it clear that his mission was not only to educate but also to entertain. Subsequent films dealt with nudist families and child sexuality (*Dein Kind –*

das unbekannte Wesen, 1970, Your Child – the Unknown Being) and group sex (*Liebe als Gesellschaftsspiel*,1972, Love as a Party Game). The innocently formulated question in the title of the seventh entry, *Was ist eigentlich Pornographie?* (1971, What, By the Way, is Pornography?) finally provided the pretext for compiling a number of (albeit heavily censored) Danish hard-core extracts, interspersed with Kolle's plea to banish censorship.

While the *Helga* and Kolle films remained relatively short-lived series franchises, Wolf Hartwig was responsible for what would become the most significant series of the West German sex film boom. Hartwig had bought the rights of the best-selling book *Schulmädchen-Report* (Schoolgirls Report, first published in the tabloid press) by Günter Hunold, which documented, through interviews, the changing sexual attitudes, aspirations, and experiences of fourteen- to eighteen-year-old girls. The resulting film, released in 1970, was a compilation of voyeuristic soft-porn episodes, linked by a framing story in which a 'reporter' gives pseudo-sociological comments and conducts 'authentic' surveys on the streets of Munich. Apart from the actor who is cast as the reporter, most other players were physically uninhibited but otherwise rather wooden amateurs, though some of them managed to have significant careers in West German cinema and television later on. The film's cinematography and editing comprises a patchwork of static shots, wobbly camera movements, and perfunctory cutting, all of this meant to contribute an immediacy and 'documentary' feel to the proceedings. The film's director, Ernst Hofbauer, had made his name earlier on in the decade with West German television's version of 'Candid Camera', and much of that series' narrational strategies (zooming in on unsuspecting passers-by, jumping between different locations, seemingly unrehearsed and unfinished scenes) found their way into *Schulmädchen-Report*. However, perhaps the film's most interesting aesthetic aspect was less its visual or narrative construction but its psychedelic musical soundtrack. The combination of a garish and sketchy *mise en scène* and the score's eerie and feverish melodies created a tabloid portrait of what may have been intended to look and sound like 'swinging' Munich, but which set up instead a deep chasm between a supposedly 'hip' and sexually transgressive (though still firmly middle-class) teenage scene and a puzzled moral majority.[39]

Requiring very few production values, the film was completed in less than three weeks. Hartwig originally offered the film on fixed-rate conditions, but Constantin did not believe in its box-office potential.[40] The film eventually had a box-office turnover of 8.5 million DM, leaving Hartwig with a profit of at least six million. During the next ten years, Rapid produced in total thirteen Schoogirls-Report sequels (which were also exported and seen by an estimated 100 million cinema-goers worldwide), as well as variations on the formula, such as *Urlaubsreport* (1971, Holiday Report) and *Krankenschwestern-Report* (1972, Nurse Report). Other producers commissioned 'reports' on, among others, housewives, pool attendants, postmen, apprentices, flight attendants, and ski instructors, clearly relishing the potential for sexual innuendo and confirming all the salacious rumours these professions invited.

Apart from the reports and the education cycles, the bawdy costume sex comedy became another significant subgenre of the sex film boom, spawning its own distinctive cycles. Prototypical was the Constantin release *Susanne, die Wirtin von der Lahn* (1968, Susan, the Innkeeper from the Lahn River), set during the Napoleonic wars in provincial Germany. Based on a fictitious character from German folklore and oral storytelling traditions, the film charted the sexual trajectory of its eponymous heroine through brothels and courtly boudoirs. An Austrian-West German-Italian-Hungarian co-production, *Susanne, die Wirtin von der Lahn* became the fourth top-grossing film in West Germany during the 1967/8 season, and the film sold well into Italy, France, and Britain, where it was released under the title *The Sweet Sins of Sexy Susan*. Between 1968 to 1973 five further Sexy Susan films were made, all of them directed by the Austrian director Franz Antel under the pseudonym François Legrand, distributed by Constantin, and starring the Hungarian actress Teri Tordai (Terry Torday) as the eponymous heroine and the French actress Pascale Petit as a countess. Antel, who had directed a number of rather undistinguished Austrian *Heimatfilme* in the 1950s was drawn to increasingly lewd material in the mid-1960s, and had an unsavoury reputation among the West German film establishment. Indeed, there were some producers who refused to work with distributors who also released material made by Antel.[41] *Sexy Susan*'s success would very much change Antel's status. Unlike other sex-film cycles, the series gave a relatively professional impression in terms of editing and cinematography, it regularly featured an international cast of established actors (which included Jeffrey Hunter, Edwige Fenech, and Margaret Lee), and it exercised care and imagination in details of decor, costumes, and narrative construction. Even Joe Hembus grudgingly conceded that the films 'at least occasionally gave the illusion of some charm and flair'.[42]

Unlike the sex reports with their contradictory messages about social acceptability and cautious sexual experimentation, the *Sexy Susan* films relished their frivolity and their status as erotic fantasies. The films' escapist settings and historical distance allowed them to be more relaxed in their attitude to sexual mores. As portrayed by the Hungarian actress Terry Torday, Sexy Susan comes across as an early nineteenth-century rebel for sexual libertinage, her exploits sometimes bearing a striking (and very probably not coincidental) resemblance to the happenings organised by students in West Germany at the time. Thus, in one instance, Sexy Susan leads a protest march of naked women through the streets to demand political changes, although the demand itself – the abolition of entertainment taxes – would, of course, hardly have agitated the generation of 1968. Compared with the empty sociological ciphers and anonymous schoolgirls of the report films, however, Sexy Susan and her female co-conspirators managed to represent a more palatable version of the sex film.

Comedy has often been regarded as one of the most culturally specific and least exportable, of European popular genres. This truism, however, does not apply to the costume sex comedies of the late 1960s which performed remarkably well across Europe. Like the contemporary British *Carry-On* films (and later the British TV farces of Benny Hill), the *Sexy Susan* series combined social and gender stereotypes, puerile innuendo, and cultural pastiche with a fairly universal sense of visual slapstick and the carnivalesque. Geoff Brown, commenting on the British release of the last entry into the series, *Frau Wirtins tolle Töchterlein* (1973, British title *Knickers Ahoy!*) gave a rather accurate summary of the main ingredients of the series:

> Admirers of Franz Antel's costume romps *The Sweet Sins of Sexy Susan* and *Sexy Susan Rides Again* will have no difficulty in recognising the Susanna of *Knickers Ahoy!*, for it is the same actress and the same lady, with her name slightly changed by the sprightly American dubbing. Within five minutes of the film's opening, however, she lies dead, victim of her own 'highly developed sense of humour', as someone generously terms it (she laughs too much at her maid and an undertaker making love in a cupboard); but she returns at odd intervals to relive her past adventures in flashback form. We also see her five attractive daughters in action, frightening a rotund monk with displays of bottoms and breasts ... But it's unlikely that audiences will follow Susanna's example and die of laughter, unless their sense of humour is developed enough to relish a naked girl riding around on a goat or a man's trouser button flying off under stress.[43]

Hartwig's and Antel's success indicates a change in the profile, backgrounds, and business strategies of West German producers during this period. Established figures, such as Brauner or Wendlandt, rather reluctantly followed the sex-film boom in order to compete. Rialto, for example, contributed to the sex-education cycle with *Die vollkommene Ehe* (1968, The Perfect Marriage) and *Das Leben zu zweit – Die Sexualität in der Ehe* (1969, Life as a Couple – Sexuality during Marriage) based on the best-selling books of Dutch gynaecologist Theodor van de Velde. These two films remained Rialto's only excursions into the sex-film genre. Wendlandt, who had initiated the two most dominant film series of the 1960s, was either unwilling or unable to follow the example of Hartwig and Antel. After the end of the Wallace and May series, Rialto's productions turned to old-fashioned comedies. By the early 1970s, Horst Wendlandt had largely suspended his production activities and turned distributor.[44]

Artur Brauner's contributions to the sex-film boom, on the other hand, attempted to give the genre a gloss of respectability and production values. Pre-dating *Helga* and the report films, CCC's first venture into the genre had been *Fanny Hill* in 1964, an adaptation of John Cleland's notorious erotic novel. Co-produced by the American company Famous Players, the film was nominally directed by Russ Meyer, who had achieved notoriety in America with his previous sex-film *Lorna* (1964). Later admirers of

Meyer's particular brand of grotesque eroticism, however, are likely to be disappointed by *Fanny Hill*. Anxious to avoid adverse public reactions, Brauner had parts of the film reshot by his co-producer Albert Zugsmith and reedited so drastically, that little erotic content (or, indeed, narrative logic) remained. In the end, the film's heroine, played by the Italian actress Letitia Roman, survived her trajectory through rather tame brothels and her encounters with comedians such as Chris Howland and Hollywood veteran Miriam Hopkins with her virginity intact.

Equally muddled was *Das ausschweifende Leben des Marquis de Sade* (1968/9, The Dissolute Life of Marquis de Sade, U.S. release title: *De Sade*), co-produced by CCC and Samuel Z. Arkoff's American International Pictures (AIP), on which three directors in succession (Cy Endfield, Roger Corman, and Gordon Hessler) worked. Despite a lurid promotion campaign, the film was essentially a straightforward costume biopic, with a respectable, if incongruous, cast that included Keir Dullea, Lilli Palmer, and John Huston. Marketed as a sex film, it unsurprisingly flopped. Leonard Maltin's *Movie and Video Guide* advises its readers that 'if you're expecting something raunchy, forget it',[45] an advice that seems to have been pre-empted by audiences in the late 1960s, who stayed away from the box office in droves.

Typical of a new breed of producer were figures such as Erwin C. Dietrich and Alois Brummer. Dietrich, an exhibitor with various cinema outlets in Switzerland, entered West German film production in 1965, compensating for his films' lack of production values and established actors with an additional amount of nudity and sexual acrobatics. Owing to the films' low production costs, Dietrich's companies Elite and Urania rarely ventured into co-productions, an exception being *Die Nichten der Frau Oberst* (1968, The Colonel's Wife and Her Nieces, allegedly based on a Guy de Maupassant novel), the best-selling West German-Italian co-production at the Italian box office in 1971.[46] In West Germany, the film's tag line was 'Banned as a book for decades. But even Maupassant did not go that far'.[47]

The career of Alois Brummer exemplifies perhaps most dramatically how weak the traditional production and distribution sector had become by the end of the 1960s. Brummer, formerly the owner of a provincial Bavarian haulage firm and a couple of small rural cinemas, specialised in the production of low-budget, simple-minded, and technically amateurish soft-porn farces with titles such as *Graf Porno und seine liebesdurstigen Töchter* (1969, Count Porno and his Nymphomaniac Daughters) which proved surprisingly successful.[48] Ignoring the previously held monopoly of the major distributors, Brummer released the films on his own. With production budgets of less than 350,000 DM, the films brought Brummer profits of about 2 million DM each. Between 1968 and 1983 Brummer (who died in 1984) independently wrote, directed, produced, and distributed around twenty-five films. His crude blend of soft porn and conventions borrowed from traditional Bavarian stage comedies and rural folklore was widely imitated by other producers, leading to a seemingly endless series of titles such as *Gejodelt wird zuhause* (1970, Yodelling at home) and *Liebesgrüsse aus der Lederhose* (1973, From the Lederhose with Love).

Peek-a-boo German Style

Watching these films today, the West German sex-film boom of the late 1960s, and particularly its scope, is difficult to comprehend. As their original cultural and social context has disappeared, the films convey a strange sense of temporal alienation, and they seem historically more remote than the exotic adventure genres that preceded them (perhaps partly because very similar formulae to the latter genre are still being provided by the ongoing James Bond series and, of course, Hollywood's action blockbusters). The Oswalt Kolle and other sex-education films may provide unintentional hilarity among younger generations of cinema-goers, while some of the *Sexy Susan* films may be appreciated for their comedy and production values. Brummer's films are plainly bizarre and grotesque, though a cult-film *aficionado* may be attracted by what could be seen as a very Teutonic equivalent of Russ Meyer. The Schoolgirls Reports and their numerous clones, on the other hand, seem to operate according to a specific code and horizon of expectations that is likely to confound most contemporary viewers, and they even seem to refuse the kind of camp appropriation or post-modern irony the Kolle or Brummer films may facilitate.

The report films of the late 1960s and early 1970s appear incoherent, elliptical and muted, marked by strangely emotionless characters, and, even in a narrowly sexual sense, unconvincing performances. Overall they frustrate rather than confirm visual pleasure and narrative expectations in a manner that, perversely, is closer to avant-garde cinema than to the conventions of popular genres. Moreover, although their perfunctory narrative structure resembles the standard of pornographic genres, they achieve neither the gloss nor the directed gaze of what could have been the cinematic equivalent of 'glamour' photographs in men's magazines, nor are the sex scenes explicit enough to pass off as 'real' pornography. They lack, of course, what the porn trade refers to as 'meat' (i.e. penetration) or 'money' (ejaculation) shots. Linda Williams has argued that 'hard core tries *not* to play peek-a-boo with either its male or its female bodies. It obsessively seeks knowledge, through a voyeuristic record of confessional, involuntary paroxysm, of the "thing" itself'.[49] An obsessive quest for knowledge is certainly at the heart of the report films and even more so in the education cycles. Yet at the same time the quest for what Williams refers to as the 'thing itself' becomes deflated, interrupted, and frustrated in the films' visual and narrative trajectories. This strategy of displacement, of course, raises the question for whom these films were originally made and what kind of function or use value they provided at the time.

Thomas Elsaesser has claimed that the sex films catered 'to a pornography clientele, largely recruited from Germany's two million immigrant workers'.[50] His argument, that 'the mainly male *Gastarbeiter* from Southern, Catholic countries' represented a 'volatile and furtive but none the less numerically quite sizeable clientele'[51] sounds suggestive, and corresponds to the success of these films in countries such as Italy and Spain. However, given that the sex films were regularly awarded prizes for reaching more than 3 million cinema-goers per film in the domestic market alone, Elsaesser's target audience appears too narrowly defined. Moreover, inasmuch as far more explicit foreign sex films (particularly from Denmark, where pornography had been legalized in 1968) became available on the West German market, albeit in a different distribution and exhibition context, one has to wonder why a 'pornography clientele' would have bothered with the comparatively tame reports or sex farces at all.

Box-office figures suggest that, rather than catering exclusively to ethnic-minority or fringe audiences, sex films attracted viewers from across the social spectrum, across the urban-rural divide, and across all ages. What is significant is that the films themselves address an implied middle-class audience, the bedrock and proclaimed core of West German society. The report films in particular emphasise the ordinariness of their characters, centring on middle-class (and in the case of the male performers, mostly middle-aged) protagonists in average surroundings. Even the sex scenes, where one would normally expect elements of fantasy or exaggeration, are firmly rooted in relatively plausible, everyday, and overall rather subdued situations. Unlike in similar genres from other countries, there seems to be no attempt to cast particularly attractive performers – in fact, the permed, portly, and mustachioed male actors so beloved of West German sex-film producers became internationally renowned as the acme of bad taste. Where sexual routine threatens to become either narratively or visually excessive, the reports frequently diffuse this with elements of comedy and farce,or provide 'scientific' and sobering instructions of 'properly' executed sexual positions. Comedy is also the mode by which the costume sex films contain possible transgression.

Georg Seesslen has suggested that the West German sex-film boom, and the reports in particular "legitimated a new liberalism. However, they also demonised what went too far. Principally the genre was about constructing a new social consensus which was less prudish but which still required its abnormal other'.[52] In other words, the genre can be seen to have provided a relatively safe outlet for sexual curiosity, which was fuelled by a more general shift in behaviour. In the late 1960s and early 1970s West German society witnessed a number of conflicting developments in sexual openness: the expansion and increased visibility of sex-shop chains under the crusading aegis of the formidable sex entrepreneur Beate Uhse (a graduate of the Nazi youth movement and a passionate aviatrix); the publication of ever more risqué tabloid papers; and the growing influence of Anglo-American popular culture on West German teenagers which manifested itself not least in a yearning for greater sexual independence. At the more alternative end of the spectrum were the various Reichian, Marcusean, or anarchist splinter communes of the student movement, staging their protest in public exhibitions of sexual non-conformism, which the West German tabloid press was only too eager to publicise with a mixture of shocked indignation and leering voyeurism. What rendered the sexual stunts of the 68ers – by today's standards rather tame and overall fairly isolated – particularly threatening was the conflation of sexual liberation and political revolution. Furthermore, as Dagmar Herzog has argued, sexual liberation in West Germany had a nationally specific vantage point and distinctive aims: 'Much of what the 68ers were actually rebelling against were their own experiences in the postfascist 1950s and the interpretations of Nazism's sexual legacies proffered by parents and political and religious leaders in that decade'.[53]

Thus, although part of the same momentum towards greater visibility in sexual matters, the sex-film wave and the actions of the 68ers had clearly divergent agendas. For the latter, sexual liberation was one of a number of means (pursued with deadly seriousness) to destroy the complacency they perceived to be characteristic of West Germany's insistence on social, sexual, and gender relations that they believed had their origins in and had helped to sustain Nazism. The reports, on the other hand, initiated a 'sensible' interest in sex and promoted the 'responsible' consumption of soft porn as an act of maturity, enlightened citizenship, and matrimonial duty, thus preserving the status quo of these social and domestic institutions, and affirming West Germany's democratic legitimacy. If one can speak of an ideological project at work in these films, it is to circumvent and suppress the dangerous link between sex, politics, and history that the 68ers addressed, while taking on board some of their more superficial attractions.

What the sex films offered their mainstream audiences were visual induction manuals for sexual efficiency, pleasure enhancement, and perhaps most importantly, new consumerist identities and lifestyles. One contemporary review tellingly compared the sex films' *mise en scène* to the presentational style of a mail-order catalogue, underlining the fact that these films were firmly placed within a consumerist agenda.[54] If there is one recurring mantra in the sex films, and one that is prevalent throughout public discourse in West Germany in the 1970s, it is the belief (a curious mélange of Freud, Marcuse, and the capitalist work ethic) that sexual freedom leads to mental and physical health, which in turn leads to greater social and economic efficiency, thus providing a blanket solution to all political ills. Thus, watching a sex film could be legitimated as an expression of worldly libertarianism or, for younger audiences, as an initiation ritual into sexual maturity (and, by implication, patriarchal hierarchies).

The Kolle and report films were explicitly advertised to function, at least in part, as 'counselling services' to sexually dysfunctional couples, and it is reasonable to assume they were used in that way by a considerable number of cinema-goers. At the same time, the sex films clearly set the rules and boundaries for sexual permissiveness. West Germany's sexually as well as politically transgressive hippie communes, not to mention any major deviation from the heterosexual norm (except for decorative lesbian scenes), are either conspicuously absent in the reports or depicted as comic or exotic aberrations. In a recent interview Hartwig showed himself unrepentant about the exclusion or stereotyping of gay characters in the series, declaring homosexuality as something personally unacceptable to him.[55] In this respect, then, Rosa von Praunheim's celebrated gay *agit-prop* film *Nicht der Homosexuelle ist pervers, sondern die Situation, in der er lebt* (1970, Not The Homosexual Is Perverse, But The Situation In Which He Lives), released at the height of the sex film boom, can almost be seen as a counter-cultural attack on this kind of (non-) representation, couched in a parodic subversion of the report films' narrative and didactic strategies and their attendant ideology of exclusion.

One reason for the success of the report films, in particular, was that, unlike 'real' pornography, they promised more than they delivered. If the West German sex films, veering between repression and libertarianism, appear in hindsight confused about their aims and intentions, this corresponded to the uncertainty of the films' audiences, who were trying to negotiate deeply ingrained moral and social conventions with an increasing pressure from the media and psychologists, among other authorities, to conform to new models of sexual and consumerist behaviour. Ironically, although the 68ers had originally set out to use sex as a weapon against a culture of commodification, they finally contributed to the consolidation of precisely the same commodification process, something, as Dagmar Herzog has documented, the West German feminist movement by the mid-1970s acutely recognised and bitterly condemned.[56]

Transformation of the West German Film Industry in the early 1970s

The sex-film boom of the late 1960s was not just a fascinating social phenomenon, it initiated significant developments in production and consumption patterns as far as West Germany's film market was concerned. It coincided with and accelerated changes in the exhibition sector, and it ultimately led to a reorientation of the West German film industry towards a more nationally and less internationally minded mode of production. Throughout the 1960s, the number of first-run, inner-city cinemas had dramatically declined. While the Karl May, Edgar Wallace, and adventure films targeted a younger market, family audiences increasingly stayed at home in front of the television set. Film producers were only too aware that colour, wide-screen formats, exotic locations, and greater sexual explicitness remained the only attractions with which film production in the 1960s could compete with the still relatively studio-bound, black and white, and family-oriented formats of television. In terms of exhibition, however, what was left were smaller provincial and suburban outlets, among them the notoriously seedy *Bahnhofskinos* (cinemas in the proximity of railway stations and red-light districts), which had either always specialised in the exploitation end of the market or had now begun to veer ever more closely towards this market segment. The cheaply available reports and Kolle films, with their transparent masquerade as serious research, provided the perfect genre for such venues, while also giving a relatively wide spectrum of audiences a designated space and a filmic format that was just about respectable enough to satisfy their sexual curiosity.

The remainder of the big urban exhibitors accelerated this process even further in the early 1970s. Large venues were subdivided into shoebox-sized multiplexes, where at least one screen was continually showing a report or a sex comedy, thus further normalising the genre as mainstream entertainment. Unlike previous genres, individual sex films had inordinately long runs in these cinemas, in some cases lasting up to more than a year. This, in turn, was detrimental to the major distributors, who had been the dominant force in the West German film industry since the 1950s. With the demise of the remaining big West German distributors, such as Gloria and Constantin, it appeared now as if Daddy's Cinema had truly gone. The production of sex films, however, continued long after the New German Cinema had consolidated itself as the officially approved version of national cinema, and they remained its abject and embarrassing other. Brummer and report films were made throughout the 1970s, although no longer possessing their initial mass appeal and increasingly displaced between the artistic aspirations of the New German Cinema, proliferating hard-core porn venues, and the by now dominant box-office presence of Hollywood. Sex-film producers responded with attempts to update their formula with variants, such as 'Ibiza reports', copying the combination of sex and glossy tourist promotion popularised by international hits such as Just Jaeckin's *Emmanuelle* (1973) and, in the wake of a late 1970s boom in zombie and cannibal films, horror-sex hybrids. Ernst Ritter von Theumer, former globe-trotting B-film producer and director in the 1960s, returned from Italian productions and increasing obscurity to team up in the late 1970s with Artur Brauner to make a truly bizarre Bavarian *Heimat*/horror hybrid, *Der Irre vom Hof* (1978, The Madman from the Farm, also known as *Die Totenschmecker* or The Deathtasters). In the 1980s, Theumer would resurface once more as the director of a few, for a short period popular, mercenary films in the *Rambo* mould, a B-film subgenre that also provided temporary refuge for fellow 1960s producer Harry Alan Towers. Not all B-film veterans remained stuck in the lower end of the market. Drawing on the profits he had made with his report films in the 1960s and 1970s, Wolf Hartwig produced two international, big-budgeted Second World War epics in 1976 and 1978, Sam Peckinpah's *Steiner – Das eiserne Kreuz/Cross of Iron*, and its sequel *Steiner – Das eiserne Kreuz, 2. Teil/Breakthrough Sergeant Steiner* (directed by Andrew V. McLaglen). Erwin C. Dietrich, in contrast, has concentrated his efforts since the late 1970s on his distribution outlet Ascot-Elite, achieving respectability and box-office success with foreign acquisitions as diverse as the action film *The Wild Geese* (1978) and, more recently, the Anglo-American comedy drama *Four Weddings and a Funeral* (1994).

As their sexual content gradually became more explicit and lurid, the sex films of the late 1970s and early 1980s now genuinely targeted a niche clientèle. The final convergence of the sex film with the hard-core industry was complete in a wholesale retreat from cinema exhibition to video distribution in the mid-1980s. If there were any producers of the old guard left peddling this type of genre, they were now firmly sidelined by a new generation of porn tycoons, such as Teresa Orlowski. Meanwhile, the cinematic back catalogue of the previous decades was sold off at cut-down prices to the newly emerging commercial TV channels, which, in the aftermath of the liberalisation of the West German television market, needed cheap fare to fill their schedule. It was on these new channels, such as RTL, Sat.1, and others, where the report films experienced a ghostly renaissance in late-night slots from the late 1980s to the mid-1990s. Whether this revival was simply a matter of cheap availability or whether there was genuine audience demand for these films (perhaps among viewers in the former GDR) is difficult to ascertain. The report films certainly did not look too much out of place in schedules that also included magazine formats produced by Playboy Publishing and game shows with striptease elements. None the less, if it could be argued that Daddy's Cinema was in the mid-1980s finally laid to rest as a viable mode of cinematic exhibition, it did so at the same time as the New German Cinema began to lose its direction. In an ironic twist to the long-standing battle between the new and the old German film and between art and commerce, the patricidal sons and daughters appeared to capitulate alongside their dissolute fathers.

Notes

1. Anon., Protest gegen Schmutzfabrik', *Berliner Morgenpost*, 30 August 1959.
2. H. Kuntze-Just, 'Die Wahrheit über Wolfgang Hartwig', *Echo der Zeit*, 23 August 1959.
3. Quoted in Anon., 'Film-Sex nicht mehr gefragt?', *Filmgeflüster*, 13 November 1962.
4. Joe Hembus, *Der deutsche Film kann gar nicht besser sein. Ein Pamphlet von gestern. Eine Abrechnung von heute*, Munich 1981, p. 10.
5. Leo Phelix and Rolf Thissen, *Pioniere und Prominente des modernen Sexfilms*, Munich 1983, pp. 214–220.
6. Cf. Stephan Buchloh, *Pervers, jugendgefährdend, staatsfeindlich. Zensur in der Ära Adenauer als Spiegel des gesellschaftlichen Klimas*, Frankfurt am Main and New York 2002.
7. *Richard Oswald. Regisseur und Produzent*, ed. Helga Belach and Wolfgang Jacobsen, Munich 1991.
8. Pam Cook, 'The Art of Exploitation, or How to Get into the Movies', *Monthly Film Bulletin*, vol. 52, 1985, p. 367.
9. Walter Kaul, *Der Kurier*, 29 August 1959, reprinted in *Filmmaterialien 9: Victor Trivas*, ed. Hans-Michael Bock and Wolfgang Jacobsen, Hamburg and Berlin 1996, pp. 37–38.
10. See *Schwarzer Traum und weisse Sklavin. Deutsch-dänische Filmbeziehungen 1910-1930*, ed. Manfred Behn, Munich 1994.
11. Cook, 'The Art of Exploitation', p. 368.

12. Anon., 'Film-Sex nicht mehr gefragt?'.
13. Ibid.
14. Barthel, *So war es wirklich*, pp. 149–150.
15. In a review of the first *Kommissar X* film, released in Britain under the title *Kiss Kiss, Kill Kill*, David Austen argued that the film was 'an extremely dull piece of sub-Bondian nonsense, and whatever little entertainment value it might have held for industrial halls in Northern Italy does not export itself to British suburban cinemas', in *Films and Filming*, vol. 15, part 3, 1968, p. 43.
16. hjw., 'Parnass – Pläne zwischen München und Ceylon', *Film-Echo/Filmwoche*, 15 October 1965, p. 6. Werner's Sinhalese partner on *Drei Gelbe Katzen* (1966, Three Yellow Cats) was P.A. Ediriweera, who had gained his expertise in international film-making through the collaboration on Anglo-American productions such as *The Bridge on the River Kwai* (1957).
17. Klaus Kunkel, 'Ein artiger James Bond. Jerry Cotton und der Bastei Verlag', in *Der Kriminalroman, Band 2*, ed. Jochen Vogt, Munich 1971, p. 559.
18. Barthel, *So war es wirklich*, p. 272.
19. Kunkel in Vogt, *Der Kriminalroman, Band 2*, pp. 566–567.
20. Ibid., p. 569.
21. Barthel, *So war es wirklich*, pp. 273–274.
22. Aspects of Towers' colourful personal and professional life are recounted in Anon., 'Harry Alan Towers', *Films and Filming*, no. 400, January 1988, p. 17.
23. Ibid.
24. Florian Pauer, *Die Edgar Wallace Filme*, Munich 1982, p. 115.
25. Christoph Nestel, *Sanders und das Schiff des Todes*. Cf. webpage: http://www.deutscher-tonfilm.de/sudsdt1.html
26. Bert Markus, 'Todestrommeln am großen Fluss', *Film-Echo/Filmwoche*, 22 May 1965, p. 14.
27. Cay van Ash and Elizabeth Sax Rohmer, *Sax Rohmer. Master of Villainy*, London 1972.
28. Barthel, *So war es wirklich*, p. 275.
29. Interview with Sax Rohmer in the *New Yorker*, 29 November 1947, quoted in Goswin Dörfler, 'Sax Rohmer's exotischer Überverbrecher', *Vampir*, vol. 21, 1980, p. 43.
30. Christopher Lee, *Tall, Dark, and Gruesome. An Autobiography*, London 1977, p. 250.
31. Reviews quoted in Dörfler, 'Sax Rohmers's exotischer Überverbrecher', p. 46.
32. German actors to appear in later entries included Heinz Drache, Götz George, Horst Frank, Wolfgang Kieling, and Harald Leipnitz.
33. Although in the German version Werner Jacobs is credited as director, it is doubtful whether he was involved in the project. In all likelihood his listing was due to national quota regulations.
34. It also recalls, however, the setting of the Hammer production *Circus of Horrors* (1960), a film that also had a German connection – in its casting of Anton Diffring and Erika Remberg.
35. Dörfler, 'Sax Rohmer's exotischer Übervrebrecher', pp. 46–47.
36. Anon., 'Kommissar X soll Jerry Cotton nicht ins Gehege kommen. Die Angebote der Verleiher müssten unterschiedlicher sein', *Film-Echo/Filmwoche* 2 March 1966, p. 4.
37. Anon., 'Deutschland klärt Italien auf!', *Film-Echo/Filmwoche*, 1 June 1968, p. 8.
38. Georg Seesslen, *Der pornographische Film*, Frankfurt and Berlin 1990, p. 175.
39. Re-released on CD in the 1990s, the soundtrack seems to have caught the mood of a new generation's appreciation for the weirder realms of 1960s 'easy listening', now rebranded under the term 'lounge-core'. In Germany, the composer Gert Wilden has seen his career revitalised in recent years, touring urban nightclubs with his synthesiser, and attracting audiences largely composed of listeners who had not been born when Wilden's soundtracks were first heard. Wilden's case is not unique in this respect. Other 1960s German film composers have also become unlikely pop icons for a new generation, including Peter Thomas (a regular contributor to the Wallace cycle) and Sigi Schwab, whose score for Jess Franco's German-Spanish horror film *Vampyros Lesbos* (1968) was used in parts for the soundtrack of Quentin Tarantino's *Jackie Brown* (1995).
40. Barthel, *So war es wirklich*, p. 152.

41. Ibid., p. 83.
42. Joe Hembus and Robert Fischer, *Der neue deutsche Film 1960–1980*, Munich 1981, pp. 204–205.
43. Geoff Brown, *Monthly Film Bulletin*, vol. 42, no. 495, April 1975, p. 81.
44. Tim Bergfelder, 'Horst Wendlandt. Produzent und Verleiher', *CineGraph. Lexikon zum deutschsprachigen Film*, ed. Hans-Michael Bock, Munich 1984– .
45. *Movie and Video Guide*, ed. Leonard Maltin, Harmondsworth 1998.
46. Phelix and Thissen, *Pioniere und Prominente des modernen Sexfilms*, p. 194.
47. Advertisement, *Film-Echo/Filmwoche*, 2 August 1968, p. 13.
48. Georg Seesslen, 'Alois Brummer', in Bock, *CineGraph*.
49. Linda Williams, *Hard Core. Power, Pleasure, and the Frenzy of the Visible*. London 1991, p. 49.
50. Thomas Elsaesser, *New German Cinema. A History*, London and Basingstoke 1989, p. 23.
51. Ibid., p. 67.
52. Seesslen, *Der pornographische Film*, pp. 180–181.
53. Dagmar Herzog, 'Pleasure, Sex, and Politics Belong Together: Post-Holocaust Memory and the Sexual Revolution in West Germany', *Critical Inquiry*, vol. 24, 1998, p. 396.
54. Anon., 'Helga und die Männer – Die sexuelle Revolution', *Film-Dienst*, April 1969.
55. Annette Miersch, *Schulmädchen-Report. Der deutsche Sexfilm der 70er Jahre*, Berlin 2003, p.18.
56. Herzog, 'Pleasure, Sex and Politics', pp. 418–425.

Chapter 10

CONCLUSION:
THE END OF AN ERA?

As the case studies in the previous chapters have shown, a combination of economic factors contributed to the demise of the popular West German film industry in the early 1970s. A perennial crisis in distribution and exhibition, endemic since the late 1950s, had reached a point where the film industry's main strategy of cheap but prolific production was no longer sustainable. Beyond purely economic factors, however, the reorientation in West German production patterns was also caused by a new agenda towards an aesthetically and politically different form of cinema, which initially was conceived as 'Young' but would eventually be termed 'New' German Cinema. At the heart of this agenda was the desire to replace a cinema of producers and distributors (decried as exemplifying Adorno's concept of the culture industry) with a cinema of *auteurs*. These were understood to be self-determined creative artists whose work moreover fulfilled a significant social function, by intervening in political issues ranging from the Vietnam War, the unresolved legacy of Germany's Nazi past, and later in the 1970s the rise of urban terrorism. It is clear that in this vision, there was not much space for either the Wendlandts and Brauners (let alone Hartwig) or the escapist genres they were producing. The aspirations towards an independent and non-commercial national art cinema corresponded to a recognition by politicians of cinema's potential to advertise the Federal Republic abroad as a functioning democracy,[1] and to contribute to political education and debate at home. It is thus no coincidence that the rise of the New German Cinema, which begins in the late 1960s with the début films of Rainer Werner Fassbinder, Werner Herzog, and Wim Wenders, coincided with the inauguration of West Germany's first postwar centre-left government in 1969.

An aesthetic as well as political redefinition of German cinema had, of course, been demanded ever since the Oberhausen Manifesto in 1962, when a group of young film-makers, under the intellectual leadership of Alexander Kluge, had announced the death of the old film, and had declared their intention to 'create the new German feature film'.[2] However, apart from Herbert Vesely's *Das Brot der frühen Jahre* (1962, The Bread of Those Early Years), which was regarded as a failure by both the proponents of a 'new' kind of cinema and the supporters of the establishment,[3] there was not much evidence of a new art-cinema movement emerging until mid-decade with the release in 1965 of Jean-Marie Straub's *Nicht versöhnt* (*Not Reconciled*), followed in 1966 by Kluge's *Abschied von Gestern* (*Yesterday Girl*), and Volker Schlöndorff's *Der junge Törless* (*Young Törless*). Of these three, Kluge's film represents perhaps the clearest prototype for the direction the New German Cinema of the 1970s would be taking – in its uncompromising political didacticism, its challenge to classical narrative strategies, its focus on issues pertaining specifically to German identity and contemporary contexts, its 'mood of melancholy self-reflection',[4] and its artisanal mode of production and distribution that circumvented the traditional film industry establishment. While Straub's and Schlöndorff's early films, meanwhile, were equally different in their formal strategies from the dominant genre cycles of the decade (very radically so in the case of Straub's *avant-garde* aesthetics), in terms of production, they still conformed to the internationalist principles that also underpinned the popular cinema of the 1960s. Straub and his wife and collaborator Danièle Huillet were French citizens, were based in Italy, and contributed to a broader idea of European art cinema (albeit German-speaking) through films that were financed as co-productions. Schlöndorff, meanwhile, had learned his trade as an assistant director for French *nouvelle vague* directors Alain Resnais and Louis Malle. Although most of his films in the late 1960s (including *Der junge Törless*) were co-productions, he later admitted to his disenchantment with this mode of production: 'I am extremely sceptical with regard to co-productions, because alongside the money you'll get, there are so many conditions that the film originally intended gets lost in the process. A film has to be concrete. This means that a German film has to be specifically German in order to be internationally successful'.[5]

Schlöndorff's comments succinctly summarise the differences in approach between the dominant West German mode of film production of the 1970s and early 1980s and the popular cinema of the 1960s, particularly with respect to strategies of multi-national collaboration, relations between the film industry and the state, and questions of popular genres. On the one hand, the films by Kluge, Fassbinder, Herzog, and Wenders certainly aimed for and achieved international critical recognition of West German cinema (especially in Western Europe and the United States). For most of the postwar period up to the mid-1960s, West German productions had bypassed or been ignored by the main European film festivals, such as Cannes and Venice, and while quite a number of popular German genre films had been distributed abroad, they had hardly helped in raising the profile of a nationally defined West German art cinema. This pattern only began to change in the 1960s with the films of the Young German Cinema, when Schlöndorff's *Der junge Törless* became the runner-up for the Golden Palm in Cannes in 1966. Kluge, meanwhile, won the Silver Lion in Venice in the same year for *Abschied von gestern,* and the Golden Lion two years later for his *Artisten in der Zirkuskuppel: Ratlos* (1968, Artists Under the Big Top: Perplexed). Perhaps ironically, what seemed to be expected abroad from West German film production was not cosmopolitanism, a strategy with which West Germany had previously hoped to religitimise itself on the world stage, but a confirmation of, in some cases, rather stereotypical expectations of 'Germanness'.

If one takes critical acclaim and success at festivals as one measure of internationalism, then on another level, production, West German cinema of the 1970s was, at least initially, rather more parochial. As Schlöndorff's quote above indicates, co-production was not one of the preferred strategies of the *auteurs* of the New German Cinema. Instead, the movement was supported primarily by a system of state subsidies, and by its relationship with public broadcasting television, both as a means of financing and as a distribution and exhibition outlet. In the process, a new dependency was created between the state authorities, the frequently politicised agendas of public broadcasters, and the indigenous film culture. The renunciation by the New German Cinema of popular genres as a means of commercial success (rather than as a primarily aesthetic concept to work with creatively, as in the case of Fassbinder's and Wenders' generic homages to melodrama, *film noir,* and the American road movie); the movement's preference of an artisanal mode of production; and the cult of the *auteur* with its occasionally élitist connotations, contributed to the breakdown of the balance that had persisted in the West German market between indigenous, transnational, and Hollywood films during the 1960s, and it allowed Hollywood to achieve a much stronger position in the West German distribution sector than it had ever had before. As the films of the New German Cinema were propagated as and came to be associated with West German cinema in its entirety, domestic mass audiences looked for popular entertainment elsewhere, and found it provided by Hollywood imports and by popular genres from other European countries. As I have argued in this book, the fact that television had paved the way for most of the previous decade in familiarising German audiences with international and especially American generic formulae only accelerated the development towards a largely Hollywood-dominated media culture and market in the 1970s.

Although the dichotomy of a national art cinema and an international entertainment industry (defined as Hollywood) did not leave much space for an indigenous popular cinema in the 1970s, the protagonists of the cinema of the 1960s found ways of adapting to these changes. Horst Wendlandt very profitably switched in the 1970s from producing Karl May and Edgar Wallace films to distribution with his new outlet Tobis (named after the defunct Nazi film company where he began his career as an apprentice in the late 1930s). Unlike Gloria and Constantin, Wendlandt tied his business strategies to the demands of a new multimedia landscape with competing as well as complementary modes of exhibition. While early Tobis acquisitions, such as a package of old Charlie Chaplin classics, were successful in their cinematic release, they became even more profitable through their repeated transmissions on television, where they fitted in perfectly in West German television's programme of film 'classics'. In the following years, Tobis concentrated almost exclusively on the acquisition of popular foreign, mostly French and Italian, films. While some of these also became box-office successes in the cinema (e.g., the action comedies with Bud Spencer and Terence Hill, French thrillers starring Jean-Paul Belmondo or Alain Delon, and Louis de Funès comedies), Tobis also negotiated the subsequent television rights.[6] In the 1980s, Tobis topped box-office records with a series of phenomenally successful films starring East Friesian comedian Otto Waalkes, who, like almost every other popular West German film star in the 1980s, had achieved his popularity on television. For these films Wendlandt reactivated Rialto as a production company. Rialto's box-office hits from the 1960s, meanwhile, the Karl May and Wallace cycles, were leased out to West German television for the first time in 1973, eliciting an enormous audience response. By contrast, only very occasionally did Wendlandt associate himself with New German Cinema projects, exceptions include Fassbinder's *Lili Marleen* (1980).

Fassbinder's collaborations with Wendlandt in the late 1970s exemplified a rare amicable arrangement between the old and the new German cinema, but also indicate the extent to which the New German Cinema itself became lured by international aspirations. Following the international profile the New German Cinema had gained but perhaps also because of a lack of domestic interest, some of the movement's most prestigious *auteurs* eventually pursued internationalist agendas – Fassbinder with his Nabokov adaptation *Despair* (1977) and his final film *Querelle* (1982); Wenders' films in the United States, from the retro-*noir Hammett* (1982) and the Baudrillardian blankness of *Paris, Texas* (1984) to his increasingly multinational films in the 1990s; Herzog's globetrotting expeditions from *Aguirre, der Zorn Gottes* (1972, Aguirre, the Wrath of God) to *Fitzcarraldo* (1982) and beyond; or Ulrike Ottinger's expeditions to Shanghai and Mongolia. Volker Schlöndorff, meanwhile, became, after his Oscar success with *Die Blechtrommel* (1980, The Tin Drum), and in an ironic reversal to the attitude he had expressed about international co-productions in the previously quoted comment, perhaps the most efficient among his generation in erasing any 'national' signatures in his work (see, e.g., *Un amour de Swann/Swann in Love*, 1984, *Death of a Salesman*, 1985, or *The Handmaid's Tale*, 1990). Schlöndorff provides a link not only between the explicitly nationally defined art cinema of the 1970s and early 1980s and the so-called Europuddings of the 1990s (see, for example, Schlöndorff's *Der Unhold/The Ogre/Le Roi des aulnes*, 1996) and the transatlantic productions of the new millennium, but also between a generation of film-makers who saw themselves as spokespersons for an entire society and nation and those German directors who have taken a more radical break from the national film industry. Examples for the latter would be those who have managed to establish themselves abroad as travelling professionals, or émigrés, from the Hollywood blockbuster-entrusted Roland Emmerich and Wolfgang Petersen to the more marginal Uli Edel and former Fassbinder protégé and American B-film *auteur* Ulli Lommel.

Looking at these films and career trajectories in a lager *durée* than simply within the framework of the *Autorenfilm* of the 1970s, there are remarkable similarities, continuities, and conjunctures yet to uncover between, on the one hand, what film history has declared *auteurs* and classics of national cinema and, on the other hand, the frequently forgotten protagonists, and ephemeral products, of the commercial film industry that I have discussed in the preceding chapters. For example, arguably the most bizarre encounter between the aesthetics of the New German Cinema and the attractions of an exploitation cinema of the kind that was once provided by Wolf Hartwig is *Die Insel der blutigen Plantage* (1982, Blood Plantation Island), an only partly ironic send-up of low-brow genres, such as prison-camp films, desert-island adventure and horror film. Made shortly after Fassbinder's death under the direction of Kurt Raab, the film features Fassbinder regulars such as Udo Kier, Peter Kern, and Barbara Valentin, whose career appears to have come full circle with this film, as she returns to the kind of role she performed in the Rapid productions of the late 1950s and early 1960s. Written by Raab and Kern, the film quite clearly shows an awareness of and personal investment in those popular traditions the official discourse on the New German Cinema tried its best to suppress over the preceding decade. In this respect, not only is *Die Insel der blutigen Plantage* a revealing 'return of the repressed' (the film has a perversely cathartic energy as it revels in its own bad taste, 'shockingly' transgressive sexual practices, aesthetic amateurism, and hysterical performances), but it also points forward to the self-reflective and post-modern horror of younger *agents provocateurs*, such as Christoph Schlingensief. In other respects too, the history I have outlined in my book and the history of the New German Cinema have converged to a remarkable degree. In the 1990s, Schlöndorff became instrumental in promoting the 'reunified' and refurbished Ufa/DEFA studio facilities at Neubabelsberg for international and big-budget co-productions, and they have since been used for the European and transatlantic films that can be seen as the most natural inheritors of the international co-productions of the 1960s.

It has become fashionable since the 1990s, particularly among the generation of film-makers who have taken over from the protagonists of the New German Cinema, to retrospectively assign blame for the decline of commercial West German film production in the early 1970s to the concept and politics of the *Autorenfilm*. Thus director Thomas Jahn has argued: 'Grandpa's cinema was not dead, the Oberhausen manifesto killed it. 1960s Germany was on its way to becoming a filmic world power ... We had everything in Germany, with the Edgar Wallace films we had the right ideas ... We have to take up where we left off in 1968'.[7] This historical scenario is too simplistic and in parts factually wrong. Jahn's comments however indicate that the Oedipal conflicts so prevalent in German cinema for decades, continue unabated.[8] The populist 'Grandchildren's Cinema' that emerged in the 1990s has mostly rejected the aspirations of the New German Cinema. Instead of following in the footsteps of Fassbinder, Herzog, Wenders, and Kluge, new directors such as Sönke Wortmann or Detlev Buck, rediscovered the gender farces of the early 1930s and 1950s, which it remade and repackaged as *Beziehungskomödien*, or relationship comedies.

After two decades of suppression, the 1950s and 1960s have returned with a vengeance in the German media landscape and have all but elbowed out the remaining vestiges of the New German Cinema. Whole German TV channels are nowadays devoted to the *Heimatfilm*, either in its 1950s variant or in new guises as sitcoms and soap operas. The Edgar Wallace films have been continuously recycled on TV already since the 1970s. Rialto produced further Wallace films in the mid- to late 1990s. The last one, *Das Schloss des Grauens* (The Castle of Terror) in 2002, not only reunited producer Horst Wendlandt with comedian Eddi Arent, but also proved to be Wendlandt's swansong – he died of cancer shortly after, aged 80.

In addition to the continued popularity of the Wallace films, there are biennial reruns of the *Sissi* films on television and other artefacts of the postwar period. A whole publishing industry has sprung up to cater for fans, with elaborate coffee-table books, while fan sites on the Internet have developed around such arcane subjects as late 1960s and early 1970s West German TV cop shows as well as Edgar Wallace films. The Karl May industry, too, goes from strength to strength – there seems to be an inexhaustible market for Karl May encyclopaedias and other, usually lavishly illustrated, books on the Rialto films, as well as countless other paraphernalia.[9] Martin Böttcher's scores continue to be evergreens in their own right; among the various collections available is a recent eight CD/book package with the collected soundtracks.[10] Apart from attesting to a continued nostalgia for the 1950s and 1960s, these ready-mades moreover provide a corrective to those who argue that the German cultural landscape has been homogenised into global audience preferences, allegedly dictated by Hollywood.

Perhaps more importantly, the 1960s not only survive as nostalgic artefacts in the new millennium, but also in the ongoing revamping of industrial outfits associated with previous decades. Horst Wendlandt's 1970s creation Tobis has become Tobis Studio Canal, and has retained its position among the top ten distributors in the German market. Matthias Wendlandt has announced after the recent death of his father that he will continue to run the family company Rialto. Elsewhere there have been generational changes too. For the Ascot-Elite Group, formerly known for their sex films, Erwin Dietrich's son Ralph has produced *Kondom des*

Grauens (Condom of Terror, 1997), a gay crime and horror comedy set and shot in New York.[11] Artur Brauner, meanwhile, still continues to produce the occasional feature film and equally continues his international reach, his most recent films being two German-Russian co-productions, *Kasachstan Lady* (2000), and *Apokalypse 99 – Anatomie eines Amokläufers* (2000, Anatomy of a Maniac). However, the most phenomenal comeback of a 1960s industrial brand name in the 1990s and 2000s has been the return of Constantin under the aegis of producer and director Bernd Eichinger. Following the demise of the old Constantin in the mid-1970s, the new company became initially associated with a group of film-makers whose populism had rendered them rather peripheral figures of the New German Cinema movement of the 1970s, but who can in retrospect be seen as the forerunners of the commercial turn in the German cinema of the 1990s, directors such as Wolfgang Petersen (*Das Boot*, 1982, *The Neverending Story*, 1984) and Uli Edel (*Christiane F – Die Kinder vom Bahnhof Zoo*, 1981). Both eventually, as mentioned above, ended up in Hollywood, which established Eichinger's contacts in the United States (in 1992, Constantin signed a co-production agreement with 20th Century Fox). The company has expanded on these international contacts ever since – in the 1990s, it has opened dependencies and offices in London, Paris, Stockholm, Copenhagen, and Dublin. This expansion was made possible in part through the alliance that Constantin forged with media mogul Leo Kirch, who became a minority partner with 25 per cent in 1986. In line with the global media industry generally, Constantin became a joint-stock company in 1999 and seems to have weathered the aftermath of the meltdown of Kirch's media empire in early 2002 remarkably well, as far as one can tell at present. While Bernd Eichinger continues to hold on to 25 per cent, Kirch's share has been bought by Highlight Communications, a Swiss media group with its own interests in film and video distribution (as well as in the negotiation of TV rights for the UEFA Champions League). A further 16 per cent share of Constantin is owned by EM-TV, a group that specialises in animated and children's programming and merchandising and whose various subsidiary interests include a 100 per cent ownership of the American-based Jim Henson Company (the 'Muppets', etc.). Constantin has thus entered the new millennium as part of a modern international media network that combines national and international film production, domestic distribution and international export, the negotiation of TV, video, and DVD rights, and merchandising.

Eichinger's business strategies, while clearly tailored to the demands of a post-digital media landscape governed to a large degree by the stock market, still remain at their core remarkably similar to the agenda his predecessors Barthel and Phillipsen pursued in the 1950s and 1960s, with a balanced company profile that combines a national and international dimension, and a production portfolio that includes European co-productions (*The Name of the Rose*, 1987; *Smilla's Sense of Snow*, 1997; *Prince Valiant*,

1997) and transatlantic endeavours that attempt to tap into the U.S. market (*The Neverending Story*, 1984; *Last Exit to Brooklyn*, 1989; *The House of the Spirits*, 1993). Particularly in the latter category, Constantin has made significant forays in recent years, culminating in the success in 2002 of the science fiction horror picture *Resident Evil*, a U.K.-U.S.-German co-production that made US$ 18 million at the American box office in the first three days after its release. Constantin's more nationally oriented films, on the other hand, have ranged in the 1990s from relatively up-market, but often rather bland, lifestyle comedies and dramas (*Der bewegte Mann/The Most Desired Man*, 1996; *Das Superweib/Super-Woman*, 1996; *Der Campus*, 1998; Eichinger's own directorial effort, *Der große Baragozy/The Great Baragozy*, 1999; *Nackt/Naked*, 2001) to low-budget comedies, which are popular with domestic and predominantly younger, audiences while being almost completely inexportable. The latter include films such as the animated feature *Werner – Beinhart* (1990), *Erkan und Stefan* (2000) and its sequel *Erkan und Stefan gegen die Mächte der Finsternis* (2002, Erkan and Stefan Against the Powers of Darkness), two showcases for a duo of popular TV comedians; and the Karl May spoof *Der Schuh des Manitu* (2001), which, with audience figures of over 11 million, is the most successful German cinema release to date. Like the Constantin of the 1960s, the company has, despite the strong personal media profile of Eichinger, overall a rather devolved approach to production and relies on external creative input, evidenced in its 1994 exclusive contract with director Sönke Wortmann. Constantin also includes under its company umbrella semi-independent smaller enterprises, such as Olga Film (whose best-known production remains Doris Dörrie's *Männer*, 1985), Moovie Entertainment (which produces the TV crime series 'Rosa Roth', starring Iris Berben), and Engram Pictures, the venture of director Rainer Matsutani (*Nur über meine Leiche* / Over My dead Body, 1995; *666 – Traue keinem, mit dem du schläfst* / Never Trust Anyone You Sleep With, 2002). All of these enterprises and film-makers share Eichinger's commitment to popular mainstream genre cinema (and television), though there are aesthetic differences between, for example, Matsutani's horror-comedy hybrids, which clearly feed on both domestic and international generic influences and styles, and Wortmann's visually and narratively pedestrian adaptations of best-selling novels and comic books, for which Eric Rentschler has coined the apt term 'cinema of consensus'.[12]

As a distributor, Constantin has managed to become one of the most significant players in the German market over the last years; by the beginning of the new millennium it outperformed not only domestic competition such as Kinowelt, Tobis Studio Canal, and Senator, but more significantly U.S. rivals such as Columbia Tristar, Buena Vista, and Warner Bros. – only United International Pictures (UIP), which distributes the products of Hollywood studios Paramount, M-G-M, Universal, and Dreamworks) did better. Of course, this performance is significantly influenced by the company's international portfolio – it is doubtful whether Constantin could achieve its position with domestic releases alone. Conversely, however, following the regeneration of domestic audience appeal for domestic films by the mid-1990s, American distributors have begun to invest in German productions (e.g., Buena Vista backed Thomas Jahn's *Knockin' on Heaven's Door*, 1997), an effect of the increasingly global media industry network which renders the discussion of a 'national' industry profile almost pointless. Audience preferences, in contrast, do occasionally differ from country to country. As with Constantin's production range, there are distinctive choices and generic preferences discernible in the twenty to twenty-five films that the company distributes annually. On the one hand, there are big-budget, international, prestige productions (*Passage to India*, 1985; *Dances With Wolves*, 1991, *Enemy At The Gates*, 2001; *K19 – The Widowmaker*, 2002), medium-budget sleepers (*The Sixth Sense*, 1999; *The Insider*, 2000), and films by slightly off-mainstream cult directors (e.g., Tim Burton's *Sleepy Hollow*, 2000; the Coens' *The Man Who Wasn't There*, 2001) or fully-fledged European art-cinema *auteurs*, such as Lars von Trier (*Dancer in the Dark*, 2000). On the other hand, Constantin is keen to reach the youth market, with gross-out highschool farces such as *American Pie* (2000), the Britney Spears vehicle *Not a Girl* (2002), and the teen comedy *Freche Biester/Slap Her She's French* (2002), which Constantin also co-produced. Moreover, these films tie in with Constantin's own domestic productions, such as *Schule* (2000) and domestic films from other production companies Constantin distributes (e.g. *Mädchen, Mädchen*, 2001). In all of these aspects, Constantin at the beginning of the twenty-first century is following the strategies of the Constantin of the 1960s. Indeed, in terms of productivity, it has nearly reached the peak of its earlier incarnation, while financially it appears more secure than the old Constantin ever was. Yet, as the Kirch disaster of 2002 has shown, the situation of the German media sector is far from stable.

The collapse of the traditional German production and distribution sector by the end of the 1960s was triggered, as I have argued in my book, by a number of international economic factors, which included the increasing discrepancy between productivity and dwindling exhibition outlets and audience figures, and the rising costs of co-productions (particularly, location shooting in formerly low-cost countries, such as Spain, Italy, and Yugoslavia). The domestic, low-budget, soft-porn boom of the late 1960s indicates the extent of West German producers' and distributors' reorientation towards national retrenchment. This crisis in the exhibition and distribution sector was a phenomenon the West German film industry shared with those in other European countries.

By the early 1970s, and particularly after the introduction of colour TV, television had irrevocably replaced the cinema as the dominant visual entertainment medium in most European countries. While the American film industry had adapted to this changed media landscape and spent most of the 1960s transforming itself into multimedia conglomerates,

European film industries, on the whole, tried to resist amalgamation and attempted to compete on increasingly unequal terms. In this respect, the temporary boom in European co-productions during the 1960s was dependent on a more global economic development. The restructuring process of the American film industry during the 1950s and 1960s (which resulted in the dissolution or transformation of established companies) resulted in a temporarily weakened control of Hollywood over European markets, which, in turn, facilitated an increased productivity (though not necessarily increased economic stability) of European industries. By the early 1970s, however, Hollywood had consolidated itself again and restated its interests in European markets. During the 1970s, the control over the West German film market was assumed by a new form of oligopoly, comprised of major American distributors and a handful of European multimedia tycoons and companies, whose main financial interests were in publishing and television (the Bertelsmann Group, Leo Kirch), while the New German Cinema was sustained primarily by what Thomas Elsaesser has termed a national media ecology, in other words, a commitment by the government towards a cinema that was explicitly understood to be 'art', rather than commercial or necessarily popular with mass audiences.[13]

Similar industry patterns were in evidence in other European countries, exemplified by the rise of Silvio Berlusconi in Italy or by the global ambitions of Rupert Murdoch. The resulting transformation of traditional film industries, based on the 'solid' contexts of locally, regionally, or nationally defined modes of production and cinematic exhibition, into a more 'virtual' mode of multinational and multimedia business interaction, of which the more recent trajectory of companies such as Constantin provide a good example, has been closely linked to the emerging technologies of initially cable and satellite TV, which instigated the shift in the 1980s from indigenous public broadcasting towards multinational commercial television (particularly in mainland Europe). An even more radical transformation of the way in which images and narratives are produced and received has commenced in the 1990s with the digital revolution, the emergence of the Internet, and the ongoing transformation of the very concept of communication, which has called into question not only traditional conceptualisations of localised or 'national' cultural production or reception but the future of cinema and television themselves as independent and exclusively designated sites of visual consumption. Like the European co-productions of the 1960s, the multimedia diversifications that have occurred since the 1970s have been motivated by explicitly global or transnational economic ambitions, and sustained by international modes of reception.

What these developments suggest is that the ultimate failure of the transnational mode of film production by the end of the 1960s may not have been the result of its lack of national specificity or indigenous base. On the contrary, television, multimedia, and Internet companies have adopted a transnational mode of production in subsequent decades as an economic necessity for competing in a changing media environment. Instead, the failure of the European film industries in the 1960s may have been largely due to their exclusive reliance on a particular exhibition context (the cinema), which, even after multinational distribution, was no longer a financially viable market or outlet in its own right. The developments of the global film economy since the 1970s have proven that the survival of cinema as a distinctive cultural and social space has become dependent on it being one designated exhibition context among a range of others and controlled, but also preserved, by multinational and multimedia interests. In this respect, the developments of the West German film industry in the 1960s and its international aspirations may thus best be understood as forming part of a wider, gradual shift in the way films are being produced, distributed, exhibited, and consumed. In other words, what makes the 1950s and 1960s a pivotal moment in media history is the emergence of a greater diversity of different media and entertainment contexts, which do not so much compete with each other as provide different, and yet coexisting temporal, spatial, and social functions.

With regard to the latter function, my analysis in the preceding chapters of popular West German film series of the 1960s and the wider patterns and legacies of cultural production to which they corresponded has suggested that my chosen case studies were not simply the meaningless confections they have been often been dismissed as, but that they actively contributed to national as well as more individual processes of self-redefinition. In the 1970s, this process articulated itself (not least through the medium film) through individual as well as collective strategies of introspection and self-interrogation. The mode of self-definition, on the other hand, that gives rise to cultural forms such as the Karl May and Edgar Wallace cycles appears to have attempted to erase the very necessity of nation as a category of belonging and self-worth, replacing this label with a utopian embrace of cosmopolitan exchange and performative identities.

Ever since the publication of Alexander and Margarete Mitscherlich's *Die Unfähigkeit zu trauern* (*The Inability to Mourn*) in the 1960s, there has been a consensus that the main psychological strategy of West Germans after 1945 with respect of the country's war crimes was a collective repression of feelings of responsibility and guilt.[14] The Mitscherlichs suggested that the only solution for West Germany to overcome its national psychosis associated with such repression was to confront and therapeutically work through its historical guilt, at the level of both the individual and national politics. Their suggestion was eventually taken up in a variety of ways in the 1970s and is also directly responsible for the soul-searching evident in the films of the New German Cinema. In the context of the Mitscherlichs' theory, one can easily see the strategies of 1960s popular cinema as being more repressive – the films' textual devices of temporal ellipsis, of uncertain topographies, and of blurred national identities all can be seen to perpetuate West Germany's amnesia over the Second World War.

As I have argued with respect of the Edgar Wallace films, these films aid in protecting their audiences to maintain the illusion of a world in which the Second World War had never happened.

The view that postwar German cinema functioned as a kind of political tranquillizer, has, of course, been a standard historical position. What I have attempted to suggest in this book is that this position is far too broad, not only in what it says about large portions of national (and international) film production, but more generally what it assumes about the psychological motivations and aspirations of an entire 'nation' (with the homogenising potential inherent in the latter term a clear indication what may be wrong with this framework). If one sidesteps the Mitscherlichs' proposal for a moment, it is, of course, entirely possible to conceive of different motivations for the diffusion of national identity in West Germany after 1945, and it is equally possible to argue that the temporary suspension of national introspection actually helped the re-democratisation of West Germany after the war and aided its reintegration into the wider international community. After all, it is worth recalling that Germany's ardent commitment to the idea of an integrated Europe originates precisely in this period. Moreover, as I have attempted to show with my various case studies, cosmopolitanism was far from being an ideologically unified or coherent concept. While the embrace of an international identity may have been prompted for some by feelings of guilt or unease about the past (or indeed the present), in the case of someone like Artur Brauner or the returning émigrés of the 1950s, the term as well as the practices of cosmopolitanism comprised a bitterly earned personal legacy of exile and persecution, a strategy of survival, and the hope for a better future.

In the reunified German media landscape (and culture more generally) of today the legacy of cosmopolitanism remains strong, and encompasses ideologically quite diverse phenomena from transnational and multi-cultural activities either at the grassroots or subsidised by the state, via European initiatives to the incursions of multinational media empires. Meanwhile, the New German Cinema's mode of intense soul-searching and national introspection has itself come under fire, challenged not only by the revival of popular genre strategies in the 1990s, but perhaps more crucially by critics who have accused the New German Cinema of having in its heyday perpetuated essentialist notions of Germanness, ignored the developments of an increasingly globalised and multicultural Germany, and failed to engage with a postcolonial world more generally – something Marie-Hélène Gutberlet has described as the movement's 'national autism'.[15] Deniz Göktürk, meanwhile, holds the same mindset responsible for the stereotypical ways in which migrants and issues of multiculturalism were represented in the German art cinema of the 1970s and 1980s, and for the structural frameworks that kept 'ethnic' film-makers in their place.[16] Thus, as the tides of political priorities have turned, it may be easier now to recognise the contribution the popular cinema of the 1960s has made not just to the history of German film, but perhaps more generally to an understanding of how certain narrative and visual conventions are used at different levels of reception in contributing to a wider perception of cultural and national identity, whether real or imagined.

Notes

1. For a discussion of this aspect of the New German Cinema, cf. John E. Davidson, *Deterritorializing the New German Cinema*, Minneapolis 1999.
2. 'The Oberhausen Manifesto', in *The European Cinema Reader*, ed. Catherine Fowler, London and New York 2002, p. 73.
3. Cf. Hester Baer, 'Negotiating the Popular and the Avant Garde: The Failure of Herbert Vesely's The Bread of Those Early Years (1962)', in *Light Motives. German Popular Film in Perspective*, ed. Randall Halle and Margaret McCarthy, Detroit 2003.
4. Thomas Elsaesser, 'The New German Cinema', in *European Cinema*, ed. Elizabeth Ezra, Oxford 2004, p. 194.
5. Quoted in *Der neue deutsche Film 1960-1980*, ed. Robert Fischer and Joe Hembus, Munich 1981, pp. 229–230.
6. Tim Bergfelder, 'Horst Wendlandt. Produzent und Verleiher', in *CineGraph. Lexikon zum deutschsprachigen Film*, ed. Hans-Michael Bock, Munich 1984–.
7. Malte Hagener, 'German Stars in the 1990s', in *The German Cinema Book*, ed. Tim Bergfelder, Erica Carter, Deniz Göktürk, London 2002, p. 104.
8. Thomas Elsaesser, 'German Cinema in the 1990s', in *The BFI Companion to German Cinema*, ed. Thomas Elsaesser and Michael Wedel, London 2000, pp. 3–16.
9. Cf., e.g., Michael Petzel, *Karl May Filmbuch*, Bamberg and Radebeul 1998; Michael Petzel, *Der Weg zum Silbersee. Dreharbeiten und Drehorte der Karl May Filme*, Berlin 2001; Michael Petzel, *Karl May Stars*, Bamberg and Radebeul 2002.
10. Cf. Martin Böttcher und andere: *Wilder Westen – Heisser Orient* (8 CDs plus book) Hambergen 2000.
11. The film was based on the gay underground comic book by Ralf König, who already provided the source for the biggest German box-office hit of the 1990s, *Der bewegte Mann* (1996, U.S. release title: *Maybe, Maybe Not*, U.K. release title: *The Most Desired Man*).
12. Eric Rentschler, 'Fom New German Cinema to the Post-Wall Cinema of Consensus', in *Cinema and Nation*, ed. Mette Hjort and Scott Mackenzie, London and New York 2000, pp. 273–274.
13. Thomas Elsaesser, *New German Cinema. A History*, London and Basingstoke 1989, p. 3.
14. Alexander and Margarete Mitscherlich, *Die Unfähigkeit zu trauern: Grundlagen kollektiven Verhaltens*, Munich 1967.
15. Marie-Hélène Gutberlet, 'In the Wilds of the German Imaginary: African Vistas', in Bergfelder et al. *The German Cinema Book*, p. 244.
16. Deniz Göktürk, 'Beyond Paternalism: Turkish-German Traffic in Cinema', in Bergfelder et al. *The German Cinema Book*, pp. 248–256.

Appendix

FILMOGRAPHY OF 1960S
GENRE CYCLES

Abbreviations:

AD: art direction
D: directed by
Dist: distribution company
F: France
GER: West-Germany
IT: Italy

M: musical score
P.c: production company
Ph: cinematography
Sc: Screenplay
SP: Spain
YUG: Yugoslavia

Note: English titles in italics indicate actual relase titles. Where no English release titles exist, literal translations are indicated in brackets after the original title.

Karl May Adaptations

Der Schatz im Silbersee/Blago u srebrnom jezeru/Le Trésor du lac d'argent
GER/YUG/F 1962. P.c: Rialto/Jadran/S.N.C. Paris. D: Harald Reinl. Sc: Harald G. Petersson; M: Martin Böttcher; Ph: Ernst W. Kalinke. Cast: Lex Barker, Pierre Brice, Herbert Lom, Karin Dor, Götz George, Eddi Arent, Ralf Wolter. German release: 12 December 1962; Dist: Constantin. British release: 1966; Dist: Planet (*The Treasure of Silver Lake*).

Winnetou I/Vinetu I/La Révolte des indiens apaches/La valle dei lunghi coltelli
GER/YUG/F/IT 1964. P.c: Rialto/Jadran/S.N.C.D.: Harald Reinl. Sc: Harald G. Petersson; M: Martin Böttcher; Ph: Ernst W. Kalinke. Cast: Lex Barker, Pierre Brice, Mario Adorf, Marie Versini, Ralf Wolter, Chris Howland. German release: 11 December 1963; Dist: Constantin. British release: 1965; Dist: BLC/British Lion (*Winnetou the Warrior*); U.S. title: *Apache Gold*.

Old Shatterhand/Old Seterhend/Les Cavaliers rouges/La battaglia di Fort Apache
GER/YUG/F/IT 1964. P.c: CCC/Avala/Criterion/Serena. D: Hugo Fregonese. Sc: Ladislas Fodor, R.A. Stemmle; M: Riz Ortolani; Ph: Siegfried Hold. Cast: Lex Barker, Pierre Brice, Daliah Lavi, Guy Madison, Ralf Wolter, Rik Battaglia. German release: 30 April 1964; Dist: Constantin. British release: 1965; Dist: Golden Era (*Apaches Last Battle*).

Winnetou II/Vinetu II/Giorni di fuoco/Le Trésor des montagnes bleues
GER/YUG/IT/F 1964. P.c: Rialto/Jadran/Atlantis/S.N.C.D.: Harald Reinl. Sc: Harald G. Petersson; M: Martin Böttcher; Ph: Ernst W. Kalinke. Cast: Lex Barker, Pierre Brice, Anthony Steel, Karin Dor, Mario Girotti, Klaus Kinski, Eddi Arent. German release: 17 September 1964; Dist: Constantin. British release: 1969; Dist: British Lion (*Last of the Renegades*).

Unter Geiern/Medju jastrebovima/Parmi les vautours/La dove scende il sole
GER/YUG/F/IT 1964. P.c: Rialto/Jadran/S. N. C./Atlantis. D: Alfred Vohrer. Sc: Eberhard Keindorff, Johanna Sibelius; M: Martin Böttcher; Ph: Karl Löb. Cast: Stewart Granger, Pierre Brice, Elke Sommer, Götz George, Sieghart Rupp, Mario Girotti. German release: 8 December 1964; Dist: Constantin. British release: 1966; Dist: BLC/British Lion (*Among Vultures*). U.S. title: *Frontier Hellcat*. Dist: Columbia.

Der Schut/Au pays des skipetars/Una carabina per Schut/Sut
GER/F/IT/YUG 1964. P.c: CCC/Criterion/Serena/Avala. D: Robert Siodmak. Sc: Georg Marischka; M: Martin Böttcher; Ph: Alexander Sekulovic. Cast: Lex Barker, Ralf Wolter, Marie Versini, Rik Battaglia, Dieter Borsche, Chris Howland. German release: 20 August 1964; Dist: Gloria. U.S. video title: *The Shoot.*

Der Schatz der Azteken (The Aztec Treasure)
GER/F/YUG 1964. P.c: CCC/Franco-London/Avala. D: Robert Siodmak. Sc: Ladislas Fodor. R.A. Stemmle, Georg Marischka; M: Erwin Halletz; Ph: Siegfried Hold. Cast: Lex Barker, Gerard Barray, Michèle Girardon, Rik Battaglia, Jeff Corey, Ralf Wolter. German release: 4 March 1965; Dist: Gloria.

Der Ölprinz/Kralj petroleja
GER/YUG 1965. P.c: Rialto/Jadran D: Harald Philipp. Sc: Fred Denger, Harald Philipp; M: Martin Böttcher; Ph: Heinz Hölscher. Cast: Stewart Granger, Pierre Brice, Macha Meril, Harald Leipnitz, Mario Girotti, Walter Barnes, Heinz Erhardt, Antje Weisgerber. German release: 27 August1965; Dist: Constantin. British release: 1969; Dist: Columbia (*Rampage at Apache Wells*).

Winnetou III/Vinetu III
GER/YUG 1965. P.c: Rialto/Jadran. D: Harald Reinl. Sc: Harald G. Petersson, J. Joachim Bartsch; M: Martin Böttcher; Ph: Ernst W. Kalinke. Cast: Lex Barker, Pierre Brice, Rik Battaglia, Sophie Hardy, Ralf Wolter, Carl Lange. German release: 14 October 1965; Dist: Constantin. British release: 1967; Dist: Columbia (*The Desperado Trail*).

Old Surehand/Lavirint smrti
GER/YUG 1965. P.c: Rialto/Jadran D: Alfred Vohrer. Sc: Fred Denger, Eberhard Keindorff/Johanna Sibelius; M: Martin Böttcher; Ph: Karl Löb. Cast: Stewart Granger, Pierre Brice, Letitia Roman, Mario Girotti, Wolfgang Lukschy. German release: 14 December 1965; Dist: Constantin. British release: 1968: Dist: Warner-Pathé (*Flaming Frontier*).

Die Pyramide des Sonnengottes (The Pyramid of the Sun God)
GER/IT/F/YUG 1965. P.c: CCC/ Serena/ Franco-London/ Avala. D: Robert Siodmak. Sc: Ladislas Fodor, R.A. Stemmle, Georg Marischka; M: Erwin Halletz; Ph: Siegfried Hold. Cast: Lex Barker, Gerard Barray, Michèle Girardon, Ralf Wolter, Rik Battaglia, Gustavo Rojo. German release: 17 April1965; Dist: Gloria.

Note: Sequel to *Der Schatz der Azteken*. In France and Italy both films were edited into a single version (French release title: *Les Mercenaires du Rio Grande*; Italian release title: *I violenti di Rio Bravo*).

Durchs wilde Kurdistan/El salvaje Kurdistan
GER/SP 1965. P.c: CCC/Balcazar. D: Franz Josef Gottlieb (uncredited: Roy Rowland, Werner Klingler). Sc: F.J. Gottlieb; M: Raimund Rosenberger; Ph: Francisco Marin. Cast: Lex Barker, Marie Versini, George Heston, Ralf Wolter, Wolfgang Lukschy, Werner Peters, Dieter Borsche, Chris Howland. German release: 28 September 1965; Dist: Gloria. British release: 1970; Dist: Golden Era (*Wild Kurdistan*).

Im Reiche des silbernen Löwen/El ataque de los kurdos (The Empire of the Silver Lion)
GER/SP 1965. P.c: CCC/Balcazar D: Franz Josef Gottlieb (uncredited: Roy Rowland, Werner Klinger)
Sc: F.J. Gottlieb; M: Raimund Rosenberger; Ph: Francisco Marin/Robert Ziller. Cast: Lex Barker, Ralf Wolter, Marie Versini, George Heston, Anne-Marie Blanc, Dieter Borsche, Chris Howland, Sieghart Rupp. German release: 31 December 1965; Dist: Nora.

Das Vermächtnis des Inka/El ultimo rey de los incas/Viva Gringo! (The Inca Legacy)
GER/SP/IT 1965. P.c: Franz Marischka/Orbita/Pea. D: Georg Marischka. Sc: Georg Marischka, Winfried Groth, Franz Marischka; M: Riz Ortolani/Angelo Francesco Lavagnino; Ph: Siegfried Hold.

Cast: Guy Madison, Rik Battaglia, Fernando Rey, Francisco Rabal, William Rothlein, Geula Nuni, Chris Howland, Heinz Erhardt, Walter Giller. German release: 9 April 1966; Dist: Nora.

Winnetou und das Halbblut Apanatschi/Apanatsi (Winnetou and the Halfbreed Apanatschi) GER/YUG 1966. P.c: Rialto/Jadran. D: Harald Philipp. Sc: Fred Denger; M: Martin Böttcher; Ph: Heinz Hölscher. Cast: Lex Barker, Pierre Brice, Uschi Glas, Götz George, Ralf Wolter, Walter Barnes. German release: 17 August 1966; Dist: Constantin.

Winnetou und sein Freund Old Firehand GER/YUG 1966. P.c: Rialto/Jadran. D: Alfred Vohrer. Sc: David De Reske, C.B. Taylor, Harald G. Petersson; M: Peter Thomas; Ph: Karl Löb. Cast: Pierre Brice, Rod Cameron, Marie Versini, Nadia Gray, Harald Leipnitz, Rik Battaglia. German release: 13 December 1966; Dist: Columbia-Bavaria. British release: 1969; Dist: Columbia (*Thunder at the Border*).

Winnetou und Old Shatterhand im Tal der Toten/Il lungo fiume del west (Winnetou and Old Shatterhand in the Valley of Death) GER/IT/YUG 1968. P.c: CCC/Jadran/S. I. P. D: Harald Reinl. Sc: Alex Berg (= Herbert Reinecker), Harald Reinl; M: Martin Böttcher; Ph: Ernst W. Kalinke. Cast: Lex Barker, Pierre Brice, Karin Dor, Rik Battaglia, Ralf Wolter, Eddi Arent. German release: 12 December 1968; Dist: Constantin.

Edgar Wallace Films

Der Frosch mit der Maske/Frøen GER/Denmark 1959. P.c: Rialto. D: Harald Reinl. Sc: Trygve Larsen (= Egon Eis), Joachim Bartsch; M: Willy Mattes; Ph: Ernst W. Kalinke; AD: Erik Aaes, Walther Rasmussen. Cast: Siegfried Lowitz, Joachim Fuchsberger, Eva Anthes, Fritz Rasp, Eddi Arent. German release: 4 September 1959; Dist: Constantin. U.S. TV title: *The Face of the Frog*. U.S. video title: *Fellowship of the Frog*.

Der rote Kreis/Den blodrøde cirkel GER/Denmark 1959. P.c: Rialto. D: Jürgen Roland. Sc: Trygve Larsen (= Egon Eis), Wolfgang Menge; M: Willy Mattes; Ph: Heinz Pehlke; AD: Erik Aaes. Cast: Karl Saebisch, Renate Ewert, Klausjürgen Wussow, Eddi Arent, Fritz Rasp. German release: 2 March 1960; Dist: Constantin. British release: 1965; Dist: D.U.K. (*The Crimson Circle*). U.S. TV title: *The Red Circle*.

Die Bande des Schreckens GER 1960. P.c: Rialto. D: Harald Reinl. Sc: Joachim Bartsch, Wolfgang Schnitzler; M: Heinz Funk; Ph: Albert Benitz; AD: Erik Aaes, Rudolf Remp. Cast: Joachim Fuchsberger, Karin Dor, Elisabeth Flickenschildt, Fritz Rasp, Eddi Arent. German release: 25 August 1960; Dist: Constantin. British release: 1962 (*The Terrible People*). Original U.S. title: *Hand of the Gallows*. U.S. video title: *The Terrible People*.

Der grüne Bogenschütze GER 1960. P.c: Rialto. D: Jürgen Roland. Sc: Wolfgang Menge, Wolfgang Schnitzler; M: Heinz Funk; Ph: Heinz Hoelscher; AD: Mathias Mathies, Ellen Schmidt. Cast: Gert Fröbe, Karin Dor, Klausjürgen Wussow, Eddi Arent, Heinz Weiß. German release: 3 February 1961; Dist: Constantin. U.S. video title: *The Green Archer*.

Der Rächer GER 1960. P.c: Kurt Ulrich. D: Karl Anton. Sc: Gustav Kampendonk, Rudolph Cartier; M: Peter Sandloff; Ph: Willi Sohm, AD: Willi A. Herrmann, Kurt Stallmach. Cast: Heinz Drache, Ingrid Van Bergen, Klaus Kinski, Ina Duscha, Siegfried Schürenberg. German release: 5 August 1960; Dist: Europa. U.S. video title: *The Avenger*.

Die toten Augen von London GER 1961. P.c: Rialto. D: Alfred Vohrer. Sc: Trygve Larsen (= Egon Eis); M: Heinz Funk; Ph: Karl Löb; AD: Matthias Matthies, Ellen Schmidt. Cast: Joachim Fuchsberger, Karin Baal, Dieter Borsche, Klaus Kinski, Eddi Arent, Wolfgang Lukschy, Ady Berber. German release: 28 March 1961; Dist: Constantin. U.S. cinema release: 1966: Dist: Magna (*The Dead Eyes of London*).

Der Fälscher von London
GER 1961. P.c: Rialto. D: Harald Reinl. Sc: Johannes Kai; M: Martin Böttcher; Ph: Karl Löb; AD: Matthias Mathies, Ellen Schmidt. Cast: Karin Dor, Hellmut Lange, Walter Rilla, Viktor de Kowa, Eddi Arent, Siegfried Lowitz, Mady Rahl. German release: 18 Auigust 1961; Dist: Constantin. U.S. video title: *The Forger of London*.

Das Geheimnis der gelben Narzissen/The Devil's Daffodil
GER/U.K. 1961. P.c: Rialto/Omnia Pictures/Donald Taylor D: Akos von Rathony. Sc: Basil Dawson, Trygve Larsen (= Egon Eis); M: Keith Papworth; Ph: Desmond Dickinson, AD: William Hutchinson. Cast: Joachim Fuchsberger (British version: William Lucas), Sabine Sesselmann (British version: Penelope Horner), Klaus Kinski (British version: Colin Jeavons), Albert Lieven, Marius Goring, Christopher Lee, Walter Gotell, Ingrid van Bergen. German release: 21 July 1961; Dist: Constantin. British release: May 1962; Dist: BLC/ British Lion/ Britannia. U.S. release: 1967: Dist: Goldstone Film Enterprises (*The Daffodil Killer* also known as *Secret of the Devil's Daffodil*).

Die seltsame Gräfin
GER 1961. P.c: Rialto. D: Josef von Baky, Jürgen Roland (uncredited). Sc: R.A. Stemmle, Curt H. Gutbrod; M: Peter Thomas; Ph: Richard Angst; AD: Helmut Nentwig, Albrecht Hennings. Cast: Joachim Fuchsberger, Brigitte Grothum, Klaus Kinski, Lil Dagover, Fritz Rasp, Eddi Arent, Marianne Hoppe. German release: 8 November 1961; Dist: Constantin. U.S. video title: *The Strange Countess*.

Das Rätsel der roten Orchidee
GER 1961. P.c: Rialto. D: Helmuth Ashley. Sc: Trygve Larsen (= Egon Eis); M: Peter Thomas; Ph: Franz Lederle; AD: Matthias Matthies, Ellen Schmidt. Cast: Adrian Hoven, Christopher Lee, Marisa Mell, Eric Pohlmann, Eddi Arent, Klaus Kinski, Walter Gotell. German release: 2 March 1962; Dist: Constantin. British title: *Gangster: London*. U.S. title: *Puzzle of the Red Orchid* also known as *The Secret of the Red Orchid*.

Die Tür mit den sieben Schlössern/La Porte aux sept serrures
GER/F 1962. P.c: Rialto/Les Films Jacques Leitienne. D: Alfred Vohrer. Sc: H.G. Petersson, Johannes Kai (= Hanns Wiedmann); M: Peter Thomas; Ph: Karl Löb; AD: Helmut Nentwig, Siegfried Mews. Cast: Heinz Drache, Sabine Sesselmann, Pinkas Braun, Klaus Kinski, Eddi Arent, Gisela Uhlen, Werner Peters, Ady Berber, Siegfried Schürenberg, Jan Hendriks. German release: 19 June 1962; Dist: Constantin. U.S. video title: *The Door with Seven Locks*.

Das Gasthaus an der Themse
GER 1962. P.c: Rialto. D: Alfred Vohrer. Sc: Trygve Larsen (= Egon Eis), H.G. Petersson; M: Martin Böttcher; Ph: Karl Löb; AD: Matthias Matthies, Ellen Schmidt. Cast: Joachim Fuchsberger, Brigitte Grothum, Elisabeth Flickenschildt, Klaus Kinski, Eddi Arent, Siegfried Schürenberg, Jan Hendriks. German release: 28 September 1962; Dist: Constantin. U.S. video title: *The Inn on the River*.

Der Fluch der gelben Schlange
GER 1963. P.c: CCC. D: Franz Josef Gottlieb. Sc: Janne Furch, F.-J. Gottlieb; M: Oskar Sala; Ph: Siegfried Hold; AD: Hans Jürgen Kiebach, Ernst Schomer. Cast: Joachim Fuchsberger, Brigitte Grothum, Pinkas Braun, Eddi Arent, Werner Peters. German release: 22 February 1963; Dist: Constantin. U.S. TV title: *The Curse of the Yellow Snake*.

Der Zinker/L'Énigme du serpent noir
GER/F 1963. P.c: Rialto/Jacques Willemetz. D: Alfred Vohrer. Sc: H.G. Petersson; M: Peter Thomas; Ph: Karl Löb; AD: Walter Kutz, Herbert Kirchhoff. Cast: Heinz Drache, Barbara Rütting, Klaus Kinski, Eddi Arent, Siegfried Schürenberg, Günther Pfitzmann, Agnes Windeck, Jan Hendriks. German release: 26 April 1963; Dist: Constantin. U.S. video title: *The Squeaker*.

Das indische Tuch
GER 1963. P.c: Rialto. D: Alfred Vohrer. Sc: Georg Hurdalek, H.G. Petersson; M: Peter Thomas; Ph: Karl Löb; AD: Wilhelm Vorwerg, Walter Kutz. Cast: Heinz Drache, Corny Collins, Hans Clarin, Elisabeth Flickenschildt, Klaus Kinski, Eddi Arent, Siegfried Schüren-berg, Ady Berber, Gisela Uhlen. German release: 13 September 1963; Dist: Constantin. U.S. video title: *The Indian Scarf.*

Der schwarze Abt
GER 1963. P.c: Rialto. D: Franz Josef Gottlieb. Sc: Johannes Kai (= Hanns Wiedmann), F.J. Gott-lieb; M: Martin Böttcher; Ph: Richard Angst; AD: Wilhelm Vorwerg, Walter Kutz, Siegfried Mews. Cast: Joachim Fuchsberger, Dieter Borsche, Charles Regnier, Grit Böttcher, Eddi Arent, Klaus Kinski, Werner Peters. German release: 5 July 1963; Dist: Constantin. U.S. video title: *The Black Abbot.*

Zimmer 13/L'Attaque du fourgon postal
GER/F 1963. P.c: Rialto/S.N.C.D: Harald Reinl. Sc: Quentin Phillips (= Will Tremper); M: Peter Thomas; Ph: Ernst W. Kalinke; AD: Wilhelm Vorwerg, Walter Kutz. Cast: Joachim Fuchsberger, Karin Dor, Walter Rilla, Eddi Arent, Siegfried Schürenberg. German release: 20 February 1964; Dist: Constantin. U.S. video title: *Room 13.*

Death Drums along the River/Todestrommeln am großen Fluss
UK/GER 1963. P.c: Hallam/Big Ben/Towers of London/Constantin. D: Lawrence Hunting-ton. Sc: Harry Alan Towers, Nicolas Roeg, Kevin Kavanagh, Lawrence Huntington. Ph: Bob Huke. Cast: Richard Todd, Marianne Koch, Albert Lieven, Walter Rilla, Vivi Bach, Robert Arden. German release: 20 December1963; Dist: Constantin. British release: 1966; Dist: Planet. U.S. TV title: *Sanders.*

Die Gruft mit dem Rätselschloß
GER 1964. P.c: Rialto. D: Franz Josef Gottlieb. Sc: R.A. Stemmle, F.J. Gottlieb; M: Peter Thomas; Ph: Richard Angst; AD: Wilhelm Vorwerg, Walter Kutz. Cast: Judith Dornys, Harald Leipnitz, Rudolf Forster, Klaus Kinski, Eddi Arent, Werner Peters, Siegfried Schürenberg. German release: 30 April 1964: Dist: Constantin. U.S. video title: *The Curse of the Hidden Vault.*

Der Hexer
GER 1964. P.c: Rialto. D: Alfred Vohrer. Sc: Herbert Reinecker; M: Peter Thomas; Ph: Karl Löb; AD: Wilhelm Vorwerg, Walter Kutz. Cast: Joachim Fuchsberger, Heinz Drache, Sophie Hardy, Siegfried Lowitz, Siegfried Schürenberg, Eddi Arent, René Deltgen, Margot Trooger. German release: 21 August 1964; Dist: Constantin. U.S. video title: *The Mysterious Magician.*

Das Verätertor/Traitor's Gate
GER/UK 1964. P.c: Rialto/Summit Films. D: Freddie Francis. Sc: John Sansom, Basil Dawson, Johannes Kai (= Hanns Wiedmann); M: Martin Böttcher; Ph: Denys Coop; AD: Tony Inglis. Cast: Albert Lieven, Margot Trooger, Eddi Arent, Klaus Kinski, Gary Raymond, Catherina von Schell, Edward Underdown. German release: 18 December1964; Dist: Constantin. British release: August 1965; Dist: BLC/Columbia. U.S. release: 1966; Dist: Columbia.

Coast of Skeletons/Sanders und das Schiff des Todes
UK/GER 1965. P.c: Towers of London. D: Robert Lynn. Sc: Anthony Scott Veitch, Peter Wel-beck (=Harry Alan Towers); Ph: Stephen Dade, Egil S. Woxholt. Cast: Richard Todd, Heinz Drache, Marianne Koch, Elga Andersen, Dietmar Schönherr, Dale Robertson. German release: 7 May1965; Dist: Constantin. British release: 1966; Dist: BLC/British Lion. U.S. release: 1966; Dist: Seven Arts.

Neues vom Hexer (Again the Ringer)
GER 1965. P.c: Rialto. D: Alfred Vohrer. Sc: Herbert Reinecker; M: Peter Thomas; Ph: Karl Löb; AD: Wilhelm Vorwerg, Walter Kutz. Cast: Heinz Drache, Barbara Rütting, Brigitte Horney, René Deltgen, Eddi Arent, Klaus Kinski, Robert Hoffmann, Siegfried Schürenberg, Margot Trooger. German release: 4 June1965; Dist: Constantin.

Der unheimliche Mönch (The Sinister Monk)
GER 1965. P.c: Rialto. D: Harald Reinl. Sc: Joachim Bartsch, Fred Denger; M: Peter Thomas; Ph: Ernst W. Kalinke; AD: Wilhelm Vorwerg, Walter Kutz. Cast: Harald Leipnitz, Karin Dor, Eddi Arent, Ilse Steppat, Siegfried Lowitz, Siegfried Schürenberg, Uschi Glas. German release: 17 December1965; Dist: Constantin.

Der Bucklige von Soho (The Hunchback of Soho)
GER 1966. P.c: Rialto. D: Alfred Vohrer. Sc: Herbert Reinecker; M: Peter Thomas; Ph: Karl Löb; AD: Wilhelm Vorwerg, Walter Kutz. Cast: Günther Stoll, Pinkas Braun, Eddi Arent, Monika Peitsch, Siegfried Schürenberg, Gisela Uhlen. German release: 6 September1966; Dist: Constantin.

Circus of Fear/Das Rätsel des silbernen Dreiecks
UK/GER 1966. P.c: Proudweeks/Circus. D: John Moxey, Werner Jacobs. Sc: Peter Welbeck (= Harry Alan Towers); M: Johnnie Douglas; Ph: Ernest Steward; AD: Frank White. Cast: Heinz Drache, Christopher Lee, Suzy Kendall, Leo Genn, Eddi Arent, Klaus Kinski, Maurice Kauffman, Anthony Newlands, Victor Maddern, Cecil Parker. German release: 29 April 1966; Dist: Constantin. British release: 1967; Dist: Warner-Pathé/Anglo Amalgamated. U.S. release: 1967; Dist: American International, U.S. title: *Psycho-Circus*.

Das Geheimnis der weißen Nonne/The Trygon Factor
GER/UK 1966. P.c: Rialto/Ian Warren. D: Cyril Frankel. Sc: Derry Quinn, Stanley Munro; M: Peter Thomas; Ph: Harry Waxman; AD: Roy Stannard, Hazel Peisel, George Best. Cast: Stewart Granger, Susan Hampshire, Sophie Hardy, Cathleen Nesbitt, Eddi Arent, Robert Morley, Brigitte Horney, Siegfried Schürenberg (British version: James Robertson Justice), Terry-Thomas. German release: 16 December 1966; Dist: Constantin. British release: July 1967; Dist: Rank.

Die blaue Hand
GER 1967. P.c: Rialto. D: Alfred Vohrer. Sc: Alex Berg (=Herbert Reinecker); M: Martin Böttcher; Ph: Ernst W. Kalinke; AD: Wilhelm Vorwerg, Walter Kutz. Cast: Klaus Kinski, Harald Leipnitz, Carl Lange, Ilse Steppat, Diana Körner, Siegfried Schürenberg. German release: 28 April 1967; Dist: Constantin. U.S. release: 1972: Dist: New World; U.S. title: *The Creature with the Blue Hand*.

Der Mönch mit der Peitsche
GER 1967. P.c: Rialto. D: Alfred Vohrer. Sc: Alex Berg (=Herbert Reinecker); M: Martin Böttcher; Ph: Karl Löb; AD: Wilhelm Vorwerg, Walter Kutz. Cast: Joachim Fuchsberger, Uschi Glas, Grit Böttcher, Siegfried Schürenberg, Jan Hendriks. German release: 11 August 1967; Dist: Constantin. U.S.-TV title: *College Girl Murders*.

Der Hund von Blackwood Castle
GER 1967. P.c: Rialto. D: Alfred Vohrer. Sc: Alex Berg (=Herbert Reinecker); M: Peter Thomas; Ph: Karl Löb; AD: Wilhelm Vorwerg, Walter Kutz. Cast: Heinz Drache, Karin Baal, Siegfried Schürenberg, Horst Tappert, Agnes Windeck, Hans Söhnker. German release: 18 January 1968; Dist: Constantin. U.S. release: 1968; Dist: Sunset International; U.S. title: *The Horror of Blackwood Castle*.

Im Banne des Unheimlichen (Spellbound by the Uncanny)
GER 1967. P.c: Rialto. D: Alfred Vohrer. Sc: Ladislas Fodor; M: Peter Thomas; Ph: Karl Löb; AD: Wilhelm Vorwerg, Walter Kutz. Cast: Joachim Fuchsberger, Siv Mattson, Wolfgang Kieling, Pinkas Braun, Claude Farell. German release: 26.4.1968; Dist: Constantin.

Der Gorilla von Soho (The Gorilla of Soho)
GER 1968. P.c: Rialto. D: Alfred Vohrer. Sc: Alfred Gregor(= Alfred Vohrer and Horst Wendlandt); M: Peter Thomas; Ph: Karl Löb; AD: Wilhelm Vorwerg, Walter Kutz. Cast: Horst Tappert, Uschi Glas, Albert Lieven, Inge Langen, Herbert Fux. German release: 27 September 1968; Dist: Constantin.

Der Mann mit dem Glasauge
GER 1968. P.c: Rialto. D: Alfred Vohrer. Sc: Paul Hengge; M: Peter Thomas; Ph: Karl Löb; AD: Wilhelm Vorwerg, Walter Kutz. Cast: Horst Tappert, Karin Hübner, Fritz Wepper, Friedel Schuster, Hubert von Meyerinck, Jan Hendriks, Christiane Krüger. German release: 21 February1969; Dist: Constantin. U.S. release: 1969; Dist: Sunset International; U.S. title: *The Man with the Glass Eye* also known as *Terror on Half Moon Street*.

Das Gesicht im Dunkeln/A doppia faccia
GER/IT 1969. P.c: Rialto/Colt Produzioni Cinematografiche S.R.L. /Mega Films. D: Riccardo Fredda. Sc: Riccardo Fredda, Paul Hengge; M: Joan Christian; Ph: Gabor Pagoni, AD: Luciano Spadoni. Cast: Klaus Kinski, Christiane Krüger, Margaret Lee, Sidney Chaplin, Günther Stoll. German release: 4 July 1969; Dist: Constantin U.S. title: *Puzzle of Horror*.

Der Teufel kam aus Akasawa/El diablo venia de Akasawa (The Devil Came From Akasawa)
GER/SP 1970. P.c: CCC/Fenix Films. D: Jess Frank (= Jesus Franco). Sc: Ladislas Fodor, Paul Andre; M: Manfred Hübler, Siegfried Schwab; Ph: Manuel Merino. Cast: Fred Williams, Susann Korda (=Soledad Miranda), Horst Tappert, Walter Rilla, Howard Vernon, Siegfried Schürenberg, Blandine Ebinger. German release: 5 March 1971; Dist: Cinerama.

Die Tote aus der Themse (The Body in the Thames)
GER 1971. P.c: Rialto. D: Harald Philipp. Sc: H.O. Gregor, Harald Philipp; M: Peter Thomas; Ph: Karl Löb; AD: Johannes Ott. Cast: Uschi Glas, Hansjörg Felmy, Werner Peters, Ivan Desny, Günther Stoll, Siegfried Schürenberg, Vadim Glowna. German release: 1 April 1971; Dist: Constantin.

Das Geheimnis der grünen Stecknadel/Cosa avete fatto a Solange?
GER/IT 1972. P.c: Rialto/Clodio Cinematografica S. P. A. /Italian International Film S.R.L.D: Massimo Dallamano. Sc: Peter M. Thouet, Bruno di Geronimo, Massimo Dallamano. M: Ennio Morricone; Ph: Aristide Massaccesi; AD: Mario Ambrosini. Cast: Joachim Fuchsberger, Karin Baal, Fabio Testi, Günther Stoll, Christine Galbo. German release: 9 March 1972; Dist: Constantin. U.S. TV title: *What Have You Done to Solange?* also known as *The Mystery of the Green Pin*.

Das Rätsel des silbernen Halbmonds/Sette orchidee macchiate di rosso
GER/IT 1972. P.c: Rialto/ Flora D: Umberto Lenzi. Sc: Paul Hengge, Umberto Lenzi; M: Riz Ortolani; Ph: Angelo Lotti. Cast: Uschi Glas, Antonio Sabato, Marisa Mell, Pier Paolo Capponi, Petra Schürmann, Rosella Falk. German release: 30 June 1972; Dist: Constantin. U.S. TV title: *The Mystery of the Silver Crescent*.

Bryan Edgar Wallace Films

Das Geheimnis der schwarzen Koffer
GER 1962. P.c: CCC. D: Werner Klingler. Sc: Percy Allen; M: Gert Wilden; Ph: Richard Angst. Cast: Joachim Hansen, Senta Berger, Hans Reiser, Chris Howland. German release: 23 February 1962; Dist: Gloria U.S. video title: *The Secret of the Black Trunk*.

Der Würger von Schloß Blackmoor
GER 1963. P.c: CCC. D: Harald Reinl. Sc: Ladislas Fodor, Gustav Kampendonk; M: Oskar Sala; Ph: Ernst W. Kalinke; Cast: Karin Dor, Ingmar Zeisberg, Walter Giller, Rudolf Fernau, Dieter Eppler. German release: 21 June 1963; Dist: Gloria. U.S. title: *The Strangler of Blackmoor Castle*.

Der Henker von London
GER 1963. P.c: CCC. D: Edwin Zbonek. Sc: R.A. Stemmle; M: Raimund Rosenberger; Ph: Richard Angst. Cast: Hansjörg Felmy, Dieter Borsche, Maria Perschy, Wolfgang Preiss, Chris Howland. German release: 22 November 1963; Dist: Columbia-Bavaria. British release: 1968 (*The Executioner of London* also known as *The Hangman of London*) U.S. release: 1965; Dist: Paramount; U.S. title: *The Mad Executioners*.

Das Phantom von Soho
GER 1963. P.c: CCC. D: Franz Josef Gottlieb. Sc: Ladislas Fodor; M: Martin Böttcher; Ph: Richard Angst. Cast: Dieter Borsche, Barbara Rütting, Hans Söhnker, Elisabeth Flickenschildt, Werner Peters, Helga Sommerfeld. German release: 14 February 1964; Dist: Gloria. British release: 1968; Dist: Golden Era (*The Phantom of Soho* also known as *Murder by Proxy*). U.S. release: 1966; Dist: Producers Releasing Organization; U.S. title: *The Phantom of Soho*.

Das Ungeheuer von London City
GER 1964. P.c: CCC. D: Edwin Zbonek. Sc: R.A. Stemmle, Bryan Edgar Wallace; M: Martin Böttcher; Ph: Siegfried Hold Cast: Hansjörg Felmy, Marianne Koch, Dietmar Schönherr, Hans Nielsen. German release: 2 July 1964; Dist: Gloria. British release: 1967; Dist: Golden Era; British title: *The Monster of London City*. U.S. release: 1967; Dist: Producers Releasing Organization; U.S. title: *The Monster of London City*.

Das siebente Opfer (The Seventh Victim)
GER 1964. P.c: CCC. D: Franz Josef Gottlieb. Sc: F.J. Gottlieb; M: Raimund Rosenberger; Ph: Richard Angst. Cast: Hansjörg Felmy, Ann Smyrner, Hans Nielsen, Hellmuth Lohner, Peter Vogel, Alice Treff, Walter Rilla, Wolfgang Lukschy. German release: 27 November 1964; Dist: Nora.

L'Uccello dalle piume di cristallo/Das Geheimnis der schwarzen Handschuhe
GER/IT 1969. P.c: CCC/SedaSpettacoli. D: Dario Argento. Sc: Dario Argento; M: Ennio Morricone; Ph: Vittorio Storraro. Cast: Tony Musante, Eva Renzi, Suzy Kendall, Werner Peters, Mario Adorf. German release: 24 June 1970; Dist: Constantin. British release: 1970 (*The Gallery Murders*, also known as *The Bird with the Crystal Plumage*, also known as *The Phantom of Terror*). U.S. release: 1969; Dist: U.M. Distributors.

Il gatto a nove code/Die neunschwänzige Katze
GER/IT/F 1971. P.c: Terra/ Seda Spettacoli/Labrador D: Dario Argento. Sc: Dario Argento/Michael Haller; M: Ennio Morricone; Ph: Erico Menczer. Cast: Karl Malden, James Franciscus, Catherine Spaak, Horst Frank, Werner Pochath. German release: 15 July 1971; Dist: Constantin. British release: 1971 (*The Cat-o-Nine Tails*).

L'Etrusco uccide ancora/Das Geheimnis des gelben Grabes
GER/YUG/IT 1971-72. P.c: CCC/Inex/Mondial Te.Fi. D: Armando Crispino. Sc: Lucio Battistrada, Armando Crispino, Lutz Elsholtz; M: Riz Ortolani; Ph: Enrico Menczer. Cast: Alex Cord, Samantha Eggar, John Marley, Horst Frank, Enzo Tarascio, Nadja Tiller. German release: 31 December 1972; Dist: Cinerama. U.S. title: *The Dead are Alive*.

Der Todesrächer von Soho (The Deadly Avenger of Soho)
GER/SP 1972. P.c: CCC/Telecine. D: Jess Frank (=Jesus Franco). Sc: Art Bernd (=Artur Brauner), Jess Frank; M: Rolf Kühn; Ph: Manuel Merino. Cast: Horst Tappert, Fred Williams, Barbara Rütting, Wolfgang Kieling, Siegfried Schürenberg. German release: 9 November 1972; Dist: Constantin.

Dr. Mabuse Films

Die tausend Augen des Dr. Mabuse
GER/F/IT 1960. P.c: CCC/ Criterion/C. E. L-Incom. D: Fritz Lang. Sc: Fritz Lang, Heinz Oskar Wuttig; M: Bert Grund, Gerhard Becker; Ph: Karl Löb. Cast: Peter van Eyck, Dawn Addams, Wolfgang Preiss, Gert Fröbe, Werner Peters. German release: 14 September1960; Dist: Prisma. British release: 1962 (*The Thousand Eyes of Dr Mabuse*, also known as *The Secret of Dr. Mabuse*, also known as *The Diabolical Dr Mabuse*).

Im Stahlnetz des Dr. Mabuse/Le Retour du Docteur Mabuse/F.B.I contro Dr. Mabuse
GER/F/IT 1961. P.c: CCC/Criterion/S.P.A. Cinematografica. D: Harald Reinl. Sc: Ladislas Fodor, Marc Behm; M: Peter Sandloff; Ph: Karl Löb. Cast: Lex Barker, Daliah Lavi, Wolfgang Preiss, Gert Fröbe, Fausto Tozzi, Werner Peters, Ady Berber. German release: 13. October 1961; Dist: Constantin. British release: 1970; Dist: Golden Era (*The Return of Dr Mabuse*).

Die unsichtbaren Krallen des Dr. Mabuse
GER 1961/1962. P.c: CCC. D: Harald Reinl. Sc: Ladislas Fodor; M: Peter Sandloff; Ph: Ernst W. Kalinke. Cast: Lex Barker, Karin Dor, Wolfgang Preiss, Siegfried Lowitz, Rudolf Fernau, Werner Peters. German release: 30 March 1962; Dist: Constantin. British release: 1965; Dist: Golden Era (*The Invisible Dr Mabuse* a.k.a. *The Invisible Horror*).

Das Testament des Dr. Mabuse
GER 1962. P.c: CCC. D: Werner Klingler. Sc: Ladislas Fodor, R.A. Stemmle; M: Raimund Rosenberger; Ph: Albert Benitz. Cast: Wolfgang Preiss, Gert Fröbe, Senta Berger, Walter Rilla, Leon Askin, Helmut Schmid. German release: 7 September 1962; Dist: Constantin British release: 1965; Dist: Golden Era (*The Testament of Dr Mabuse*).

Scotland Yard jagt Dr. Mabuse (Scotland Yard Chases Dr Mabuse)
GER 1963. P.c: CCC. D: Paul May. Sc: Ladislas Fodor; M: Rolf Wilhelm; Ph: Nenad Jovicic. Cast: Peter van Eyck, Sabine Bethmann, Dieter Borsche, Klaus Kinski, Walter Rilla, Werner Peters, Wolfgang Lukschy. German release: 20 September 1963; Dist: Gloria.

Die Todesstrahlen des Dr. Mabuse/Les rayons mortels du Docteur Mabuse/
I raggi mortali del Dottore Mabuse
GER/F/1T 1964. P.c: CCC/ Franco-London/Serena. D: Hugo Fregonese. Sc: Ladislas Fodor; M: Oskar Sala, Carlos Diemhammer; Ph: Riccardo Pallottini. Cast: Peter van Eyck, Yvonne Fourneaux, O.E. Hasse, Yoko Tani, Wolfgang Preiss, Walter Rilla, Leo Genn, Robert Beatty. German release: 18 September 1964; Dist: Gloria.

Kommissar X Films

Kommissar X: Jagd auf unbekannt/Dodici donne d'oro
GER/IT/YUG 1965. P.c: Parnass/Metheus/Avala. D: Frank Kramer (= Gianfranco Parolini). Sc: Giovanni Simonelli, Frank Kramer, Werner Hauff; M: Mladen Gutesha; Ph: Francesco Izzarelli. Cast: Tony Kendall (= Luciano Stella), Brad Harris, Maria Perschy, Christa Linder, Nicola Popovic. German release: 11 March 1966; Dist: Gloria. British release: 1968; Dist: Gala (*Kiss, Kiss, Kill, Kill*).

Kommissar X: Drei gelbe Katzen/Operazione 3 gatti gialli
AUSTRIA/GER/IT/F 1966. P.c: Danubia/Danny/Parnass/Jacques Willemetz/Filmedis. D: Rudolf Zehetgruber. Sc: Rudolf Zehetgruber; Ph: Klaus von Rautenfeld. Cast: Tony Kendall (= Luciano Stella), Brad Harris, Ann Smyrner, Corny Collins, Siegfried Rauch. German release: 17 May 1966: Dist: Gloria. U.S. video title: *Death is Nimble, Death is Quick*.

Kommissar X: In den Klauen des goldenen Drachen/ Agente Joe Walker. Operazione Estreme Oriente
(Inspector X and the Claws of the Golden Dragon)
GER/AUSTRIA/IT/YUG 1966. P.c: Parnass/ Cinesecolo/ Avala D: Frank Kramer (= Gianfranco Parolini). Sc: Stefan Gommermann, Frank Kramer; Ph: Francesco Izzarelli. Cast: Tony Kendall (= Luciano Stella), Brad Harris, Barbara Frey, Luisa Rivelli, Gisela Hahn, Ernst F. Fürbringer. German release: 30 September1966; Dist: Constantin.

Kommissar X: Drei grüne Hunde/ Commissaire X traque les chiens verts
GER/IT/F/Lebanon/Hungary 1967. P.c: Parnass/ Cinesecolo/ C.F.F.P./ Kassar/ Hungaro. D: Rudolf Zehetgruber. Sc: Rudolf Zehetgruber: M: Francesco de Masi; Ph: Baldi Schwarze. Cast: Tony Kendall (= Luciano Stella), Brad Harris, Olly Schoberova, Dietmar Schönherr, Sabine Su, Samson Burke. German release: 7 April 1967; Dist: Constantin. U.S. video title: *Death Trip*.

Kommissar X: Drei blaue Panther/Gangsters per un massacro (Inspector X: Three Blue Panthers)
GER/IT/Canada 1967. P.c: Parnass/PEA/I.P.S.D.: Frank Kramer (= Gianfranco Parolini). Sc: Robert F. Atkinson, Günter Rudorf, Giovanni Simonelli; M: Francesco de Masi; Ph: Rolf Kästel, Francesco Izzarelli. Cast: Tony Kendall (= Luciano Stella), Corny Collins, Brad Harris, Siegfried Rauch, Hannelore Auer, Erika Blanc. German release: 4 April 1968. Dist: Constantin.

Kommissar X: Drei goldene Schlangen (Inspector X: Three Golden Snakes)
GER/IT/U.S./Thailand 1968. P.c: Terra/Regina/ G. L A. /Taitri Mtr. D: Roberto Mauri. Sc:
James Brewer, Robert F. Atkinson, Manfred R. Köhler; Ph: Francesco Izzarelli. Cast: Tony
Kendall (= Luciano Stella), Monica Pardo, Loni Heuser, Brad Harris, Herbert Fux. German
release: 18 April 1969. Dist: Constantin.

Kommissar X jagt die roten Tiger/ F.B.I. – Operazione Pakistan (Inspector X and the Red Tigers)
GER/IT/Pakistan 1971. P.c: Divina/ Regina/ Virginia/ Montana D: Harald Reinl. Sc: Werner
Hauff, Klaus R.E. von Schwarze, Werner P. Zibaso; Ph: Francesco Izzarelli. Cast: Tony Kendall
(= Luciano Stella), Brad Harris, Gisela Hahn, Rainer Basedow. German release: 20.8.1971.
Dist: Constantin.

Jerry Cotton Films

Schüsse aus dem Geigenkasten. Fall Nr. 1/ Agente segreto Jerry Cotton: Operazione Uragano
GER/F/IT 1965. P.c: Allianz/Constantin/Astoria D: Fritz Umgelter. Sc: Georg Hurdalek; M:
Peter Thomas; Ph: Albert Benitz. Cast: George Nader, Heinz Weiß, Richard Münch, Sylvia Pas-
cal. German release: 6 May 1965; Dist: Constantin. British release: 1966; Dist: D.U.K. (*Tread Softly*).

Mordnacht in Manhattan. Fall Nr. 2 (Murderous Night in Manhattan)
GER 1965. P.c: Allianz/Constantin. D: Harald Philipp. Sc: Alex Berg (= Herbert Reinecker);
Ph: Walter Tuch. Cast: George Nader, Heinz Weiß, Richard Münch, Monika Grimm, Silvia
Solar. German release: 25 November 1965; Dist: Constantin.

Um null Uhr schnappt die Falle zu. Fall Nr. 3 (The Trap Shuts at Midnight)
GER 1965. P.c: Allianz/Constantin. D: Harald Philipp. Sc: Kurt Nachmann, Fred Denger; M:
Peter Thomas; Ph: Helmut Meewes. Cast: George Nader, Horst Frank, Richard Münch,
Dominique Wilms. German release: 4 March 1966. Dist: Constantin.

Die Rechnung – eiskalt serviert. Fall Nr. 4 (Ice-Cold Reckoning)
GER/F 1966. P.c: Allianz/Constantin/Prodex. D: Helmuth Ashley. Sc: Georg Hurdalek; Ph:
Franz X. Lederle. Cast: George Nader, Heinz Weiß, Richard Münch, Yvonne Monlaur, Horst
Tappert, Walter Rilla. German release: 25 August 1966; Dist: Constantin.

Der Mörderclub von Brooklyn. Fall Nr. 5 (The Murder Club in Brooklyn)
GER/IT 1966. P.c: Allianz/ Constantin/ Associate D: Werner Jacobs. Sc: Alex Berg (= Herbert
Reinecker); M: Peter Thomas; Ph: Franz X. Lederle. Cast: George Nader, Heinz Weiß, Helga
Anders, Karel Stepanek. German release: 17 March 1967; Dist: Constantin.

Dynamit in grüner Seide. Fall Nr. 6/ Il piu grande colpo delta malavita americana (Dynamite and
Green Silk)
GER/IT 1967. PC: Allianz/Constantin/Associate. D: Harald Reinl. Sc: Rolf Schulz, Christa
Stern; Ph: Franz X. Lederle. Cast: George Nader, Heinz Weiß, Silvia Solar, Claus Holm, Gün-
ther Schramm, Marlies Draeger, Käthe Haack, Dieter Eppler. German release: 23 February
1968; Dist: Constantin.

Der Tod im roten Jaguar. Fall Nr. 7 (Death in a Red Jaguar)
GER/IT 1968. P.c: Allianz/Constantin/Associate. D: Harald Reinl. Sc: Alex Berg (= Herbert
Reinecker); Ph: Franz X. Lederle. Cast: George Nader, Heinz Weiß, Grit Böttcher, Carl Lange,
Ilse Steppat, Karin Schröder, Richard Münch. German release: 15 August 1968; Dist: Con-
stantin.

Todesschüsse am Broadway. Fall Nr. 8 (Deadly Bullets on Broadway)
GER 1968/69. P.c: Allianz/Terra D: Harald Reinl. Sc: Rolf Schulz, Christa Stern; Ph: Heinz
Hölscher. Cast: George Nader, Heinz Weiß, Heidy Bohlen, Michaela May, Mika Balok. Ger-
man release: 26 March 1969; Dist: Constantin.

Fu Manchu Films

The Face of Fu Manchu/Ich, Dr. Fu Manchu
UK/GER 1965. P.c: Hallam/Constantin. D: Don Sharp. Sc: Peter Welbeck (= Harry Alan Towers); M: Christopher Whelen (German version: Gert Wilden); Ph: Ernest Steward. Cast: Christopher Lee, Nigel Green, Joachim Fuchsberger, Karin Dor, Walter Rilla, Tsai Chin, James Robertson Justice. German release: 6 August 1965; Dist: Constantin. British release: November 1965; Dist: Warner-Pathé/Anglo-Amalgamated.

The Brides of Fu Manchu/Die 13 Sklavinnen des Dr. Fu Manchu
UK/GER 1966. P.c: Hallam/Constantin. D: Don Sharp. Sc: Peter Welbeck (= Harry Alan Towers); Ph: Ernest Steward. Cast: Christopher Lee, Douglas Wilmer, Heinz Drache, Marie Versini, Tsai Chin, Harald Leipnitz, Howard Marion Crawford, Rupert Davies. German release: 2.9.1966; Dist: Constantin British release: December 1966. Dist: Warner-Pathé.

The Vengeance of Fu Manchu/Die Rache des Dr. Fu Manchu
GER/UK 1967. P.c: Constantin/Fu Manchu Films. D: Jeremy Summers. Sc: Peter Welbeck (= Harry Alan Towers); M: Malcolm Lockyer; Ph: John von Kotze. Cast: Christopher Lee, Douglas Wilmer, Howard Marion Crawford, Horst Frank, Maria Rohm, Tsai Chin, Wolfgang Kieling, Peter Carsten, Suzanne Roquette, Tony Ferrer, Noel Trevarthen. German release: 26 May 1967; Dist: Constantin.. British release: 3 December 1967: Dist: Warner-Pathé.

The Blood of Fu Manchu/Der Todeskuß des Dr. Fu Manchu/Fu Manchu y el beso de muerte/ Kiss and Kill
GER/SP/U.S. 1968. P.c: Terra/Ada/Udastex. D: Jess Franco (= Jesus Franco). Sc: Peter Welbeck (= Harry Alan Towers); M: Daniel White; Ph: Manuel Merino. Cast: Christopher Lee, Richard Greene, Götz George, Shirley Eaton, Maria Rohm, Tsai Chin, Loni von Friedl, Howard Marion Crawford, Ricardo Palacios, Frances Kahn, Isaura de Oliveira. German release: 23 August1968; Dist: Constantin.

The Castle of Fu Manchu/Die Folterkammer des Dr. Fu Manchu/El castillo de Fu Manchu
GER/SP/IT/UK 1968. P.c: Terra/Balcazar/Italian International/Towers of London. D: Jess Franco (= Jesus Franco). Sc: Peter Welbeck (= Harry Alan Towers); M: Carlo Camilleri; Ph: Manuel Merino. Cast: Christopher Lee, Richard Greene, Tsai Chin, Günther Stoll, Maria Perschy. German release: 30 May 1969; Dist: Constantin. British release: 1972, Dist: M-G-M/EMI; U.S. title: *Assignment Istanbul*, also known as *The Torture Chamber of Fu Manchu*.

Angélique Films

Angélique, Marquise des Anges/Angelique
F/GER/IT 1964. P.c: Borderie/Gloria/Francos/Fono. D: Bernard Borderie. Sc: Claude Brulé, Louis Agotay; M: Michel Magne; Ph: Henri Persin. Cast: Michèle Mercier, Robert Hossein, Dieter Borsche, Claude Giraud, Giuliano Gemma, Rosalba Neri, Renate Ewert. German release: 18 December 1964, Dist: Gloria. British release: October 1967 (*Angelique*).

Merveilleuse Angélique/ Angelique 2.Teil
F/GER/IT 1964. P.c: Borderie/Gloria/Francos/Liber. D: Bernard Borderie Sc: Claude Brulé, Louis Agotay; M: Michel Magne; Ph: Henri Persin. Cast: Michèle Mercier, Claude Giraud, Charles Regnier, Jean-Louis Trintignant, Ernst Schröder. German release: 30 July 1965; Dist: Gloria. British release: 1968; (*Angelique – The Road to Versailles* also known as *Licence for Love*).

Angélique et le roi/Angelique und der König (Angélique and the King)
F/GER/IT 1965. P.c: Borderie/Gloria/Francos/Fono/CICC. D: Bernard Borderie. Sc: Bernard Borderie, Claude Brulé, Francis Kosne; M: Michel Magne; Ph: Henri Persin. Cast: Michèle Mercier, Robert Hossein, Jean Rochefort, Samy Frey, Estella Blain. German release: 3 March 1966; Dist: Gloria.

Indomptable Angélique/Unbezähmbare Angelique (Untamable Angélique)
F/GER/IT 1967. P.c: Gloria/Francos/CICC/Cinephonic/Fono Roma. D: Bernard Borderie.
Sc: Pascal Jardin, Francis Cosne, Bernard Borderie; M: Michel Magne; Ph: Henri Persin. Cast:
Michèle Mercier, Robert Hossein, Bruno Dietrich, Roger Picaut, Christian Rode. German
release: 15 December 1967; Dist: Gloria.

Angélique et le sultan/Angelique und der Sultan (Angélique and the Sultan)
F/GER/IT 1967. P.c: Gloria/Francos/Borderie/Cinephonic/Fono Roma. D: Bernard Bor-
derie. Sc: Pascal Jardin, Bernard Borderie, Francis Cosne; M: Michel Magne; Ph: Henri Persin.
Cast: Michèle Mercier, Robert Hossein, Jean-Claude Pascal, Helmut Schneider, Roger Pigaut,
Ettore Manni, Jacques Santi. German release: 9 August 1968; Dist: Gloria.

Sexy Susan (Frau Wirtin) Cycle

Susanne, die Wirtin von der Lahn/Il dolci vizi della casta Susanna
GER/Austria/IT/Hungary 1968. P.c: Neue Delta/Aico/Hungarofilm. D: François Legrand (=
Franz Antel). Sc: Kurt Nachmann; M: Johannes Fehring (= Gianni Ferrio); Ph: Siegfried Hold.
Cast: Pascale Petit, Terry Torday, Mike Marshall, Harald Leipnitz, Claus Ringer, Jacques Her-
lin, Hannelore Auer, Oskar Sima, Günther Philipp, Judith Dornys. German release: 16 January
1968; Dist: Constantin British release: 1968 (*The Sweet Sins of Sexy Susan*).

Frau Wirtin hat auch einen Grafen
GER/Austria/IT/Hungary 1968. P.c: Terra/Neue Delta/Aico/Hungarofilm D: François
Legrand (= Franz Antel). Sc: Kurt Nachmann, Günter Ebert; M: Gianni Ferrio; Ph: Hanns
Matula. Cast: Terry Torday, Jeffrey Hunter, Pascale Petit, Gustav Knuth, Jacques Herlin, Har-
ald Leipnitz, Hannelore Auer, Ralf Wolter, Edwige Fenech. Geman release: 26 November1968;
Dist: Constantin. British release: 1969 (*Sexy Susan Sins Again*).

Frau Wirtin hat auch eine Nichte
GER/Austria/IT 1969. P.c: Terra/Neue Delta/Aico. D: François Legrand (= Franz Antel). Sc:
Kurt Nachmann, Günter Ebert; M: Gianni Ferrio; Ph: Hanns Matula. Cast: Terry Torday, Clau-
dio Brook, Margaret Lee, Jacques Herlin, Heinrich Schweiger, Lando Buzzanca, Karl-Michael
Vogler, Ralf Wolter, Edwige Fenech. German release: 16 April 1969; Dist: Constantin. British
release: 1971 (*House of Pleasure*).

Frau Wirtin bläst auch gern Trompete
GER/Austria/IT/Hungary 1970. P.c: Terra/Neue Delta/Italian International/Mafilm D:
François Legrand (= Franz Antel). Sc: Kurt Nachmann; M: Gianni Ferrio; Ph: Hanns Matula.
Cast: Terry Torday, Harald Leipnitz, Glenn Saxson, Jacques Herlin, Willy Millowitsch, Rudolf
Prack, Rudolf Schündler, Andrea Rau. German release: 27 February 1970; Dist: Constantin.
British release: 1972 (*Sexy Susan Knows How…*).

Frau Wirtin treibt es jetzt noch toller (The Innkeeper Has Gotten Even Wilder)
GER/Austria 1970. P.c: Terra/Neue Delta. D: François Legrand (= Franz Antel). Sc: Kurt
Nachmann, August Rieger; M: Gerhard Heinz; Ph: Hanns Matula. Cast: Terry Torday, Glenn
Saxson, Günther Philipp, Jacques Herlin, Paul Löwinger. German release: 25 September 1970;
Dist: Constantin.

Frau Wirtins tolle Töchterlein
GER/IT 1973. P.c: Malory/Cinemar. D: François Legrand (= Franz Antel) Sc: Kurt Nachmann;
M: Stelvio Cipriani; Ph: Siegfried Hold. Cast: Terry Torday, Gabriele Tinti, Femy Benussi, Paul
Löwinger, Marika Mindzenthy, Maja Hoppe, Margot Hielscher, Jacques Herlin. German
release: 19 April 1973; Dist: Constantin. British release: 1975; Dist: Border (*Knickers Ahoy!*).

BIBLIOGRAPHY

Books

Allan, S. and J. Sandford, edS. *DEFA: East German Cinema, 1946-1992*, New York and Oxford 1999.

Austin, T. *Hollywood, Hype and Audiences. Selling and Watching Popular Film in the 1990s*, Manchester 2002.

Balio, T., ed. *The American Film Industry*, Madison 1985.

Barr, C. *Ealing Studios*, 2nd edition, London 1993.

Barthel, M. *So war es wirklich. Der deutsche Nachkriegsfilm*, Munich 1986.

Becker, J.-P. *Sherlock Holmes und Co. Essays zur englischen und amerikanischen Detektivliteratur*, Munich 1975.

Behn, M., ed. *Schwarzer Traum und weiße Sklavin: Deutsch-dänische Filmbeziehungen 1910–1930*, Munich 1994.

Belach, H. and W. Jacobsen *Richard Oswald. Regisseur und Produzent*, Munich 1991.

Berger, J., H.-P. Reichmann and R. Worschech, eds. *Zwischen Gestern und Morgen. Westdeutscher Nachkriegsfilm, 1946–1962*, Frankfurt-on-Main 1989.

Bergfelder, T., E. Carter and D. Göktürk, eds. *The German Cinema Book*, London 2002.

Bertram, T., ed. *Der rote Korsar. Traumwelt Kino der fünfziger und sechziger Jahre*, Essen 1998.

Bessen, U., ed. *Trümmer und Träume. Nachkriegszeit und fünfziger Jahre auf Zelluloid*, Bochum 1989.

Bliersbach, G. *So grün war die Heide. Der deutsche Nachkriegsfilm in neuer Sicht*, Weinheim and Basle 1985.

Bloch, E. *Verfremdungen I*, Frankfurt-on-Main 1963.

Bock, H.-M., ed. *CineGraph. Lexikon zum deutschsprachigen Film*, Munich 1984–.

Bock, H.-M. and W. Jacobsen, eds. *Filmmaterialien 7: Heinz Pehlke, Kamera*, Hamburg and Berlin 1995.

———. *Filmmaterialien 9: Victor Trivas*, Hamburg and Berlin 1996.

Bock, H.-M. and C. Lenssen, eds. *Joe May. Regisseur und Produzent*, Munich 1991.

Bock, H.-M. and M. Töteberg, eds. *Das Ufa Buch*, Frankfurt-on-Main 1992.

Bongartz, B. *Von Caligari zu Hiter – von Hitler zu Dr. Mabuse? Eine 'psychologische' Geschichte des deutschen Films von 1946 bis 1960*, Münster 1992.

Bordwell, D., J. Staiger and K. Thompson *The Classical Hollywood Cinema. Film Style and Mode of Production to 1960*, London 1985.

Brennicke, I. and J. Hembus *Klassiker des deutschen Stummfilms, 1910-1930*, Munich 1983.

Brüne, K., ed. *Lexikon des internationalen Films*, Reinbek 1991.

Buchloh, S. *Pervers, jugendgefährdend, staatsfeindlich. Zensur in der Ära Adenauer als Spiegel des gesellschaftlichen Klimas*, Frankfurt-on-Main and New York 2002.

Buscombe, E. and R.E. Pearson, eds. *Back in the Saddle Again. New Essays on the Western*, London 1998.

Byg, B. and B. Moore, eds. *Moving Images of East Germany*, Washington 2002.

Calloway, C.G., G. Gemünden and S. Zantop, eds. *Germans and Indians. Fantasies, Encounters, Projections*, Lincoln and London 2002.

Cargnelli, C. and M. Omasta, eds. *Aufbruch ins Ungewisse. Bd.1: Österreichische Filmschaffende in der Emigration vor 1945*, Vienna 1993.
———. *Aufbruch ins Ungewisse. Bd.2: Lexikon, Tributes, Selbstzeugnisse*, Vienna 1993.
Carter, E. *How German is She? Postwar West German Reconstruction and the Consuming Woman*, Ann Arbor 1997.
Christ, M. *Von Tarzan bis Old Shatterhand. Lex Barker und seine Filme*, Tuningen 1995.
Clark, T. *Der Filmpate. Der Fall des Leo Kirch*, Munich 2002.
Cook, P. *Fashioning the Nation. Costume and Identity in British Cinema*, London 1996.
Corrigan, T. *New German Cinema. The Displaced Image*, Austin 1983.
Curran, J. and V. Porter, eds. *British Cinema History*, London 1983.
Davidson, J.E. *Deterritorializing the New German Cinema*, Minneapolis 1999.
Dillmann-Kühn, C. *Artur Brauner und die CCC. Filmgeschäft, Produktionsalltag, Studiogeschichte 1946–1990*, Frankfurt-on-Main 1990.
Dixon, W.W. *The Charm of Evil. The Life and Films of Terence Fisher*, New York 1991.
Donald, J., ed. *Fantasy and the Cinema*, London 1989.
Dost, M., F. Hopf and A. Kluge, *Filmwirtschaft in der BRD und in Europa. Götterdämmerung in Raten*, Munich 1973.
Dyer, R. and G. Vincendeau, eds. *Popular European Cinema*, London and New York 1992.
Ellwood, D.W. and R. Kroes, eds. *Hollywood in Europe. Experiences of a Cultural Hegemony*, Amsterdam 1994.
Elsaesser, T. *New German Cinema. A History*, London and Basingstoke 1989.
———. *Weimar Cinema and After. Germany's Historical Imaginary*, London and New York 2000.
Elsaesser, T. and M. Wedel, eds. *A Second Life. German Cinema's First Decades*, Amsterdam 1996.
———. *The BFI Companion to German Cinema*, London 2000.
Ezra, E., ed. *European Cinema*, Oxford 2004.
Farin, M. and G. Scholdt, eds. *Dr. Mabuse – Medium des Bösen*, 3 vols. Hamburg 1994.
Fehrenbach, H. *Cinema in Democratizing Germany. Reconstructing National Identity after Hitler*, Chapel Hill and London 1995.
Filmstatistisches Jahrbuch, published by the Spitzenorganisation der deutschen Filmwirtschaft (SPIO).
Fischer, R. and J. Hembus, *Der neue deutsche Film 1960-1980*, Munich 1981.
Fowler, C., ed. *The European Cinema Reader*, London and New York 2002.
Frayling, C. *Spaghetti Westerns*, London and New York 1981 (2nd edn, London 1999).
Garncarz, J. *Filmfassungen. Eine Theorie signifikanter Filmvariation*, Frankfurt-on-Main and New York 1992.
———. 'Populäres Kino in Deutschland. Internationalisierung einer Filmkultur, 1925–1990', unpublished Habilitationsschrift, University of Cologne, 1996.
Ginsberg, T. and K.M. Thompson, eds. *Perspectives on German Cinema*, New York 1996.
Göktürk, D. *Künstler, Cowboys, Ingenieure. Kultur- und mediengeschichtliche Studien zu deutschen Amerika-Texten 1912–1920*, Munich 1998.
Guback, T. *The International Film Industry*, Bloomington 1969.
Gunning, T. *The Films of Fritz Lang. Allegories of Vision and Modernity*, London 2000.
Hake, S. *German National Cinema*, London and New York 2002.
———. *Popular Cinema of the Third Reich*, Austin 2002.
Halle, R. and M. McCarthy, eds. *Light Motives. German Popular Film in Perspective*, Detroit 2003.
Hansen, M., *Babel and Babylon: Spectatorship in American Silent Film*, Cambridge 1991.
Hardt, U. *From Caligari to California. Eric Pommer's Life in the International Film Wars*, Providence and Oxford, 1996.
Harper, S. *Picturing the Past. The Rise and Fall of the British Costume Film*, London 1994.
Hembus, C. and M. Nüchtern, ed. *Luggi Waldleitner. Fast ein Leben für den Film*, Munich 1983.
Hembus, J. *Der deutsche Film kann gar nicht beser sein. Ein Pamphlet von gestern. Eine Abrechnung von heute*, Munich 1981.
Herrwerth, T. *Partys, Pop und Petting. Die Sixties im Spiegel der Bravo*, Marburg 1997.
Hickethier, K. *Geschichte des deutschen Fernsehens*, Stuttgart and Weimar 1998.
Higson, A., ed. *Dissolving Views. Key Writings on British Cinema*, London 1996.
Hill, J. and P.C. Gibson, eds. *The Oxford Guide to Film Studies*, Oxford 1998.

Hill, J., and M. McLoone, eds. *Big Picture, Small Screen. The Relationship between Film and Television*, Luton 1996.

Hill, J., M. McLoone and P. Hainsworth, eds. *Border Crossing. Film in Ireland, Britain and Europe*, London and Dublin 1994.

Hjort M. and S. McKenzie, eds. *Cinema and Nation*, London and New York 2000.

Hobsch, M. *Liebe, Tanz, und 1000 Schlagerfilme*, Berlin 1998.

Horak, J.-C. *Fluchtpunkt Hollywood. Eine Dokumentation zur Filmemigration nach 1933*, Münster 1986.

Humphreys, P.J. *Media and Media Policy in Germany. The Press and Broadcasting since 1945*, 2nd edn, Oxford and Providence, 1994.

Hutchings, P. *Terence Fisher*, Manchester 2001.

Infield, G. *Hitler's Secret Life: The Mysteries of the Eagle's Nest*, New York 1979.

Jacobsen, W. *Erich Pommer. Ein Produzent macht Filmgeschichte*, Berlin 1989.

———. ed. *Babelsberg. Ein Filmstudio, 1912–1992*, Berlin 1992.

Jacobsen, W., A. Kaes and H.-H. Prinzler, eds. *Geschichte des deutschen Films*, Stuttgart and Weimar 1993.

Jacobsen, W. and H.-H. Prinzler, eds. *Käutner*, Berlin 1992.

———. eds. *Siodmak Bros.: Berlin – Paris – London – Hollywood*, Berlin 1998.

Jansen, P.W. and W. Schütte, eds. *Fritz Lang*, Munich and Vienna 1976.

Jary, M. *Traumfabriken made in Germany: Die Geschichte des deutschen Nachkriegsfilms 1945–1960*, Berlin 1993.

Kaes, A. *M*, London 2000.

Kaschuba, W., ed. *Der deutsche Heimatfilm. Bildwelten und Weltbilder*, Tübingen 1989.

Kastner, J. *Das grosse Karl May Buch*, Bergisch-Gladbach 1992.

King, L.J. *Bestsellers by Design. Vicki Baum and the House of Ullstein*, Detroit 1988.

Kiss, R.J. 'The Doppelgänger in Wilhelmine Cinema (1895–1914): Modernity, Audiences and Identity in Turn-of-the-Century Germany', unpublished Ph.D. thesis, University of Warwick, 2000.

Klinger, B. *Melodrama and Meaning. History, Culture, and the Films of Douglas Sirk*, Bloomington 1994.

Klussmeier, G. and H. Paul, *Karl May. Biographie in Dokumenten und Bildern*, Hildesheim 1987.

Koepnick, L. *The Dark Mirror. German Cinema between Hitler and Hollywood*, Berkeley 2002.

Korte, H. *Der Spielfilm und das Ende der Weimarer Republik: Ein rezeptionshistorischer Versuch*, Göttingen 1998.

Kracauer, S. *From Caligari to Hitler. A Psychological History of the German Film*, Princeton 1947.

———. *'Schriften 1*, Frankfurt-on-Main 1971.

Kramp, J. *Hallo! Hier spricht Edgar Wallace. Die Geschichte der deutschen Kriminalfilmserie von 1959–1972*, Berlin 1998.

Kreimeier, K. *Kino und Filmindustrie in der BRD. Ideologieproduktion und Klassenwirklichkeit*, Kronberg 1973.

———. *Die Ufa Story. Geschichte eines Filmkonzerns*, Munich 1992.

———. *The Ufa Story: A History of Germany's Greatest Film Company, 1918-1945*, New York 1996.

Kuhn, A. *Cinema, Censorship and Sexuality*, London 1988.

Lane, M. *Edgar Wallace. The Biography of a Phenomenon*, London 1938.

Lembach, J. *The Standing of the German Cinema in Great Britain after 1945*, Lampeter 2003.

Lee, C. *Tall, Dark, and Gruesome. An Autobiography*, London 1977.

Longhurst, D., ed., *Gender, Genre, and Narrative Pleasure*, London, Boston, and Sydney 1989.

Martin, L., ed. *Movie and Video Guide*, Harmondsworth 1998.

Marshall, B. and Stilwell, R., ed. *Musicals – Hollywood and Beyond*, Bristol 2000.

McCarthy M. and Halle, R., eds. *Light Motives. Popular German Cinema*, Detroit 2003.

Miersch, A. *Schulmädchen-Report. Der deutsche Sexfilm der 70er Jahre*, Berlin 2003.

Mitscherlich, A. and M. Mitscherlich *Die Unfähigkeit zu trauern: Grundlagen kollektiven Verhaltens*, Munich 1967.

Moran, A., ed. *Film Policy. International, National and Regional Perspectives*, London and New York 1996.

Mückenberger, C. and Jordan, G., eds. *'Sie sehen selbst, sie hören selbst': Die DEFA von ihren Anfängen bis 1949*, Marburg 1994.

Müllender, B. and A. Nollenheidt, eds. *Am Fuss der blauen Berge. Die Flimmerkiste in den sechziger Jahren*, Essen 1994.

Müller, C. and H. Segeberg, eds. *Die Modellierung des Kinofilms*, Munich 1998.

Murphy, R., ed. *The British Cinema Book*, 2nd edn, London 2001.

Nusser, P. *Der Kriminalroman*, Stuttgart 1980.

Orbanz, E. and Prinzler, H.-H., *Staudte*, Berlin 1992.

Orwell, G. *The Collected Essays, Journalism, and Letters of George Orwell, vol. III, As I Please, 1943–1945*, London 1968.

Pauer, F. *Die Edgar Wallace Filme*, Munich 1982.

Petley, J. *Capital and Culture. German Cinema 1933–1945*, London 1979.

Petzel, M. *Karl May Filmbuch*, Bamberg and Radebeul 1998.

————. *Der Weg zum Silbersee. Dreharbeiten und Drehorte der Karl May Filme*, Berlin 2001.

————. *Karl May Stars*, Bamberg and Radebeul 2002.

Petzel, M. and J. Wehnert, *Das neue Lexikon rund um Karl May. Leben – Bücher – Filme – Fans*, Berlin 2002.

Pflaum, H.G. and H.-H. Prinzler, *Cinema in the Federal Republic of Germany*, Munich and Vienna 1983.

Phelix, L. and R. Thissen, *Pioniere und Prominente des modernen Sexfilms*, Munich 1983.

Pleyer, P. *Deutscher Nachkriegsfilm 1946-1948*, Münster 1965.

Pommerin, R., ed. *The American Impact on Postwar Germany*, Providence and Oxford 1995.

Reichmann, H.-P. and R. Worschech, eds. *Abschied von Gestern. Bundesdeutscher Film der sechziger und siebziger Jahre*, Frankfurt-on-Main 1991.

Reinhardt, G. *Der Apfel fiel vom Stamm. Anekdoten und andere Wahrheiten aus meinem Leben*, Munich 1992.

Said, E.W. *Orientalism*, London 1978.

Schanze, H. and B. Zimmermann, eds. *Das Fernsehen und die Künste*, Munich 1994.

Schaudig, M., ed. *Positionen deutscher Filmgeschichte: 100 Jahre Kinematographie: Strukturen, Diskurse, Kontexte*, Munich 1996.

Schenk, R., ed. *Das zweite Leben der Filmstadt Babelsberg, DEFA 1946-1992*, Berlin 1994.

Schlüpmann, H. *Die Unheimlichkeit des Blicks. Das Drama des frühen deutschen Kinos*, Frankfurt-on-Main 1990.

Schmidt, A. *Sitara und der Weg dorthin: Eine Studie über Wesen, Werk, & Wirkung KARL MAY's*, Karlsruhe 1963.

Schmieding, W. *Kunst oder Kasse: Der Ärger mit dem deutschen Film*, Hamburg 1961.

Schneider, T.M. 'Genre and Ideology in the Popular German Cinema 1950-1972', unpublished Ph.D. thesis, University of Southern California 1994.

Schöning, J., ed. *London Calling. Deutsche im britischen Film der dreissiger Jahre*, Munich 1993.

————. ed. *Fantaisies russes: Russische Filmemacher in Berlin und Paris 1920–1930*, Munich 1995.

————. ed. *Triviale Tropen. Exotische Reise-und Abenteuerfilme aus Deutschland 1919–1939*, Munich 1997.

Seesslen, G. *Der pornographische Film*, Frankfurt-on-Main and Berlin 1990.

Seidl, C. *Der deutsche Film der fünfziger Jahre*, Munich 1987.

Shandley, R.R. *Rubble Films. German Cinema in the Shadow of the Third Reich*, Philadelphia 2001.

Siepmann, E. and I. Lusk, eds. *Bikini. Die fünfziger Jahre. Kalter Krieg und Capri-Sonne*, Reinbek 1983.

Silberman, M. *German Cinema: Texts in Context*, Detroit 1995.

Siodmak, R. *Zwischen Berlin und Hollywood. Erinnerungen eines grossen Filmregisseurs*, ed. H.C. Blumenberg, Berlin 1980.

Stacey, J. *Star Gazing. Hollywood Cinema and Female Spectatorship*, London 1994.

Staiger, J. *Interpreting Films. Studies in the Historical Reception of American Cinema*, Princeton 1992.

Steiner, G. *Die Heimatmacher: Kino in Österreich 1946-1966*, Vienna 1987.

Sturm, S. and A. Wohlgemuth, eds. *Hallo? Berlin? Ici Paris! Deutsche-französische Filmbeziehungen 1918–1939*, Munich 1996.

Tatar, M. *Lustmord. Sexual Murder in Weimar Germany*, Princeton 1995.

Theuerkauf, H. *Goebbels Filmerbe: Das Geschäft mit unveröffentlichten Ufa-Filmen*, Berlin 1998.

Theweleit, K. *Männerphantasien*, Frankfurt-on-Main 1978.

Thode-Arora, H. *Für fünfzig Pfennig um die Welt. Die Hagenbeckschen Völkerschauen*, Frankfurt-on-Main and New York 1989.

Thompson, K. *Exporting Entertainment. America in the World Film Market 1907-1934*, London 1986.

Tses, C. *Der Hexer, der Zinker, und andere Mörder. Hinter den Kulissen der Edgar Wallace Filme*, Essen 2002.

Unucka, C., ed. *Karl May im Film*, Hebertshausen 1991.

Urry, J. *The Tourist Gaze. Leisure and Travel in Contemporary Societies*, London 1990.

Van Ash, C. and E.S. Rohmer, *Sax Rohmer. Master of Villainy*, London 1972.

Vincendeau, G., ed. *Encyclopedia of European Cinema*, London 1995.

Vogt, J., ed. *Der Kriminalroman*, 2 vols., Munich 1971.

Von Wilpert, G. *Lexikon der Weltliteratur, Band I: Autoren*; Stuttgart 1975.

Watson, C. *Snobbery and Violence. Crime Stories and their Audience*, London 1971.

Williams, A. and G. Shaw, eds. *Tourism and Economic Development. Western European Experiences*, London and New York 1988.

Williams, L. *Hard Core. Power, Pleasure, and the Frenzy of the Visible*, London 1991.

Wohlgschaft, H. *Grobe Karl-May-Biographie: Leben und Werk*, Paderborn 1994.

Wollschläger, H. *Karl May. Grundriss eines gebrochenen Lebens*, Zurich 1976.

Wolf, K. *Ich bin ja heut so glücklich*, Munich 2001.

Journal Articles, Press Reviews, and Trade Paper Reports:

Anon., 'Stimmen aus Parkett und Rang: Man mag keine Ruinen', *Der Spiegel*, 6 January 1946.

———. 'Männer für Sentiment – Frauen für Sensationen', *WAZ*, 16 December 1949.

———. 'Ilse Kubaschewski. Det greift ans Herz', *Der Spiegel*, 23 January 1957.

———. 'Abschied von den Wolken', *Filmdienst*, no. 8616, 1959.

———. 'Protest gegen Schmutzfabrik', *Berliner Morgenpost*, 30 August 1959.

———. 'Kleine Fische sind unverkäuflich', *Film-Echo*, 25 February 1960.

———. 'Film: Renate Müller: Liebling der Götter', *Der Spiegel*, no. 13, 30 March 1960.

———. 'Constantin: 12 deutsche und 10 ausländische Filme', *Film-Echo*, 13 August 1960.

———. 'Beispiel kulturwirtschaftlicher Förderung', *Film-Echo*, 3 December 1960.

———. 'Thema Coproduktionen. Ein Filmkapitel unterschiedlicher Wertschätzung', *Film-Echo*, no. 49, 21 June 1961.

———. 'Ein Toter sucht seinen Mörder', *Filmdienst*, no.11473, 1962.

———. 'Sherlock Holmes und das Halsband des Todes', *Filmdienst*, no.11619, 1962

———. 'The Devil's Daffodil', *Monthly Film Bulletin*, vol. 29, no. 340, May 1962.

———. 'Karl der Deutsche', *Der Spiegel*, 12 September 1962.

———. 'CCC Films of London in Reciprocal Coin, Distrib Deal with German Co', *Variety*, 12 September 1962.

———. 'Film-Sex nicht mehr gefragt?', *Filmgeflüster*, 13 November 1962.

———. 'French Union Secretary's Warning on Common Market', *Film and Television Technician*, December 1962.

———. 'Wie entsteht eine Coproduktion?', *Film-Echo/Filmwoche*, 13 March 1963, continued on 3 April 1963.

———. 'Edgar Wallace ohne Ende', *Frankfurter Rundschau*, 16 September 1963.

———. 'Reise zu Winnetou', *Bravo*, no. 38, 22 September 1963.

———. 'Station Six Sahara', *Monthly Film Bulletin*, vol. 30, no. 357, October 1963.

———. 'Old Shatterhand triumphiert', *Bravo*, no. 40, 6 October 1963.

———. 'Keine Frau für Pierre Brice', *Bravo*, no. 42, 20 October 1963.

———. 'Vengeance' *Monthly Film Bulletin*, vol. 30, no. 359, December 1963.

———. 'Karl May Sensationen – aber nicht nur für Filmproduzenten', *Ringpress-feature* 1964.

———. 'Constantins 3,5 Millionen-Programm', *Film-Echo/Filmwoche*, 8 April 1964.

———. 'Besuch bei Dreharbeiten: Der Hexer', *Film-Echo/Filmwoche*, 19 June 1964.

———. 'Winnetou III', *Illustrierter Film-Kurier*, no. 66, 1965.

————. 'The Crimson Circle', *Monthly Film Bulletin*, vol. 32, no. 373, February 1965.

————. 'Winnetous Tod', *Bravo*, no. 30, 25 July 1965.

————. 'Traitor's Gate', *Monthly Film Bulletin*, vol. 32, no. 379, August 1965.

————. 'Pierre Brice als Vorbild', *Film-Echo/Filmwoche*, 5 November1965.

————. 'Singend auf Kriegspfad', *Bravo*, no. 48, 22 November 1965.

————. 'Lage hoffnungslos – aber nicht ernst', *Filmdienst*, no. 13844, 1966.

————. 'The Treasure of Silver Lake', *Kine-Weekly*, 3 March 1966.

————. 'The Treasure of Silver Lake', *Monthly Film Bulletin*, vol. 33, no. 387, April 1966.

————. 'Die Exportsituation des deutschen Films', *Film-Echo/Filmwoche*, 25 June 1966.

————. 'Das Geheimnis der weissen Nonne', *Filmkritik*, no. 3, 1967.

————. 'Leserbrief', *Bravo*, no.14, 27 March 1967.

————. "Leserbrief', *Bravo*, no. 18, 24 April 1967.

————. 'Unverwüstlich: James Bond-Edgar Wallace-Jerry Cotton', *Film-Echo/Filmwoche*, 22 December 1967.

————. 'Goldene Leinwand für den 25. Wallace-Krimi', *Film-Echo/Filmwoche*, 17 January 1968.

————. 'Goldene Leinwand für Wendlandt und Wallace', *Film-Echo/Filmwoche*, 26 January 1968.

————. 'Sherlock Holmes and the Deadly Necklace', *Monthly Film Bulletin*, vol. 35, no. 410, March 1968.

————. 'Helga und die Männer – Die sexuelle Revolution', *Filmdienst*, April 1969.

————. 'Harry Alan Towers', *Films and Filming*, no. 400, January 1988.

Asper, H. G. and Horak, J.C. 'Three Smart Guys: How a Few Penniless German émigrés saved Universal Studios', *Film History*, vol. 11, 1999.

Augstein, R., 'Weiter Weg zu Winnetou', *Der Spiegel*, no. 18, 1 May 1995.

Austen, D. 'Kiss, Kiss, Kill, Kill', *Films and Filming*, vol. 15, 1968.

———— 'Continental Westerns', *Films and Filming*, vol. 17, 1971.

Axtmann, H. 'Informativer Besuch in Verleihhäusern', *Film-Echo/Filmwoche*, 17 December 1966.

————. 'Internationale Zusammenarbeit als zwingendes Gebot', *Film-Echo/Filmwoche*, 23 June 1967.

Bean, R., 'Sex, Guns, and May', *Films and Filming*, vol. 11, part 6, 1965.

————. 'Way Out West in Yugoslavia', *Films and Filming*, vol. 11, part 8, 1965.

Bender, R. G., 'Ist der deutsche Kriminalfilm tot?', *Westfälische Rundschau*, 30 January 1960.

Bergfelder, T. 'Reframing European Cinema. Concepts and Agendas for the Historiography of European Film', in *Lähikuva*, no. 4, 1998.

Birch, M.J. 'The Popular Fiction Industry. Market, Formula, Ideology', in *Journal of Popular Culture*, vol. 21, part 3, 1987.

Cole, S., 'Danger Ahead', *Film and Television Technician*, January 1962.

Cook, C. 'Germany's Wild West Author: A Researcher's Guide to Karl May', *German Studies Review*, vol. 5, part 1, 1982.

Cook, P. 'The Art of Exploitation, or How to Get into the Movies', *Monthly Film Bulletin*, vol. 52, 1985.

Cracroft, R.H. 'The American West of Karl May', *American Quarterly*, vol.19, no. 2, Summer 1967.

Dillmann, C. 'Treffpunkt Berlin, Artur Brauners Zusammenarbeit mit Emigranten', *Film-Exil*, no. 3, 1993.

Dörfler, G.'Sax Rohmers exotischer Überverbrecher', *Vampir*, vol. 21, 1980.

Eyles, A. 'Winnetou the Warrior', *Films and Filming*, vol. 11, part 7, 1965.

F.E., 'Was heisst Europäischer Film?', *Film-Echo*, 6 July 1960.

Fischer, K. J. 'Relationen wie bei einem Eisberg', *Film-Echo/Filmwoche*, 23 December 1966.

Gifford, D. 'Nolan's Edgar Wallace', *Films in Review*, vol.18, no. 5, 1967.

Gnuva, P. 'Hinter den Wasserschleiern von Plitvice', *Illustrierter Film-Kurier*, 'Winnetou III', no. 66, 1965.

Gunning, T. 'An Aesthetic of Astonishment: Early Film and the (In)credulous Spectator', *Art and Text*, vol. 34, Spring 1989.

Gutberlet, M.H. and H. Ziegler, 'Re-educate Germany by Film', *Frauen und Film*, no. 61, March 2000.

Helm, L. 'Land der Urlaubs-Sehnsucht: Winnetous Jagdgründe', in 'Winnetou und das Halbblut Apanatschi', *Ringpress-feature*, 1966.

Herzberg, G. 'Das Gesicht im Dunkeln', *Film-Echo/Filmwoche*, 25 July 1969.

Herzog, D. 'Pleasure, Sex, and Politics Belong Together: Post-Holocaust Memory and the Sexual Revolution in West Germany', *Critical Inquiry*, vol. 24, 1998.

H.H., 'Unternehmungslust Marke Wendlandt', *Saarbrücker Zeitung*, 7 March 1969.

hkf, 'Exporterfolg für Karl May', *Film-Echo/Filmwoche*, 17 August 1963.

hjw, 'Gloria: 64/65 aufwendiger denn je', *Film-Echo/Filmwoche*, 16 May 1964.

———. 'Parnass – Pläne zwischen München und Ceylon', *Film-Echo/Filmwoche*, 15 October 1965.

Höhn, H. 'Teenagers Leinwandwunsch: Winnetou darf nicht sterben', *Der Kurier/Der Tag*, 30 July 1964

Hoppe, U. 'Interview mit George Nader: Jerry Cotton tut mir leid', *Bravo*, no. 24, 6 June 1966.

Jäckel, A., 'Dual Nationality Film Productions in Europe after 1945', *Historical Journal of Film, Radio and Television*, vol. 23, no. 3, 2003.

Jenkins, H. 'The First Fifty Days of Labour Rule', *Film and Television Technician*, January 1965.

Käutner, H. 'Demontage der Traumfabrik', *Film-Echo*, no. 5, June 1947.

kn, 'Das Rätsel des silbernen Halbmonds', *Der Tagesspiegel*, 9 August 1972.

Kuester, M. 'American Indians and German Indians. Perspectives of Doom in Cooper and May', *Western American Literature*, vol. 23, part 3, 1988.

Kuntze-Just, H. 'Die Wahrheit über Wolfgang Hartwig', *Echo der Zeit*, 23 August 1959.

Leitner, Reg.Dr. 'Das deutsch-spanische Filmabkommen', *Film-Echo*, 3 December 1960.

Leonhardt, R.W. 'Mit Schreiben Millionen verdient', *Die Zeit*, no.15, 4 April 1975.

Loiperdinger, M. 'Amerikanisierung im Kino? Hollywood und das westdeutsche Publikum der fünfziger Jahre', *Theaterzeitschrift*, no. 28, Summer 1989.

Mann, K. 'Karl May: Hitler's Literary Mentor', *Kenyon Review*, no. 2, 1940.

Markus, B.'Todestrommeln am großen Fluss', *Film-Echo/Filmwoche*, 22 May 1965.

Morlock, M., 'May-Regen', *Der Spiegel*, 23 September 1964.

N.W., 'James Bond – Das Phänomen', *Film-Echo/Filmwoche*, 7 April 1965.

Newman, K., 'Thirty Years in Another Town: The History of Italian Exploitation', *Monthly Film Bulletin*, vol. 53, no. 624, January 1986.

nn, 'Kommissar X soll Jerry Cotton nicht ins Gehege kommen. Die Angebote der Verleiher müssten unterschiedlicher sein', *Film-Echo/Filmwoche*, 2 March 1966.

Nolan, J.E. 'West Germany's Edgar Wallace Wave', *Films in Review*, vol. 14, part 6, 1963.

———. 'Edgar Wallace: His Literary Pop-eries, Unread for Decades, Are Being Revived on Film', *Films in Review*, vol. 18, no. 2, 1967.

Peck, R. 'The Banning of *Titanic*: A Study of British Post-war Film Censorship in Germany', *Historical Journal of Film, Radio, and Television*, vol. 20. no. 3, 2000.

Pitts, M.R. 'The Cinema of Edgar Wallace', *Classic Images*, nos.126–128, December 1985 – February 1986.

R.F., 'Winnetou ist tot', *Münchner Merkur*, 19 October 1965.

R.H., 'Der düstere Rächer im sonnigen Rom', *Abendzeitung München*, 1 July 1972.

Schneider, T. 'Somewhere Else: The Popular German Cinema of the 1960s', in *Yearbook of Comparative and General Literature*, no. 40, Bloomington 1992.

Schulte, C.C. 'Coproduktionen sichern Europas Film', *Film-Echo/Filmwoche*, 22 January 1965.

Seesslen, G. 'Edgar Wallace. Made in Germany', *epd film*, vol. 6, June 1986.

Smyth, R. 'Wurst Wallace', *Observer*, 14 February 1982.

Sudendorf, W. 'Ich wollte nach Europa, nicht nach Deutschland', *Film-Exil*, no. 3, 1993.

Thomasius, J.W., 'Produzent sagt der Nachtausgabe: Höchste Zeit für Film-EWG', *Frankfurter Nachtausgabe*, 24 April 1963.

Von Feilitzsch, H. 'Karl May: the Wild West as Seen in Germany', *Journal of Popular Culture*, vol. 27, part 3, 1993.

Wasem, E. 'Der Erzieher und der Wildwestfilm', *Jugend-Film-Fernsehen*, vol. 6, no. 1, 1962.

———. 'Kriminalspiele und Kriminalfilme im Fernsehen', *Jugend-Film-Fernsehen*, vol. 8, no.1, 1964.

Zucker, W. 'Edgar Wallace', *Die Weltbühne*, vol. 23, no. 49, 6 December 1927.

INDEX

A

Abe Lincoln in Illinois (1940) 23
Abschied von den Wolken (1959)
110–11
Abschied von Gestern (1966)
238–39
Absent-Minded Professor, The
(1961) 59
Action in the North Atlantic (1943)
23
Adenauer, Konrad 209
A doppia faccia (1969) 161
Adorf, Mario 184
Adorno, Theodor W. 2, 237
Adventure films (film genre) 66,
69, 212–14, 229, 232
'Adventures of Rin Tin Tin, The'
(TV series) 95
Aes, Erik 150
African Queen (1951) 48
Aguirre, der Zorn Gottes (1972) 240
Air Force (1943) 23
Aktion Saubere Leinwand 36,
224
Albers, Hans 28, 32, 94, 110, 114,
181
Aleichem, Sholem 133
Alexander, Georg 145
Alexander, Peter 44, 65
Allen, Irving 133
Alliance Cinématographique
Européenne (A.C.E.; film
company) 128
Allianz (film company) 85, 215
American International Pictures
(AIP, film company) 228
American Pie (2000) 245
Amici per la pelle (1955) 99
Amour de Swann, Un (1984) 240
Anatomy of a Murder (1958) 97
Anderson, 'Broncho' Billy 180
Anderson, Lindsay 159
Andersson, Harriet 118
Andress, Ursula 67
Angeli, Pier 136n51
Angélique (1964) 79–81
Änglar, finns dom? (1960) 59
Anglo-Amalgamated (film com-
pany) 132
Angst, Richard 122, 131, 150, 152
Annakin, Ken 59
Année dernière à Marienbad, L'
(1962) 83
Antel, Franz 226–27

Antonioni, Michelangelo 58, 79
Apfel ist ab, Der (1948) 29
*Apokalypse 99 – Anatomie eines
Amokläufers* (2000) 243
Arbeitsgemeinschaft der
öffentlich-rechtlichen Rund-
funkanstalten der Bundesre-
publik Deutschland (ARD,
West German public broad-
casting institution) 89, 94, 98,
99
Arent, Eddi 145, 156, 158, 159,
160, 166, 184, 221–22, 242
Argento, Dario 162
Arkoff, Samuel Z. 228
Arna, Lissy 145
Arsenic and Old Lace (1944) 48
Artisten in der Zirkuskuppel: Ratlos
(1968) 239
Association of Cinema and Tele-
vision Technicians (ACCT) 57,
132
Atlantik (distribution company)
73
Atlas (distribution company) 73,
223
Audience preferences 22–23,
28–29, 31–35, 46–49, 59–60,
95–100, 195
Auf den Trümmern des Paradieses
(1921) 180
Auger, Claudine 67
*Ausschweifende Leben des Marquis
de Sade, Das* (1968/69) 228
Austen, David 235n15
Avala (film company) 133
'Avengers, The' (TV series) 96, 97
*Axel Munthe, der Arzt von San
Michele* (1962) 79

B

Baal, Karin 46
Back, Henri 57
Bailey, David 134
Baker, Carroll 128–29, 136n51
Baky, Josef von 27, 28
Bande des Schreckens, Die (1960)
149
Bannen, Ian 128–29
Banquet des fraudeurs, Le (1951) 62
Bardot, Brigitte 63, 133, 195
Barker, Lex 151, 183–84, 188, 189,
190, 192, 193–96, 198, 219
Barr, Charles 89
Barthel, Manfred 81, 83, 183, 215

Barthel, Waldfried 82, 86, 243
Bathing Beauty (1944) 46
Battaglia, Rik 184
Battle of the River Plate (1958) 47
Baum, Vicki 63, 111, 144
Bava, Mario 160
Bavaria (film company and stu-
dio) 24, 27, 71, 75, 76, 90. *See
also* Columbia-Bavaria
Bean, Robin 83, 168, 191
Beatty, Robert 151
Beatty, Warren 136n24
Becker, Jens Peter 140
Belmondo, Jean-Paul 240
Ben-Hur (1959) 59
Benzoni, Juliette 80
Berben, Iris 244
Berger, Jürgen 38
Bergfilm (film genre) 41
Bergman, Ingmar 59, 73, 211
Bergman, Ingrid 32–33
Berliner Ballade (1948) 29
Berlusconi, Silvio 246
Berolina (production company)
76
Bertelsmann (media company)
26, 73–74, 86–87, 90, 246
Best Years of Our Lives, The (1946)
32
Bewegte Mann, Der (1996) 244
Bezencenet, Peter 217
Beziehungskomödie (film genre)
242
Bianchi, Daniela 67
Big Heat, The (1953) 119
Birch, M.J. 141
Birgel, Willy 32
Bis fünf nach zwölf (1953) 208
Black Narcissus (1947) 37
Blackboard Jungle (1955) 45
Blaue Engel, Der (1930) 26
Blauvogel (1978) 203
Blechtrommel, Die (1980) 240
Bleierne Zeit, Die (1981) 21
Bloch, Ernst 169n37, 174
Blow-Up (1966) 58, 59
*Blue Angel, The. See Blaue Engel,
Der*
Bocaccio 70 (1962) 63
Bolognini, Mauro 208
'Bonanza' (TV series) 96
Boot, Das (1982) 243
Borderie, Bernard de 80
Bordwell, David 164, 187

Borsche, Dieter 79, 93, 130
Borsody, Hans von 152
Böttcher, Martin 150, 158, 184, 186, 187, 188, 192, 242
Boy Cried Murder, The (1965/66) 133
Boyer, Charles 32–33, 46
Brandlmeier, Thomas 121
Brando, Marlon 45–46
Braun, Eva 209
Braun, Harald 27
Brauner, Artur 5, 11, 13, 14, 26, 65, 90–91, 105–35, 138, 151, 188, 189, 207, 208, 227–28, 233, 237, 243
Bravo (teenage magazine) 44, 96, 98, 193–96, 198, 199, 202
Brecht, Bertolt 78, 143, 174
Bressart, Felix 112
Breuer, Siegfried 46
Brice, Pierre 183–84, 188, 189, 190, 193–96, 198, 201, 205n38, 206n75
Brides of Fu Manchu, The (1966) 220
Bridge on the River Kwai, The (1958) 47
Brighton Rock (1948) 22
British Broadcasting Corporation (BBC) 89, 95
British Lion (film company) 127, 129, 142, 145, 189
British presence in the postwar West German film market 20–23, 46–47, 59–60, 71, 72
Broccoli, Albert 135
Broken Arrow (1950) 202
Bronston, Samuel 53, 135
Brooks, Louise 143
Brot der frühen Jahre, Das (1962) 238
Brown, Geoff 227
Bruce, Nigel 131
Brummer, Alois 228–29
Brüne, Klaus 94
Buchholz, Horst 46, 213
Büchse der Pandora, Die (1929) 143, 148
Buck, Detlev 242
Buddenbrooks (1959) 58, 110
Bulworth (1998) 136n24
Buñuel, Luis 83
Burn, Witch, Burn (1970) 81
Byrnes, Edd 96
C
Cabinet des Dr Caligari, Das (1919) 26, 28, 144, 210–11
Calvert, Phyllis 33
Cameron, Rod 184
Campus, Der (1998) 244
Canaris (1954) 108
Captain Sindbad (1963) 71
Caravan (1946) 22
Carol, Martine 208
Carry-On (film series) 227
Carstairs, John Paddy 127
Carter, Erica 7, 47
Cartier, Rudolph. *See* Katscher, Rudolf

Casablanca (1942) 48, 99
Castle of Fu Manchu, The (1968) 222
Cathérine – Il suffit d'un amour (1968) 80
Cavell, Edith 141
CCC-London (film company) 13, 127–35
Celi, Adolfo 67
Centfox (distribution company) 71, 72
Central Cinema Company (CCC; film company) 5, 14, 26, 76, 90–91, 105–35, 138, 151, 162, 188, 189, 207
Centre National de la Ciné-matographie (CNC) 56
Cervi, Gino 122
Chandler, Raymond 140
Chaplin, Charles 240
Chase, James Hadley 151
Cheyenne Autumn (1963) 202
Christian-Jaque 208
Christiane F. – Wir Kinder vom Bahnhof Zoo (1981) 243
Christine (1959) 63
CineGraph (Research Centre) 4
'Circus Boy' (TV series) 95
Circus of Fear (1966) 151, 220–22
Ciudad sin hombres (1968) 220
Clemens, Brian 128, 133, 137n69
Cleopatra (1962) 151
Clift, Montgomery 61
Coast of Skeletons (1964) 151, 219
Cochran, Steve 219
Cole, Sidney 57
Collins, Joan 136n51
Columbia (film company) 71, 77, 189
Columbia-Bavaria (distribution company) 71, 73
Comedy (film genre) 68–69
Committee of European Film Industries (CICE) 54
Commonwealth United (media company) 74, 87
Confidential (gossip magazine) 194
Connery, Sean 133, 195
Conny und Peter machen Musik (1960) 46
Conquest (1938) 46
Constantin (film company) 12, 72, 80, 81, 82–87, 92, 153, 161, 184, 189, 198, 207, 212, 215, 216–17, 223, 225, 226, 233, 239, 243–45, 246
Constantine, Eddie 83
Contribution of returning émi-grés to postwar West German cinema 108–25
Cook, Colleen 174, 176, 177
Cook, Pam 22–23, 209–10, 211
Coop, Denys 158
Cooper, James Fenimore 175, 177
Co-productions (policies, strate-gies, agreements) 53, 55–58, 61–64, 78–80, 84–85, 125–35, 156–62, 212–13, 214–16, 216–22, 238–39, 240, 243–44

Corman, Roger 211, 212, 228
Corrigan, Timothy 1
Cortese, Valentina 79
Cosa avete fatto a Solange? (1972) 161
Courths-Mahler, Hedwig 22
Cracroft, Richard 177–78
Cream – Schwabing Report (1970) 223
Crime film (film genre) 67, 69
Crimson Circle, The (1929) See *Rote Kreis, Der* (1929)
Crimson Circle, The (1959) See *Rote Kreis, Der* (1959)
Critical neglect of post- World War II West German cinema 1–4
Critical studies on popular Euro-pean cinema 4–7
Crosby, Bing 32–33
Cry of the City (1948) 118
Cul-de-sac (1966) 134
Czinner, Paul 75
D
Dagover, Lil 156
Dahlke, Paul 115
Dallamano, Massimo 160
Dancer in the Dark (2000) 245
Dances With Wolves (1991) 245
D'Arcy, Alex 211, 212
Darrieux, Danielle 33
Dassin, Jules 158
Daves, Delmer 191, 202
Davis Jr, Sammy 78
Dawson, Basil 157
Day, Doris 59, 195
Dean, James 45–46, 193, 195
Dearden, Basil 21, 158
Death Drums Along the River (1963) 151, 217–19
Death of a Salesman (1985) 240
DEFA (film studio) 3, 24, 203
Defector, The (1966) 61
Dein Kind – Das unbekannte Wesen (1970) 224–25
Deine Frau – Das unbekannte Wesen (1968) 224
Delon, Alain 240
DeMille, Cecil B. 46, 184, 185
Deppe, Hans 3
Desny, Ivan 152
Despair (1977) 240
Deutsch, Ernst 46
Deutscher Filmpreis (film award) 58
Deutsches Filmmuseum Frank-furt (DIF) 5, 105
Devil's Agent, The (1961) 127–28
Devil's Daffodil, The See *Geheimnis der gelben Narzissen, Das*
Dickens, Charles 22
Dickinson, Desmond 157
Diehl, Carl Ludwig 145
Diessl, Gustav 42
Dieterle, William 108, 122, 123, 126, 138
Dietrich, Erwin C. 228, 233–34, 242
Dietrich, Marlene 32–33

Dietrich, Ralph 242–43
Dillmann, Claudia 5, 106, 112, 115, 117, 118, 125
Distribution 71–87, 237
Divina (production company) 75, 85
Dix, Otto 143
Dmytryk, Edward 133
Doctor Zhivago (1965) 59
Dolce Vita, La (1959) 78
Donovan's Brain (1953) 129, 130
Doppelgänger, Der (1934) 145, 146
Dor, Karin 152, 153, 220
Douglas, Kirk 60–61, 115
Doyle, Sir Arthur Conan 130–31, 134, 143
Dr Crippen an Bord (1942) 146
Dr Mabuse, der Spieler (1922) 124, 144
Dr Mabuse film series 123, 151–52, 219
Drache, Heinz 83, 153, 155, 160, 221, 235n32
Drei von der Tankstelle, Die (1930) 109
Dreigroschenoper, Die (1962) 78
Droop, Adolf 179
Droop, Marie Luise 179
Dullea, Keir 228
Du Rififi chez les homes (1956) 158
Durbridge, Francis 93, 151
Durch die Wüste (1936/37) 180–81
Durchs wilde Kurdistan (1965) 188
Duvivier, Julien 62
E
Eagle-Lion (film company) 20
Eaton, Shirley 220
Eckelkamp, Hanns 73, 223
Edel, Uli 241, 243
Edgar Wallace film series 11, 13, 65, 67, 80, 82, 84, 85, 86, 92, 93, 94, 109, 115, 121, 123, 125, 126, 130, 138–68, 172–73, 179, 183, 184, 187, 200, 202, 209, 217, 219, 220–22, 232, 239–40, 242, 247, 248. *See also* Wallace, Edgar
Ehe der Maria Braun, Die (1978) 75
Ehe im Schatten (1947) 32
Eichberg (film company) 127
Eichberg, Richard 119, 120, 122
Eichinger, Bernd 87, 243–45
Einstein, Albert 174
Eis, Egon 109, 145, 149–50
Eis, Otto 145
Ekberg, Anita 136n51
El Cid (1961) 53
Elf Jahre und ein Tag (1963) 115
Elliott, Denholm 128–29
Elsaesser, Thomas 5, 84, 144, 164, 229–30, 246
Emmanuelle (1973) 233
Emmerich, Roland 241
Emnid (Market research institute) 30–35, 46
Endfield, Cy 228
Endstation Rote Laterne (1959) 211
Enemy At The Gates (2001) 245

Engel auf Erden, Ein See Madame Ange
Englische Heirat, Die (1934) 112
Epilog – Das Geheimnis der Orplid (1949/50) 148
Erhardt, Heinz 110, 131, 184
Erkan und Stefan (2000) 244
Erkan und Stefan gegen die Mächte der Finsternis (2002) 244
Erskine, Rosalind 133
Ertogrul, Musshin-Bey 180
Erzähl mir nichts (1964) 214
Escale à Orly (1955) 62–63
Es geschah am hellichten Tag (1958) 126, 148
Escapism 3–4, 22–23, 48–49, 147–48, 166–68, 248
Europa (distribution company) 73
Europa, Europa. See Hitlerjunge Salomon
European Economic Community (EEC) 54, 55, 58
European spy thriller (film genre) 67, 69, 86, 207, 213–16. *See also* James Bond, Kommissar X, Jerry Cotton
European Union (EU) 55
Eurovision Song Contest 44, 95
Exhibition 81, 232–33, 237
Exoticism 119–23, 212–15, 216–20
Export situation of West German productions 60–61
Export-Union 56, 60
Eyck, Peter van 111–12, 114, 128, 129, 130, 133
Eyles, Allen 191
F
Fabiola (1948) 32
Face of Fu Manchu, The (1965) 220
Fairbanks, Douglas 32, 34
Fall of the Roman Empire, The (1964) 53
Fall Rabanser, Der (1950) 148
Fan Culture 193–96
Fanck, Arnold 184, 197
Fanny Hill (1965) 80, 227–28
Fantômas (film series) 125, 219
Fassbinder, Rainer Werner 75, 209, 237, 238, 239, 240, 241, 242
'FBI' (television series) 216
Fédération internationale des associations des producteurs de films (FIAPF) 55
Fehrenbach, Heide 6, 21, 23, 30, 33–35, 37, 45, 47
Feilitzsch, Heribert von 175
Félix, Maria 125
Fellini, Federico 57, 78, 83, 94
Felmy, Hansjörg 83, 129
Fenech, Edwige 226
Ferienfilm (film genre) 42
Fernandel 63
Fernsehfilm (TV genre) 91–92
Fernsehroman (TV genre) 92
Fernsehspiel (TV genre) 91–92
Fiddler on the Roof (musical) 133

Film ohne Titel (1947) 29
Film State subsidy 39, 58–59, 74
Filmbewertungsstelle der Länder (FBW) 38, 58
Filmförderungsgesetz 74
Finch, Peter 47
Fischer, O.W. 63, 65, 78, 79, 195
Fisher, Terence 128, 131
Fitzcarraldo (1982) 240
Flickenschildt, Elisabeth 152, 155
'Flipper' (TV series) 95
Fluch der gelben Schlange, Der (1963) 151
Fodor, Ladislas 137n69
Forbes, Bryan 128
Ford, Aleksander 107
Ford, John 95, 172, 191, 202
Foreign reception of West German productions 149, 189–93
Forst, Willi 94
Forster, Rudolf 156
Förster vom Silberwald (1954) 43, 47
Four Weddings and a Funeral (1994) 234
Fourneaux, Yvonne 151
F.P.1 antwortet nicht (1932) 129
Francis, Freddie 128, 129–30, 158
Franco, Jesus 66, 222, 223, 235n39
Franju, Georges 210
Frank, Horst 210, 213, 235n32
Frankel, Cyril 159
Frankenstein (1931) 210
Frau Wirtin cycle. *See* Sexy Susan film
Frau Wirtins tolle Töchterlein (1973) 227
Frayling, Christopher 66, 82, 192
Fregola (1948) 31
Fregonese, Hugo 188
Freiwillige Selbstkontrolle (FSK) 37, 208
Freud, Siegmund 231
Frieda (1948) 21
Fritsch, Willy 114
Fröbe, Gert 67, 125
Froboess, Cornelia ("Conny") 46, 209
From Russia With Love (1962) 151
Frosch mit der Maske, Der (1959) 149
Frozen Alive (1964) 133
Fu Manchu (film series) 84, 125, 219–20
Fuchsberger, Joachim 83, 153, 155, 157, 160, 220
Fuller, Robert 96, 98
Funès, Louis de 63, 83, 240
Fünf unter Verdacht (1949) 148
'Fury' (TV series) 95
G
Gable, Clark 32
Gainsborough melodrama 22, 71
Gans von Sedan, Die (1959) 63
Garbo, Greta 32–34, 46
Garncarz, Joseph 5, 31, 34, 48, 84
Gasthaus an der Themse, Das (1962) 166

Geheimnis der gelben Narzissen, Das (1961) 157, 158, 170n51
Geheimnis der grünen Stecknadel, Das. See Cosa avete fatto a Solange?
Geheimnis der schwarzen Handschuhe, Das. See Uccello dalle piume di cristallo, L'
Geheimnis der weissen Nonne, Das. See Trygon Factor, The
Gejodelt wird zuhause (1970) 229
Generational and gender differentiation among audiences 31–35, 45–46, 47, 96–98, 193–96
Genghis Khan (1964/65) 133
Genn, Leo 151
Genre criticism 8–10, 162–68
German western (film genre) 67, 172–204. *See also* Karl May film series
Gerstäcker, Friedrich 175
Gesicht im Dunkeln, Das. See A doppia faccia
Giallo (Italian crime film genre) 160–62
Gloria (distribution company) 12, 72, 74–81, 82, 83, 85, 207, 212, 219, 233, 239
Goebbels, Joseph 108, 114
Goethe, Johann Wolfgang von 174
Going My Way (1944) 23
Göktürk, Deniz 175, 180, 248
Goldene Leinwand (film award) 59, 80, 18
Goldfinger (1964) 220
Goldmann (publisher) 144, 146, 147, 153–54, 164
Golon, Anne 79
Gone With the Wind (1939) 21
Göring, Hermann 116
Gottlieb, Franz Josef 152
Gottschalk, Hans 91
Graf, Robert 114
Graf Porno und seine liebesdurstigen Töchter (1969) 228
Grand Hotel (1932) 111
Grand Hôtel (1959). *See Menschen im Hotel*
Grand Jeu, Le (1953) 118
Granger, Stewart 32–33, 50n40, 159, 184
Grapes of Wrath, The (1940) 21
Great Expectations (1946) 22
Greatest Show on Earth, The (1952) 46
Green, Guy 127
Greene, Hugh Charleton 89
Grey, Zane 189
Grob, Norbert 163
Grosse Baragozy, Der (1999) 244
Grosse Unbekannte, Der (1927) 144
Grosz, George 143
Grün ist die Heide (1951) 76
Grüne Bogenschütze, Der (1960) 149, 154
Grüter, Alexander 59

Guback, Thomas 5
Guinness, Alec 115
Gunn, Victor 151
Gunning, Tom 122–23, 124, 171n83
'Gunsmoke' (TV series) 96
Gutberlet, Marie-Hélène 248
Gutowski, Gene 126, 127, 129, 132, 133, 134, 135

H
Haack, Käthe 62
Haarmann, Fritz 143, 156, 169n25
Habe, Hans 127
Hagener, Malte 162
Hake, Sabine 111, 166
Halbstarken, Die (1956) 46, 213
'Halstuch, Das' (TV serial) 93
Hamlet (1948) 32
Hammer (film company) 132, 158, 160, 222
Hammett (1982) 240
Hampshire, Susan
Handmaid's Tale, The (1990) 240
Harbou, Thea von 119, 174
Hardt, Ursula 23, 30
Harlan, Veit 33
Harnack, Falk 107
Harper, Sue 22
Hart, William S. 180
Hartwig, Wolf C. 14, 83, 84, 208–14, 222, 223, 225, 227, 232, 233, 237, 241
Harvey, Laurence 118
Harvey, Lilian 114
Hauptmann, Gerhart 110, 118
Hawks, Howard 95, 191
Hayworth, Rita 33
Head, The See Nackte und der Satan, Die
Heimatfilm (film genre) 2, 3, 4, 7, 9, 11, 34, 40–44, 45, 47, 48, 64, 66, 76, 79, 80, 84, 108, 114, 117, 123, 138, 148, 181, 184, 197, 198, 199, 226, 242
Heisser Hafen Hong Kong (1962) 212–13
Heist film (film genre) 158
Helga (1967) 85, 223–24, 227
Helga und Michael (1968) 224
Helga und die Männer – Die sexuelle Revolution (1969) 224
Hellman, Carol 60, 126
Hellman, Marcel 60, 126
Helm, Lutz 198
Help! (1965) 59
Hembus, Joe 119, 164, 208, 226
Herbig, Michael 174
Héros sont fatigues, Les (1955) 125
Herrin der Welt (1919) 122
Herrin der Welt (1959/60) 122, 123, 126, 138
Herrin von Atlantis, Die (1932) 129
Herrwerth, Thommi 195
Herzkönig (1947) 106
Herzog, Dagmar 231, 232
Herzog, Roman 174
Herzog, Werner 156, 237, 238, 240, 242

Hesse, Sebastian 143
Hessler, Gordon 228
Heuss, Theodor 174
Hexer, Der (1965) 153, 154, 155
Heywood, Anne 130
High Adventure (1962) 217
High and the Mighty, The (1954) 111
'High Chapparal' (TV series) 96
Hill, Benny 227
Hill, James 133
Hill, Terence 240
Hitchcock, Alfred 21, 46, 48
Hitler, Adolf 174, 209
Hitlerjunge Salomon (1990) 107
Hodder and Stoughton (publisher) 141–42, 144
Hofbauer, Ernst 213, 225
Hofrat Geiger (1948) 31
Holiday film. *See Ferienfilm*
Holland, Agnieszka 107
Hölle von Macao, Die (1966) 132
Hollywood's presence in the West German market 5, 20–21, 23, 30, 32–35, 46, 59–60, 71–73, 74, 78, 239, 246
Holm, Claus 42
Holt, Seth 128–29, 132
Hopkins, Miriam 228
Horak, Jan-Christopher 109, 116
Hörbiger, Paul 46, 145
Horkheimer, Max 2
Horn, Camilla 145
Horner, Penelope 157
Horror (film genre) 68
Horrors of Spider Island See Toter hing im Netz, Ein
House of the Spirits, The (1993) 244
Hoven, Adrian 81
How to Marry a Millionaire (1954) 212
Howland, Chris 152, 184, 228
Hubschmid, Paul 119
Hudson, Rock 195
Huillet, Danièle 238
Human Comedy, The (1943) 23
Hund von Blackwood Castle, Der (1968) 153
Hunde, wollt ihr ewig leben (1958) 92, 108
Hunold, Günter 225
Hunter, Jeffrey 226
Huntington, Lawrence 217
Huston, John 228
Hutchings, Peter 160
Huxley, Aldous 127
Hyer, Martha 122
I
I Confess (1952) 48
I Hired a Contract Killer (1990) 136n24
I tre volti (1964) 79
Ich hab mein Herz in Heidelberg verloren (1952) 117
Il Bastardo (1968) 61
Il gatto a nove code (1971) 162
Im Reiche des silbernen Löwen (1965) 188

Im Stahlnetz des Dr Mabuse (1961) 151
Indianerfilm (film genre) 203
Indische Grabmal (1937/38) 119–20, 122
Indische Grabmal, Das (1921) 119–20, 122. *See also Tiger von Eschnapur, Der*
Indische Grabmal, Das (1959) 119–23
Indische Tuch, Das (1963) 154
Information Control Division (ICD) 20, 21
Insel der Amazonen (1960) 211
Insel der blutigen Plantage, Die (1982) 241
Insider, The (2000) 245
Inter (distribution company) 73
Interessengemeinschaft deutscher Filmexporteure 60
Invitation (1952) 110
Irgendwo in Berlin (1946) 29
Irre vom Hof, Der (1978) 233

J
Jacques, Norbert 123–24, 151, 152
Jadran (film company) 184
Jahn, Thomas 241–42, 245
James Bond (film series) 59, 65, 67, 94, 125, 135, 151, 160, 193, 207, 213, 214–16, 219, 222, 229
Jeavons, Colin 157
Jenkins, Hugh 57
Jerry Cotton (film series) 84, 85, 86, 92, 194, 215–16, 222
Jessner, Leopold 143
'Jeux sans frontières' (TV game show) 95
Jones, Jennifer 32
Junge Törless, Der (1966) 238
Jungen Tiger von Hongkong, Die (1969) 213–14, 223
Jürgens, Curd 63, 76, 78, 125

K
K19 – The Widowmaker (2002) 245
Kafka, Franz 63
Kaiser und das Wäschermädel, Der (1957) 117
Kaiserin von China, Die (1953) 125
Kaiserwalzer (1953) 76
Kalinke, Ernst W. 150, 152, 157, 184
Kampf um Rom (1968) 118
Karl May film series 11, 13, 65, 80, 82, 84, 85, 86, 92, 93, 94, 96–97, 118, 121, 123, 126, 138–39, 172–73, 181–204, 209, 217, 232, 239–40, 242, 247. *See also* May, Karl
Kasachstan Lady (2000) 243
Katia (1960) 63, 118
Katscher, Rudolf 145
Kaufmann, Christine 115, 209
Kaurismäki, Aki 136n24
Käutner, Helmut 3, 26. 29–30, 33, 71
Kendall, Tony. *See* Stella, Luciano
Kennedy, John F. 193
Kern, Peter 241

Kettelhut, Erich 125
Kieling, Wolfgang 155, 235n32
Kier, Udo 81, 241
Killers, The (1945) 118
King, Henry 172
King Kong (1933) 142
King of Kings (1961) 53
Kings of the Road (1975) 82
Kinsey, Alfred 224
Kinski, Klaus 65, 85, 156, 157, 158, 160, 161, 165, 221
Kinski, Nastassja 134
Kirch, Leo 98–99, 243, 245, 246
Kiss Kiss, Kill Kill. See Kommissar X – Jagd auf unbekannt
Klein-Rogge, Rudolf 124
Klingler, Werner 151
Kluge, Alexander 224, 237–239, 242
Knef, Hildegard 32–33, 219
Knickers Ahoy!. See Frau Wirtins tolle Töchterlein
Knife in the Water. See Noz w Wodzie
Knockin' on Heaven's Door (1997) 245
Koch, Marianne 85, 218
Kohl, Helmut 174
Kolle, Oswalt 224–25, 229, 231
Kommissar X (film series) 84, 85, 214–15, 222, 223
Kommissar X – Jagd auf unbekannt (1965) 235n15
Kondom des Grauens (1997) 242–243
König, Ralf 249–11
Königin Luise (1957) 112
Korczak, Janusz 127
Korda, Alexander 127, 217
Koster, Henry 109
Kracauer, Siegfried 2, 8, 14n5, 124, 139, 143, 144, 146, 162, 164, 180
Krahl, Hilde 32
Kräly, Hanns 109
Kramer, Frank. *See* Parolini, Gianfranco
Krankenschwestern-Report (1972) 225
Kraus, Peter 46
Krause, Georg 212
Krause, Willy 114
Kreimeier, Klaus 25, 33
Kristl, Vlado 1, 2, 14n7
Krüger, Christiane 161
Krüger, Hardy 47, 63, 195
Kubaschewski, Hans 75, 76–78
Kubaschewski, Ilse 74–81
Kubrick, Stanley 60, 208, 212
Kulenkampff, Hans-Joachim 96
Kulturfilm (film genre) 93, 121, 218
Kürten, Peter 143
Küster, Martin 178
Kutz, Walter 150
Kwan, Nancy 132

L
Lady and the Monster, The (1943) 129, 130
Lady Hamilton (1968) 223
Lamac, Carl 145
Landon, Mike 96
Lang, Fritz 13, 108, 119–25, 126, 134, 143, 145, 151, 174
Lange, Erwin 184, 197
'Laramie' (TV series) 96, 98
'Lassie' (TV series) 95
Last Exit to Brooklyn (1989) 244
Last Laugh, The See Letzte Mann, Der
Last Year at Marienbad See Année dernière à Marienbad, L'
Lausbubengeschichten (1964) 71
Lavi, Daliah 151, 188
League of Gentlemen, The (1960) 158
Lean, David 22, 59
Leander, Zarah 32–33, 76
Leben zu zweit – Die Sexualität in der Ehe, Das (1969) 227
Lee, Belinda 212
Lee, Christopher 130, 131, 157, 220, 221
Lee, Margaret 161, 226
Leidenschaftliche Blümchen (1977) 134
Lemmy Caution (film series) 83
Lemon popsicle (film series) 137n71
Lenya, Lotte 67
Lenzi, Umberto 160
Leone, Sergio 85, 192
Lester, Henry 131, 133, 134
Lester, Richard 59
Letzte Fussgänger, Der (1960) 110
Letzte Mann, Der (1926) 26
Leuwerik, Ruth 76, 112–14, 115, 195, 209
Liebe 47 (1949) 32
Liebe als Gesellschaftsspiel (1972) 225
Liebesgrüsse aus der Lederhose (1973) 229
Liebling der Götter (1960) 111–15
Lied geht um die Welt, Ein (1933) 117
Lied geht um die Welt, Ein (1958) 117
Lieven, Albert 157, 158
Lili Marleen (1980) 240
Lindgren, Astrid 65
Lingen, Theo 32, 117, 120, 145, 181
Little Caesar (1931) 146
Löb, Karl 125, 150, 157
Lockwood, Margaret 33
Loder, John 144
Loewen (distribution company) 73
Lom, Herbert 81, 184, 190
Lommel, Ulli 241
Longest Day, The (1962) 151
Lord (distribution company) 73
Loren, Sophia 195

Lorna (1964) 227
Lorre, Peter 143, 148, 156
Love Bug, The (1969) 60
Love Story (1944) 22
Lover Come Back (1961) 59
Löwe von Bablyon, Der (1959) 181
Lucas, William 157
Lucrèce Borgia (1952) 208
Ludwig (1972) 78
Ludwig II (1955) 78, 112
Luft, Friedrich 28
Lugosi, Bela 180
Lutz, Hartmut 201, 202
Lynn, Robert 217
M
M – Eine Stadt sucht einen Mörder (1930) 122, 143, 148
Mackie, Philip 129
Macnee, Patrick 96
Madame Ange (1959) 63
Madame Curie (1943) 23
Mädchen hinter Gittern (1949) 106
Mädchen in Uniform (1931) 108
Mädchen in Uniform (1958) 108
Mädchen, Mädchen (2001) 245
Mädchen Rosemarie, Das (1958) 209
Madonna of the Seven Moons (1946) 22, 31, 32
Magic Bow, The (1946) 22
Magnificent Men in their Flying Machines, The (1965) 59
Malle, Louis 238
Malleson, Miles 130
Maltese Falcon, The (1941) 23
Maltin, Leonard 228
'Man from U.N.C.L.E., The' (TV series) 96
Man lebt nur einmal (1952) 117
Man Who Bought London, The (1916) 141
Man Who Changed His Mind, The (1928) 145
Man Who Wasn't There, The (2001) 245
Mann, Anthony 172
Mann, der seinen Mörder sucht, Der (1931) 117
Mann, der Sherlock Holmes war, Der (1937) 146
Mann, Klaus 175
Mann, Thomas 58, 110, 127, 174
Mara, Lya 145
Marais, Jean 32, 63
Marcuse, Herbert 231
Maret, Jean 128–29
Marianne de ma jeunesse (1954) 62
Marischka, Georg 181
Mason, James 32–33
Matsutani, Rainer 244
Maupassant, Guy de 228
Maur, Meinhart 180
Maurus, Gerda 145
May, Joe 119, 120, 122
May, Karl 138, 173–79, 181, 182–83, 189, 193, 201, 202, 203, 204 *See also* Karl May film series

May, Klara 179
McCallum, David 96
McGuire, Dorothy 110
McLoone, Martin 96, 99
Mein Vater, der Schauspieler (1956) 118
Mémoires de la vache Yolande, Les (1950) 116
Menschen im Hotel (1959) 111
Mercier, Henri 119
Mercier, Michèle 79
Mercouri, Melina 136n51
Merton Park (film company) 149, 152, 160, 220–21
Metro-Goldwyn-Mayer (M-G-M; film company) 71, 72
Metropolis (1927) 26, 122
Meyer, Russ 227–28
Million Eyes of Su-Muru (1967) 220
Millowitsch, Willy 96
Ministerio del turismo e dello spettacolo 56
Minnelli, Vincente 110
Mitic, Gojko 203
Mitscherlich, Alexander 247
Mitscherlich, Margarete 247
Moltke, Johannes von 7, 40–42
Monroe, Marilyn 212
Montand, Yves 125
Moore, Roger 96
Mörder sind unter uns, Die (1946) 26, 28, 29
Mordprozess Dr Jordan (1949) 148
Morgan, Michèle 32, 63
Morituri (1947/8) 106, 111
Morley, Robert 159
Morricone, Ennio 192
Moser, Hans 94
Most Desired Man, The. See Bewegte Mann, Der
Motion Picture Association of America (MPAA) 21, 55
Motion Picture Export Association (MPEA) 21, 30, 46
Mountain film. *See* Bergfilm
Mozambique (1964) 219
Müller, Renate 111–15
Münchhausen (1942) 27, 28
Murderers Are Among Us, The. See Mörder sind unter uns, Die
Murdoch, Rupert 246
Murnau, F.W. 208
'My Three Sons' (TV series) 95
N
Nachts wenn der Teufel kam (1957) 118, 148
Nackt (2001) 244
Nackte und der Satan, Die (1959) 210–11, 212
Nader, George 194, 215
Name of the Rose, The (1987) 243
Nanook of the North (1922) 93
National Identity 33–35, 40–43, 48–49, 162–68, 200–204, 229–32, 247–49
Navy Comes Through, The (1942) 23

Nenno, Nancy 43
Nesbitt, Cathleen 159
Neubach, Ernst 13, 108, 116–17, 118, 128, 136n24
Neue Constantin (film company) 87
Neuer Filmverleih (distribution company) 73
Neues vom Hexer (1966) 154, 165, 167
Neverending Story, The (1984) 243, 244
'New Adventures of Martin Kane, The' (television series) 217
New German Cinema 1, 2, 10, 73, 74, 82, 208, 224, 233, 234, 237–42, 247–48
Newman, Kim 66
Nibelungen, Die (1924) 125, 145
Nibelungen, Die (1966) 136n45
Nicht der Homosexuelle ist pervers, sondern die Situation, in der er lebt (1970) 232
Nicht versöhnt (1965) 238
Nichten der Frau Oberst, Die (1968) 228
Nielsen, Asta 143
Ninotchka (1939) 33
Noa, Manfred 144
Nolan, Jack Edmund 162, 163, 167
Nora (distribution company) 74
Nordwestdeutscher Rundfunk (NWDR, West German broadcasting station) 89
Nosferatu (1921) 144
Nosseck, Max 108
Not a Girl (2002) 245
Notorious (1946) 48
Notte di Cabiria, Le (1957) 94
Nous sommes tous les assassins (1952) 97
Noz w Wodzie (1962) 83
Nur über meine Leiche (1995) 244
Nurse and Martyr (1915) 141
O
Oberhausen Manifesto 1, 5, 7, 241
Office of the U.S. Military Government for Germany (OMGUS) 20
Office of War Information (OWI) 21
Ogre, The See Unhold, Der
Old Shatterhand (1964) 188, 190
Old Surehand (1965) 190, 197
Oliver Twist (1948) 22
Olivier, Laurence 32
Ölprinz, Der (1965) 190
On demande un assassin (1949) 117
Once Upon a Time in the West (1968) 192
Ondra, Anny 145
100 Men and a Girl (1938) 109
One That Got Away, The (1958) 47
Operetta (film genre) 64, 76
Organisation for European Economic Cooperation (OEEC) 54

Orlowski, Teresa 234
Orwell, George 140
Osmy dzien tygodnia (1957) 107, 127
Oswald, Gerd 108
Oswald, Richard 108, 209
Otro Fu Manchu, El (1945) 219
Ottinger, Ulrike 240

P
Pabst, G.W. 108, 129, 143, 156
Paget, Debra 119, 122
Pallas (distribution company) 74
Pallos, Steven 127, 157
Palmer, Lilli 76, 228
Paluzzi Luciana 67
Pandora's Box. *See Büchse der Pandora, Die*
Papworth, Keith 157
Paramount (film company) 71, 72
Paris, Texas (1984) 240
Parker, Cecil 222
Parnass (film company) 214, 223
Parolini, Gianfranco 214
Pasolini, Pier Paolo 57
Passage to India (1985) 245
Patalas, Enno 122–23
Paths of Glory (1957) 60
Pauer, Florian 142, 161
Peckinpah, Sam 233
Peking Medallion, The. *See Hölle von Macao, Die*
Perkins, Anthony 195
'Persuaders, The' (TV series) 96
Petersen, Wolfgang 241, 243
Petersson, Harald G. 184
Petit, Pascale 226
Phantom Speaks, The (1944) 129
Philippe, Gérard 63
Phillips, Leslie 162
Phillipsen, Preben 82, 85, 138, 149, 243
Pièges (1938) 116
Piel, Harry 181
Piran (distribution company) 73
Planet (film company) 189
Pochath, Werner 213–14
Poe, Edgar Allan 156
Poitier, Sidney 45
Polanski, Roman 83, 134
Polonsky, Abraham 134
Pommer, Erich 26–30, 36
Ponti, Carlo 53, 135
Ponto, Erich 46
Powell, Michael 37
Prack, Rudolf 42
Praunheim, Rosa von 232
Preiss, Wolfgang 107, 122, 124
Presle, Micheline 122
Presley, Elvis 45, 193
Pressburger, Emeric 37
Prévert, Jacques 21
Prince Valiant (1997) 243–44
Prinzessin von St. Wolfgang, Die (1957) 117
Prisma (distribution company) 73
Private Lives of Sherlock Holmes, The (1970) 134
Privatsekretärin, Die (1931) 108,

112, 135n12
Privatsekretärin, Die (1953) 108, 135n12
Procès, Le (1962) 63
Production Code Administration (PCA) 36
Prümm, Karl 91, 118–19
Pulver, Lieselotte 209
Pyramide des Sonnengottes, Die (1964) 188

Q
Quabus, Günther 97
Querelle (1982) 240
Quinn, Freddy 44

R
Raab, Kurt 241
Rächer, Der (1960) 145, 151
Rahl, Mady 115
Rank Organisation (film company) 20, 22–23, 71, 72, 149
Rank, J. Arthur 20, 33
Rapid (film company) 14, 84, 85, 208–14, 223
Rasp, Fritz 145, 149, 156
Rathbone, Basil 130
Rathony, Akos von 157
Rätsel des silbernen Dreiecks, Das. *See Circus of Fear*
Rätsel des silbernen Halbmonds, Das (1972) 161
Ratten, Die (1955) 118
'Raumpatrouille' (TV series) 93
Rebecca (1940) 46
Rebel Flight to Cuba. *See Abschied von den Wolken*
Rebel Without a Cause (1955) 45, 96
Reception studies 10–11
Reconstruction of the West German film industry after World War II 24–27
Red River (1948) 95, 98
Regnier, Charles 155
Regulation of film content 36–39
Reinecker, Herbert 150
Reinhardt, Gottfried 13, 108, 110–16, 125, 134
Reinhardt, Max 108, 109, 110, 144
Reinl, Harald 3, 149, 151, 152, 184, 185, 195, 197
Reisz, Karel 159
Remakes 108, 116–17, 119–23, 125, 151
Remberg, Erika 152
Rentschler, Eric 244
Republic (film company) 78
Repulsion (1965) 134
Resident Evil (2002) 244
Resnais, Alain 83, 208, 238
Reyer, Walter 122
Rhein-Main-Film (film company) 61
Rialto (film company) 13, 14, 82, 85, 92, 138, 149, 152, 153, 156, 157, 158, 160, 161, 162, 172, 181, 183, 184, 185, 188, 189, 190, 191, 193, 198, 199, 200, 201, 204, 207, 217, 219, 220–21, 227, 240, 242

Richard, Jean 63
Richardson, Tony 159
Richter, Paul 145
Rigg, Diana 96
Rilla, Walter 218, 220
Robeson, Paul 217
Rock Around the Clock (1956) 45
Roeg, Nicolas 217
Rohmer, Sax 140, 219–20
Rökk, Marika 31, 32, 76
Roland, Jürgen 3, 83, 93, 213
Rolf Torring (film series) 84, 213, 215, 222
Roma, Citta Aperta (1945) 28
Roman, Letitia 228
Romance of a Horsethief (1971) 134
Rome, Stewart 145
Rooney, Mickey 219
Rosay, Françoise 62
Rossellini, Roberto 28
Rote Kreis, Der (1929) 145
Rote Kreis, Der (1959) 149
Rotha, Paul 21
Rough and the Smooth, The (1959) 118
Roxy (production company) 76
Rubble film. *See Trümmerfilm*
Rühmann, Heinz 94
Runaway productions 53–54
Rupp, Sieghart 85
Rütting, Barbara 152

S
Saad, Margit 152
Sabine und die 100 Männer (1960) 109, 110
Sabu 122
Said, Edward 121
Sailer, Toni 66
'Saint, The' (TV series) 96
Salgari, Emilio 197
Samson und der Schatz der Inkas (1964) 66
San Remo Festival 44
Sanders of the River (1935) 217
Sanders und das Schiff des Todes See Coast of Skeletons
Sans tambour ni trompète See Gans von Sedan, Die
Satan lockt mit Liebe, Der (1959) 211
Sauerkraut western. *See German western*
Scarface (1931) 146
Schatz der Azteken, Der (1964) 188
Schatz im Silbersee, Der (1962) 67, 181, 184–88, 189, 190, 192, 198
Schell, Maria 63, 76, 209
Schiaffino, Rossana 79
Schlagerfilm (film genre) 44–46, 48
Schlingensief, Christoph 241
Schlöndorff, Volker 224, 238, 239, 240–41
Schlüpmann, Heide 143
Schlüter, Gisela 120
Schmidt, Arno 174
Schmidt, Joseph 117
Schneider, Irmela 99

Schneider, Romy 40, 63, 65, 118
Schneider, Sascha 180
Schneider, Tassilo 7–9, 163–64, 199, 200, 202
Schorcht (distribution company) 73
Schorcht, Kurt 73
Schroth, Hannelore 114
Schuh des Manitu (2001) 174, 244
Schule (2000) 245
Schulmädchen-Report (film series) 84, 225–26, 227, 229–32
Schürenberg, Siegfried 156, 160, 222
Schüsse aus dem Geigenkasten (1965) 216
Schut, Der (1964) 188
Schwab, Sigi 235n39
Schwarzwaldmädel (1950) 42
Schweitzer, Albert 193
Schwiers, Ellen 130
Scotland Yard jagt Dr Mabuse (1963) 152
'Sea Hunt' (TV series) 96
Sealsfield, Charles 175
Seberg, Jean 136n51
Secret Cities (1962) 217
Seesslen, Georg 42, 48, 224, 230
Seitz, Franz 16n38
Sekely, Steven 108, 125
Seltsame Gräfin, Die (1961) 156
Sender Freies Berlin (SFB, Berlin-based broadcaster) 91
Sesselmann, Sabine 157
Sette orchidee macchiate di rosso. See *Rätsel des silbernen Halbmonds, Das*
'77 Sunset Strip' (TV series) 96
Sex film (film genre) 68, 69, 83, 86, 207, 222–32, 232–34
Sexuelle Partnerschaft (1968) 224
Sexy Susan film (film series) 226–27, 229
Shadow of a Doubt (1943) 23
Shakespeare, William 127
Shalako (1968) 133
Shandley, Robert 6, 107
Sherlock Holmes and the Deadly Necklace. See Sherlock Holmes und das Halsband des Todes
Sherlock Holmes und das Halsband des Todes (1962) 128, 129, 130–32, 137n69
Sieg, Katrin 201–202, 203
Siegel-Monopol (distribution company) 75
Signal rouge, Le (1948) 116
Simmons, Jean 33
Siodmak, Curt 129, 131
Siodmak, Robert 108, 116, 118–19, 125, 129, 134, 148, 188
Sirk, Douglas 115
Sissi (1955) 40, 63, 242
Sittenfilm (film genre) 209, 223
Situation Hopeless – But Not Serious (1965) 115
666 – Traue keinem, mit dem du schläfst (2002) 244

Sixth Sense, The (1999) 245
Sjömann, Vilgot 211
Sklavenkarawane, Die (1958) 181
Skolimowski, Jerzy 134
Slap Her She's French (2002) 245
Sleepy Hollow (2000) 245
Smilla's Sense of Snow (1997) 243
Smyth, Robin 142, 147, 162, 163
Söderbaum, Kristina 32, 76
Söhnker, Hans 130
Solveg, Maria 145
Sommer, Elke 132, 209
Song of Bernadette, The (1943) 23, 32, 34
SOS Sahara (1938) 128
'Soweit die Füsse tragen' (TV serial, 1959) 92
Spaak, Charles 62
Spaghetti western (film genre) 65, 67, 85, 173, 192
Spencer, Bud 240
Spiegel, Sam 135
Spiral Staircase, The (1945) 118
Spitzenorganisation der deutschen Filmwirtschaft (SPIO) 59
Stack, Robert 132
Stadt ohne Mitleid See Town without Pity
'Stahlnetz' (TV series) 92, 93
Stapenhorst, Günther 26–27
Stark, Lothar 180
Station Six-Sahara (1962) 128–29, 130, 134
Staudte, Wolfgang 3, 78
Steckel, Leonhard 108
Steel, Anthony 184
Steiner – Das eiserne Kreuz (1976) 233
Steiner – Das eiserne Kreuz, 2. Teil (1978) 233
Stella (distribution company) 73
Stella, Luciano 215
Stern von Rio (1940) 125
Stern von Rio (1954/55) 125
Sternberg, Josef von 21
Stevens, George 172
Stewart, Robert 129
Stoll, Sir Oswald 141
Story of Three Loves, The (1953) 108, 110
Strada, La (1954) 83
Straub, Jean-Marie 238
Stresemann (1956) 58
Stroheim, Erich von 116
Stross, Raymond 128, 130, 133
Study in Terror, A (1965) 134
Süddeutscher Rundfunk (SDR, West German broadcaster) 90, 91
Sudendorf, Werner 115
Sullivans, The (1944) 23
Sünderin, Die (1950) 37
Superweib, Das (1996) 244
Suprema confessione (1956) 126
Susanne, die Wirtin von der Lahn (1968) 226, 227

Sweet Sins of Sexy Susan, The See Susanne, die Wirtin von der Lahn
T
Tabu (1931) 208
Tani, Yoko 151
Tarantino, Quentin 235n39
Tatar, Maria 143
Tausend Augen des Dr. Mabuse, Die (1960) 119, 124–25, 151
Tefi (film company) 214
Television and the West German film industry 88–100
Terra (film company in the 1930s and 1940s) 24–25, 75
Terra (production company in the 1960s) 85
Terry-Thomas 159
Testament des Dr Mabuse, Das (1932) 124
Testament des Dr Mabuse, Das (1962) 151
Teufel kam aus Akasawa, Der (1970) 151
Teufelsanbeter, Die (1921)
Tevye und seine sieben Töchter (1967/68) 133
Theumer, Ernst Ritter von 214, 222, 223, 233
Theweleit, Klaus 177
Thiele, Wilhelm 108, 109–10
Thier, Erich 146, 147
Thiery, Fritz 27
Third Man, The (1949) 46
Thoma, Ludwig 71
Thomalla, Georg 181
Thomas, Peter 150, 235n39
Thompson, Carlos 122
Thompson, Kristin 5
3-Groschenoper, Die (1931) 143, 156
Tiger von Eschnapur (1921). See *Das indische Grabmal* (1921)
Tiger von Eschnapur (1937/38) 119–20, 122
Tiger von Eschnapur, Der (1958) 119–23
Tiller, Nadja 209
Tobis (film company of the 1930s and 1940s) 24–25, 75, 125, 138, 181, 239
Tobis (distribution company from the 1970s onwards) 239–40, 242
Todd, Richard 217
Todeskarawane, Die (1921) 180
Todesmühlen, Die (1945) 21
Todesstrahlen des Dr Mabuse, Die (1964) 152
Todestrommeln am grossen Fluss. See *Death Drums Along the River*
Torday, Terry 226
Toten Augen von London, Die (1961) 155
Toter hing im Netz, Ein (1959) 210–211

Toter sucht seinen Mörder, Ein. See Vengeance
Tourbillon (1952) 117
Tourism and the tourist gaze 41–44, 180–81, 196–200, 218–19
Towers, Harry Alan 14, 84, 85, 135, 216–22, 223, 233
Towers of London (film company) 216–22
Town without Pity (1960) 115
Traitor's Gate. See Verrätertor, Das
Tread Softly. See Schüsse aus dem Geigenkasten
Trenker, Luis 181
Trial, The. See Procès, Le
Trivas, Victor 212
Tromba (1949) 31
Trooger, Margot 65
Trotta, Margarete von 21
Trümmerfilm (film genre) 6, 27–30, 106
Trygon Factor, The (1966) 159
Tsai Chin 220
Tumulto de paixoes (1958) 126
Tür mit den sieben Schlössern, Die (1962) 157
Turm der verbotenen Liebe, Der (1968) 223
24 Hours To Kill (1965) 219
20. Juli, Der (1955) 107, 111
Two-Faced Woman (1941) 33
Tystnaden (1963) 59, 211
U
Uccello dalle piume di cristallo, L' (1969) 162
Ufa (Babelsberg and Tempelhof studios) 24, 90. *See also* DEFA
Ufa (production company; style, star system and legacy) 22, 26, 28, 31, 32, 33, 39, 75, 76, 82, 94, 108, 110, 111, 115, 117, 128
UFI (Ufa Film GmbH; film company) 20, 24–26, 39, 73, 75, 76, 94
Uhse, Beate 230
Ulrich, Kurt 16n38, 76, 151
Umgelter, Fritz 92, 213
Und immer ruft das Herz (1959) 126
Und über uns der Himmel (1947) 28
Unhold, Der (1996) 240
Unifrance 56
Union (distribution company) 73
Unitalia 56
United Artists (film company) 61, 67, 71
Universal (film company) 71
Unsichtbaren Krallen des Dr Mabuse, Die (1962) 152
Unter Geiern (1965) 191
'Untouchables, The' (TV series) 92, 96, 216
Unucka, Christian 193
Urlaubsreport (1971) 225
Urry, John 199

V
Vajda, Ladislao 108, 126, 148
Vajda, Ladislaus ("Laszlo") 108, 148
Valente, Caterina 44
Valentin, Barbara 209, 211, 241
Veidt, Conrad 48, 120, 122, 156, 210
Velde, Theodor van de 227
Vengeance (1962) 128, 129–30
Vengeance of Fu Manchu (1967) 220
Ventura, Lino 78, 122
Verband deutscher Filmproduzenten 60
Verband deutscher Filmverleiher 60
Verboten! (1958) 21
Verlorene, Der (1951) 148
Verlorene Gesicht, Das (1948) 31
Verne, Jules 117
Verrätertor, Das (1964) 157–59, 166–67, 170n51, 221
Versini, Marie 188, 195–96
Vesely, Herbert 238
Victim Five (1964) 219
Viktor und Viktoria (1933) 112
Viridiana (1961) 83
Visconti, Luchino 57, 63, 78
Vohrer, Alfred 3, 149, 184
Vollkommene Ehe, Die (1968) 227
Vor Sonnenuntergang (1956) 110
Vorwerg, Wilhelm 150
W
Waalkes, Otto 240
'Wagon Train' (TV series) 96
Waldleitner, Luggi 16n38, 75, 76
Wallace, Bryan Edgar 152, 162
Wallace, Edgar 140–43, 144–45, 147–48, 217. *See also* Edgar Wallace film series
Walt Disney (film company) 71
Walters, Thorley 130
War film (film genre) 47
Warm, Hermann 211
Warner Bros. (film company) 61, 71, 76
Warner-Pathé (distributor) 189
Was ist eigentlich Pornographie? (1971) 225
Watson, Colin 140
Waynberg, Sam 134, 137n71
Wedekind, Frank 143
Weidenmann, Alfred 110
Weiß, Ulrich 203
Welles, Orson 57, 63, 118
Wellman, William 111
Wenders, Wim 82, 237, 238, 239, 240, 242
Wendlandt, Horst 83, 85, 86, 138, 149, 153, 159, 161, 162, 172, 181, 183, 185, 189, 192, 195–96, 207, 208, 227, 237, 239–40, 242
Wendlandt, Matthias 242
Wenn die Conny mit dem Peter (1958) 46
Werfel, Franz 23
Werner – Beinhart (1990) 244

Werner, Theo Maria 214, 222, 223
West German cinema in the 1950s 6–7, 36–49, 53–64
West German film industry during the occupation period (1945–1949) 6, 19–35
Westdeutscher Rundfunk (WDR, West German public broadcaster) 90
Western European Union (WEU) 54
Wicked Lady, The (1945) 22
Wiedmann, Hanns 150
Wien-Film (film company) 181
Wild Geese, The (1978) 234
Wild One, The (1954) 45
Wilden, Gert 235n39
Wilder, Billy 21, 50n25, 134
Williams, Esther 46
Williams, Guy 72
Williams, Linda 229
Window, The (1949) 133
Winnetou I (1963) 188, 190, 191, 192, 194–95
Winnetou II (1964) 190, 197
Winnetou III (1965) 190, 195–96, 197
Winnetou und das Halbblut Apanatschi (1966) 189
Winnetou und Old Shatterhand im Tal der Toten (1968) 189
Winnetou und sein Freund Old Firehand (1966) 189, 195
Winterstein, Frank 131, 137n69
Wisbar, Frank 108
Wolf, Konrad 3
Wolf Man, The (1941) 129
Wolter, Ralf 184
Woman in the Window, The (1945) 119
Woods, Robert 213
Wortmann, Sönke 242, 244
Writers Guild of America 132
Wunder der Liebe, Das (1968) 224
Würger von Schloss Blackmoor, Der (1963) 152
Wyler, William 32
Y
Yeux sans visage, Les (1959) 210
York, Eugen 106
Young Tom Edison (1940) 23
Z
Zelnik, Friedrich 145
Zeugin aus der Hölle (1965) 133
Zielinski, Siegfried 91, 95
Ziemann, Sonja 76, 126, 135n12
Zimmer 13 (1963) 157
Zinker, Der (1931) 145
Zinker, Der (1963) 157
Zugsmith, Albert 228
Zweites Deutsches Fernsehen (ZDF, West German public broadcaster) 90, 94, 98